Tl

MW01025544

The Peoples of Africa

General Editor: Parker Shipton

This series is about the African peoples from their origins to the present day. Drawing on archaeological, historical and anthropological evidence, each volume looks at a particular group's culture, society and history.

Approaches will vary according to the subject and the nature of evidence. Volumes concerned mainly with culturally discrete peoples will be complemented by accounts which focus primarily on the historical period, on African nations and contemporary peoples. The overall aim of the series is to offer a comprehensive and up-to-date picture of the African peoples, in books which are at once scholarly and accessible.

Already published

The Shona and their Neighbours*
David Beach

The Berbers*
Michael Brett and Elizabeth Fentress

The Peoples of the Middle Niger*
Rod McIntosh

The Ethiopians*
Richard Pankhurst

The Egyptians*
Barbara Watterson

The Swahili
Mark Horton and John Middleton

In preparation

The Peoples of Kenya
John Middleton

* Indicates title commissioned under the general editorship of Dr David Phillipson of Gonville and Caius College, Cambridge

The Berbers

Michael Brett and Elizabeth Fentress

Blackwell
Publishing

© 1996, 1997 by Michael Brett and Elizabeth Fentress

BLACKWELL PUBLISHING
350 Main Street, Malden, MA 02148-5020, USA
9600 Garsington Road, Oxford OX4 2DQ, UK
550 Swanston Street, Carlton, Victoria 3053, Australia

The right of Michael Brett and Elizabeth Fentress to be identified as the Authors of
this Work has been asserted in accordance with the UK Copyright, Designs, and
Patents Act 1988.

All rights reserved. No part of this publication may be reproduced, stored in a
retrieval system, or transmitted, in any form or by any means, electronic, mechanical,
photocopying, recording or otherwise, except as permitted by the UK Copyright,
Designs, and Patents Act 1988, without the prior permission of the publisher.

First published 1996
First published in paperback 1997

10   2007

Library of Congress Cataloging-in-Publication Data
Brett, Michael.
        The Berbers / Michael Brett and Elizabeth Fentress.
            p.   cm. — (The Peoples of Africa)
        Includes bibliographical references (p.) and index.
        ISBN 978-0-631-16852-2 (hbk) — ISBN 978-0-631-20767-2 (pbk)
            1. Berbers.   2. Africa, North–Social life and customs.
        1. Fentress, Elizabeth. II. Title. III. Series.
        DT193.5.B45B74   1996
        961'.004933 — dc20   94–35110
                                                         CIP

A catalogue record for this title is available from the British Library.

Set in 11 on 12.5 pt Sabon
by Best-set Typesetter Ltd, Hong Kong

The publisher's policy is to use permanent paper from mills that operate a sustainable
forestry policy, and which has been manufactured from pulp processed using
acid-free and elementary chlorine-free practices. Furthermore, the publisher ensures
that the text paper and cover board used have met acceptable environmental
accreditation standards.

For further information on
Blackwell Publishing, visit our website:
www.blackwellpublishing.com

For Yvonne and James

Contents

Plates

Figures

Maps

Series Editors' Preface

The Peoples of Africa series has been designed to provide reliable and up-to-date accounts of what is known about the development and antecedents of the diverse populations in that continent, and about their relations with others near or far. It is hoped that the series will enjoy a wide readership in many parts of the world, including Africa itself.

This series has counterparts relating to other continents, and it may be appropriate to discuss here aspects specific to a series dealing with Africa. Africa is a continent of contrasts – not only in its physical environments and in the life-styles and economies of its peoples, but also in the extent to which writing has influenced its development and recorded its past. Parts of Egypt have one of the longest histories of literacy in the world; on the other hand, some interior regions – notably in south-central Africa – remained wholly unrecorded in writing up to a hundred years ago. The historical significance of this contrast has been both varied and far-reaching.

The books in this series variously combine perspectives of archaeology, anthropology and history. It will be obvious that someone studying the past of a non-literate people will adopt techniques very different from those that are at the disposal of historians who can base their work on written sources. The relevance of archaeology is by no means restricted to non-literate contexts, but it is clearly a pre-eminent means of illustrating even the comparatively recent past in those parts of Africa where writing was not employed. It may be less obvious to those not familiar with Africa that non-literate peoples were by no means ignorant of their past, traditional knowledge about which was often preserved and orally transmitted through several generations, albeit not infrequently subject to change – conscious or unconscious – in the light of contemporary circumstances. Further clues about the non-literate African past can be obtained from studying the distributions and interrelationships of modern languages. Each of these approaches presents its own problems, and has its own potential to illustrate particular aspects of the past.

Each volume in the series is a specialist's attempt to condense, and to order, a large and diverse body of scholarship on a way of life. The series describes both changes and continuities, relating historic processes occurring at all levels of scale, from the domestic to the intercontinental. The changing definitions and self-definitions of peoples, in the light of new communications and sensitive ethnic and national politics, pose difficult problems for theory and description. More often than not it is debatable where, and when, one population ends and another begins. Situating African societies flexibly in time and space, and taking account of continual movements, anomalies, and complexities in their cultures, these volumes attempt to convey some sense of the continent's great variety, to dispel myths about its essential character or its plight, and to introduce fresh and thoughtful perspectives on its role in human history.

DAVID W. PHILLIPSON
PARKER SHIPTON

Preface

This book is the product of a collaboration between two authors, an archaeologist (Elizabeth Fentress) and an historian (Michael Brett). We were responsible, respectively, for chapters 1, 2, 6 and 7, and for chapters 3, 4 and 5, but we have each benefited from the other's revision.

We are indebted to Ali Aït Kaci, Dida Badi, Nacera Benseddik and Ahmed Toufiq for their precious information on the life of modern-day Berbers, to James Fentress, David Hart and Chris Wickham for their critical comments on parts of the text and their constant encouragement, and to Derek Kennet and Sergio Fontana for their photographs.

Introduction

They belong to a powerful, formidable, brave and numerous people; a true people like so many others the world has seen – like the Arabs, the Persians, the Greeks and the Romans.

The men who belong to this family of peoples have inhabited the Maghreb since the beginning.

Ibn Khaldūn

In 1980 the cancellation by Algerian authorities of a lecture on Berber poetry was followed by widespread rioting and a series of demonstrations which came to be known as the 'Berber spring'. The 'Berber Cultural Movement' which grew up around this curiously romantic beginning has had as much resonance in France as it has in Algeria, but is unknown outside the French-speaking world. No general book on the Berbers is available in English. One of the most unfortunate consequences of this is the total ignorance in both Great Britain and the United States of the existence of the Berbers. In an interview with an American historian who holds that the Roman emperor Septimius Severus was black, a journalist recently asked whether he wasn't Berber, and received the simple answer, 'What's that?'[1] This book is intended as a step towards answering the question, and perhaps towards a modification of the idea that Mediterranean history can be divided between black Africans and white Europeans.

Although they are a minority within the Maghreb, the area in which Berber speakers are found is immense, and testifies to the size of the original population (see map 0.1). Today, these areas are best described as mountainous islands in a vast sea of Arabic.

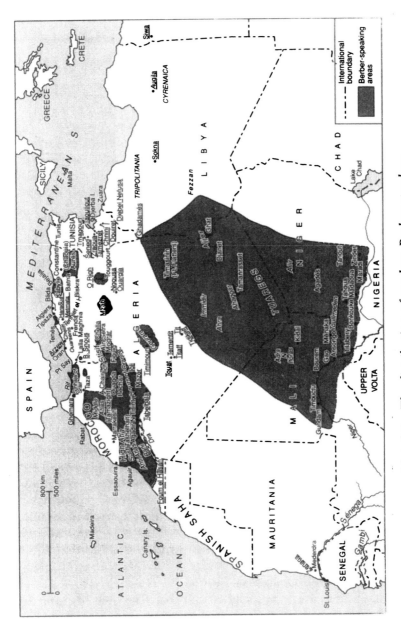

*Map 0.1 The distribution of modern Berber speakers
(Adapted from G. Camps, Les Berbères. Mémoire et identité, Paris, 1980)*

Small groups are found at Siwa, in the western desert of Egypt, and in the Fezzan in southern Libya. An archipelago of Berber-speaking villages runs from the Jebel Nefousa in Libya through south-eastern Tunisia to the island of Djerba, where several communities of Berber speakers follow the puritanical Ibadite Islamic sect. Although fairly distinctive in this area, in Tunisia as a whole, Berber speakers constitute less than 1 per cent of the population. Larger groups are found in the coastal chain of mountains which marks the African coast from northern Tunisia to Morocco, particularly in Kabylia, between Annaba and Algiers, with a few groups in the Dahra area west of Algiers. South of the mountains, the inhabitants of the high plains are almost exclusively Arab speaking until just north of the Aures mountains, a massive, compact block which separates the high plains from the Sahara. These are inhabited by the Shawiya, who speak a dialect of the same name. Further south lie the oases of the Mzab, whose five villages are lived in by the Ibadite Berbers who fled there to escape persecution further north.

In all, Berber speakers constitute perhaps 20 per cent of Algeria's population. Of these, a few are the Tuareg (*sing.* Targui) in Tamenrasset in the far south, who speak their own dialects. These are perhaps the richest of the Berber dialects and the least contaminated by Arabic. The Tuareg occupy an immense area of the Sahara, from the Hoggar and Tassili to Northern Niger, Mali and Burkina Faso. Estimates of their numbers vary between 600,000 and 1,600,000, depending on who is counting and who is counted, but the bulk of them are found in the south.

Moroccan Berber speakers constitute over 40 per cent of the population. Three distinct dialects are spoken: *dhamazighth* in the Rif mountains of northern Morocco, *tamazight* in the High Atlas, where the largest number of Berber speakers are concentrated, and *tashilit* in the Sūs Valley and Anti-Atlas, inhabited by groups known collectively as the Shallūḥ or Chleuh. Except in the case of the deep Sahara, Berber languages are concentrated in the mountainous areas which have best resisted Arabization.

There is little doubt that the whole of North Africa spoke Berber languages at one time, while in the middle ages they occupied much of Spain and Sicily as well. But just as the dialects are often mutually incomprehensible, so the people themselves are extremely heterogeneous: the existence of an ethnically unified 'people' is no more demonstrable for the past than it is today.

Indeed, there are a bewildering number of cultures, economies and physical characteristics.

At best we can define Berbers as Mediterranean. In terms of their physical anthropology they are more closely related to Sicilians, Spaniards and Egyptians than to Nigerians, Saudi Arabians or Ethiopians: more precise characteristics are conspicuous by their absence, as a recent attempt at mapping a broad range of genetic traits has shown.[2] We are thus immediately thrown into the problem of whom we are going to call a Berber, and why.

The most common response is linguistic: Berbers are defined as people speaking Berber languages. Indeed, one of the things that sets the Berbers apart is their language, whose sibilant, aspirated sounds are highly distinct from any other language spoken in the Mediterranean. This was often commented on in the past, and a common myth links the odd-sounding language to the name 'Berber'. One version is that given by Ibn Khaldūn:

> Their language is not only foreign but of a special kind, which is why they are called Berbers. It is said of Ifrīqish son of Qays son of Ṣayfī, [...] that he encountered this strange race with its peculiar tongue and struck with amazement exclaimed 'What a *barbara* you have!' For this reason they were called Berbers.[3]

In fact, the Berber dialects are part of the language group, the Afro-Asiatic, which comprises the Semitic languages and Ancient Egyptian. The Berber dialects vary widely, but they are all recognizably Berber; a modern Targui can, with some difficulty, understand a Kabyle (although not vice versa). Further, Berber languages are rarely used by outsiders: Arabic is the dominant language in North Africa, and there would be little reason for a non-Berber to learn the language today. Thus the ability to speak a Berber language gives us an objective basis for asserting that a given individual is a Berber.[4] This definition is both transparent and convenient, but on closer examination proves more than a little restrictive. Today, a man born in France and exclusively francophone might easily refer to himself as a Berber, while the Roman author Apuleius, about whose ability to speak a Berber language we have no evidence whatsoever, claimed to be 'half-Numidian and half-Gaetulian' – both of which were, as we shall see, Berber communities. Thus both men would ascribe themselves to Berber groups on a non-linguistic basis. In ancient ethnography the languages of the North African tribes were rarely mentioned, and may not have been perceived as linguistically unified. The ability to speak a Berber language is thus only one of the characteristics of groups who consider themselves Berbers, or are considered to be so by others. Today it is the principal characteristic – and indeed the revival of the Berber language is the most important aspect of the new affirmation of Berber culture – but if we restrict ourselves to a linguistic definition of Berbers when discussing their history there will be few groups we can discuss with certainty.

A cultural definition appears more promising, but when applied to the past becomes unsatisfactory. Unfortunately, this is a common procedure: perceptions of Berber culture derived from modern anthropology are often casually back-projected to antiquity. Worse, they are then used to justify a judgement that Berbers were culturally immobile. The circularity of the argument is evident: if we look for Berbers in the Roman period only in mountain villages in which we find them today it will be easy, but hardly legitimate, to show that Berbers in antiquity were identical to modern inhabitants of the Aures or Kabylia.

The least unsatisfactory solution seems to be to use the term 'Berber' in the broader sense of those groups who were perceived to be indigenous North Africans, both in antiquity and in the middle ages, as well as anyone who is still perceived that way today.

Of course, even the use of the name 'Berber' is somewhat arbitrary: it is of external origin, and certainly not a Berber word.[5] How did the Berbers distinguish themselves from other groups? How did they refer to themselves in the past? The word for Berber today is either '*Tamazight*' or '*Imazighen*', the first referring to their language, the second to the people who use it. Both have been recently adopted throughout North Africa, although their first attestations are only known from Moroccan dialects and until 1945 did not spread outside them. There is, however, some evidence that the term was used more widely in the classical period. Under the Romans the tribal name 'Mazices' and its variations has been shown to be far too widespread to refer to a specific tribe: it is probably a cognate of Imazighen, and it may have been one of

the terms used to refer to indigenous Africans in general.[6] Leo
Africanus, writing in the sixteenth century, claimed that the word
is related to the term for free,[7] so that 'Imazighen', like 'Franks',
would mean 'the free men'. Although this derivation has recently
been disputed, principally on the grounds that there is no modern
term meaning 'free' related to the root MZC,[8] it remains possible.
Further, the Tuareg word for 'noble' – and free in the sense of 'not
vassal' – is *amajegh*, another cognate. The binomial noble/free
gives us a self-image that is perhaps the closest we can come to a
universal Berber trait. It is not random or tied to a specific historical moment. Thus in the mid-tenth century the following dialogue
is reported with the Kutāma people of eastern Kabylia:

> 'Who is in command of your affairs?'
> 'Each man of us is his own master, although each tribe has its
> elders, and advisers in matters of (religious) conduct, to whom we
> take our disputes; and whoever loses must accept the judgement
> against him, or suffer the wrath of the whole community.'
> 'Are you in fact a single people?'
> 'We are certainly all Kutāma, although divided into various
> tribes, clans and families.'
> 'And are you close to each other?'
> 'Yes, there is no great distance between us.'
> 'But are you united?'
> 'No; we fight each other and then make peace, and make peace
> with one group while we fight another. That's our way.'
> 'Do you unite if a foreign enemy attacks?'
> 'No-one has ever made it necessary, because of our numbers and
> the fastness of our land.'[9]

Many themes are evident in this passage which will be treated
later: the distinctions between self, family, clan, tribe, and people,
the emphasis on personal freedom and the apparent absence of a
state. All of these risk being taken as Berber universals. It is,
however, more appropriate to treat them as themes, which emerge
differently according to the specific historical context. We are less
interested in 'what Berbers are like' than in attempting to describe
the characteristics of Berbers in a given period. Until recent times
this was unnecessary: everyone knew that Berbers never changed,
indeed, 'Berber permanence' was a central tenet of much of the
history of North Africa: Theodore Mommsen wrote that 'One
foreign domination follows another, bringing new civilizations.
The Berbers remain like the palms in the oasis and the sands of the

desert.' And yet any more than superficial examination shows that Berbers *do* change: their economies and political systems under the Romans have little in common with those of the twentieth century.

The Berber peoples did not develop in a vacuum, and their history must be put into its North African context: the Punic settlers, the Romans and the Arabs all were integrated into North African society, and in large parts controlled it. This has caused two dangerous distortions; first, that the history of North Africa has tended to be exclusively that of the events which involved the conquerors; and second, that the Berbers themselves have been treated as more or less a-historic, a people without history. In this way diachrony becomes a property of the conquerors, while the conquered have the right, at best, to the synchronic studies of anthropology. The role of Berbers as protagonists in their own history has been lost in the process.

We thus aim to give a clear account of Berber history – an aim not different from that of Ibn Khaldūn, but carried out with rather different means. There are no serious modern texts which deal with the whole of Berber history, although there exist a few popular histories written for Berbers and filled with oppressive imperialists and freedom-fighting Donatists. Notable exceptions to the studied ignorance about the Berbers in modern historiography are found in the work of two French scholars, the archaeologist Gabriel Camps and the historian Jehan Desanges. The former has been one of the fathers of modern North African prehistory and, by founding the Institut d'Etudes Berbères at the University of Aix-en-Provence and the *Encyclopédie berbère*, a patron of the modern Berber cultural movement. The latter has contributed enormously to our knowledge of North African tribes both inside and outside the frontiers of the classical period. Another salutary step away from the traditional view was made in the 1970s by Marcel Benabou, whose book on African resistance to the Romans placed the Berbers at the centre of the stage, not only in a military sense, but also as people who significantly influenced the culture and religion of Roman North Africa.[10] However, this step was not followed up. Writing about Berbers after the Arab conquest is still, today, not politically correct in the Maghreb. There are a number of reasons for this. One, perhaps the most important, is a commonly felt desire for the unity of Islam through its sacred language, Arabic. Further, the attempt by the French to create a Berber 'fifth column' in the Maghreb to support their rule was quite rightly rejected by the nationalist movement. Finally, a substantial current of the left has always tried to suppress ethnic differences.[11]

The problems inherent in discussing the Berbers become compounded when we turn to their material culture and ethnography. Here, it is harder to avoid generalities; generalities which will certainly be false in some of the patchwork of Berber peoples. But these generalities are, at least, more complex than the observations that Berbers are segmentary, anarchic and immobile, which have been so frequent in the past. Modern social anthropology – the splendid work of Montagne, Gellner, Hart, Bourdieu, Colonna and others – has inevitably focused on a single region. Few studies have treated Berber ethnographic themes across North Africa as a whole, even the most evident ones such as habitat, magic or political structures.[12] Yet striking unities do exist and are worth bringing out.

Very little of our work is based on first-hand ethnographic research, for neither of us is an anthropologist. Although we have both spent much time in the Maghreb, neither of us is equally well-versed in all parts of it, and the balance of the book is perhaps more on Tunisia and, particularly, Algeria than on Libya and Morocco. This is, however, a correction to the disproportionate share of space that Morocco has received in English publications.

A final problem is the rate of change since the 1960s, when with the independence of Algeria much of its traditional culture began to disappear. During the colonial period, areas such as Kabylia had enclosed themselves in immobility, relying on tradition to protect themselves from the imperialism of French culture – although Kabylia had always had privileged access to what little education was offered to Algerians.[13] But the participation of many women in the fight for independence left them loath to take up where their mothers left off. With independence and the greater availability of a university education, Kabylia took up its chances for economic improvement, as much for women as for men. In so far as women had been the primary repositories for traditional culture this is showing its effects: the traditional house is not being copied in concrete but discarded for more European models, and the traditional way of life is being seriously questioned. At the same time, however, the *ideal* of Berber culture has become a major political and cultural fact.

Little work has been done on this transition. We thus risk treating as contemporary accounts of behaviour which are more than thirty years out of date. But concomitant with this transition has been the emergence of Berber scholars in the school which took its lead from the protean Mouloud Mammeri, symbol and chief protagonist of the revival of Berber culture. The son of an *amousnaw*, or sage, he was descended from a line of poets, whose oral tradition he published and revived. One of a number of important authors writing in French who came to prominence in the post-war years – Kateb Yacine, Jean Amrouch, Mouloud Feraoun – Mammeri became increasingly interested in the whole field of Berber history and culture, from prehistory and anthropology to literature and linguistics. With the work of his school and of the Centre for Anthropological, Prehistoric and Ethnographic Research (CRAPE) which he directed, we are moving towards a specifically Berber history and anthropology, as opposed to an ethnography coloured by European preconceptions, tailored to European categories. It is perhaps the long tradition of cultural duality – the ability to assimilate the hegemonic culture without suppressing the traditional culture – which has permitted Berber scholars this double view, the meta-level without which it is impossible to study oneself. We ourselves can hardly offer a 'Berber view', but we have tried to use material written by Berbers as much as possible.

1

Berbers in Antiquity

In defining Berbers as indigenous North Africans we have begged
the question of their origins. It is thus worthwhile to summarize
briefly the archaeological evidence for North African prehistory.
This is not an easy task: prehistorians disagree on it, and the
evidence is complex – although there is little doubt that the reality
was more complex still.

The earliest type of *Homo sapiens* in the Maghreb is a North
African equivalent of the Cro-Magnons in Europe. It was earlier
thought that this type, known as 'Mekta-Afalou', had split off
from the Cro-Magnons, moving from Asia into North Africa
while the Cro-Magnons moved into Europe. This has recently
been disputed and an indigenous development from the
Neanderthals proposed. However, an indigenous development remains to be proven, as there are no intermediate types known
from North Africa.[1]

Capsian Stone Industries

Around 7,000BC the eastern Maghreb saw the development of a
new stone industry, known as 'Capsian' from the site at which it
was first studied, El Mekta near Gafsa, ancient Capsa, in southern
Tunisia. Capsian tools – generally beautifully retouched microliths
– were associated with the presence of large quantities of ash and
snail shells, which suggest that snails were the principal source of
protein, and were probably consumed boiled. Several sites have
also produced small anthropomorphic sculptures, both in stone

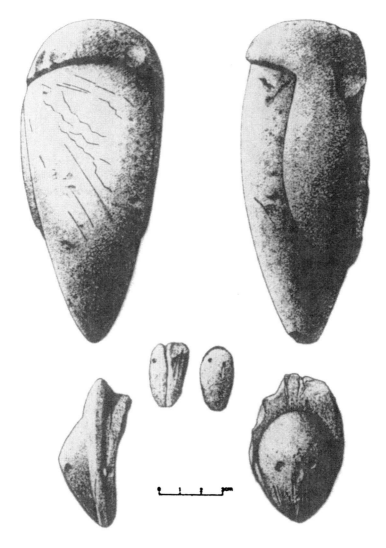

Plate 1.1   Anthropomorphic stone figures from El Mekta
(From R. Horn and C. Rüger, Die Numider: Reiter und Könige nördlich der Sahara, Bonn, 1979)

(El Mekta) and in coarsely fired clay (Afalou in Algeria), while decorated ostrich shell beads are also characteristic.[2] Again, there are no immediate local predecessors of this type of site, and a diffusion from the eastern Mediterranean has been proposed. It has been suggested by the prehistorian Gabriel Camps that we can see in the new types associated with the Capsian a sort of proto-Berber population which would have migrated to the Maghreb during this period.[3] However, skeletal material shows that many of the people associated with these sites belong to the original 'Mekta' type, and thus it is hard to postulate an entirely new group of people. The physical variability of the skeletons associated with Capsian sites suggests that we are not dealing with a single immigration, but with a series of small groups. In general, however, the individuals were tall (1.74 m on average) and long-headed, with high foreheads: Camps' characterization of them as 'proto-Mediterraneans' is loose but effective.

The Neolithic in the Maghreb

The transition to the neolithic is anything but clear-cut. It is certain that it occurred much earlier in the south. Radiocarbon dates of around 7,000BC from the southern Sahara and the Sahel, in such areas as the Tassili and the Hoggar, show a remarkable contemporaneity with those in the Eastern Sahara as far as the Nile. It has recently been suggested that the wet period which began after 7,000BC made this area inhabitable for the first time in several millennia, and allowed it to be occupied by food-producing people. Alternatively, the drying out of certain areas encouraged the domestication of cattle. There is increasing evidence to suggest that this domestication was in no way linked to the Near Eastern neolithic, and indeed that the introduction of food production in the Nile Valley took place from the west rather than from the east. In the lower Nile Valley itself there are no neolithic sites before around 4,000BC – possibly because no technology was available to deal with the river's floods.[4] Pottery seems to have been produced in the southern Sahara as early as the middle of the seventh millennium, and may even be the predecessor of pottery production in the Near East.[5]

The Sudanese-Saharan neolithic seems to have had little connection with the north, however. In the Tell, the cultivable area

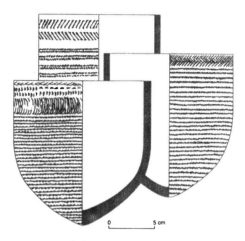

Figure 1.1   Neolithic pottery from Hassi Mouilah
(From G. Camps, Aux origines de la Berbérie: monuments et rites
funéraires protohistoriques, *Paris, 1961)*

between the Sahara and the Mediterranean, the transition was
much more gradual and piecemeal, and seems to have begun at
more or less the same time as in the lower Nile – although one cave
site in Cyrenaica has a much earlier date.[6] Much of the Maghreb
appears to have been rather conservative. In eastern Algeria, particularly in mountainous areas, we find neolithic sites which retain
many elements of the epi-palaeolithic Capsian tradition. Skeletons
who still strongly resemble the Mekta type are found in seasonally
occupied rock shelters. Pottery was used and animals herded, but
the tool industries show little development from the Capsian.[7] One
of the problems, of course, is that the division between epi-
palaeolithic and neolithic is not as neat as was once assumed. Just
as some groups integrated the use of pottery and domestic animals
into what was essentially a palaeolithic lifestyle, so many apparently epi-paleolithic groups ,may have been carrying out some
cultivation or intensive gathering of wild grains, as the polished
sickles of the Capsian seem to show. The physical anthropology of
the neolithic is equally weak on clear divisions between techniques
and peoples: what little we know seems to show that the population of the Maghreb was composite, including various racial
elements.

The Spread of Berber Language

In an interesting model for the spread of the Indo-European languages across Europe, Colin Renfrew has proposed their diffusion by the steady progress of neolithic agriculture. The geometric increase in the productivity of the land allowed a population growth which gradually expanded westwards, displacing or absorbing the mesolithic populations.[8] Curiously, he retains the older model of immigration from a heartland for Semitic speakers who, he suggests, moved outwards from the Arabian peninsula around the third millennium BC, ultimately outnumbering and absorbing earlier language groups such as Sumerian. However, if we examine a map of the Afro-Asiatic languages – the eastern Semitic group, Kushitic, Egyptian and Berber – both the centrality of the Nile Valley and the difficulty of positing the Arabian peninsula as a 'heartland' become evident. There has never been any suggestion that the Nile Valley was populated from the Arabian peninsula, nor of any major shift in its population. It seems intellectually more satisfying to suggest that the advent of the neolithic in the lower Nile Valley and the delta area caused a major rise in

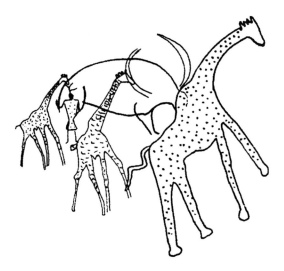

Figure 1.2   Domesticating the giraffe
(From A. Muzzolini, L'Art rupestre préhistorique des Massifs Centraux saharien, Oxford, 1986)

its population density, and a consequent spin-off to the east and north-west of groups of people who carried the new techniques, and a related language, with them. This would explain the presence of these groups in the Arabian peninsula as well as in North Africa.[9] The climatic conditions during this period would have made the movement outward from the Nile a far less forbidding enterprise than it would be today.[10]

This suggestion cannot, at the moment, be more than speculative. Archaeological evidence for a consistent movement of people is lacking, while, unlike the Indo-European languages, the Afro-Aslatic family as a whole has received little study.[11] Only the most rudimentary comparative studies exist, and thus any diagram of the relationships between them is impossible. The one statement we can make is that the Berber languages are all remarkably similar, which suggests that their spread across North Africa was relatively uniform and did not occur over a great period of time. The break between them and old Egyptian (related to modern Coptic) could be explained by the physical barrier of the eastern desert, which became more and more impassable as the Sahara dried out. Again, this would suggest that the separation of the two had taken place *before* the definitive drying out of the Sahara between 2,500 and 2,000BC.[12]

Mediterranean Connections

The Nile, however, was certainly not the only point of reference for North Africa. From the fourth millennium onwards one can begin to see contacts with the Mediterranean islands and with the Iberian peninsula: obsidian from Lipari appears in northern Tunisia, while shell-decorated pottery and, at the beginning of the bronze age, bell beakers similar to Iberian types are found in northern Morocco. In the high Atlas numerous engravings of Iberian daggers and halberds attest that contacts continued throughout the bronze age.[13] There is no evidence for major immigration from these areas, but again the continuous arrival of small groups is probable. Dolmens in northern Tunisia and eastern Algeria recall Maltese prototypes, while late bronze age chamber tombs on Cap Bon have clearly Sicilian origins. This is the last 'archaeological' moment in which the Berbers – or the Berber language – could have arrived: Camps sporadically holds

the view that the earliest Berbers migrated from the eastern
Mediterranean during the bronze age, along with the chamber
tombs, the dolmens and pottery styles acquired in Sicily.[14] This,
again, is hard to prove, as we cannot find 'proto-Berbers' anywhere else.

The North African tell at the beginning of the second millennium thus presents a picture not very different from the rest of the
western Mediterranean: farmers with a strong pastoral element in
their economy and fairly elaborate cemeteries. There is, however,
little evidence for the production and working of metal: no bronze

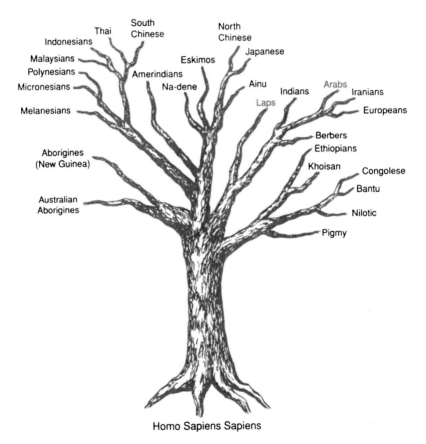

*Figure 1.3 Tree of world populations, showing the relationship
between the language and genetic groups
(From L. Cavalli-Sforza, P. Menozzi and A. Piazza,* History and Geography of Human Genes, *Princeton, N.J., 1994)*

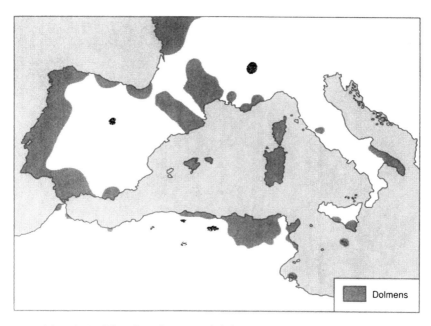

Map 1.1   The distribution of dolmens in the Mediterranean
(From G. Camps, Aux origines de la Berbérie: monuments et rites
funéraires protohistoriques, *Paris, 1961)*

weapons have been found in eastern Algeria or Tunisia. While we assume that by this time Berber languages were established throughout North Africa, there is no good evidence of exactly how this took place. Our only certainty is that the population by the second millennium was extremely heterogeneous, with a range of Mediterranean types mixed with some descendants of the original, possibly indigenous, 'Mekta' type.

The Sahara and the Garamantes

The really original aspect of the North African prehistoric cultures is evident not on the Mediterranean coast but in the Sahara, in the highlands of Tibesti and Tassili, the Hoggar and west to the Atlantic coast. In these areas, and to a lesser extent in Kabylia and the Saharan Atlas, are found numerous elaborate rock carvings and paintings. From these we can deduce much, not only about the

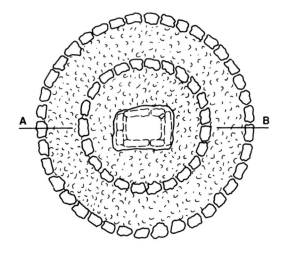

Section **AB**

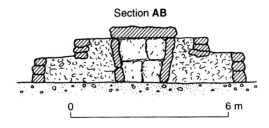

0   6 m

Figure 1.4   Dolmen from Sigus, Algeria
(From G. Camps, Aux origines de la Berbérie: monuments et rites
funéraires protohistoriques, *Paris, 1961)*

economy of the people which produced them, but also about their
social organization.[15] At the beginning of the neolithic period the
climate of this area was radically different from modern conditions. Although it certainly did not resemble a tropical
jungle, it was much wetter than in historic times. The chain of
depressions running across the southern Sahara was filled with
shallow lakes, while the highlands were forested. A neolithic civilization combining fishing with stock raising grew up here whose
connections are far closer to the Sudan than to the Capsian to the
north. The people were negroid, as both their rare skeletons and
the splendid frescos they painted on the cliffs of the Tassili range

demonstrate. Their economy was largely pastoral, and many of the frescos show large herds of cattle. At some time, perhaps around the end of the second millennium, frescos begin to show elongated white men with characteristic long hair and pointed beards. Some confirmation of this racial shift comes from physical anthropology, although the skeletons seem to show closer resemblance to groups from the upper Nile Valley than to contemporary material from the Maghreb.[16]

By the middle of the second millennium the frescos show men using horses to pull light war chariots, armed with spears and wearing kilts similar to those of the Egyptians. The chariots could be drawn by as many as four horses, but two were more common:

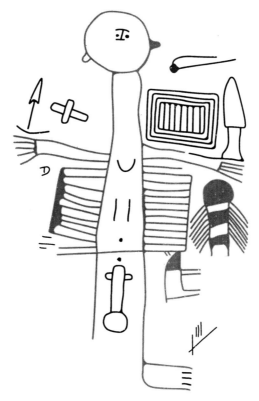

Figure 1.5   Bronze Age engraving of a warrior from the High Atlas (From G. Camps, Encyclopédie berbère, *vol. x, Paris, 1991)*

Figure 1.6   Jackal-headed dancers from the Tibesti
(From J. Leclant and P. Huard, 'La culture des chasseurs du Nil et du
Sahara', Mémoirs du Centre des Recherches Anthropologiques,
Préhistorique et Ethnographiques, *29, 1980)*

these are generally depicted in a 'flying' gallop. As Camps points
out, the chariots were almost certainly aimed at enhancing the
prestige of their users rather than for transporting goods.[17] Recently, A. Smith has suggested that the frescos themselves represent a hermetic, priestly discourse aimed at perpetuating the social
hierarchy.[18] Masked, shaman-like figures are common, although
some scenes certainly represent the ordinary life of the group. For
the first time women are shown on relatively equal terms with
men, while in a well-known engraving a man is shown happily
playing with a child.[19]

What appears to have taken place is that the domestication of
the horse gave the Mediterranean groups in North Africa infinitely
greater mobility than they had had before. They were thus able to
exploit the now arid steppe areas of the Sahara for an increasingly
nomadic pastoralism. Both the new technology and their more
stratified society enabled them to subjugate the existing black
population, whose flourishing civilization had since around
2,500bc been put under ever-increasing stress by the drying out of
the Sahara.

There seems to be little doubt that we are dealing here with a warrior aristocracy which had gained ascendency over the black groups of the Sahara: this is the first instance of a pattern which has been repeated until the present day. The equation of the new group with the modern Tuareg is facile, and effectively

Figure 1.7   Hunters on an engraving from Tassili n'Ajjer (From G. Camps, Encyclopédie berbère, *vol. VI, Paris, 1989)*

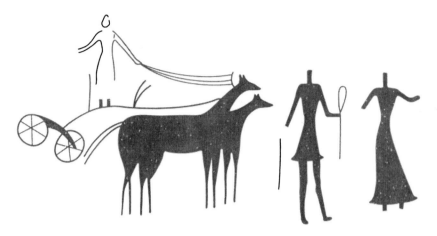

Figure 1.8   Chariot from the Wadi Zigza
(From A. Muzzolini, L'Art rupestre préhistorique des Massifs Centraux
saharien, *Oxford, 1986)*

unprovable, but there is no doubt that their hierarchic structure, with a warrior caste which probably exploited black cultivators, was similar.

Evidence from the Tassili frescos receives striking confirmation from paintings in Egyptian tombs of the thirteenth century, which show 'Libyans' – 'Libu' and 'Mashwash' – wearing kilts and ostrich feather head-dresses, their hair falling in elaborate locks as far as their shoulders, their beards short and pointed and their faces covered with tattoos or, more likely, ritual scars (plate 1.2). These would have been the northern equivalent of the groups in Tassili; they apparently had trading contact with the Egyptians, eventually settling in the far-western areas of the delta. In 1,220BC and again in 1,180 they invaded the delta, and the extraordinary figures of 9,300 and 28,000 Libyans are recorded as having been killed on these two occasions. Their political centralization is indicated by the references to a chief, or king, and there are also some references to towns.[20]

It is with part of this group, the Garamantes of the Fezzan in the Libyan desert mentioned by Herodotus, that the Saharan Berbers first came to the notice of the ancient world. The historian tells us that they are 'an exceedingly populous nation . . . The Garamantes go in four-horse chariots hunting the cave-dwelling Aethiopians.'[21] The Garamantes are also the first protohistoric peoples of the

Maghreb whose settlement sites are known archaeologically. The valleys of the Fezzan are extremely rich in archaeological sites: Caputo counted 59,686 tombs in the 1950s,[22] while villages and towns of all dates are numerous. Excavations at the plateau of Zinchecra between 1965 and 1973 revealed a small hut settlement dating from as early as 1,000BC. Dry stone gave way to mud brick somewhere around the middle of the millennium, when the site covered as much as 8 ha, defended by a wall across the neck of the plateau. It continued to grow, moving to the slopes outside the defended settlement, and the latest houses appear to be built in stone. At the end of the first millennium BC Zinchecra seems to have been replaced by the large site at Garama/Germa in the valley bottom.[23]

Palaeobotanical evidence shows that both breadwheat and barley were cultivated near the site, while seeds of marsh species seem to suggest that the valley was far wetter than it appears today – a conclusion which is supported by the presence of breadwheat alongside the more resistant barley. Sheep were apparently kept on

Plate 1.2   Libyans on an Egyptian tomb: note the 'dreadlocks' and tattoos
(From O. Bates, The Eastern Libyans, *London, 1914)*

the site. The village was thus a mixed farming community, without a visible hierarchy within the settlement itself – indeed, we have no evidence that the farming population was not, in fact, black. Physical anthropology of the later tombs shows a mix of racial types, with some 'negroid' and some 'Mediterranean' people.[24] The warrior aristocracy is archaeologically invisible in the early period, although by the second century AD the presence of 'villas' and of large, well-built tombs at Germa shows a fairly pronounced hierarchy. The development of Germa as a central place probably also reflects the centralization of power in the society, and references in Roman authors to the 'king' of the Garamantes underline this point.[25]

Punic North Africa and the Berber Kingdoms

If the principal contacts of the Garamantes were probably Egyptian, the foundation of Carthage by the Phoenicians at the end of the ninth century BC made a far more lasting cultural impact on the inhabitants of the northern Maghreb. Initially at least, Carthage did not aspire to a land empire, but her influence over northern Tunisia cannot be underestimated, and smaller ports along the coast as far as Lixus in Morocco provided a capillary contact with the peoples of the interior.

The earliest settlement at Carthage was restrained by a treaty with the 'Libyans' (as non-Punic Africans were called) from expanding her territory beyond the small strip of land on which the city is sited.[26] Her livelihood depended on her trade rather than on her territorial empire. Even Cap Bon, the large peninsula to the south of the city, was not occupied by Carthage until the fifth century, when large towers seem to have replaced earlier Libyan sites, and the town of Kerkouane was founded on the south coast.[27] By the time of Agathocles' invasion in 310BC, Carthage controlled much of northern Tunisia, and there is talk of rich estates and of large numbers of slaves,[28] while during the third century a fully fledged empire was established, controlling much of Tunisia and eastern Algeria.

The effect of this activity on the African populations can hardly be underestimated. What we seem to see, quite apart from the growing political control and domination by Carthage, is a process of emulation and competition which slowly transformed

Berber society even outside the zone of Punic control. The first aspect of this transformation was apparently political. As early as the end of the fourth century we begin to hear of Libyan 'kings', such as Aelymas, with whom the Sicilian Greek general Agathocles treated.[29] It is logical that the reaction to the growing territorial consolidation of Carthage should have been the formation of larger territorial entities by the Berbers. As such kingdoms emerged throughout the Mediterranean in the Hellenistic age the Berbers followed suit. We perceive this transformation first in the new name applied to them by the Carthaginians: outside the territory controlled by Carthage, peopled by 'Libyphoenicians', were the 'Numidians'. By the end of the third century BC the Numidians were divided into three kingdoms: the Massyli, the Masaesyli and the Mauri. The history of these kingdoms is particularly interesting in that this was one of the rare times that development in the Maghreb took place without significant political interference from elsewhere.

In around 220BC the area of modern Morocco was peopled by the 'Mauri', and ruled by a somewhat shadowy king called Baga. By far the largest of the three kingdoms was that of the Masaesyli, covering roughly the northern half of modern Algeria. This was ruled by Syphax from two capital cities, Siga, near Oran in western Algeria, and Cirta, modern Constantine, in eastern Algeria. The kingdom of the Massyli, ruled by Gaia, the father of Masinissa, is generally held to have been south of Constantine, but there is some evidence that it extended along a line of salt lakes and oases all the way to the Tunisian coast at Gabes, and from there down to the Lesser Syrtis: as we shall see, the Massyli clearly had some contacts with the Greek world, and possibly directly with Alexandria. Indeed, a curious series of coins dating from around 241 bears in Greek the legend 'Libyans': we may see here the remains of Aelymas' kingdom, which could have been absorbed into that of Masinissa at a later date.[30]

Syphax and Masinissa

In the course of the second Punic war both Syphax and Masinissa played important roles, and the Numidians were clearly regarded both by the Romans and the Carthaginians as people requiring careful handling. Syphax disposed of a vast cavalry and, inspired

Figure 1.9   Masinissa
(From R. Horn and C. Rüger, Die Numider: Reiter und Könige nördlich
der Sahara, *Bonn, 1979)*

by the Roman example, created infantry units which he used with
success against the Carthaginians. Masinissa, too, learned his military technique with the Romans, with whom he campaigned in his
youth in Spain. Although both were nominally allies of the
Romans, they were permanently at war with each other: Masinissa
tended to be on the losing side, although he managed again and
again to escape when defeated and to raise a new army. On one
occasion he retired as far as the Lesser Syrtis, making contact with
the Garamantes.

   The major shift in balance was caused by the alliance of Syphax
with the Carthaginians after his marriage to Sophonisba, daughter
of the Punic general Hasdrubal. She persuaded her husband to go
over to her father's side: from this point on, the contest between
the Numidian kings became a sideshow to the Roman–
Carthaginian struggle. Masinissa, with Roman help, was eventually victorious and, once Syphax was taken prisoner by the
Romans, Masinissa managed to annex at least the eastern half of
the kingdom of the Masaesyli. From that time the names of these
kingdoms became subsumed under the general heading of
Numidia. Masinissa, who reigned for the next sixty years, and his
successors became known as the kings of the Numidians rather
than of the smaller sub-groupings of Massyli and Masaesyli.[31]

It is interesting that both of these kings were treated, by the Romans as well as the Carthaginians, with all the honour due to Hellenistic monarchs. Syphax was awarded the curule chair and other ornaments of a Roman triumph at the same time as the Ptolemys in acknowledgement of their status as friendly, or client, kings.[32] After his victory, Masinissa received the same insignia, as well as a golden patera, an ivory sceptre, the purple cloak of a Roman military commander and equestrian arms. This was not simply condescension: Masinissa was also recognized as one of their own by other Hellenistic rulers. Statues were erected to him at Delos by the Rhodians and Athenians, as well as by Nicomedes of Bithynia.[33] He was a hero on a large scale: like many subsequent Berber leaders, Masinissa charmed his biographers. Dashing, athletic, crafty and passionate in his youth, in his old age he acquired more regal attributes. As an established king, he carefully cultivated the image of the perfect Hellenistic monarch through his coinage and the participation of at least one of his sons in the Panathenaic games. The language of the court remained Punic, however, as did religious practices. Indeed, the extent of community between the Carthaginians and the Numidians is underlined by Livy, in whose account Sophonisba falls at the feet of the victorious Masinissa and pleads with him that she should not fall into Roman hands saying, 'I should have preferred to trust the word of a Numidian, born in Africa like myself, to that of a foreigner' (Livy, xxx, xii, 15).

Royal Tombs

This Numidian fusion of the dominant cultures of the Mediterranean is best demonstrated by a series of tombs built by the Numidian kings and some of the nobles. The earliest of these is the Medracen, just north of the Aures mountains (plate 1.2). Although sited in the centre of a vast cemetery whose tumuli are similar to all the protohistoric tombs of the area, the cultural context of the Medracen is very different indeed. It has recently been suggested that the giant tumulus in well-cut ashlar masonry, with its sixty attached Doric columns and Egyptian 'throat' cornice, referred directly to the tomb of Alexander at Alexandria and was, indeed, probably created by craftsmen from the Greek east.[34] Radiocarbon dates it to the third century, although in that it is generally held to

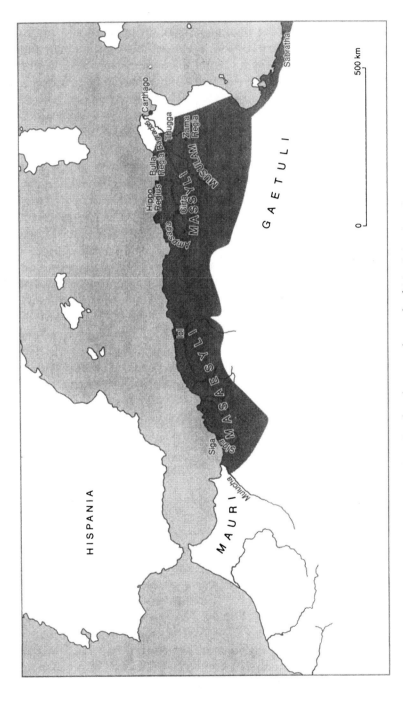

Map 1.2   North Africa at the end of Masinissa's reign
(From G. Camps, Aux origines de la Berbérie, Masinissa ou les débuts de l'histoire, Algiers, 1961)

Plate 1.3 The Medracen
(From R. Horn and C. Rüger, Die Numider: Reiter und Könige nördlich der Sahara, *Bonn, 1979)*

have been built for Masinissa, it is systematically down-dated by half a century. Whether it is the tomb of Masinissa or, more probably, that of his father Gaia, its siting in the southern part of their kingdom is interesting, demonstrating a control over man-power and resources – over 29 tonnes of lead was used in the construction of the tomb – which the standard account of semi-savage Numidians hardly takes into account.

Equally striking is a series of tower tombs, of which the best known is that built for Syphax at Siga, and possibly used by his son Vermina after Syphax's death in Italy. This combines Hellen-istic elements into a complex of three storeys, topped by a convex pyramid. Similar tombs were built for Masinissa's grandson Micipsa at the Souma a el Kroub, and for nobles at Thugga,

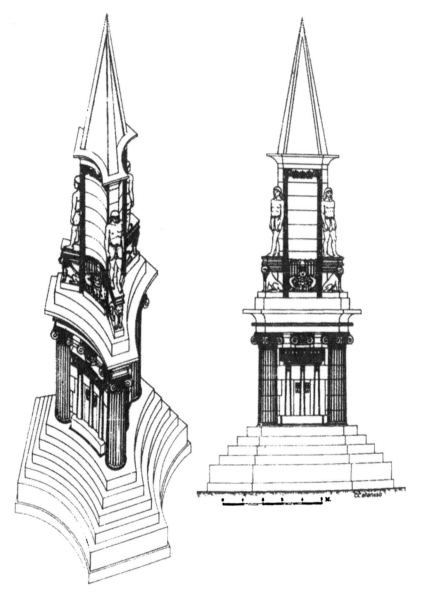

Figure 1.10 Tower tomb from Sabratha (after Rakob)
(From R. Horn and C. Rüger, Die Numider: Reiter und Könige nördlich
der Sahara, Bonn, 1979)

Plate 1.4 Model of the tomb of Syphax at Siga (reconstruction F. Rakob)
(From R. Horn and C. Rüger, Die Numider: Reiter und Könige nördlich der Sahara, *Bonn, 1979)*

Sabratha and on the island of Djerba.[35] Tower tombs of the same type are found as far south as the Fezzan in the first century AD.[36] These tombs display an evident iconographic unity: although the prototype was probably the Greek heröon, or hero's monument, the tower tombs seem to have become one of the major symbols of nobility within the Numidian and Libyan heartlands. Just as Masinissa (or his father Gaia) used the massive symbolism of Alexander for his own purposes, so the tower tomb of Syphax was emulated by the kings and nobles right across North Africa, from Siga to the Fezzan, over a period of 200 years.

North Africa under the Numidian Kings

Although at the top of the hierarchy there seems to have been a creative use of Mediterranean cultures, we have far less evidence for what was going on in the countryside. Besides their royal families, what did these kingdoms consist of? Archaeology tells us little, although new evidence is beginning to emerge for a series of villages scattered over the arable land of the Tell.[37] These were hut settlements, generally defended by a wall across the neck of a spur. Evidently most of the population lived in these: when Masinissa began his attempt to regain his father's kingdom Numidians 'flocked to him from the fields and the villages'.[38] Further south, in the predesert, the economy was probably pastoral, and there are few traces of settlement before the first century BC.[39]

Some sites were larger and can be properly classified as cities. Of these, those in Mauretania are the best known archaeologically. At Volubilis in the interior are found imposing city walls and an apparently orthogonal plan.[40] Banasa shows a succession of buildings in *tabiya*, or mud walling, which date from the third century BC or earlier, as well as a flourishing pottery industry,[41] while Tamuda (Tetouan) again has an orthogonal plan, at least from the middle of the second century BC. Of Siga, the western capital of Syphax, however, we know little beyond the royal tomb.[42]

In Southern Numidia, the territory of the Massyli, is found the site of Ichoukane which, while apparently more primitive than the Moroccan examples, is none the less large (at least 20 ha) and well fortified, with a double enceinte of dry stone, and clearly visible roads. Surface finds of black glaze ware testify to its occupation in the third or second century.[43] Cirta was apparently occupied by Punic-style houses with olive presses,[44] and continued to play the role of capital city. Four other cities – Thimida, Bulla, Hippo and Zama – are qualified as 'Regia', although only the last was a capital. Theveste (modern Tebessa) is identified with the 'Hecatompylos' which is said to have given up 3,000 hostages in the middle of the third century BC.[45]

In general, however, in spite of a multitude of toponyms, the evidence suggests that the Numidian landscape continued to be one of villages, practising mixed farming and paying tribute in kind. This tribute was probably collected in royal granaries, for which we have evidence in a later period in various places –

Mactar, Thala, Capsa, Suthul and Calama. The surplus produced was sufficient for Masinissa to export grain to the Romans in Greece and to gain fame as the man who developed wheat cultivation in North Africa. Inside the former Punic territories Masinissa held vast estates, although their absence outside these areas suggests that the individual ownership of land was influenced by Punic practice.[46] Outside this area tribute probably remained the principal mode of appropriation of wealth. There is, however, little or no evidence for the growth of institutions other than tribute linking the villages with the monarchs.

The situation was thus in many ways comparable to that of Ptolemaic Egypt: a large number of small farming communities ruled by a bi-cultural, bi-lingual court. The bulk of the cities were coastal, and their main market language was probably Punic – indeed, it is clear that Punic was the language of the countryside around Hippo Regius as late as the time of St Augustine. Under the superficial structure of the Numidian state, however, tribal social structures probably remained strong. This is an obvious instance of Gellner's model of social relationships in agrarian societies: while the elite was able to communicate with the neighbouring elites, their cultural differentiation from the peasants was strongly marked, and their connections with them based on kinship rather than on state structures.[47]

Tribes and the State

From the second Punic War onward we begin to hear of indigenous tribes inside Numidia as historical entities: the elder Pliny states that some 463 of these gave allegiance to Rome.[48] That not all of these are listed by Pliny is perhaps lucky; there are enough difficulties in any attempt to discover the location, size or structure of the tribes that we do know. It is probable that the Berbers in the classical period were organized in agnatic kinship groups, in Gellner's term, 'segmentary patrilineal peoples', characteristic of tribal society.[49] Villages might be composed of such extended family groups, sub-divided into clans. But the tendency of clans within a village to feud with each other inhibits the formation of very large units, and makes it difficult for the society to transcend the level of organization of the village itself. It is this split between the indigenous, agnatic structures of the villages and the king –

Hellenistic monarch rather than tribal leader – which may have impeded the development of a state with highly articulated administrative structure. This disjunction is common in tribal societies and flourishes in the literature on the Berbers: thus Montagne contrasts two antithetical types: the 'egalitarian' tribal republics, on the one hand, and the autocratic tyranny of the caids, on the other.[50] There is no evident progression from the relatively anarchic tribal structures to the Hellenistic state: nor, indeed, is there any reason to expect it. From what we have seen, the development of the Hellenistic monarchies in North Africa between the fourth and first centuries BC occurred in emulation of the major polities and was in no way a spontaneous occurrence.

Much modern theory has centred on the tendency for the neighbours of emerging states to emulate the new models they provide, and to take measures to resist the growth of their military power.[51] Berber tribal society from the seventh century onwards was peripheral to two such states, Carthage and, subsequently, Rome. The military resources which these were able to command found a counterweight in the development of the Numidian cavalry (not surprisingly the first thing we hear about in ancient authors), a cavalry which could then be used by the paramount tribal leaders to coerce their own people and raid their neighbours. By the time of Masinissa this cavalry was the primary resource of the state. According to Strabo: 'The kings are much occupied with the breeding of horses, thus 100,000 foals in a year have been counted with a census.'[52] Horses were ridden bareback and bridleless, and the Numidian mercenaries were being used as Roman auxiliaries by the second century BC. Livy leaves a splendid description of an early second-century troop of 800 Numidian horse: 'horses and men were tiny and gaunt; the riders unequipped and unarmed, except that they carried javelins with them; the horses without bridles, their very motion being the ugly gait of animals running with stiff necks and outstretched heads'.[53] These cavalry units were extra-tribal, and provided an important link between the emerging state and its people.

Dreaming in Tombs: the Cult of the Dead

The political disjunction between the Hellenistic kings and their tribes may also be traced on a religious level: alongside a profoundly rooted cult of the god Baal Hammon, adopted as much, perhaps, from Egypt as from the Carthaginians (the Punic goddess Tanit is singularly absent), there were probably a vast number of local gods and lesser spirits who do not even form part of the same pantheon, still less a coherent belief structure. On another level, however, this apparent disjunction found a resolution in the occupation by the kings of a role in communication with the supernatural. This is a classic feature of the Asiatic, tributary state and is evident in the case of the Numidian kings, who seem to have taken over the important cult of the dead. This cult was one of the distinguishing characteristics of Berbers in antiquity. Their dead were certainly connected with the fertility of the soil and probably exercised some control over the future. Thus Pomponius Mela says that 'The Augilae consider the spirits of their ancestors gods, they swear by these and consult them as oracles, and, having made their requests, treat the dreams of those who sleep in their tombs as responses.' As Camps has shown, provision of chambers for this practice is a standard trait of Berber tombs, from prehistory onwards.[54]

More elaborate shrines are sometimes found. In the extraordinary sanctuary of Slonta in the highlands of Cyrenaica the walls were covered with an intricate jumble of carvings showing numerous people in attitudes of worship, as well as snakes, lizards, horses' heads and, towards the centre of the room, an altar topped by the representation of four pigs.[55] Behind the altar a small, possibly natural, niche was decorated with disembodied heads. A bench, probably for sleeping, ran along one wall, while a separate chamber may also have been used for the same purpose. Both chambers were originally roofed. Outside are small stone altars pierced with basins, of a type normally associated with funerary cults. The funerary elements are mixed with fairly clear references to fertility – enlarged sexual members, for instance. This complicated iconography and the provision of space for sleepers to dream – the practice is called incubation – suggest that the sanctuary was used for communication with the dead and also suggests the role of the spirits in ensuring human fertility.

Now, if both funerary chapels, such as Slonta, and ancestral tombs were regarded as fundamental links to the supernatural, it is not surprising that tombs are the major monuments left by the Berber kings. Although the form is Hellenistic, their massive size suggests that the dead kings occupied a role as super-ancestors,

Figure 1.11   The sanctuary at Slonta
(From M. Luni, 'Il santuario rupestre libyco delle imagini a Slonta
(Cirenaica)', Cirene e i Libyi, **12,** 415–18)

monopolizing communication with the spirits and acting as intermediaries in the vital connection between spirits and fertility.
While we have no evidence that the monarchs were deified in life,
after death they were certainly sanctified: Micipsa's tombstone
refers to him as the 'living of the living', and to Masinissa as
'among the gods', while a Roman-period stele was erected to
king Juba, promoted to a deity in death. It is in this quality that
they had a 'right' to tribute, a right which could if necessary be
enforced by the use of arms.[56]

The Development of Indigenous Civil Institutions

Although the initial development of the monarchy appears to us as a qualitative leap, under pressure from neighbouring polities, there is some evidence of a subsequent move towards the use of specifically Berber cultural forms and institutions. This is clearest in the large number of inscriptions in the Libyan alphabet which were produced from at least the fourth century BC. The inscriptions use a simplified Semitic alphabet, highly symmetrical and orthogonal. As in Punic, vowels are not transcribed. It is an ideal epigraphic alphabet, but ill-adapted to cursive texts. The rare official texts tended to be written, like Punic, from right to left, while funerary inscriptions are generally inscribed in columns, read from either the bottom or the top. The use of this script was extremely widespread, stretching from the Fezzan to the Canary islands: a form of it survives today among the Tuareg under the name of Tifinagh, and its use is being revived in Kabylia. Although long texts are rare, and the bulk of the inscriptions are funerary, one long bilingual Punic/Libyan inscription does exist, and this is well

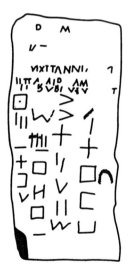

Figure 1.12   Bilingual Latin/Libyan inscription from Morocco (From L. Galand, Langue et littérature berbère (vingt-cinq ans d'études), *Paris, 1979)*

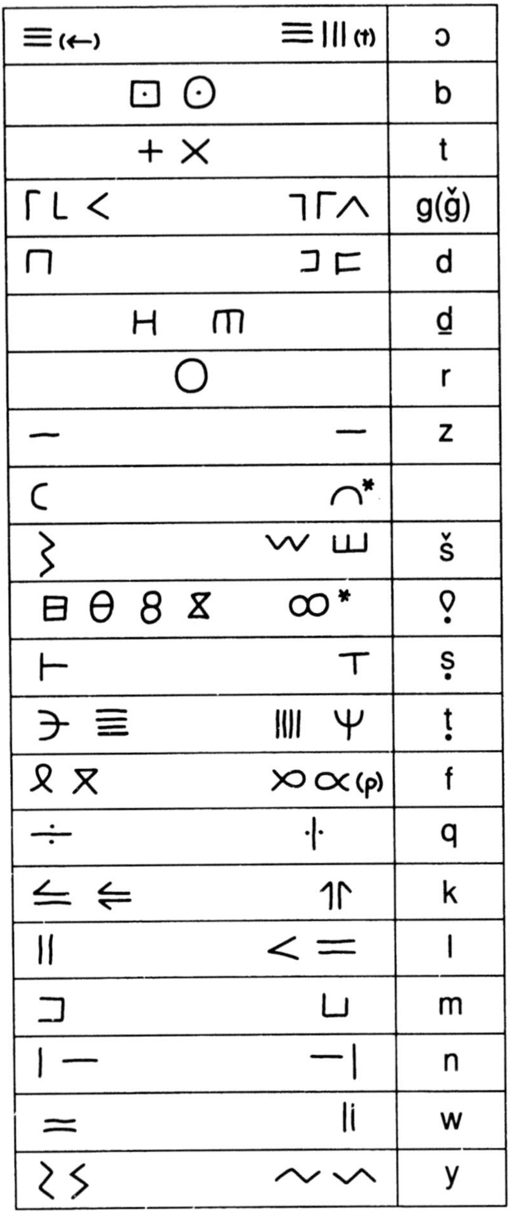

≡ (←)	≡ ||| (↑)	ɔ
▫ ⊙		b
+ ×		t
⌐ L <	⌐ ⌐ ∧	g(ǧ)
⊓	⊐ ⊏	d
H �III		ḏ
○		r
—	—	z
⊂	∩*	
⟩	w ⊔⊐	š
⊟ θ 8 ⅀	∞*	ʠ
⊢	⊤	ṣ
⟍ ≡	|||| Ψ	ṭ
⅄ ⅄	✕ ∝ (p)	f
÷	·|·	q
≤ ⇐	⇑⇗	k
||	< =	l
⊐	⊔	m
	—	—|	n
≈	|i	w
⟩⟨	∼ ⌄	y

Figure 1.13 The Libyan alphabet

worth examining for the evidence it gives us for the development of Numidian institutions. The text comes from Thugga, modern Dougga in Tunisia, which by the middle of the second century had been subtracted from the control of Carthage, either by Masinissa or by Micipsa. The translation given by the editors[57] is as follows:

1   The citizens of Thugga have built this temple to the king (GLD) Masinissa, son of the king Gaia, son of the sufete Zilasan, in the year ten of Micipsa.
2   The year of the GLD Safot, son of the GLD Afsan. The leaders of 100 being Sanak, son of Banai, [son of Sanak] and Safot, son of Ganam, son of Tanakwa.
3   The MSSKWI being Magon, son of Iaristan, son of Sadylan; the GZBI being Magon, son of Safot, leader of 100, son of the GLD Abdesmun.
4   The GLDGIML being Zumar, son of Masnaf, son of Abdesmun; the Prefect in charge of construction being Maqelo, son of the king Asyan, son of the king Magon.
5   In charge of this work: Asyan, son of Ankikan, son of Patas, and Aris, son of Safot, son of Sanak.
6   The builders are: Hanno, son of Iatonbaal, son of Hannibaal, and Niptasan, son of Safot.

It is immediately obvious that while most, but not all, of the personal names are Punic, the titles are not: this is our first glimpse of the development of institutions not directly derived from Punic practice. The most obvious of these is the title GLD. Now GLD can only be translated as ruler – in fact, it is a direct cognate of the modern Berber term Aguellid, or paramount tribal chief. The position of GLD seems to be hereditary, as almost all GLDs have fathers with that title. But the large numbers of holders of this post within what seems to be a period of about three generations suggests that it is not a permanent job, while the fact that most of these are not apparently related has suggested to most commentators that the position is similar to that of an eponymous magistrate, possibly annual, and corresponding to the Punic sufete (although the Punic text does not translate the word in this way). Now, it seems more than coincidental that almost all the holders of the temporary post should be descended from other such holders. It seems possible to suggest that those eligible for the position GLD at Thugga were the heads of their families, and that the position rotated through the principal families of the town. This would be clearly related to the modern Berber practice of rotating chieftainships.

We have no way of guessing the functions of the other officials, but it seems fair to say that the city institutions were relatively complex, and had existed at least since the reign of Masinissa. That they were of indigenous origin is suggested by the fact that the Punic text refrains from translating them, and simply transliterates the Libyan words. The Thugga bilingual and associated texts, then, are evidence for a certain indigenous development of civic institutions. Unfortunately, Thugga is unique. There are no similar inscriptions from other towns: what evidence we have suggests that most of the Numidian towns were governed by sufetes. Higher administration was carried out by members of the king's families, rather than by agents of coherent administrative structures.

Written Language

What the Thugga bilingual does show, however, is that the Libyan language and script were gradually coming into their own as official forms of expression. In the tenth year of Micipsa's reign (138 BC) there was obviously a literate component of the urban population which expressed itself in Berber and not in Punic. How far the use of the Libyan alphabet spread into the countryside is evident from the distribution of its inscriptions: many are found in the wilder areas along the Tunisian–Algerian border, and the vast majority come from rural rather than from urban contexts. The practice of inscribing texts was probably picked up from their neighbours: as Benabou has pointed out, Libyan inscriptions are normally found in areas where either Punic or Roman epigraphy is also present, and it appears to have developed concurrently with the use of these in funerary contexts.[58] Various elements of Punic iconography – solar discs, palms, pinecones and so on – are also borrowed. There is, however, a strong possibility that in an earlier period the texts were painted, rather than inscribed, and have not survived. Certainly they were spread to the Sahara at a very early date, and often accompany the frescos showing chariots.[59] The use of the Libyan alphabet and language appears assertive and symbolic rather than functional, a characteristic which it retains to the present day in the use of Tifinagh for love-letters. Outside the main centres of power, it was used for the tombstones of the tribal leaders. The kings, however, expressed themselves in Punic, as we know from Micipsa's tombstone.

In the years which followed the establishment of Masinissa's kingdom there is thus some evidence for the integration of indigenous forms into what started out as a Hellenistic monarchy with a highly Punicized culture. Like all Berber states since, it was essentially bilingual and bicultural and put this duality to good use. Far from the ephemeral entities described by many modern authors, the African states were relatively solid: Masinissa ruled for over sixty years, Micipsa for thirty, and it would have been surprising if their kingdoms had not developed in the meantime. But if this development did exist it was cut short by the events of the end of the century, when the actions of Masinissa's grandson Jugurtha gave the Romans the occasion to annex a large part of Masinissa's old kingdom.

Jugurtha

The history of the next hundred years is one in which the events in Africa became ever more entwined with the politics of the Roman state. By the middle of the first century AD the whole of North Africa was absorbed into the empire. This did not take place without a struggle, however.

The Jugurthine war was in many ways a paradigm for future wars: in it we can see most of the essential characteristics of Berber military resistance. Like Syphax and Masinissa, Jugurtha combined the military skills learned while fighting with the Roman troops with the classically Numidian use of cavalry and guerrilla tactics.

The political geography of North Africa at the end of Micipsa's reign was essentially quadripartite. In 146, at the end of the third Punic war, Rome had annexed Carthage's territories, creating the province of *Africa* and leaving to Masinissa much of the land he had appropriated in the intervening period, as well as his own Numidian kingdom. To the west, in Mauretania, was found the kingdom of Bocchus, while in a long band along the pre-desert lived the Gaetulians. Although it is often proposed that this group of tribes were exclusively nomadic pastoralists, there is in fact no solid evidence for this; indeed, Strabo refers to scattered habitations in the territory of the Gaetulians, while '*oppida Gaetulorum*' are found in the *Bellum Africum*.[60] Their principal characteristic seems instead to have been that they lay outside the two great kingdoms of Numidia and Mauretania, and resisted any attempts to tax or control them. They occupied an intermediate zone between the Numidians and the Garamantes, and may at this period have been developing into a coalition, in emulation of their northern neighbours. They certainly considered themselves distinct from the Numidians: as late as the second century AD Apuleius could stress the structural opposition between the two, referring to himself as 'half Numidian, half Gaetulian', and comparing himself to Cyrus who was 'half Mede and half Persian'.[61]

In 118BC Micipsa, son of Masinissa, bequeathed his kingdom to his two legitimate sons, Hiempsal and Aderbal, and, on the recommendation of Scipio Aemilianus, to Jugurtha, illegitimate son of his younger brother. Jugurtha followed in his grandfather's footsteps – he had charmed Scipio at the battle of Numantia with his courage and skill – but unlike Masinissa he did not get away with it, and Sallust represents him as more scurrilous than crafty.

After his father's death, Jugurtha promptly killed one cousin and attacked the other in Cirta, the capital. During the capture of the city a number of Roman merchants were killed. The whole episode violated agreements with Rome, and despite Jugurtha's attempts to bribe members of the Senate to accept his *fait accompli*, war was declared in 111BC. The main Roman aim seems to have been the restoration of order: no 'imperialist' ambitions are obvious, but an armed struggle between the various Numidian factions was clearly inconvenient to the orderly progress of Roman trade.

After some initial successes Jugurtha was forced to flee to the Gaetuli, where he raised an army and made contact with the Mauretanian king, his father-in-law, Bocchus. The capture by Marius of his treasury, and by Metellus of most of his kingdom, left Jugurtha without any Numidian troops, but he continued to carry out a certain amount of guerrilla warfare. It was the treachery of king Bocchus, who handed Jugurtha to the Romans, which brought the war to an end, rather than any defeat in battle.[62]

Throughout the war the Romans pursued a policy of plunder and terrorism, burning fields, villages and towns and massacring the civilian population.[63] In 107BC Marius burned the town of Capsa, which had surrendered, massacred its male inhabitants and sold the rest into slavery. He did this because the place was 'convenient for Jugurtha', and its people 'changeable, untrustworthy, and not to be coerced by fear or by favour'. It cannot be supposed that this treatment endeared Rome to the Numidians.

Towards Annexation: Kings, Tribal Leaders and Romans

Between the capture of Jugurtha and Caesar's African war the Roman presence outside their province became increasingly felt. To the small groups of merchants found in Numidian cities outside the province were added groups of veterans in the Medjerda valley. The kingship, which had passed from Jugurtha to his weakminded brother Gauda, to Gauda's son Hiempsal II, and then to his son Juba (plate 1.5), seems still to have been relatively stable and prosperous. The first suggestion that Numidia should become the property of the Romans, made in 50BC, was a piece of fairly transparent opportunism and not immediately successful. But the alliance of Juba I with the faction of Pompey proved to be decisive for the end of his kingdom: Juba was defeated by Caesar at Thapsus in 46BC and his territory divided. The area around Cirta as far as the sea was given to the mercenary Sittius, who had defeated the remainder of the Numidian army, while the rest of Numidia was joined to the old province of Africa. When Bocchus II, the Mauretanian king, willed his kingdom to Octavian in 33BC most of North Africa fell into Roman hands.

The Clients: Juba II and Cleopatra Selene

This was not, however, the end of the Berber kingdoms. Mauretania was treated less as a province than as a convenient place to settle colonies and give land to deserving veterans. In 25BC it was given to Juba II, a son of Juba I who had been brought up in Rome by Augustus and married off to Cleopatra Selene, daughter of Cleopatra and Mark Anthony. His kingdom contrasts

Plate 1.5   Juba I
(From R. Horn and C. Rüger, Die Numider: Reiter und Könige nördlich
der Sahara, *Bonn, 1979)*

in many ways with that of his ancestors, although certain similarities remain. The most obvious of these is its conscious Hellenism – not surprising when even Augustus was modelling himself
on Alexander. Indeed, this was a Hellenism filtered through Rome.
Like Augustus, Juba constructed a royal tomb for himself which
referred to that of Alexander. This is the so-called '*tombeau de la*

Chrétienne' just outside Tipasa, to the east of his capital at Iol. It is bigger, if less well constructed, than the earlier Medracen. Other Hellenistic references, such as the cult of Isis, were even more specific, and may be traced to the formidable Cleopatra – who was, after all, a Ptolemy, and a descendant of one of Alexander's generals. Statues were erected to Juba and his son Ptolemy in a gymnasium at Athens.[64] His new capital at Iol Caesarea was decorated with Italian marble and laid out according to the latest ideas in Roman town planning.[65] Juba also seems to have attempted to establish an entirely alien economic system at Caesarea: over half of the inscriptions of this period refer to Greek slaves or, at least, slaves with what their patrons thought were Greek names.[66] As we have little or no evidence for the widespread use of slaves elsewhere in North Africa, and as in Caesarea itself the practice did not survive, it is tempting to think that slaves served less in an economic context than as a form of status symbol – although we may doubt Juba's ability to raise sufficient tribute from the Mauretanians to keep himself in Roman style. The initial influx of slaves must be due in part to Caesarea's ambitions as a Mediterranean capital: their subsequent disappearance may only be explained by the fact that slavery was ill-adapted to the tribal economic structures of Caesarea's territory.

With Juba we thus have a classic example of an artificial monarchy: imposed by Rome on an area which his family had never governed, his kingdom lacks any reference to its indigenous culture. There is no trace of the integration of Berber, Punic and Hellenistic which we can see in the monarchies of Masinissa and Micipsa: indeed, one searches in vain at Caesarea for traces of

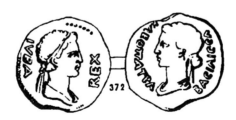

Figure 1.14   Juba II, with his wife Cleopatra Selene
(From J. Mazard, Corpus Nummorum Numidiae Mauretaniaeque, *Paris, 1955)*

anything particularly African. Juba II is one of the most note-
worthy examples of the complete co-option of an African aristo-
crat into the Roman structure. He is hardly the last.

There is some evidence that this monarchy did not go down well
with its subjects: between AD3 and 6 the Gaetulians and a tribe
known as the Musulamians, from the region of Theveste, engaged
in a rebellion which was put down jointly by Juba II and a Roman
general. Cassius Dio records the reasons for the revolt as the anger
of the Gaetulians at Juba II for submitting to the Romans, and
their refusal to do likewise.[67] As we have seen, the Gaetulians
consistently opposed the Numidian kings, and refused to be taxed
by them.

Tacfarinas and the Musulamian Revolt

A direct consequence of this revolt was the stationing of a Roman
legion at Ammaedara, in the territory of the Musulamians, and the
construction in AD14 of a road linking it to the coast. Scarcely was
the new road finished when the next revolt broke out, and it is
hard not to see a connection between the two. The winter camp
was established in tribal territory, and there is some evidence that
the Romans had begun to survey and parcel out the tribal land.
Indeed, the rebels insistently demanded a 'seat' and a land grant –
not the action of nomads, but of a group which feared the appropriation of its territory.

The revolt of the Musulamians comes into better focus than that
of the Gaetulians. Tacfarinas, the rebel leader, was a deserter from
a Numidian auxiliary force, who gathered around himself a group
of men and trained them in Roman military tactics. So successful
was this that he became the chief of the Musulamians and started
a general rising against Rome in AD17. They were joined by the
Gaetulians, along with some 'Mauri' and the Cinithians from
the coast near Gigthis.[68] Thus for the second time in fifteen years
the entire southern border of North Africa was in revolt. The story
of the uprising is familiar: Tacfarinas, consistently defeated in
battle, always managed to escape and adopt guerrilla tactics while
raising a new army among the tribes. He was painted in far less
sympathetic terms than earlier rebels by Tacitus, for as he was not
of royal blood he was obviously a bandit and his offers to treat
were considered presumption. But by AD24 it was complained
in Rome that fully three triumphs had been celebrated over

Figure 1.15 Ptolemy of Mauretania
(From J. Mazard, Corpus Nummorum Numidiae Mauretaniaeque, *Paris, 1955)*

Tacfarinas, who continued to pillage Africa undisturbed. Several things had worked in his favour, principally the arrival on the Mauretanian throne of Juba II's son Ptolemy. Weak-chinned and incompetent, Ptolemy managed to annoy the Mauretanians into joining the revolt. The rebellion thus became general, as even the king of the Garamantes started actively supporting Tacfarinas. Although it was widespread it proved ephemeral: a decisive victory by the Roman general Dolabella and the destruction of Tacfarinas and the greater part of his army in eastern Mauretania brought to an end the last serious attempt to maintain at least some of North Africa free of Roman control. But this rebellion is significant in that it shows the extraordinary unity both of purpose and of communications between the various groups of indigenous North Africa: it is as if all of Gaul had risen at once against the Romans. Again, we can see the potential for unified organization which periodically emerged during the Roman period.

With the murder of Ptolemy in AD40 the emperor Caligula eliminated the last Berber kingdom in Africa. The revolt which this inspired in Mauretania was echoed by the Musulamians in southern Numidia: this was the last tribal revolt recorded in Numidia for two centuries, although sporadic disturbances probably continued throughout the first century.

The Eclipse of the Berber Kingdoms

The history of the last three centuries before Christ thus shows fairly clearly that the Numidian and Mauretanian kingdoms were states in every sense of the word: they were not 'supertribes', to use

Montagne's term, nor were they the temporary agglomerations of charismatic chiefs. Partially, of course, this was the result of the standard Roman practice of meddling in the affairs of its client kingdoms, but the fact that the Numidian state was controlled by a single dynasty throughout this period says much for the essentially stable relationship between the dynasty and its subjects, a relationship which may have contained a significant proportion of religious awe. The major element of instability was, however, characteristically Berber: it was the lack of any natural succession or clear principle of primogeniture. Thus Masinissa's kingdom, on Scipio's advice, was divided between his sons Micipsa, Gulussa and Mastanabal (although Micipsa was probably paramount[69]). Micipsa disastrously left his to Jugurtha, Hiempsal and Adherbal. Gauda left his to Mastanabal and Hiempsal II, and so on.[70] As we shall see, problems continued to arise from this lack of a concept of primogeniture. On the other hand, there has been no trace of the disunity which is generally held to derive from the instability of Berber segmentary social structure.

A second element of disruption is visible in those tribes, such as the Gaetulians, who refused to pay tribute to the kings. This is another Berber theme: both Montagne and Gellner speak of the *Makhzan* tribes of Morocco as 'the inner circle who extracted taxes, as opposed to the middle circle who had taxes extracted from them, and the outer circle, in the *bilād al-sība*, or uncontrolled lands, who refused to allow taxes to be extracted from them.[71] The adjective *Regiani*, which is applied to the tribes Suburbures and Musuni, could be suggested to have the same meaning as *Makhzan*: royal, or of the government. It is perhaps significant that the tribute-paying tribes, like the royal estates, were found in areas which were cultivated early on, and it is likely that tribute was easier to collect from cultivators than from pastoralists, as the tributary relationship between cultivated land and the king was clearer to settled agriculturalists than to tribes such as the Gaetulians which were largely (though not entirely) nomadic.

What is perhaps most striking about the last five centuries before Roman rule is the speed of the transformation of African society. The rapid formation of states, the development of urban structures and of a written language all testify to the ability of the African populations to adapt to and exploit new situations. It is less clear how far these transformations affected the basic nuclei of society: the family and the clan, or their beliefs. We know, for instance, that some groups remained polygamous throughout the Roman period.[72] In the same way, a belief in the powers of the spirits of the ancestors was not eclipsed by the introduction of new gods – Hammon, or Tanit – but existed in parallel with them. It is this same duality, or readiness to adopt new cultural forms while retaining the old on a more intimate level, which characterizes the period of Roman colonization.

2

The Empire and the Other:
Romans and Berbers

It is not the purpose of this book to give even an outline political history of the seven centuries during which North Africa was Roman: the theme of the Romans in North Africa has been well covered elsewhere.[1] But we cannot fall into the other trap, that of simply telling the story of the victims of Roman imperialism, as if there were no other role for the Berbers to play. What is interesting about North Africa is that it gives a very vivid and full range of the types of relationship possible between Rome and its subject peoples in the early empire. On the one hand, Africa produced emperors, on the other, an ever-renewable crop of rebellious tribes, whose religion and culture remained only partially influenced by the hegemony of Rome. The possible relationships between Africans and Romans were numerous: we shall examine a few of them here.

Co-option: Becoming a Roman

As with most of its empire, the policy of Rome appears to have been to co-opt the tribal leaders, and through them to control the tribes, thus maintaining, for a while at least, traditional forms of domination. There appears to have been no lack of minor chiefs willing to co-operate. The advantages were obvious: a *princeps* could obtain Roman citizenship and have his *de facto* power transformed into a high-status, legitimate position.

We have some epigraphic traces of Numidian aristocrats turned Roman citizens: in an inscription from a tombstone found near

Sicca we find a woman called 'Plancina, first lady of the Numidians, of kingly stock'.[2] She was the wife of Quintus [A]rruntius Mas[cel], whose cognomen betrays similar origins, but whose Roman name shows that he was granted citizenship. From Gigthis, in southern Tunisia, comes a second-century dedication to Lucius Memmius Pacatus, who 'stood out among his people'. The fact that this was erected by the tribe of the Cinithians, and that Pacatus is himself called 'Cinithius', demonstrates that he was one of them, although the family went on to achieve senatorial rank.[3] At the veteran colony of Sitifis founded at the end of the first century AD in eastern Mauretania, just south of the Kabylia mountains, we find the inscription of a *prin[ceps] gentis*, probably of the Musunian tribe.[4] His name, Flavius, indicates that he received citizenship under the Flavians, and thus before the foundation of the colony. Here, the tribal chief appears to have acted as an intermediary in the romanization and urbanization of his followers.

The most striking example of Roman policy towards tribal leaders comes from the town of Banasa, in Mauretania Tingitana. Here a bronze tablet records two letters granting citizenship to the family of Julianus, of the Zegrensian tribe. The first, addressed by the emperor Marcus Aurelius to the Roman governor of the province in the middle of the second century, reads:

We have read the petition of Julian the Zegrensian which was attached to your letter, and although Roman citizenship, except when it has been called forth by a member of the chief's family with very great services in the tribe is not wont to be granted to those tribesmen, nevertheless since you assert that he is one of the leading men of his people and is very loyal in his readiness to be of help to our affairs, and since we think that there are not many families among the Zegrensians who can make equal boasts concerning their services, whereas we wish that very many be impelled to emulate Julian because of the honour conferred by us upon his house, we do not hesitate to grant the citizenship, without impairment of the law of the tribe, to him himself, to his wife Ziddina, likewise to his children Julian, Maximus, Maximinus, Diogenianus.[5]

This splendid mixture of resigned distrust and practical politics shows how the process of co-option was viewed by the Romans themselves. Certainly it was advantageous for the family of Julian:

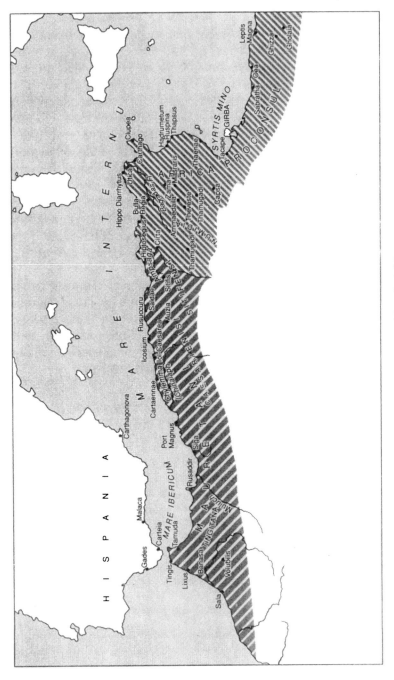

Map 2.1   Roman North Africa

although the first citizen was simply head of 'one of the leading families', his son became *princeps* of the tribe, and we may guess that this appointment was more likely to have been effected by the Romans than by his fellow countrymen.

Another advantage which came from accepting a role in the Roman province was probably the privatization of tribal land. This was hardly a new phenomenon: we have seen that Masinissa held vast estates in *Africa Nova*, and it has recently been suggested the monumental tombs found in much of the Medjerda Valley were erected by indigenous landlords on what may formerly have been tribal land.[6] The relations of production probably continued much as before: surplus produced by the tribe was now acquired by the landlord not as tribute but as rent. The result, as far as the peasant was concerned, was much the same, but the landlord probably possessed more coercive power over the peasants than that which accrued to him by customary law. Further, in so far as he was able to sell their crops, he could now participate fully in the monetary economy of the cities.

The culture of Roman Africa was overwhelmingly urban, and if indigenous aristocrats became major landholders, it was in the town that they spent their wealth.[7] Culturally, or at least epigraphically and archaeologically, they became indistinguishable from any other Roman citizen. It is here that a major contradiction arises. It is very hard to tell in the case of a given individual whether he had Punic, African or immigrant origins. In some cases the name helps, but in the vast majority we simply do not know. The successful African is perfectly camouflaged and only chance remarks, such as that of Apuleius mentioned above or of the schoolteacher from Cirta who declared his origins to be *de sanguine Mauro*, from Moorish blood, help us to see that some of the urban upper classes had Berber origins, but we are unable to quantify them.[8]

The case of the Septimii of Leptis Magna illustrates a particularly successful family *cursus*.[9] In the first century AD the family formed part of the municipal upper classes, and may have been made citizens by the legate of the III Augustan legion, Septimius Flaccus, whose *nomen* they took. One branch then emigrated to Italy, where it held land in Veii, near Rome, and achieved senatorial rank by the second century. This Italian connection was maintained and exploited by the branch of the family which remained in Tripolitania. A Lucius Septimius Severus played a major role in the elevation of Leptis to the rank of colony, serving first as sufete and then, under the new romanized constitution, as *duumvir*. His son, Septimius Geta, was a local notable who facilitated his grandson Severus' promotion to the senate and, in AD193, to the purple. Romans sneered at his halting Latin and his reliance on dreams[10] (shades of the Augilae at their ancestors' tombs) but his African origins showed best in the extraordinary energy he devoted to the promotion of Africa's cities and the expansion of its borders. Severus' reign is one of the high points of Roman rule in Africa. By any measure – new buildings, new men in the senate, pottery production, the expansion of the market in African oil – it can be considered the African age of the empire. This cannot in any way be construed as a form of *revanche*; rather, it is the end result of a process of co-option which had made the governed equate their self-interests entirely with that of the governors.

Berbers in the Army

Just as the aristocracy were willing to co-operate with Rome if they were given the right sort of position in their cities and eventually in the empire as a whole, the creation of auxiliary units of Numidian cavalry gave a new role to an important component in African society, one which brought with it both status and a road to Roman citizenship, for veterans of auxiliary units had an automatic right to citizenship. Further, service in the army could lead to land grants on retirement or reasonably substantial retirement bonuses. The auxiliaries thus in some respects served as schools of Roman life and were probably an important resource for the Berber communities. They maintained, however, an important aspect of the indigenous culture: its involvement in fighting. The status of a knight in an auxiliary *ala* was not far distant from that of the mounted, bridleless warriors of the past, as a series of decorated tombstones shows. A similar grafting of an indigenous military culture on to an imperial army was found in this century in India, when the Gurkha regiments were recruited from independent states outside the frontier, and formed a source of income and prestige for their recruits – and, indirectly, for the independent states themselves.

  At the top of the military structure could be found some notable individuals, such as Lusius Quietus, a 'Maurus' who came to prominence as head of a cavalry contingent, sacking cities in Trajàn's Parthian War. He rose to the rank of consul, and was put in charge of crushing the revolt of the Mesopotamian Jews, a task which he carried out with notable ferocity. Governor of Judaea in AD117, he was executed in the next year for plotting against Hadrian. On Trajan's column he appears at the head of his troops, who are distinguished by their flowing corkscrew curls. His career demonstrates the growing importance of African cavalry units and their leaders within the army, and the route it formed to success on Roman terms.

The Roman army was not composed solely of auxiliaries. Until the third century the principal instrument of Roman control in Africa was the third Augustan legion, which manned the frontiers between Tripolitania and Numidia. It was, like all Roman legions, recruited entirely from Roman citizens, and in the first century was in every sense a foreign body in Africa. However, in the course of the second century, and particularly in the third, Africans were recruited into the legion in large numbers: as their origins became more local the soldiers, based in southern Numidia, identified more directly with the civilian population. Officers would have siblings in the local aristocracy, while soldiers came from successful peasant families in the neighbourhood. The purchase of army supplies would have had important economic effects on the areas in which army camps were found, not least the immission of a substantial quantity of silver into the local economy.[11] This gradual union between the police and the policed is a curious but undeniable phenomenon of Roman rule in North Africa. The very fact that the whole vast Numidian frontier was controlled by a single legion of (ideally) 5,000 men with perhaps as many auxiliaries gives us ample proof that the natives were not continually restless. That the army was an instrument of social control is obvious – and we shall see it in action further west – but it is also clear that it contributed to the more general co-option of the local population. Like city life, it gave another frame of reference to the individual, outside his tribal or family loyalties.

Peasants and Property Relations

The Roman tendency to leave native customary property relations relatively intact while using the cities as the principal means of extracting taxes is particularly evident in North Africa. As we have seen, the Numidian kings received tribute from their subjects, and within the old Carthaginian territory Masinissa founded large private estates. Other nobles probably had rights over the tribute from individual villages: it has recently been shown that there is a clear topographical relationship between large, 'noble' tombs and indigenous villages in the ancient territory of Carthage, and the tombs may express ownership of some kind.[12] Vitruvius had a friend, described as a 'son of Masinissa' (which would have been difficult chronologically, but the sense that he was of the royal family is clear), who owned an oppidum called Ismuc, along with all its fields.[13] He may have had even more extensive rights over the village, as he discussed the possibility of breeding imported slaves there so as to profit from the fact that the local water made children wondrously sweet-voiced. Now, we have little evidence for the private ownership of land away from Punic territory, although Pliny tells us that land in the oasis of Tacape, miraculously fertile and productive, was extremely expensive.[14] There is, however, a relationship between the conditions of land use and their relation to land ownership. Irrigated farming is regularly associated with individual private property, while pasture land with its vaguer boundaries may be more generally associated with a clan or a tribe. We might thus expect a mixed structure, with a complicated system of rights which could range from the private ownership of a single tree to the tribal rights over winter pasture in the desert.

Our knowledge of estates in Roman North Africa reflects both aspects of these property relations, although the most detailed evidence comes from estates owned by the emperor rather than by local aristocrats. The landowners were structurally similar to the emperor, and the addition of the imperial administration simply added another tier to the process of extracting the peasant's surplus. A series of inscriptions from the Medjerda valley in Tunisia has done much to elucidate the nature of the imperial estates.[15] In a sense, they depict a pre-Roman, tributary situation to which a new, Roman level of administration has been added. Individual estates were let to a *conductor*, or head lessee, at a fixed rent for a five-year period. He would be entitled to the rents from the tenants, or *coloni*, who farmed the land on a share-cropping basis. The *coloni* would also be required to provide several days of labour service a year for the 'home farm' run directly by the *conductor*. This system was modified by a ruling referred to on the inscriptions as the *lex Manciana*. Uncultivated land could be claimed by any tenant willing to improve it by bringing it under cultivation. Figs, olives and vines newly planted on this land would be rent free for a number of years while immature, after which normal rents would prevail. The *lex Hadriana* modified the tenure of these cultivations by making them alienable by sale or inheritance, and by extending the rent-free period. Imperial procurators oversaw the functioning of these estates, mediating in disputes between the *coloni* and the *conductores* and generally looking after the interests of the owner.

The system is thus one in which tenants were encouraged to invest in the development of the estate by the grant of property rights over the trees which they planted. After the rent-free period they still had to pay a proportion of the crop to the *conductor*. The marketing of the crop was up to the *conductor*, whose cash rent was fixed and not dependent on the harvest. The peasants themselves would have sold any remaining surplus on the local periodic market, where they would have bought anything they could not produce themselves. As long as peasants were in short supply their conditions were thus not particularly arduous: they were free to sell up and leave the estate, and could increase their capital with time. The system, which seems to have been unique to Africa, created an increasing surplus of olive oil, reflected in the wide distribution of African oil amphorae, and a category of small *possessores*, whose own holdings linked them to the estates but drew them away from any property which might have been held in common by a kinship group.

The history of settlement in various parts of North Africa seems to demonstrate this gradual loosening of the strength of tribal groups. This is a history which a number of recent archaeological surveys is beginning to fill out. They show the gradual development of peasant farming both in the areas settled from Punic times and in the more marginal lands of the pre-desert, where intensive labour on irrigation was required to make farming possible.

In Tripolitania, two major projects have given us a particularly clear image of settlement in the Roman period.[16] Tripolitania divides fairly neatly into three zones: the coastal plain, the Gebel or high plateau to the south whose scarce rainfall still allows some cultivation, and the pre-desert to the south-east where agriculture must be irrigated to be viable. Close to the coast, finds of numerous olive farms show the basis of the wealth of the aristocracies of towns such as Leptis Magna. Here, although a system of tenants paying rent in kind might have prevailed, the importance of olive oil as a cash crop gave their owners an interest in the direct management of their estates, and many of the farms closest to the town may have been cultivated by slaves.[17] This development of great estates producing olives was precocious, probably starting as early as the first century BC. Further south a large number of farms are found in the river valleys of the Wadis Sofeggin and Zemzem and in the smaller valley systems running into the Syrtis.[18] These areas, like Southern Tunisia, probably underwent a changeover from pastoral nomadism in the late first century AD. Immense labour was put into the land to catch as much as possible of the run-off with dams and terracing. The farms were isolated or grouped in hamlets of five or six houses. Some of the larger farms had dependencies, but in general they appear to be the sort of exploitations which would be run by an extended family. We know from various sources, not least the archives of the soldiers on the frontiers, that some of these farms were inhabited by a people called the Maces, who were regarded as peaceable by the Romans.[19] The large amounts of imported pottery found on these sites show that they participated in the Roman market economy, and they may have served as intermediaries in communications with the Garamantes beyond the frontiers.[20]

One important group of farms is found at Ghirza, in the valley of the Wadi Zemzem some 180 km due south of Leptis Magna. Here a number of castle-like buildings with numerous rooms and large courtyards are flanked by smaller buildings, huts, and enclosures for stock.[21] The major families erected elaborate mausoleums for themselves, decorated with vivid scenes of ploughing (with camels and oxen), threshing and winnowing, lion, hare and cheetah hunts, ostriches, camels and caravans, horsemen, executions and battles. An inscription which mentions the sacrifice of fifty-one bulls and thirty-eight goats (all male) indicates the importance of pastoralism in their economy. They probably enjoyed a large degree of autonomy, and their inscriptions proclaim a command of Latin rather different from the rest of the area, where neo-Punic is the dominant epigraphic language.[22] In all the rural areas, however, the people recorded bear Libyan names.

A survey near Thelepte, in southern Tunisia, shows a more gradual development of settlement patterns in the area.[23] An economy with a major component of pastoral nomadism in the

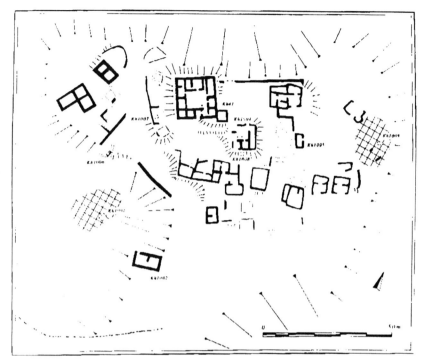

Figure 2.1   Third-century farming settlement with 'big house' from the Libyan desert
(*From D. Welsby, 'ULVS XX: the Gsur and associated settlements',* Libyan Studies, 23, 1992)

period before Roman rule seems to have given way to settled agriculture in the course of the first century AD. The first settlements, near the Roman colonies of Cillium and Thelepte, were fairly large agglomerations, and it was not until the third and fourth centuries that scattered villas, farms and hamlets started to emerge – perhaps signs that the peasants were moving towards a more individual cultivation of the land. The farms had olive presses, enclosures for animals and field systems, suggesting a relative balance between the cultivation of grain and olives and stock raising.[24]

To the west, in Mauretania Sitifensis, settlement patterns were radically different. We have no trace of the sort of hierarchies visible in Tripolitania and Africa Proconsularis. The amount of land occupied by imperial estates increased, but the form of its exploitation appears to have been different. Here, the peasants were grouped in large *castella* under the direct control of an imperial procurator who managed the estates: we do not have any evidence as to whether they were sharecroppers or some other form of labourers. The principal crop was wheat, and we can see no signs of the development of arboriculture so obvious in Africa and Numidia.[25]

The territory of Cherchel – Juba II's capital of Iol Caesarea – has also been intensively surveyed.[26] What emerges is a fascinating mosaic of settlement types. Both on the coast and in the richer mountain valleys are found farms and villas whose construction and oil presses relate them to the urban economy. On the worst lands, villages which may or may not have been composed of tenants huddle over poor fields and upland pastures. These evidently played little role in the urban, market economy, and produced almost exclusively for their own subsistence.[27] This was probably the pattern further west, where urban centres became fewer and the areas under direct Roman control more limited.

Finally, we know something of the rural settlement in Mauretania Tingitana, thanks to the work of R. Rebuffat.[28] The province as a whole was thinly settled, with few cities and large zones of mountain and forest. In the valley of the Oued Sebou, east of the inland town of Banasa, rural settlement was already developing in the first century BC, during the time of Juba II. Occupation of small farms, with little settlement hierarchy, grew through the second century AD, but appears to have stagnated in the third century. In the late empire, although direct Roman control was withdrawn as early as AD280, the cities were evidently still occupied. However, identifiable pottery is no longer found on rural sites, which points to a growing isolation from the market if not to an actual desertion of the countryside.

There is thus a fair amount of variation both in settlement and in modes of production, although most of the farmers probably participated in the market to some extent, as finds of pottery and metalwork show. The free peasant is perhaps the rarest category, found outside the areas occupied by cities and imperial estates, near the frontiers and in the mountain valleys. Most other farmers were tenants, either individual or collective, and their surplus production was probably extracted in kind, although local periodic markets would have provided some entry into the monetary economy. There was probably a certain amount of crossing-over between the categories – a peasant might own a few fields outright and cultivate others as a tenant on an estate or as an itinerant harvester. Others might save up sufficient capital to establish themselves as large landowners in their own right. Best known of these (but how typical was he?) is the poor-boy-made-good whose story is told on an inscription from Mactar:

> I was born into a poor family; my father had neither income nor house. From my birth I have always cultivated my field: neither I nor my land ever rested. As the season ripened the crop I was the first to cut my sheaves. When groups of harvesters gathered in the fields of Cirta in Numidia, or near the mountain of Jupiter, then I was the first in the field; then, leaving my country I harvested for others for twelve years, under the burning sun; for eleven years I led a gang of harvesters, cutting with our sickles the wheat in the fields of Numidia. By working, and by knowing how to be content with little, I became the owner of a villa and master of an estate; the house lacks for nothing in riches. I have even achieved honours: I was called to the senate of my city, and from peasant I became censor. I have seen my children and grandchildren born and grow up. My life has passed in honour, unblemished by any crime. Learn, mortals, to live a blameless life, for even thus a man deserves to die who has lived without treachery.[29]

Tribes and the Unregenerate

The first three categories of Roman African – aristocrats, cavalry and soldiers, and peasants – all had some sort of positive inducement to co-operate with the new order. They did this, it seems, almost individually: by becoming a knight in a Roman auxiliary force the new military loyalty took the place of the old tribal affiliation. Peasants appear to have identified with their village or estate, but the more successful they were the farther they moved from the tribal context. This is evident in the names they gave their children: in the second and third centuries AD, Berber names are recorded almost exclusively in the lowest (recording) classes, and then are more common for women than for men. But all our evidence suggests that many tribes persisted through the empire, and indeed that tribal structures emerged in the fourth century just as strong as before. The Roman treatment of the tribes thus deserves close examination.[30]

In Africa, as in other frontier provinces, the conquest of territory was succeeded by a period in which its tribal occupants were cantonned into limited tribal lands, and occasionally split into small sub-sections so as to prevent future collusion and revolt. Our evidence for this process is derived from the boundary stones set up by the legionary legate at the moment a particular tribe was assigned a territory. In the pre-desert of southern Tunisia the tribe of the Nybgenii, mentioned by Ptolemy, was established on a vast, arid patch of land south of the oasis of Tacape. Under Trajan, the Musulamians were officially granted a portion of what had been their territory in the pre-Roman period. How far was the delimitation of a tribal territory in a particular area a recognition of the *status quo* – that is, an attempt to order an existing situation rather than a radical displacement of a tribal group?

The case of the Nybgenii is fairly clear. The creation of their reserve took place in the context of the survey by the army of the whole of southern Tunisia.[31] The object of this process could be described as the definition of separate parcels of territory for the purposes of determining ownership and consequently taxation. Not only were the Nybgenii included in this, but also the towns of Tacape and Capsa. Land not assigned to these might become the property of private individuals or of the emperor. Now, the participation of the Nybgenii on the same footing as the two *municipia* indicates that they had a similar status: they were recognized as a *civitas stipendaria* and constituted a legal entity. Their capital was situated in the oasis of Telmin, the *Civitas Nybgenorum* or, as it was known in the third century, Turris Tamalleni. By AD100 the *Civitas Nybgenorum* was constructing a road to Capsa and it was made a *municipium* by Hadrian. This rapid development seems to suggest another instance of co-option, not of an individual but of a whole tribal group. The removal of the tribal name from the settlement – mirrored at Thubursicu Numidarum, which became plain Thubursicu by the third century – suggests that the tribal association was not felt appropriate to a new Roman *municipium*.

The case of the Musulamians is somewhat different.[32] The *limitatio* of their territory occurred at a time when large estates under private ownership were already established in the area. It is possible that formal boundary divisions were established after a series of disputes over the encroachment of these estates, legitimizing the expropriations which had already taken place but limiting future ones. In the centre of their territory lies their old capital of Theveste, now a newly refounded veteran colony. What was the relationship between the new colony and the tribe? And who administered their territory? The answers to these questions remain entirely obscure, although since auxiliary troops were already being raised from the tribe during this period a certain number of Musulamians must have become eligible for citizenship. Again, as members of the tribe were brought into the market economy we can probably see the slow substitution of economic relations for those based, even ideally, on kinship.

Evidence for administrative structures of the Berber tribes and villages comes from a number of inscriptions from the area of the old kingdom of Masinissa. This is the institution of the *undecemprimi*, or council of notables, which we find in the *Gens Saboidum*, the *Gens Bacchuiana*, at Mactar and a number of smaller towns. Sometimes they were simply referred to as *primores*, as at Sicca, while at the *castellum* of Tituli a dedication to Neptune was put up by the elders, or *seniores*, together with the *plebs* and *magister*, suggesting a community with a council of elders headed by an (elected?) chief: as we shall see, this is a pattern frequently found in modern Berber villages.[33] The major difference between this and the modern form, however, is that beside the *seniores* we continue to find traces of hereditary kings, for example the '*rex gentis Ucutamani*' who is known from the little Kabylia – the first trace of a tribe, the Kutāma, which would one day sweep the Fatimid dynasty to power.[34]

Elsewhere, particularly in Numidia and the Kabylia mountains, the situation appears to have been quite different. There, far from being given autonomous status, the tribes were governed by a Roman prefect, probably a young soldier establishing himself as an administrator. Such was Lucius Calpurnius Fabatus, prefect of the 'six nations of Gaetuli found in Numidia' at the time of Trajan,[35] or the man who was both prefect of a cavalry *ala* and of the *gens Mazices* in the valley of the Chelif.[36] These prefects certainly had some hand in recruiting auxiliaries, but whether they had direct administrative responsibilities over the tribes is open to doubt. When a tribe was deemed civilized, which we can see expressed by the transformation of its status to *civitas*, its administration was certainly left to its own members – the *principes*, which have been discussed above, or *magistri*. By the late empire many of the tribes were still run by prefects, although these were

no longer foreign but came from the tribes themselves. In a letter
of St Augustine we read that some of the tribes 'are attached to the
Roman territories without their own kings but, at their heads,
prefects chosen by the Roman empire'. Inscriptions from the third
and fourth century give the names of various of these – M.
Aurelius Masaisilen; Aurelius Urbanus Mastlius, or Gerrasu – and
there is no doubt of their cultural affiliation.[37] They had themselves represented on their tombstones, mounted, carrying spears
and shields, and sometimes followed by other horsemen. The most
famous such stele is that of Abizar. His name is written in the
Libyan alphabet next to his upraised right hand, which holds a
spherical object. In his left hand he holds a round shield and three
javelins, while in front of the horse runs a large bird – probably an
ostrich which he is hunting. The carving is primitive, but the
iconography combines that of the late Roman noble, represented
on horseback while hunting, with one of the symbols of African

Figure 2.2   Stele of Abizar, from Kabylia
(From P.-A. Février, 'L'art funéraire et les images des chefs indigènes
dans la Kabylie antique', Actes du premier congrès d'études des cultures
Méditerranéennes d'influence arabo-berbère, *Malta, 1972, pp. 152–74)*

nobility, the ostrich, whose plumes decorated the heads of the Garamantes and who retained a powerful symbolic reference for the Tuaregs in this century.[38]

With these prefects, half tribal chiefs, half Roman administrators, we come to the most interesting type of relationship between Roman and Berber, a relationship in which there is apparently no hope of progress towards identity or co-option or even any particular hope of tribute. Rather, there is an overwhelming desire to keep on good terms with tribes whose ill will would be at best annoying, at worst disastrous. There were ritual and symbolic means of codifying these relationships. A series of eleven altars and inscriptions dating between c.AD170 and AD280 record the 'colloquia' and peace treaties between the Roman governors of Mauretania Tingitana and the tribe of the Baquates.[39] It is clear from these that the Baquates were autonomous, although they may have been used as intermediaries to control their neighbours.

The leaders of these 'client tribes' might be granted the insignia which we first saw given to Syphax and Masinissa: sceptres, coronets and robes.[40] The tribal leaders were referred to as *principes*, and Rome was prepared to treat them as 'equals' by entering into treaty relationships with them – the Baquates are referred to as a 'confederate tribe' (*gens foederata*) – and recognizing their noble status. This symbolic codification of the 'client king' relationship became increasingly important to tribal society. In AD533, after the Byzantine reconquest, we find a local chief requesting the 'client king' set of honours so that he would be accepted *by his own subjects*. Procopius says 'according to Moorish custom, no one can rule even if he is the enemy of the Romans before the Romans give him the symbols of government. Now, they had already received these from the Vandals, but did not consider their power sure.' The honours consisted of 'a silver-gilt staff, a silver headdress like a sort of crown made of silver bands, a white mantle attached to the right shoulder by a gold pin, like a thessalian chlamys, and gold shoes'.[41] Rome had become a source of legitimation on its periphery, outside the areas which it effectively controlled.

When power over the internal tribes was effectively transferred to their own leaders this same symbolic relationship was called into play. From one of the Ghirza tombs comes a sculpture representing just such a chief, seated in a curule chair and holding a cup and a sceptre or scroll, while smaller figures offer him wine and, possibly, tribute (plate 2.1). The tomb from which it comes dates to the fourth century, and the names recorded – M[archius] Chullam, Varnychsin, Marchius Nimmire and Marchius [M?]accurasa – are a mixture of Roman, Punic and Libyan.[42] These ambiguous princes, often referred to in Tripolitania as *tribuni*,[43] are heirs of the Numidian chief in other important ways. At Ghirza was sited a major temple of a Semitic type, the only known cult centre in the pre-desert.[44] Indeed, the god worshipped at the site may have given the settlement his name, as we know that the nomadic tribes of fourth and fifth century Tripolitania adored the god Gurzil.[45] The use of the temple well into the sixth century, and a corresponding lack of evidence for Christianity,[46] argues that the dominant family at Ghirza had not only temporal power over the area but also some wider ranging claim to spiritual power.

Tribes outside the frontier were carefully watched, and much of the activity of the soldiers on the frontiers seems to have consisted of this kind of surveillance. We have evidence of it from a series of ostraka, or sherds on which notes were taken, from the fort of Gholaia in the Libyan desert.[47] One sherd reports the entry (into Roman territory) of 'Garamantes bearing barley, four mules and

Plate 2.1   Chieftain from Tomb N at Ghirza
(From O. Brogan and D. Smith, Ghirza: A Libyan Settlement in the
Roman Period, *Tripoli, 1984)*

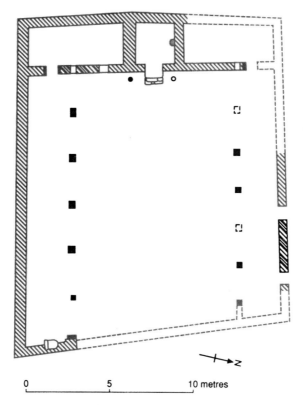

Figure 2.3   The sanctuary of Gurzil at Ghirza
(From O. Brogan and D. Smith, Ghirza: A Libyan Settlement in the
Roman Period, *Tripoli, 1984)*

four asses'; another of 'Garamantes leading four asses'. One of the
functions of the frontier zone, or *limes*, with its long walls, ditches,
and small signal stations in front of it, was apparently to act as a
semi-permeable membrane for the tribes who nomadized in and
out of Roman territory.[48]

Cycles of Aggression

Of course, not all relationships with the peripheral tribes were so
well ordered. From the second century onwards, Mauretania,
Southern Numidia and then Tripolitania were shaken by revolts
and external raiding parties which required a military response.

These are, at last, relations of pure antagonism. How did they arise? The answers are complex but closely tied to responses to the overt behaviour of the Romans. To the expansion and consolidation of the frontiers under Hadrian can be added a tendency to expansion on the part of the cities themselves. From the Algerian coast comes an inscription defining the territory of the town of Igilgili, and warning the tribe of the Zimizes that 'they no longer have the right to use these lands'.[49] In AD112, before they were brought into a more stable relationship with Rome, the Baquates raided the coastal town of Cartenna – possibly, as Benabou suggests, in reaction to a move towards their own territory.[50] Another cause of tribal resentment in those areas outside the effective control of the empire was almost certainly slaving. A customs tariff from the south-eastern borders of Mauretania mentions a tax on slaves, which suggests they were being brought up from the south.[51] A geography called the *Expositio Totius Mundus et Gentium* names slaves as the principal export of Mauretania, while among the newly discovered letters of St Augustine we find one in which he complains bitterly that 'Those commonly called slave-merchants are so numerous in Africa that they empty a large part of the countryside of its population, and export to provinces

Figure 2.4   Late Roman estates: the castellum of Kaoua
(From S. Gsell, Monuments antiques de l'Algérie, Paris, 1901, vol. I)

overseas those they buy, and who are almost all free men'. For these, especially the Christians among them, he feels the utmost pity, for who can resist these 'merchants who do not deal in animals but in men, not in barbarians but in Romans'? By the time of St Augustine, then, the slave trade was expanding to the Roman heartlands – but it is clear that the trade in *barbarians* (read tribesmen) was looked on as normal and raids outside the frontier condoned.[52] One of the effects of these raids, as it emerges from the same letter, was the reverse: small-scale barbarian raids on isolated hamlets, whose prisoners were either sold to the same merchants or held for ransom outside the province. This might result in a punitive expedition against the tribesmen, thus creating a spiral of predatory conduct and violence which would have been a continuous irritant along the frontier. Finally, the Roman cities were rich; sometimes, as in the case of Leptis Magna, offensively so. In periods of unrest, or of temporary military weakness on the part of Rome, the prizes were evidently tempting.

Mauretania Tingitana was probably the most unstable of all the African provinces, but we know little about the actual events which led the Romans to give it up as early as the reign of Diocletian. At the end of the second century we can see a general strengthening of the frontiers. In Numidia the frontiers were strengthened under Septimius Severus, and a line of forts thrust down into the Saharan Atlas, an area which was probably fairly densely populated. At the same time we have references to Severus' victory over 'warlike and ferocious tribes' near Leptis Magna, in Tripolitania,[53] and the great oasis forts, Gholaia (Bu Ngem), Gheriat el Garbia and possibly Ghadames constructed at the beginning of the third century were probably a reaction to this menace.[54]

By the middle of the third century Mauretania Caesariensis was the centre of a full-scale war against a confederation led by the tribe of the Bavares, who apparently lived both in the mountains within the Roman province and to the south-west of the Hodna basin.[55] Significantly, our first sign of unrest is a letter of AD253 from St Cyprian deploring the kidnapping of Christians by barbarians. A series of skirmishes and Roman victories occupied the next few years, until in 259 the four 'kings' of the Bavares were joined by the five tribes of the Quinquegentanei and the tribe of Faraxen, the *'gentiles Fraxinenses'*. Although the revolt was put down by 263, it had flared up again by the end of the century.

These cycles of violence with the tribes on the frontiers were a problem never effectively resolved: as we shall see, they continued with ever-increasing ferocity into the late empire. They created conditions of increasing insecurity in the countryside, while maintaining the glamour of the warrior ethos even within the areas of provinces which were most heavily Romanized.

The Late Empire and the Rebirth of Berber Kingdoms

Anyone familiar with the archaeology of North Africa associates the fourth century with a period of astonishing material brilliance, rivalled only by the Severan period.[56] But there is a difference: while at the beginning of the third century an extraordinary amount of money was put into public building, in the fourth the most striking monuments are private houses, whose huge reception rooms were decorated with splendid mosaics. As elsewhere in

*Plate 2.2   The noble estate: mosaic from an estate near Carthage
(Photo: D. Kennet; Museum of Carthage)*

the empire, wealth was becoming ever more concentrated in the hands of a few, but those few were very wealthy indeed. In a town such as Djemila, Roman Cuicul, south of little Kabylia, just four or five great houses seem to have been the homes of the major families of the period.[57] All were of course landlords, with estates to which the peasants were ever more closely tied. The class of small decurions had not disappeared altogether, however, and some social mobility was still possible. The most obvious example of this is St Augustine, himself the son of a minor decurion in a small provincial town: his mother's name, Monica, is Berber, and suggests that she came of African stock.[58]

The conditions of the rural population were probably significantly worse than in the preceding centuries. Although the tenants on the great estates were still legally free to leave, de facto they were almost entirely tied to the landowner. Thus in one letter Augustine asks whether a landlord can sell his tenants into slavery.[59] On the other hand, although undoubtedly abused, the rural population was not diminishing. A recent survey of Southern Numidia has demonstrated that almost all farms were still occupied in the fifth and sixth centuries, while in central Tunisia a survey has shown continuous renewal of rural property into the fifth century.[60] But these surveys can tell us nothing about the relationships of power, and it is doubtful that all the farmers were independent. It is probable that with the increase in population pressure the landlords or lessees could effectively call the tune, and while the customary laws about the planting of new trees on uncultivated land still existed, peasants had in fact fewer opportunities to improve their lot.[61]

The growth in the personal power of the landlords was not restricted to the urbanized part of the population. In mountains such as those of Kabylia the sort of dominance we can see on 'urban' senatorial estates took on a more traditional face. One of the most significant tribal disturbances in the fourth century centred around the family of a Mauretanian *princeps*, Flavius Nubel. We know of him both from the history of Ammianus Marcellinus, as a 'little king most powerful among the Moorish tribes' and, from an inscription, as the builder of a church near Rusguniae in which was placed a supposed fragment of the true cross.[62] The inscription describes him as son of a man with equestrian rank and as the prefect of a cavalry unit – again, the cavalry provides a link between the native aristocracy and the Roman

state. He had both a wife, Nonnica, and concubines, an arrange-
ment that can be seen as a Christianized version of polygamy. By
these he had a number of children whose names indicate the
cultural ambivalence – if not the conscious strategy – of a family
with one foot in the Roman camp and the other planted firmly in
tribal society. One was called Gildo, clearly derived from the
Libyan root GLD which, we have seen, means ruler. The names of
the other sons included the Latin Firmus and Dius, the Berber
Mascazel and Sammac, while the only daughter we know of bears
the Greek name Cyria.

The material wealth of Nubel's children was matched by a great
fluency in Roman culture. At some time before AD371 Sammac
erected a metric inscription at his estate, Petra, in which the first
and last letters of each line, read vertically, give the acrostic
'*Praedium Sammacis*' (Sammac's estate): Ammianus describes
the estate as 'built like a city', and the cultural reference of the
inscription is urban as well:

> With prudence he establishes a stronghold of eternal peace, and
> with faith he guards everywhere the Roman state, making strong
> the mountain by the river with fortifications, and this stronghold he
> calls by the name of Petra. At last the tribes of the region, eager to
> put down war, have joined as your allies, Sammac, so that strength
> united with faith in all duties shall always be joined to Romulus'
> triumphs.[63]

Sammac thus claims to have made the neighbouring tribes lay
down their arms and make peace with Rome. He is a mediator
between the two elements in the society, and boasts of it. There is
also a more menacing subtext: the tribes are Sammac's allies, not
Rome's, and will do his bidding.

The beginning of Firmus' revolt was not unlike that of
Jugurtha's: accused of murdering his brother Sammac, who was
supported by the Roman authorities, he found himself forced to
take up arms against them. With him fought all his other brothers
with the exception of Gildo, who took the Roman side.

Now, a recent analysis of this war has made it very clear that
this was no more a class struggle than was the war against
Jugurtha.[64] Nor is it a case of Berber versus Roman. Rather, the
war against Firmus was a dynastic struggle pitching one lot of
African nobles, with their tribes, against another. But the existence
of unquestioningly loyal tribesmen on the great estates of these

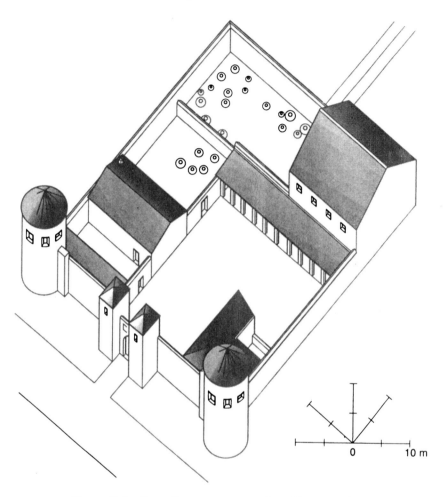

Figure 2.5 Late Roman estates: the villa at Nador
(From Anselmino et al., Il Castellum di Nador, *Rome, 1989)*

nobles shows that little of the personal and tributary relationships within the African tribes had changed. Just as in the past, the nobles offered protection in exchange for tribute and military service. Their castles sheltered their tribesmen against raids, not only by other tribes but also, perhaps, by the Romans, for whom the *barbari* could be legally enslaved. This relationship between nobles and tribes was, of course, beneficial to both. Members of Nubel's family by now occupied key roles in Roman provincial

*Plate 2.3   A Roman perfume flask showing a Garamantian captive: the
lines on his cheeks probably represent ritual scars
(Photo: S. Fontana)*

administration, but much of this was due to their unquestionable
personal power, and this was based as much on the armed might
which they could command on occasion as on their fluency in
Roman cultural forms and their ability to communicate as equals
with the rest of the Roman elite. They had, if they survived, the
best of both worlds.

Firmus' brother Gildo, who revolted in 396, was even more
tightly interlocked with the empire. His daughter Salvina was
married to a nephew of the emperor, and at the time of his revolt
he had been appointed *comes*, or count, of Africa. During his short
secession he behaved in all ways as a 'Roman' ruler, holding court
and striking coins with his image.[65] His immense wealth put him
on a par with the great families of the empire: more than a regional

potentate, he was a member of its inner circle. However, he did not long survive his defection, and the manner of his defeat was appropriate: just as Gildo had been used against Firmus thirty years before, so he was himself defeated by one of his brothers, Mascazel.

The two parallel stories of Nubel's heirs bring us back to a theme discussed in the first chapter: the undoubted effect of the lack of a tradition of primogeniture. Just as the succession to Micipsa was disputed because of the lack of a clear successor, so Nubel's succession split his power and estates among his progeny, each one of which seems to have become chief of a separate tribal or territorial grouping: Mascazel of the Tyndenses, Dius of the Masinissenses and so on.[66] This continual fracturing of power between generations seems to have been one of the factors that prevented the formation of major blocs under dynastic control. Historians and anthropologists have spent much time on the determinants of the balanced anarchy of the mountain tribes, but the constraints on the transmission of personal power have been given very little consideration. It was not so much the 'democratic' or segmentary institutions of the underlying structure as the difficulty of passing on accumulated power to his heirs that thwarted any possibility of the consolidation of Nubel's kingdom in Kabylia.

Archaeologically, we know little of this society. Survey in the Belezma has revealed fortified structures in the mountains, with associated hamlets, which appear to date to the fifth century.[67] Numerous inscriptions refer to the construction of '*centenaria*'. The term originally referred to small forts, but it was taken over by the builders of fortified farmhouses, such as that of Marcus Caecilius Bumupal in Tripolitania or of Marcus Aurelius Masaisilen in Kabylia, with an associated village and church. In the Wadi Sofeggin, in Tripolitania, Flavius Nasama and his son, Macrinus, built a *centenarium* to guard and protect all the region.[68] The grandest of them all was Kaoua[69] in Mauretania, with a Greek cross plan surrounded by two circular walls (figure 2.4). Over the door were found a series of low reliefs: a man with a dagger, a gazelle and a chi-rho, as well as an inscription reading SPES IN DEO FERINI AMEN.

Contemporary with these emerging castles, however, were splendid villas, which we find depicted on mosaics such as the well-known series showing the estate of Lord Julius. One of these found in the last century at Oued Athmenia, west of Cirta, had a huge peristyle court for its stables of thoroughbreds, and extremely elaborate baths. Now, these societies were certainly interlinked, and it is probable that the senatorial proprietor of an 'urban' villa would have had clients in the more tribal areas whose strongholds would have presented an altogether more uncouth aspect, but whose own peasants could be transformed into an effective fighting unit. The Numidian cavalry was still a weapon to be reckoned with, but it was increasingly found in private hands.

The Threat from the Desert

Another sort of tribal conflict occurred in Tripolitania at this time; it can be seen as a worsening of the sort of external tribal wars we saw earlier. This was the destruction of Leptis Magna at the hands of a tribe called the Austuriani, recorded by the historian Ammianus Marcellinus.[70] An important recent study of this tribe suggests that, along with the Leuathae, the Austuriani derived from the tribe of the Nasamones, recorded as early as Herodotus as nomadizing between the Syrtis and the oasis of Augila.[71] One of their number, who had attempted to raise the settled peoples inside the Roman province against the cities, was burnt at the stake by the authorities. The first raid occurred in AD363. On the refusal of the Count of Africa, Romanus, to counterattack unless supplied with 4,000 camels, the raids were repeated until the defeat of the Austuriani in AD367 – although since their raids continued during the next forty years the defeat cannot have been definitive.[72] This, then, is an example of an attack on the province by a Berber tribe living outside it, but with close contact with other Berber tribes such as the Maces who lived within Roman territory and may have participated in the raids.

The effect of the Vandal conquest of AD429–440 on tribal society seems initially to have been little more than a change of patrons, giving the nobles new and not necessarily more reliable possibilities for alliance and discord. However, the legitimation which the Roman state made possible disappeared along with their power to enforce it, and there is evidence that both the pre-desert and the mountain areas escaped altogether from any effective control. Indeed, Corippus speaks of the happiness known by Africa under Vandal rule.[73] It is not until the Byzantine reconquest over one hundred years later that we get a detailed picture of the situation in North Africa, and it is clear from Procopius that by then much of the periphery – the Aures, the Hodna, most of Tripolitania and all of Mauretania west of Caesarea – was in the hands of tribal chiefs.[74]

What these tribal kingdoms consisted of is very unclear. In Tripolitania, the Leuathae had probably moved from their original base – perhaps the oasis of Augila – to take control over most of the Gebel, with their capital at the religious centre of Ghirza.[75] They appear at the head of a vast coalition of tribes arrayed against the Byzantines in revenge for the murder of seventy-nine of their leaders.[76] They were certainly pastoralists, but although some of the tribes possessed camels the presence of numerous cows in their herds suggests that they were not fully nomadic. It is in fact far more likely that they comprised both transhumants and the remains of the sedentary communities of the pre-desert.[77] The successful war carried out by the Byzantine general John Troglyta against this coalition is vividly depicted by the contemporary poet Corippus in the *Johannidos*: defeated, the Leuathae were probably pushed back to the Syrtis, and the temple at Ghirza was destroyed in the middle of the century.

Desert Kingdoms

In Mauretania the situation was more complex. Traditionally, it has been assumed that the area outside Vandal control was divided up into a number of small states, each with its own leader.[78] However, an inscription found at Altava, in western Mauretania, far outside Vandal or Roman control, referred to a 'king of the Moors and the Romans' in AD 508, while in the Aures another king 'never broke faith with the Romans'.[79] The theme is familiar: powerful, independent nobles who assume the recognition of the Roman state and may, according to circumstances, ally with it, or take on the role of mediator between it and the tribes. These monarchies are often said to be 'shadowy' or 'ephemeral', but this must be because we have no historical accounts of them, nothing to throw light on them. For all we know, they may have had effective control over large numbers of people. This, indeed, is the theory of Camps, who believes that Mauretania was ruled by a stable dynasty.[80] The inscription of Altava does indeed mention

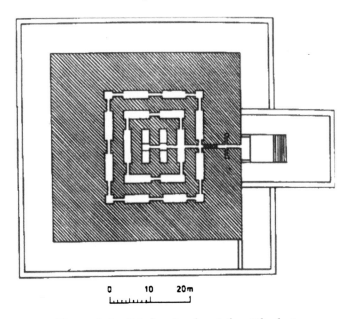

Figure 2.6   Djedar A, plan (after Khadra)
(From R. Horn and C. Rüger, Die Numider: Reiter und Könige nördlich
der Sahara, *Bonn, 1979)*

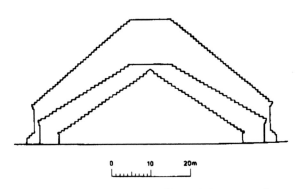

*Figure 2.7   A comparison of the profiles of the Mausoleum at Tipasa,
the Medracen and Djedar A*
(From R. Horn and C. Rüger, Die Numider: Reiter und Könige nördlich
der Sahara, *Bonn, 1979)*

prefects and a procurator of the 'king', and seems to suggest an administration based on Roman tradition. Another indication that these 'kingdoms' were not, in fact, petty chiefdoms is, again, the presence of huge monumental tombs. These are the Djedar, built in two cemeteries near Tiaret, in an area only briefly under Roman control.[81] They consist of large stepped pyramids, with elaborate funeral chambers as well as external altars, chapels and other annexes. They are decorated with the 'noble' iconography we have already seen on the stele of Abizar – ostrich hunts, with horses, as well as lion hunts. The earliest was constructed at some time in the fifth century, as we know from a fragment of an inscription, which also seems to say that it was made for one 'Egregius', a 'dux'.[82] Like the inscription of Altava, this inscription seems to have carried the provincial year – or the number of years since the foundation of the Roman province: there is thus no doubt that the rulers of Mauretania believed themselves to be simply continuing the administration of the province, now independent of Roman rule. The cemetery – and the dynasty? – continued in use for at least a century, as radiocarbon dates taken from another Djedar show.

We have no evidence for the origins of this group, but the type of tomb seems to derive from those known from Saharan prehistory, and it is not impossible that there was at this time a northward movement of the Saharan tribes and their establishment in the Aures and the Hodna.

Byzantine Rule and the End of the African City

Although after the Byzantine reconquest in AD530 order was progressively restored, one fundamental aspect of the relationship between the African nobles and the empire had changed, and this was the possibility of absorbing them or, indeed, of treating them on any other terms but as enemies or equals. For one thing, the language of government was now the alien Greek of the Byzantine empire: they were now no longer bilingual in the hegemonic language. Moreover, the symbolic value of the city had faded – or, indeed, had taken on a different sense. Thus Timgad was destroyed (or at least partially so) by tribes from the Aures 'so that the Romans would have no excuse for coming near us again'.[83] There has been much discussion of the continuity of African cities in the sixth and seventh centuries, discussion which tends to lay a somewhat excessive weight on the presence or absence of a sherd, or of a bishop at a church council.[84] There is little doubt that occupation continued in some form on most urban sites. Even in the far west, at Volubilis, where Roman officials hadn't been seen since the end of the third century, we can find Latin inscriptions and new city walls in the sixth century.[85] But what form did the occupation of these cities take? The African city, which by the fourth century had become the residence of a few major land-owners and a remnant of the decurion class, no longer showed any evidence whatsoever for an urban aristocracy. The major monu-ments in any townscape were the Byzantine fort, built in general out of the ruins of the forum, and one or more fourth- or fifth-century basilicas. Only at Carthage do we have evidence for new building and a resident aristocracy, but even there quarters which were fully urban as late as the fifth century were occupied by rubbish and huts in the seventh.[86] Elsewhere, inertia and a wealth of building material maintained some population in the old towns, but by any definition they had become villages, with parish churches, a small garrison, the occasional tax or rent collector, but without a local hierarchy, a network of services or an administrat-ive structure. At this point the kinship and tribal structures which had ceased to be a primary source of reference during the Roman empire, and had re-emerged as the power bases of the elite in the late empire, became the dominant form of identification wherever one lived. As general insecurity drove the scattered farms from the landscape, the rural population found shelter under the wing of the local chiefs or their 'urban' counterpart, the Byzantine forts. With the replacement of the state by the personal power of chiefs – including, of course, chiefs who were symbolically invested by the state – and the concentration of all settlement inside walls, the encastellation of North Africa was complete.

3

The Unification of North Africa by Islam

The Berbers in Arabic literature, to quote the title of Harry Norris's book,[1] is almost the only way in which we see the great majority of North Africans, apart from their material remains, from the time of the Arab conquests in the seventh and eighth centuries down to the beginning of modern times. Arabic effortlessly replaced Latin and Greek as the language of civilization from Tripoli to Tangiers, imposing upon the native inhabitants yet another frame of mind and expression. Arabic literature on the subject of the Berbers was nevertheless far more substantial than that of either Latin or Greek, and culminated in the late fourteenth century in a work which has already been quoted on the subject of Berber origins, the *Kitāb al-'Ibar* or 'Universal History' of Ibn Khaldūn.[2] This vast compendium of information on the races of mankind began as a treatise on the Berbers, who continue to fill most of the last two volumes, in second place only to the Arabs.[3] They do so through the great dynasties to which they gave rise in the Middle Ages – the Almoravids, the Almohads, the Ḥafṣids, the Ziyanids and the Marinids, at whose court Ibn Khaldūn began his career. He himself came from an old Arab family of Seville, but his patronage by the Berber rulers of Fes induced him to take up the traditional theme of the *mafākhir al-Barbar*, 'the boasts of the Berbers', and turn it over the years into the inspiration of one of the great books of all time. The despised natives of the Muslim West thus found their supreme literary monument in the language of their conquerors seven hundred years earlier.

The Arab Conquerors

They did so because the dynasties and their glorification were a cultural as well as a political response to the invaders from the east. The Arabs in the seventh and early eighth centuries were the last of the great Barbarians, those peoples from outside the Roman empire who spoke neither Latin nor Greek, but whose military energies had delivered the whole of western Europe into the hands of the Visigoths and the Ostrogoths, the Anglo-Saxons and the Franks, and now incorporated the whole of Egypt and North Africa into a vast new empire centred on Syria and Iraq. On the face of it, this empire in North Africa slipped straight into the mould of its predecessor. The Byzantine province of Africa became the Arab province of Ifrīqiya, although the capital was transferred from Carthage to Qayrawān (Kairouan), inland on the edge of the steppe to the south. From Qayrawān the armies advanced through the old Roman Mauretanias to Tangier and on across the Straits of Gibraltar to Toledo. By 715 the Arab empire stretched to the Pyrenees. In North Africa, however, it conformed exactly to the limits of Rome. Neglected by the Vandals and only partially restored by Constantinople, the line of the old Roman frontier, cutting diagonally across the uplands of the Atlas, first corralled and then funnelled the charge of the conquerors westwards from Egypt and onwards into Spain.

Nevertheless, the Arabs were different from both the Romans and the Byzantines. They were invaders and conquerors because they were the citizens of a new religious community, whose destiny was to rule the world. According to legend, the great hero of the conquest of North Africa, 'Uqba ibn Nāf'i, the founder of Qayrawān about 670, rode his horse into the Atlantic crying: 'Oh God! if the sea had not prevented me, I would have coursed on for ever like Alexander the Great, upholding your faith and fighting all who disbelieved!'[4] In this dramatic declaration he epitomized the Arabs' vision of themselves as a chosen people and of the rest of humanity as folk to be conquered and subjected. Its meaning for the people of North Africa, however, was not quite so simple. Categorized as Christian, and thus located in a hierarchy of beliefs from the Dīn Allah or Worship of God at the top, down through the other creeds of the Bible to sheer paganism at the bottom, the Latin-speaking population of Byzantine Africa was placed under the protection of the Arabs and allowed to keep its religion in return for the payment of a poll-tax. Only a minority of Berbers, on the other hand, were deemed eligible for this subject status. The majority were considered pagan; when fought and conquered, they were obliged to make their *islām* or submission to the Arabs on terms which placed them in bondage to the victors. In doing so, however, they also made their Islam or submission to the God of the Arabs and entered, however humbly, as Muslims into His community. Classified in this way, they were given a name, and thus for the first time were identified as a nation, a people, a race. The term 'barbarian', which the Romans had foisted upon this miscellaneous collection of tribes on the strength of their incomprehensible dialects, was rendered into Arabic as Barbar, and elevated into the proper name of a branch of the human race descended from Noah and his sons.[5] As the Barbar or Berbers, the people themselves acquired an objective existence.

For the purpose of the conquest, a vital principle was thereby established, with far-reaching implications. In the first place, although the actual treatment of the Berbers by the Arabs continued the traditional discrimination of the Classical period against peoples beyond the pale of civilization, Islam now created a presumption in their favour, as people within the bounds of the faith. Moreover, since this presumption was exercised on behalf of populations many if not most of whom lay beyond the old *limes* or frontier, North Africa in its entirety was for the first time embraced by the philosophy of the dominant culture and brought within its scope. It was the beginning of a revolution.

The Conquest of North Africa

Before that could happen, the Berbers had to be conquered; and that was not easy. The Arabs first encountered the Berbers to the west of Egypt; and it was there in Cyrenaica that they first treated them as *kuffār*, 'unbelievers', in order to procure both a tribute in slaves and a supply of recruits to the army. These objectives were subsequently disavowed, and the enslavement of the Berbers was justified as a punishment for rebellion after their original capitulation; but this was an argument of the eighth or ninth century to explain a previous practice at variance with Islamic law.[6] The objectives themselves were not mutually exclusive, for male slaves could be converted into troops. The systematic enlistment of Berbers as *mawālī*, or 'clients', into the regiments of the army was necessary to provide the Arabs with the manpower they required for the conquest of North Africa and eventually Spain. The crucial battle was the protracted struggle for Byzantine Africa. In 647 a raiding force from Egypt defeated and killed the Byzantine exarch Gregory at Sufetula, or Sbeitla, putting paid to his designs on the imperial crown at Constantinople and, in large measure, to Byzantine control of the country from Carthage. When the Arabs returned to the attack from their base as Tripoli in the 660s, they were confronted by a number of Berber princes, a number of King Arthurs claiming the land for themselves.

When 'Uqba ibn Nāf'i established his headquarters in the heart of Byzantine Africa about 670, it was as a *qayrawān* or caravan, a halt at the head of the desert road from Egypt, at the foot of the highlands to the north and west. Laid out foursquare – north, south, east and west, like a Roman legionary camp – it formed a *miṣr* or garrison city for the occupation of the country by the Arabs and their Berber freedmen. But not until the end of the century was it securely in the hands of the invaders, able to grow into the permanent city of Qayrawān. Its first ten years or so were dominated by the alliance between Abū 'l-Muhājir, 'Uqba's successor, and Kasīla (more commonly Kusayla), who appears in the Arabic sources as chief of the Awrāba. In this capacity he has been variously identified with Numidia and the Mauretanian 'kingdom' of the Djedar.[7] It seems probable that whoever he was, he attempted to use the Arabs in order to put himself on the throne of Africa, perhaps in the name of Islam. According to the Arabic sources, which are all very much later than the event and describe what happened from the invaders' point of view, when 'Uqba was reappointed in place of Abū 'l-Muhājir in 681, Kasīla was imprisoned and humiliated while the conquering hero led his legendary dash to the Atlantic. Nevertheless he escaped and, at the head of a coalition of tribesmen and Byzantines, slaughtered his captor near Biskra in the Djerid. The *qayrawān* of the Arabs would then have become the *takirwan* or 'place of assembly' of the Berbers, the capital of Kasīla, who reigned over the country for two or three years as a Muslim monarch until defeated and killed by an army from Egypt in 686.[8]

Even so, Kasīla was the victim of a punitive expedition rather than of a return of the Arabs in force. This return was delayed for

ten more years until Ḥasan ibn al-Nuʿmān came to capture
Carthage in 695, only to confront a fresh enemy. While Carthage
was at once recovered by the Byzantine fleet, Ḥasan himself was
routed by the Kāhina, the prophetess identified with the Jarāwa
people of the Aures mountains. Her dramatic figure, with stream-
ing hair and the gift of second sight, has been regarded in turn as
Jewish, Christian and typically Berber in her role as a North
African Boadicea, doomed to fight the foreign enemy to the last in
full knowledge of her fate.[9] What is certain is that her prophecy of
Ḥasan's eventual victory is the whole purpose of her existence in
the earliest substantial source, the ninth-century work of Ibn ʿAbd
al-Ḥakam.[10] What she sees are the messages hidden in a loaf of
bread and the saddle of a horse, sent back to Ḥasan by the captive
Arab Khālid whom she has adopted as her son. What she foresees
is that eventually Khālid will introduce her own sons, his adoptive
brothers, into the armies of the conqueror.[11] What we have, in
fact, is the rump of a legend explaining the glorious destiny of at
least one Berber prince (her elder son) as the commander of Berber
troops in the Arab army; contained within it is the key to the
Arabs' eventual success.

When we find the story repeated in the fourteenth-century
Bayān of Ibn ʿIdhārī, we are told that after Ḥasan's final victory
over the queen at a place to the west of the Aures mountains called
the Kāhina's Well:

> Many Berber tribes had surrendered to Ḥasan, but he had
> only accepted their surrender on condition that they supplied him
> with twelve thousand horsemen for the holy war. On that condition
> he had received their submission to God, and entrusted six thou-
> sand each of their warriors to the two sons of the Kāhina, sending
> them off with the Arabs to fight the Byzantines and the pagan
> Berbers.[12]

No more is heard of the sons of the Kāhina, but some ten years
later the tale is told of Ḥasan's successor, Mūsā ibn Nuṣayr:

> He raided westwards as far as Tangier, pursuing the fleeing Berbers,
> whom he killed or captured until they surrendered and obeyed the
> governor he appointed over them. Tangier and its region he left in
> charge of his *mawlā* or client, Ṭāriq, at the head of seventeen
> thousand Arabs and twelve thousand Berbers, ordering the Arabs
> to teach the Berbers the Qurʾān and instruct them in the faith.[13]

Ṭāriq, who gave his name to Jabal Ṭāriq, the Rock of Gibraltar, is himself little more than a name. Figuring in the literature as a Berber from the Djerid in southern Tunisia, beginning his career as a prisoner of war and becoming the *mawlā* or freedman of the Arab general,[14] he is nevertheless the kind of Berber commander envisaged by the legend of the Kāhina. At the head of his twelve thousand, he may indeed be the same person, the man for whom the legend was designed.

However that may be, these traditions make clear that the secret of Arab success was not simply victory in the long struggle for Byzantine Africa, but the massive recruitment of Berbers which that victory entailed. That recruitment in turn necessitated the advance into Spain to satisfy the demands of this composite horde of Arabs and Berbers for fresh conquests and fresh booty. Having recaptured Carthage about 698, Ḥasan ibn al-Nuʿmān destroyed it and replaced it with Tunis a few miles away. The *qayrawān/takirwan* finally became Qayrawān, the new capital city of old Byzantine Africa, which was now resurrected as the Arab province of Ifrīqiya. When Ḥasan was replaced by Mūsā ibn Nuṣayr in 705, the new governor had both the means and the pressing motive for a great leap forwards. Passing through Tlemcen in western Algeria, the onrush he released reached Tangier in 710, and under the command of Ṭāriq crossed into Spain in the following year. Ṭāriq's victory over the Visigothic king Roderic entailed the rapid collapse of the Visigothic kingdom, and the annexation of the greater part of Spain to the Arab empire. By 720 the armies were crossing the eastern Pyrenees to occupy Narbonne. Only their celebrated defeat by Charles Martel at Poitiers in 732 marked the limit of their expansion.[15]

In this way, although the career of Arab conquest in North Africa stayed for the most part firmly within the boundaries of the old Roman empire, the Berbers took advantage of their new national and religious identity to stream out of their homeland into Spain and even France, joining the Arabs not simply as pressed men but as volunteers. Meanwhile in North Africa itself, the Arabs did at least begin to penetrate the lands beyond the *limes*, which the Romans had refused to conquer. The legendary charge of ʿUqba ibn Nāfʿi into the Atlantic, at the limit of a campaign to conquer the whole of North Africa, may have been yet another myth, invented at a later date to establish the Islamic credentials of the entire Berber nation, whether or not they had all been subjected by the Companions or near-Companions of the Prophet.[16] But at some early stage, the Arabs did indeed conquer the old Garamantes of the Fezzan in Libya, and left them firmly Muslim; and further to the west the garrison city of Tlemcen on the way to Tangier became the headquarters of a campaign in the 730s to conquer the Sūs, the border of the desert to the east and south of the Moroccan Atlas, as far as Agadir. These great adventures eventually combined to give real substance to the concept of an Islamic Berber nation, but not before both had been truncated by revolt.

The Revolt of the Berbers

The great revolt of the Berbers in the middle of the eighth century sprang directly from the ambiguity in their status as tribute-paying subjects and militant members of the community of their conquerors. From the time of Kasīla until the conquest of Spain was complete, the advantages of their *islām*, their submission, seem progressively to have outweighed the disadvantages. The story of the Kāhina, prophesying her own death at the hands of the Arabs and the future of her sons in their service, is a celebration of the alliance of the two nations. But these sons, and Ṭāriq himself, vanish without trace from the record of subsequent events, while the Kāhina herself remains as a legendary destroyer who laid waste the land.[17] Meanwhile frightful condemnations of the Berbers are put into the mouth of the Prophet,[18] only to be matched by his praises of their simple faith.[19] These shifting images of staunch friendship and bitter hostility to the religion of God reflect the antagonism between Berbers and Arabs which came to the fore once the Spanish honeymoon was over and the imperial government at Damascus endeavoured to hold its North African subjects to the terms of their original capitulation. Their daughters were demanded for the slave markets of the East, while their sheep were killed for Persian lambskins.[20] Their remedy lay in rejecting their *islām*, their submission to the Arabs, in the name of their Islam, their submission to God.

The revolt which began at Tangier in 740 had simmered for twenty years, ever since the new governor Yazīd had branded his Berber guards, the freedmen of Mūsā ibn Nuṣayr, like slaves, with their name and regiment on their forearms. They cut him down at prayer.[21] About 731 Munnuza, the Berber commander who garrisoned the passes across the Pyrenees to Narbonne, conspired with the Frankish duke Eudo of Aquitaine to overthrow the Arabs because of the way they were treating his people in North Africa. Although his revolt was suppressed, it throws new light on the defeat of the Arabs by Charles Martel in 732: despite their aggression, they may already have been on the defensive, victims of the growing conflict within their ranks.[22]

The great explosion of 740, however, was symptomatic of much more general discontent with the rule of the Caliphs of the Umayyad dynasty at Damascus; it was indeed the beginning of ten revolutionary years which culminated in 750 in the replacement of the Umayyads by the 'Abbasids in faraway Iraq. In the wider context of the empire as a whole, the resentment of the Berbers was shared by many others, including the poorer Arabs. It found its religious expression in Kharijism, the belief that the sinner, including the sinful ruler, had renounced his faith and was therefore worthy of death. Only the best Muslim was entitled to govern the community, irrespective of race. The Kharijism which inspired the revolt in the Maghrib was common to both Arabs and Berbers in the army, and had as its initial purpose the elevation of a new Caliph to the throne.

The spontaneity of the outbreak right across North Africa ensured its immediate success. Arab governors, generals and their armies were defeated and, in the case of the elite force sent out from Damascus under Kulthum and Balj in 741, massacred by a horde of naked Berbers, wearing only trousers and wielding slings.[23] Qayrawān itself barely survived. Al-Andalus or Spain was cut off from the rest of the empire, and relapsed into anarchy. But spontaneity was the undoing of the revolution; too many new Caliphs sprang up. It was never likely that the rebels would be able to sweep eastwards to Damascus. The Arab aristocracy managed to cling fast to Ifrīqiya, and after some thirty years of continuous warfare, the province was back in the hands of governors appointed by the 'Abbasid Caliph of Baghdad.

The Colonization of the Maghreb

The scene in the Muslim West in the 770s was nevertheless very different.[24] The political unity of Islam had been destroyed. Muslim Spain was independent under a refugee prince of the Umayyads; so were Tlemcen and northern Morocco, where the arrival of a second refugee from the East in 788 established the Idrisid dynasty in the newly founded capital city of Fes. In the same way, the religious unity of the faithful had been broken. The failure of the revolt to take power in Ifrīqiya, let alone Syria, had converted Kharijism from a contender for the name of Islam itself into the creed of sectarian separatists. These separatists were in turn divided into the Ṣufriyya or 'Yellows', who ruled at Tlemcen (to 790) and at Sijilmāsa in south-eastern Morocco, and the Ibāḍiyya or 'Whites', who had set up their own Imamate or religious government at Tahert in western Algeria. Despite the division, the authority of this Imamate stretched for a thousand miles eastwards across the Sahara to Zawīla in the Fezzan. Its following in North Africa was now exclusively Berber, although the Imams of the Rustumid dynasty at Tahert were Iranian in origin; they were recognized by the Ibāḍīs in Iraq; and their capital, like Zawīla, attracted a miscellany of immigrants from the East. In this way, although the centres of political power in the Maghreb remained to the north of the Roman frontier, the population beyond the *limes* to the south was already extensively defined by the new religion in a way that no longer owed anything to the imperial government of the original Arab invaders.

It owed everything to commercial enterprise. At Zawīla, the demand of the Arabs for Berber slaves had been converted into the demand of the Muslim world for blacks from the lands of the Central Sudan to the south of the Sahara. When al-Ya'qūbī visited the Fezzan in the late ninth century, he found the Ibāḍiyya systematically engaged in the import of slaves supplied by the kings of the Sudan, and their export to Ifrīqiya and Egypt.[25] This long-distance trade, reported by a long-distance traveller, is symptomatic of the economic revolution effected by the Arab conquests, which had incorporated the declining economy of late Classical North Africa, as well as the cycles of trade between the desert and the savannah of tropical Africa,[26] into a vast commercial network from the Atlantic to China and from the Equator almost to the Arctic.[27] The systematic development of trans-Saharan trade, made possible by the combination of market forces to the north of the desert with the spread of camel-herding in the desert itself,[28] was something new. For the first time an economic premium had been placed upon the Sahara, elevating it high over the horizon of North Africa's affairs.

This was equally true much further to the west, where the same commercial instinct dictated the occupation of southern Morocco. What we find when the picture becomes clear in the ninth century, not least in the work of al-Yaʿqūbī,[29] is the appearance of a string of oasis cities south-east and south of the High Atlas: Sijilmāsa in the valley of the Tafilelt, Tāmdult in the mountains of the Anti-Atlas, and Iglī in the valley of the Sous, ending at Māssa on the Atlantic south of Agadir. These cities represented so many colonies of Muslim immigrants from the north, part conquerors whose settlements were their capitals, part merchants anxious to exploit the silver of the Anti-Atlas, and increasingly the gold of the Western Sudan which came across the Sahara from Ghana, the land of gold. The cities themselves were connected by caravan trails back to Tlemcen, Tahert and Ifrīqiya, across the Middle Atlas to the Idrisid capital at Fes, and across the High Atlas to the Berber city of Aghmat. By sea they were connected to the old Roman and now Islamic frontier town of Salé by a chain of little ports along the Atlantic coast. By sea or by land, these routes ran on into Spain and the Levant, and thence to the Indies.[30] The long-distance trade of the Islamic world had reached out to encircle all those lands of Morocco excluded from the Roman empire, bringing them materially within the grasp of its civilization.[31]

That grasp was specifically Muslim. Islam had emerged from the great Berber revolt divided but dominant, a religion of the Law, no longer the preserve of soldiers but of scholars. Its rules and regulations, obligations, permissions and prohibitions supplied the framework for the dynamic growth of the new society, in which the old armies melted into a mixture of foreign slaves, local militias and tribal warriors, and the inhabitants of the garrison cities turned into a civilian, subject population. The antagonism between Arabs and Berbers continued, but the original distinction between members and non-members of a ruling race broke down. In its place the faith became the principle of state formation, settlement, trade and trade relations. Along the highways into and out of Spain, inland and on the coast, northern Morocco and western Algeria filled up with new cities, large and small, each one the capital of some Idrisid prince. Immigrants from east and west mingled with immigrants from the tribal countryside in the souk below the mosque and the citadel, where the *muḥtasib* or market inspector 'commanded the right and forbade the wrong' on behalf of the *qāḍī* or judge. Under their insistent pressure, the community of the faithful steadily developed into a cross-section of the population, and increasingly into the population as a whole.

The tribal Berbers of western Algeria and northern Morocco seem eagerly to have welcomed the establishment of a Muslim market town in their midst, and to have professed the faith quite happily to gain admission.[32] In southern Morocco and the northern Sahara, on the other hand, the confrontation between the colonists from the north and a Berber population which had never been incorporated into the Arab empire was much sharper. On the Day of Judgment, said a tradition of the Prophet reported by al-Bakrī, the High Atlas along with all its people will be led to Hell like a bride to her groom.[33] *Ribāṭs*, or garrisons of zealous militants,[34] appeared at Salé, Qūz to the north of the High Atlas, and Māssa to the south, holding the thin line of the Muslim frontier against the peoples of the interior, where in the mountains they worshipped a ram.[35] In the oases, Sijilmāsa was founded by Ṣufrī Kharijites from the direction of Tlemcen who forcibly resettled the population of the neighbourhood within its walls.[36] For Berbers like these, the profession of faith was necessary to avoid hostilities and, as in the north, to admit them to trade in

Figure 3.1   Kutāma Berber warrior
(Drawing from Fatimid plate in the National Museum of Islamic Art,
Kairouan)

the Muslim market place. Where the city itself was not a Muslim
foundation, such as Aghmat close to the site of Marrakesh,
Muslim merchants are likely to have established their own market
as the nucleus of a second city nearby.[37] This practice became
familiar south of the Sahara, where the kings were initially
all pagan.[38] North of the desert, however, paganism had little
future in a world dominated by Islam, not only economically and
politically, but also ideologically. To the tribal Berber population,
the original model of the militant Muslim community conquering
and living off the wealth of the vanquished remained profoundly
attractive. In the course of the ninth century the Berbers south of
Salé, never conquered and never colonized, responded to the call
of an imitation Prophet who offered them an imitation Qur'ān, in
Berber, and led them in an imitation holy war upon their neighbours, Muslim and pagan alike. They called themselves the
Barghawāṭa, and they flourished for some two hundred years in
the Chaouia, inland from modern Casablanca.[39] At the time of
their establishment, they prefigured a much more important development in Islam itself.

The Revolution of Abū 'Abd Allah

Ifrīqiya under the Aghlabids, the Arab dynasty which had become
independent of Baghdad in 800, was ruled by a monarch who
presided over two distinct societies. On the one hand were the
inhabitants of Qayrawān, Tunis, Tripoli and the smaller cities of
the agricultural lowlands, an urban and rural population settling
down to a law-abiding existence under the administration of
governors and judges appointed by the Amir. On the other were
the Berber tribes of the mountainous uplands of Numidia. In the
aftermath of the great Kharijite rebellion, these were treated as
Muslim to the extent of calling their taxes *ṣadaqāt* or alms, but
such Islamic offerings were simply tributes extracted by military
expeditions. Muslim they might be, but in their state of tribal
nature, governing themselves by the customs of the feud, the
family and the elders, they could hardly be said to live by the
Law. They were repressed rather than administered by the Muslim
state, through Arab militias stationed along the main highways
westwards to Tahert, Tlemcen, Tangier and Spain. The situation
was more Byzantine than Roman, and fraught with danger. As

Muslims faced by the oppression of a Muslim regime, the tribes were peculiarly susceptible to the appeal of the Muslim zealot who preached both for and against the political order: for the right which it represented and against the wrong that it did. If the Kharijites had retired from the fray, others had not. At the end of the ninth century there appeared among the Kutāma the prophetic figure of Abū ʿAbd Allah, come to announce the imminence of the Mahdi, the Muslim Messiah, sent by God to sweep away all tyrannies and restore the golden age of divine justice, when the unrighteous would perish and good Muslims receive their reward.

The Kutāma were conceivably the Ucutumani of the Byzantine period,[40] more certainly the population of old Numidia, down to the famous cavalry, spreading out from the mountains of Little Kabylia across the high plains to the Aures. Worked upon by the missionary from the East, they made a new *islām* or submission to enter into a new Muslim community under the direction of this new prophet as judge and commander. Paradoxically, therefore, they transformed themselves from a stateless tribal people into the subjects of a dictator who formed them, like the original Arab believers, into an army which in 909 swept the Aghlabids from power.

It was an astonishing demonstration of the forces unleashed by Islam in North Africa. Their victory had nothing to do with specific doctrines, which in this case proved to be the familiar claim of the descendants of Muḥammad, his daughter Fāṭima and her husband ʿAlī to the Caliphate. It had much more to do with the structural militancy of tribal society, mobilized by a militant messianism for a specific kind of revolution. The revolution in question was certainly not egalitarian. Like that of the Arabs against whose dynasties it was directed, it meant the overturning of old hierarchies by new elites, a new people for a new vocation to conquer and rule. While it succeeded almost to perfection, therefore, the revolt of the Kutāma failed to do more than establish them as the army of a new prince whose regime was in fact little different from its predecessor. The Mahdi ʿAbd Allah, who came to the throne of Ifrīqiya as the first Imam and Caliph of the Fatimid dynasty, simply continued the trend towards absolute monarchy, requiring nothing but obedience from the *raʿiyya* or flock of his subjects. But to bring such a monarch to power was in itself a tremendous achievement. For the first time, Berber clan-

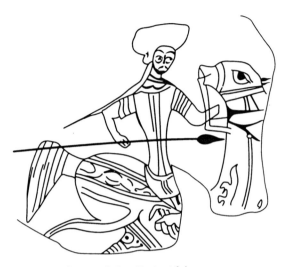

Figure 3.2   Fatimid huntsman
(Drawing from Fatimid plate in National Museum of Islamic Art,
Kairouan)

nishness had become the agent rather than the enemy of civilization in the Maghreb.[41]

For this reason, although the Fatimids ruled in Ifrīqiya and then
in Egypt for over 250 years as one of the great dynasties of Islam,
their fundamental importance for North Africa remained the
revolution which had brought them to power, and the revolutions
which they themselves provoked. The Fatimid revolution at the
beginning of the tenth century was the first of three which by the
end of the twelfth century had changed the whole political face of
North Africa from an essentially Roman division of the country
into an essentially Islamic unity. The revolution itself took place in
Ifrīqiya, and therefore within the old Roman *limes*; but it set in
motion a series of repercussions as far away as the western Sahara,
because the appeal of the Muslim holy man on which it was based
was common to the whole of Berber tribal society in the presence
of Islam – creed, way of life and civilization. In the zealous
preacher, Islam in North Africa found the means to do what the
Romans had refused to attempt: to seize upon Berber tribalism
and use it for the purpose of the dominant civilization. In so doing,
it found the means to bring al-Andalus, the European *'udwa* or
'bank' of the Muslim West, back into the fold of a great North
African empire.

The Breakup of Ifrīqiya

Between the Fatimids and the creation of that empire in the second half of the eleventh century, however, lay a hundred years of military conflict which extended the range of Berber armies from Damascus in Syria to Santiago de Compostela in Spain, but finished by reducing the Muslim West to political atoms. Within thirty or forty years of their triumph, the Fatimids were at risk from an imitation of their revolution by the messianic Abū Yazīd, 'the Man on a Donkey', an extreme Kharijite who preached his own cause to the Berbers of the Aures mountains. They survived an invasion of legendary savagery only because of the strength of their new fortress city of Mahdia on the east coast of Tunisia, and the loyalty of their Berber troops and allies. Instead, they made a fearful example of their enemy's corpse, stuffing the skin of the man they called the Dajjāl or Antichrist with straw for public exhibition. Taking advantage of this apocalyptic triumph, however, the dynasty then turned away from its designs upon North Africa to pursue its long-term ambition to rule the entire Muslim world in place of the decadent ʿAbbasid Caliphs of Baghdad. In 969–72 the Fatimids abandoned Ifrīqiya for Egypt, taking the Kutāma with them as the basis of their army in the East for the next fifty years. Old Numidia thus became a kind of Switzerland or Nepal, a reservoir of mercenaries serving far away from their homeland.

As for Ifrīqiya, its government was left to the Zirids, Ṣanhāja Berber chieftains from the western borders of Ifrīqiya, who from their stronghold of Ashīr in the highlands south of Algiers had carried the holy war of their masters westwards as far as Morocco, and back into Ifrīqiya to the defeat of Abū Yazīd. With the departure of the Fatimids they became the first great Berber dynasty in North Africa,[42] residing at Qayrawān while their cousins the Ḥammadids took command of the central Maghrib. There Ḥammād built his Qalʿa or Citadel, an astonishing eyrie overlooking the strategic point where the caravan routes to the north and south of the Aures converged for the onward journey to Tahert, Tlemcen and the west.[43] In this way Ifrīqiya itself began to break up, its political structure beginning to reflect more clearly the ancient dichotomy between what Braudel calls 'a land of ordered civilization' to the east and a 'dense and rustic region . . . amazingly uncivilized' to the west.[44] It

Figure 3.3   Fatimid warriors
(Drawings from wall-tile from Fatimid palace of Sabra outside
Qayrawan, in National Museum of Islamic Art, Kairouan)

was a political development rather than a religious achievement,
leading to disintegration rather than unity at the hands of native
rulers.

The crisis came in the middle of the eleventh century, when the
Zirid sultan Mu'izz ibn Bādīs attempted to win the approval of his
subjects by severing his links with Cairo, only to be defeated by
nomadic bedouin at the battle of Ḥaydarān in 1052, and promptly
deserted by his Ṣanhāja kinsmen and the citizens of towns like
Tunis. In 1057 he abandoned Qayrawān for Mahdia on the coast.
As the great city shrank into political insignificance, the state of
Ifrīqiya, which the Arabs had taken over from the Byzantines,
crumbled away. The Qalʿa of the Banū Ḥammād fell into ruin as
the Ḥammadids moved down to the port of Bijaya. The heirs of

Kasīla and the Kāhina, Berber princes who had eventually won the monarchy of Africa for themselves, failed to preserve the inheritance they had at last achieved.[45]

Still further to the west, the attempts of the Fatimids and their Zirid viceroys to conquer Morocco resulted in a similar political restructuring. The Fatimid revolution had swept away the Kharijite principalities of Tahert and Sijilmāsa, driving the Ibādis to take refuge in the northern Sahara. The Idrisids likewise were evicted from their strongholds; their place was taken by Zanāta Berbers fighting on behalf of the Umayyad Caliphate at Cordoba against the Ṣanhāja tribesmen of Zīrī ibn Manād and his sons. A hundred and fifty years after their arrival in al-Andalus, the Umayyads of Cordoba had been on the point of extinction when the Fatimids came to power, but they rallied remarkably under the Amir ʿAbd al-Rahmān III, who celebrated the restoration of his power and authority in 929 by claiming the Caliphate from both the ʿAbbasids and the Fatimids. With the support of his dynasty, Zanāta warlords took control of Tlemcen, Sijilmāsa and Fes, which they held long after the Fatimids had departed and the Caliphate at Cordoba itself had collapsed.

If the Umayyad Caliphate at Cordoba had been created as a counterblast to the imperialism of the Fatimids in Ifrīqiya, its collapse in 1009 owed much to its involvement in the warfare across the Straits. Large numbers of Berbers had been recruited into the armies of Cordoba, especially by the Ḥājib or Chamberlain Almanzor, 'the Conqueror', the minister who was the real ruler of Spain from 976 to his death in 1002. They gave him the power to crush all opposition, and the prestige of a holy warrior which he derived from his annual campaigns against the Christian kingdoms to the north. Zanāta from northern Morocco and western Algeria were joined by rebellious refugees from the Fatimids and the Zirids in Ifrīqiya: all 'new' Berbers quite distinct from the 'old' Berbers settled in the mountains to the north, east and west of Toledo since the original invasion of the peninsula, and almost as alien in al-Andalus as the Kutāma in Egypt. Most came as tribesmen with their families to form a foreign horde apart from the native population of the country, with whom they were bitterly unpopular. Hatred of the favour they enjoyed from the great minister and his family underlay the revolution which overthrew Almanzor's grandson Sanchuelo in 1009; the occasion was his order to wear the Berber turban in place of

the long many-coloured hoods which distinguished the officers
of state from the common people.[46] But the result was a protracted
civil war between the rival *ṭā'ifas* or factions of the army and
the aristocracy, which by 1031 had put paid to the Umayyad
dynasty, the Caliphate and Cordoba itself as the capital of the
country. In their place appeared a multitude of city-states ruled by
the Mulūk al-Ṭawā'if or Kings of the Factions, many of whom
were Berber. The Afṭasids at Badajoz and the Zannunids or Dhu
'l-Nunids[47] at Toledo were Berbers from the original settlement,
while the Zirids at Granada headed the list of recent immigrants at
Carmona, Ronda, Silves, Arcos, Mertola and Moron in the south
and south-west. Right across North Africa and well into Spain, the
direct and indirect effect of Fatimid imperialism had been the
establishment of Berbers in the place of Arabs at the head of more
or less petty states, matched by the decomposition of central
government and exposure of the entire region to invasion and
conquest.[48]

In Spain, the relentless harrying of the Christian north by
Almanzor, who had brought to Cordoba the bells from the
shrine of St James at Compostela, had repressed but not stunted
the continuous growth of the kingdoms and counties of the
Asturias, Leon, Castile, Navarre, Aragon and Catalonia, that ran
right across the north of the country from Galicia to the Mediterranean. Societies organized for war, as they have been aptly
called,[49] they had since their formation in the ninth century
pushed steadily south to colonize land on the ill-defined frontier
of al-Andalus. Coupled with this basic hunger for territory was
the much grander ambition of a wholly Christian Spain,
which eventually led to the term *Reconquista*, or Reconquest,
to describe what was in fact a slow conquest of Muslim by
Christian Spaniards, as a return to national independence following the expulsion of the foreign Arabs with their foreign faith.
In between the hunger and the ambition was a willingness to
profit from the divisions of Muslim Spain. The collapse of the
Caliphate at Cordoba first allowed the King of Navarre to dominate the Mulūk al-Ṭawā'if, and then the King of Castile to attack.
In 1085 Alfonso VI took the city of Toledo, the old Visigothic
capital of the country, from the Dhu 'l-Nunids, and with it
the centre of the peninsula. Al-Andalus, like Ifrīqiya, was in
disarray.[50]

The Almoravids

Nevertheless, the nerve of enthusiasm touched by the preaching of the Fatimid missionary in the tribal population of the Maghrib was still very much alive. It responded even more effectively to the equally prophetic figure of Ibn Yāsīn, militant holy man of southern Morocco who, in the middle of the eleventh century, went south to preach the duty to 'command the right and forbid the wrong' to the Berber nomads of the western Sahara. Arising on the desert frontier of Islam, where the *murābiṭūn* or men of the *ribāṭ* were on their guard against the abomination of paganism, the blasphemy of the Barghawāṭa and the falsehoods of the Ibāḍiyya, his mission was more than a distant echo of the Fatimid revolution. Typologically, it was exactly the same: targeting a people at their own request for instruction in the word of God, and converting them into a new Muslim community living strictly by the Holy Law under the rigorous direction of their religious overseer. Doctrinally, however, it was directly and deliberately opposed, following the lead of the jurists of the Maliki school at Qayrawān, who insisted that they, rather than the Fatimid Imam, were the true authorities for the Law of God on earth. The mission took place in the 1040s, the years in which these jurists urged the Zirid sultan Muʿizz ibn Bādīs to make his fatal break with Cairo; and it succeeded at precisely the time when Muʿizz was defeated and central government in Ifrīqiya broke down. At the moment of political collapse in the ancient heartland of civilization in North Africa, a radical movement for the creation of a grand new Muslim order in the Muslim West arose at the opposite extreme of the Maghrib, as far from that heartland as it was possible to be.

The Almoravids, as the followers of Ibn Yāsīn are known in English, have aroused the interest of West Africanists almost more than that of North Africanists, so that the scrutiny of their origins in the desert has frequently been divorced from the study of their empire in Morocco and Spain. Underlying the distinction is the fact that the principal source for the origins of the movement, the contemporary al-Bakrī, was writing in 1068, immediately before the Almoravids finally emerged from the Sahara to conquer the North. The hiatus this creates in the record means that the circumstances surrounding the foundation of Marrakesh as the capital of the new empire in 1070 are buried in legend, and must be reconstructed from much later accounts. Without al-Bakrī, on the other hand, the problem would be far worse, and the achievement of the Almoravids in the perspective of Europe as well as Africa far harder to place. Through the mildly astonished eyes of this highly cultured Cordoban, unbiased by awareness of the prodigious consequences to come, we see something of the alien ferocity of the Berber whose zeal later overturned the world with which he was familiar.[51]

Unlike the Fatimid missionary Abū 'Abd Allah, who had preached the coming of the Mahdi to the Kutāma, 'Abd Allah ibn Yāsīn of the Gazūla people of the Moroccan Sahara was nothing if not a Berber. He may well have started life as a convert to Islam, taking the Muslim name of 'Abd Allah, 'Servant of God', 'the Son of Yā Sīn', at his entry into the *ribāṭ* of his master Waggāg ibn Zalwī in the Sūs. Yā Sīn, the Arabic letters Y and S, are the mysterious title of a Sūra of the Qur'ān, making 'Abd Allah an offspring of the Book rather than the son of a man. Intentionally or not, the opening lines of the Sūra were prophetic of his destiny:

Yā Sīn,
By the Book that prescribes and ordains,
You are one of those that are sent
Upon a straight road,

Plate 3.1 Almoravid gold dīnār of 457/1065, from Sijilmasa. The margin of the obverse (left) reads: 'Whosoever seeks a religion other than Islam, it shall not be accepted from him, and in the Hereafter he shall be lost' (Qur'ān 3: 85)
(Courtesy of the Trustees of the British Museum)

A revelation of the Mighty, the Merciful,
To warn a people whose fathers have not been warned,
leaving them heedless and unaware . . .
(Qur'ān xxxvi. 1–6)

Certainly he was chosen by his master Waggāg, on the instruction
of *his* master, the jurist Abū 'Imrān al-Fāsī at Qayrawān, to go
down into the desert at the request of the chieftain Yaḥyā ibn
Ibrāhīm to summon the Gudāla and the Lamtūna to the *ribāṭ*, the
community of *murābiṭūn*, those 'bound together' for the holy war
upon ignorance and opposition to the word of God. The binding
was merciless: Ibn Yāsīn was determined to impose the law upon
his tribal flock, reducing them to strict equality and absolute
obedience. Under the heading, 'Peculiar principles of Ibn Yāsīn',
al-Bakrī relates:

> When a man joins the cause and repents for his past misdeeds they
> say to him: 'You have committed in your youth many sins, so it is
> necessary that you be subjected to the punishment stipulated by the
> Law, and so purified from your transgressions.' The stipulated
> punishment for an adulterer is 100 lashes, for a slanderer 80 lashes;
> for a drunkard likewise. . . . It is in the same way that they treat
> those whom they have vanquished and compelled to join their holy
> war (sc. *ribāṭ* or cause). Yet if they know that he has killed someone
> they kill him, regardless of whether he came to them voluntarily,
> repenting, or was compelled to do so while openly recalcitrant. His
> repentance does not profit him, nor is his regret of any avail. Those
> who fail to attend the Friday prayer receive twenty lashes, and
> those who omit one genuflection five . . . .[52]

But the preaching was also ignorant: Ibn Yāsīn's own knowledge of the Law was primitive; objections were raised, and he was
driven to treat his opponents as apostates, killing them for abandoning the faith. The Gudāla eventually refused his call, but
the Lamtūna finally accepted, becoming in consequence al-
Murābiṭūn, 'the Men of the Ribāṭ', dedicated to the fight against
the enemy; in other words, against everything outside the Law of
God. The enemy in question was paganism on the one hand,
Christianity on the other, but still more important, Islam in any
shape that did not conform to the precepts of the Maliki school of
Sunnism at Qayrawān. Such a definition of iniquity embraced, on
the one hand, the Fatimid belief in the supreme authority of the
Imam; on the other, the exclusive doctrines of the Kharijites,

which in their treatment of the sinner as an apostate, worthy of death, were very close to Ibn Yāsīn's execution of his opponents. Still more important, it included the nominal Islam of Berber peoples whose faith, such as it was, did not yet impinge upon their traditional rules of conduct. Such were the various tribes of the Sahara.

They were known as the Mulaththamūn, the People of the Lithām or Veil, still worn by the Berber Tuareg of the central Sahara and by the Arabized Blue Men of the western desert, so-called from the deep indigo dye of the cloth, which stains the skin. Among the races of the Berbers, they were classed as Ṣanhāja as distinct from Zanāta, although their affinity with the mountain Ṣanhāja of the Zirids is not clear. They were a warrior aristocracy of camel-herding nomads, dominating a servile population of cultivators in the palm groves of the oases, and deeply involved in the gold and salt trade of the western Sudan. Awdaghast, the oasis city on the southern edge of the desert where the caravans rendez-voused for the onward journey into the Black empire of Ghana, had belonged to them before it was taken over by the kings of Ghana, and had filled up with Zanāta from Sijilmāsa and Ibāḍīs from Sedrata in the deserts of Ifrīqiya.[53] This change of fortune from the great days of their overlord Tīnbārutān, whose legend reached the ears of the geographer Ibn Ḥawqal in the tenth century, was undoubtedly a motive behind their acceptance of Ibn Yāsīn, whose first great exploits were the capture of Sijilmāsa from the Zanāta and the sack of Awdaghast, 1053–7. In this way, the Lamtūna and their allies gained control of the desert, despite their defeat by the Gudāla on the haunted battlefield of Tabafarala,[54] where the dead lay unburied with their weapons and the voices of the muezzins continued to summon the faithful to prayer.

With Sijilmāsa secured, Ibn Yāsīn crossed the High Atlas to occupy Aghmat and attack the Barghawāṭa. Despite all the legends of 'Uqba ibn Nāf'i, it was the first time that a Muslim army had attempted the conquest, as distinct from the commercial penetra-tion, of the land within the arc of the High and Middle Atlas as far north as Salé; and it failed. The false Islam of the Barghawāṭa and the militancy of their movement set the prophet of the Almoravids an example and a challenge which he could not ignore; but in 1059 he was killed in battle against them. His tomb at Keriflet near Rabat immediately became a place of pilgrimage;[55] but ten

Figure 3.4   The Western Sahara, showing the Almoravid commander Abu Bakr, riding his camel, and with a whip of knotted cords. Sijilmasa is in the ring below the High Atlas at the top, and Marrakesh above it (From the fourteenth-century portolan of Mecia de Viladesta, Bibliothèque Nationale, Paris)

years later, says al-Bakrī, the Almoravids under his successor, the Lamtūna chieftain Abū Bakr ibn ʿUmar, were divided, and their power was confined to the desert. There is no hint of anything to come.

Abū Bakr figures on the Catalan maps of the fourteenth century as a giant on a camel, wearing the veil and wielding a whip of knotted cords (see figure 3.4). But he is mentioned only briefly by al-Bakrī; and though coins were struck in his name at Sijilmāsa until 1085, he is known only for his alleged conquest of Ghana in 1076,[56] and for his foundation of Marrakesh in 1070.[57] This was certainly a subject of legend:

Zaynab the beautiful, so it was said, was the queen of Aghmat to the north of the High Atlas. Wooed by all, she refused, saying that

only the man who ruled the whole of the Maghrib would marry
her. Those she rejected hated her as a witch with second sight, to
whom the genies from below the earth would speak. But when Abū
Bakr, chief of the Ṣanhāja of the desert to the south of the mountains, presented himself, she agreed. Leading him blindfold underground, she showed him by the light of a candle a mighty hoard of
treasure which God had given to him by her hand. Then in the same
way she brought him out. On his return to the desert to fight his
enemies, however, he gave Zaynab in marriage to his cousin Yūsuf
ibn Tāshfīn. From the city of Marrakesh which Abū Bakr had
founded close to Aghmat, Yūsuf conquered Morocco. When Abū
Bakr came back from the south, he found the gates closed against
him. He retired permanently into the Sahara, while Yūsuf advanced
into Spain. Thus the prophecy of the princess was fulfilled.[58]

However it happened, Marrakesh, the Qaṣr al-Ḥajar or Fortress
of Stone, was built as a *miṣr* or garrison city a few miles from the
old twin city of Aghmat, where the old Muslim merchant community to which Zaynab reputedly belonged continued to fore-
gather.[59] As the headquarters of the Almoravid army in the north,

*Plate 3.2   View over Marrakesh, the capital of the Almoravids and the
Almohads
(From W.B. Harris,* Tafilet, *London, 1895)*

it became the base from which its commander Yūsuf ibn Tāshfīn finally overcame the Barghawāṭa, and went on to capture both Fes and Tlemcen in the 1070s. After 1085 his name replaces that of Abū Bakr on the Almoravid coinage, a clear sign that he had assumed supreme command of the movement. More than that: the coins bear witness to the imperialism of the leaders as rulers of the Maghreb in the name of Sunnī Islam after the failure of the Zirids in the 1050s. The gold dinars first struck in the name of Abū Bakr at Sijilmāsa in 1058 bear the same Qur'ānic verse as those minted over the previous ten years at Qayrawān by Mū'izz ibn Bādis to proclaim his rejection of the Fatimids:

> Whoever seeks a religion other than Islam, it shall not be accepted from him, and in the Hereafter he shall perish.   (Qur'ān III. 85)[60]

The verse epitomizes the religious mission to extirpate all forms of unbelief; but the coin is a symbol of state. In 1085, when Abū Bakr's name appears for the last time, the Almoravid state in Morocco had become an empire stretching into western Algeria, while Yūsuf, its Amir, stood on the threshold of supreme power in the Muslim West.

The Almoravid and Almohad Empire

In 1085 Alfonso VI of Castile captured Toledo, and the *'ulamā'*, the men of religion in al-Andalus, appealed to Yūsuf to save Islam in the Peninsula from the Christian threat and the feebleness of the Mulūk al-Ṭawā'if. Yūsuf had resisted the attempts of these petty monarchs to draw him into their country as their ally and saviour over the past four years. But in response to this religious appeal on behalf of the Muslim community, the Almoravids inflicted a crushing defeat on the Castilians at the battle of Zallāqa in 1086. The Almoravids themselves are described by al-Bakrī as a phalanx of infantry, the first rank armed with pikes and those behind with javelins, never retreating, never pursuing, standing firm or steadily advancing, the image of *murābiṭūn* bound together in a common cause.[61] A minority fought on horseback or on camels, which terrified the enemy, as did the sound of their drums, for which the Almoravids were famous. Victory over the Zanāta in North Africa, however, had enabled them to levy a more substantial

*Plate 3.3   The Mosque of Ibn Tūmārt, Mahdi of the Almohads, at
Tinmāl
(Photo: Vivienne Sharp)*

force of cavalry for the final charge; and it was a balanced force which survived the flight of the Mulūk al-Ṭawā'if from the battlefield to win an epic victory.[62]

It did not lead to the recovery of Toledo. Instead, Yūsuf returned to Morocco for four years; and when the Almoravids came back in 1090, it was to remove the Mulūk al-Ṭawā'if one by one, sending them into exile at Aghmat. By the end of the century, only the north-east held out. Valencia, which in the midst of the political confusion had fallen into the hands of the legendary Castilian hero El Cid, was not occupied until 1102, and Zaragoza not until 1110. A vast new empire had nevertheless come into existence on either side of the Straits of Gibralter with two novel, and vital, features. In the first place its rulers were Berber. With the title of Commander of the Muslims, Yūsuf ibn Tāshfīn represented a final victory for the belief introduced by the Kharijites to vindicate the opposition of the Muslim Barbar to the Caliphate of the Umayyads, that the government of the community belonged to the most godly, whatever his race or lineage. At best with a limited knowledge of Arabic, swathed in the blue veil of the Saharans, Yūsuf was a striking emblem of the accomplishment of Islam in opening the way for the most remote tribesman to scale the heights of power and authority with no Arab or descendant of the Prophet to raise him up.

Just as striking, however, was the capital of his empire, Marrakesh. The new imperial city was located far beyond the old *limes*, and thus far beyond the pale of Classical, and indeed of early Islamic, civilization in North Africa. It stood in a land of barbarians with no native tradition of state organization. Yet now that land served as a base for the conquest of the old Roman territories to the north, and for their incorporation into a new state structure whose centre of gravity was away to the south. It was the logical, if paradoxical conclusion of the Arab invasion 400 years before, with its identification of a Berber race to be fought until it accepted God.

No sooner was this structure in place than the Almoravids themselves were swept away. During the long reign of Yūsuf's pious son ʿAlī, 1106–42, the puritanism, power and privilege of these exotic Saharans alienated the *raʿiyya* or flock of their subjects by a mixture of fanaticism, arrogance, obscurantism and corruption. In the famous words of ʿAbd al-Wāḥid al-Marrākushī, who celebrated their downfall:

The Commander of the Muslims, ʿAlī ibn Yūsuf ibn Tāshfīn, followed his father in waging the holy war for the defence of the land. But while his conduct was good, his intentions excellent, his soul pure and far from doing wrong, he was more of an ascetic or a hermit than a king or a conqueror. So strong was his preference for the scholars of the holy law, that no decision, great or small, was ever taken without their advice, giving them quite unheard-of influence . . . Thus from the moment of his accession the state was deranged and evils multiplied, as the Almoravids seized power for themselves, each claiming a better right to rule than the Amir. Even worse, their wives took charge, involving themselves in every vice, not least the drinking of wine and prostitution. And all this time the Commander of the Muslims grew more feeble and neglectful, content with the name of Amir and the proceeds of taxation as he withdrew into his religion, praying by night and fasting by day. So the welfare of his subjects was utterly ignored, and Andalus reverted to its former state, until there arose the call of the prophet Ibn Tūmart in the Sūs.[63]

Al-Marrākushī was a chronicler of the Muwaḥḥidūn or Almohads, 'the Unitarians', the movement founded by Ibn Tūmart in 1122 to combat the tyranny, immorality, even infidelity of the Almoravids in preferring the doctrines of the Maliki school to the Qurʾān itself. Within five years of the death of ʿAlī in 1142 they had overthrown his regime. The last, greatest and most sophisticated of the three great revolutions began in exactly the same way as its predecessor, among the Maṣmūda peoples of the High Atlas in the mountains above the capital city of Marrakesh. A third prophet, Ibn Tūmart, returned to his homeland in southern Morocco from his education in the East, first as a moralist, then as the Mahdi in person. His mission to command the right and forbid the wrong became the directive of God to trace the faith back to its original roots in the revelation, overgrown with the ramifications of the Sunnī jurisprudence by which Ibn Yāsīn had lived and died.

So he roused his fellow tribesmen to challenge the masters of the plain below, just as the Fatimid *dāʿī* Abū ʿAbd Allah had stirred up the Kutāma against the Aghlabids of Ifrīqiya. At Tinmel, high in the valley of the Nfiss at the foot of the Tizi N'Test, the pass across the High Atlas from Marrakesh to Taroudant in the valley of the Sous, he transformed yet another 'stateless' Berber society into a new Muslim community under religious and military discipline, which formed an army to fight in God's name. Under his successor, his disciple and Caliph 'Abd al-Mu'min, this army took Marrakesh from the Almoravids in 1147, and proceeded to conquer not only their empire in Morocco and Spain but Ifrīqiya as well. In this way, although the Almoravids were massacred, their achievement was upheld. The extension of their dominions to the whole of the Maghrib completed the work that Yūsuf ibn Tāshfīn had begun. By the year 1200 the old political division of North Africa, inherited by the Arabs from the Romans, had been finally overcome; and overcome, moreover, not from the old starting-point of civilization at Carthage/Tunis in the far north-east, but from the new city of Marrakesh, a point of departure diametrically opposed to it in the far south-west.[64]

The Almohad empire was a considerable advance upon the simple Berberism, simple tribalism, simple legalism, of the Almoravids. Ibn Tūmart had claims to be the most advanced scholar of his age; his successor 'Abd al-Mu'min was no tribal chieftain but his favourite disciple. Berbers they may both have been, but their faith had provided them not only with the force but also the learning to take command of the great civilization that Islam in the Maghreb had become. In place of the exotic Saharans, whose menfolk never abandoned their veils but whose highly influential women went abroad in Berber fashion with bare faces, they installed a regime that more closely matched their subjects' expectations of Islamic monarchy. 'Abd al-Mu'min, 'the Servant of the Faithful One' (i.e. God), took the Caliphal title of Amīr al-Mu'minīn, or Commander of the Faithful, in his capacity as heir to the Mahdi and ruler over the community in God's name. Where the Almoravids had enslaved themselves to the legal rulings of the Maliki school of jurisprudence, the Almohads boasted their own theology in the works of the Mahdi, written in Berber and subsequently translated into Arabic, an appeal like that of the Protestant Reformation to the people at large as well as to the highest principles of the faith.[65] Moreover, where Yūsuf ibn Tāshfīn and his son 'Alī had been content to rely upon the independent opinions of the Maliki jurists, 'Abd al-Mu'min, the founder of the Almohad dynasty, created his own imperial staff of scholars out of the younger generation of Ibn Tūmart's disciples. Their education in the doctrine of the movement was expanded into the military training of a privileged corps of administrators, the *ṭalabā'*, 'students', or *ḥuffāẓ*, 'memorizers', of the works of the Mahdi.[66] After 'Abd al-Mu'min's death in 1163, his sons and successors

Plate 3.4   Detail from Mosque of Ibn Tūmārt, Tīnmāl
(Photo: Michael Brett)

made Seville into the second capital of the empire, where they extended their patronage not so much to the schoolmen as to the more broadly learned circles of the peninsula. The Almohad Caliphs of the second half of the twelfth century presided over a distinguished court of physicians, philosophers and scientists headed by the Aristotelian Ibn Rushd, or Averroes as he was known in the Latin West. At a time when the monarchy was committed by its zeal to the continued defence of Islam against the Christian kingdoms of the north, it was their learning which was passing in translation to the schools of Paris and so into the intellectual life of northern Europe.

The Almohads themselves, whose tribal regiments were the rank and file of the community, were commanded by their own aristocracy of shaykhs and *mizwār*s or *muḥtasib*s: those with the duty to 'command the right and forbid the wrong'. The original organization of these headmen into councils of ten and fifty, modelled perhaps on tribal or village practice, is not wholly clear, but served on the one hand to maintain an army of tribal reservists, and on the other, to create an influential nobility, whose most notable family gave rise to the independent dynasty of the Ḥafṣids at Tunis in the thirteenth century.[67] Soldiers, statesmen and scholars, the shaykhs of the Almohads seem to have blended with the corps of *ṭalabā'*, but continued to keep their distance from the dynasty as guardians of the doctrine of the Mahdi, as commanders of the army, and as governors of the realm. The doctrine of the Mahdi was meant to supersede all other versions of Islam, and in accordance with his prophetic purpose, some attempt was made to impose it upon the population at large as the one true faith for the community, not simply the rulers.[68] If the attempt failed, it was because both the nobility and the monarchy remained stubbornly elitist; because they quarrelled over the inheritance of the Mahdi, and the right to rule in his name; and because in the end the empire proved too large to defend successfully against its enemies in Spain and in North Africa.

The greatest monuments to the Almoravids and the Almohads are the mosques which set their stamp upon the cities they created or conquered. Those of Algiers, Tlemcen and the world-famous Mosque of the Qarawiyyīn at Fes are Almoravid; that of the Almoravid Amir 'Alī ibn Yūsuf at Marrakesh was destroyed by 'Abd al-Mu'min and only rebuilt in the nineteenth century. But on the site of the Almoravid palace at the other end of the old city stands its replacement, the Kutubiyya Mosque of the Almohads, who also built the great mosques of Seville and Rabat. All are masterpieces of the Andalusian style which the two dynasties elevated into the art of their empire; but the Mosque of Ḥasan at Rabat is unfinished, and the Great Mosque of Seville has been converted into the cathedral, its minaret turned into a bell tower complete with weathervane – la Giralda. Both are reminders that the monuments of the empire itself are not religious but military: the great walls of Marrakesh, Fes and Seville, and the Ribāṭ al-Fatḥ or Fortress of Victory, which has given its name to Rabat (while changing its own to the Qaṣba of the Udaya). Triumphal and majestic with their imperial gates, these fortifications nevertheless bear witness to the fact that, once the empire had been conquered and created, its priority was defence.

Not only Seville but the whole of southern Spain is replete with Almohad castellations, witness to the relentless advance of the Christians from the north. For the conquest of the empire, 'Abd al-Mu'min had created a superb military machine, a combination of all races, arms and types of soldier by land and sea, with the logistical capacity to operate over the immense distances from

*Plate 3.5   The Kutubiyya Mosque, Marrakesh, first great symbol of the
Almohads
(From W.B. Harris, Tafilet, London, 1895)*

Tripoli in the east to Lisbon in the west. The campaign which
recaptured the Ifrīqiyan fortress of Mahdia from the Normans of
Sicily in 1159–60 was a masterly operation in which the fleet
sailed along the coast from the Straits in company with the army
marching overland from Morocco along a well-prepared route.[69]
The morale and discipline of the Almohads extended to all the
contingents levied from the Caliph's dominions as he mobilized
the whole of the Muslim community for war upon the infidel.
Together with the material resources of the state, that morale was

nevertheless increasingly taxed by the repeated demands of a monarchy driven on to the defensive.

When 'Abd al-Mu'min ascended the Rock of Gibraltar in 1161, he was the monarch of all he surveyed:

> Ignore the sun, think Saturn's measure short;
> see on the mountaintop the peak of peaks.[70]

In 1184 his son and successor Yūsuf died of wounds at the un- successful siege of Santarem, attempting to halt the incursions of the kings of Castile and Portugal, which had reached as far south as Malaga. At the same time the empire in North Africa was threatened by the mercurial attacks of the Banū Ghāniya, Almoravids who had fled from the Balearic islands to Ifrīqiya, where they campaigned successfully for twenty years. Faced with a war on two fronts, the Almohad armies swung to and fro from end to end of the empire, winning the great battle of Alarcos in 1195, but coming finally to grief at Las Navas de Tolosa in 1212, annihilated by a combined host of Crusaders, Castilians and Aragonese.[71] It was the beginning of the end. By 1250 almost the whole of Muslim Spain, including Seville, was in the hands of Portugal, Castile and Aragon; only Granada remained Moorish until 1492. Ifrīqiya was independent once again under an Almohad shaykh, the founder of the Ḥafṣid dynasty; Tlemcen was controlled by a tribal chieftain, the founder of the 'Abd al-Wadids or Ziyanids; while the dynasty of 'Abd al-Mu'min was itself under threat from the Marinids, Berber nomads from eastern Morocco who had captured Fes and finally took Marrakesh in 1269. The political unity of the Maghreb was at an end; moreover, since the Marinids preferred to make Fes their capital instead of Marrakesh, the centre of political gravity in North Africa had shifted back to the north.

The Almohad Legacy

Yet the legacy of the Almohads lived on, not simply in the fact that all three of the dynasties which succeeded them were Berber. The Ḥafṣids at Tunis were indeed Almohads who prolonged the life of the movement for a further 250 years, only gradually abandoning its distinctive doctrines for those of the Malikite school of Sunnī

Plate 3.6   Almohad silver dirham from Tlemcen, no date. The reverse (right) reads: 'God is our Lord; Muhammad is our Prophet; the Mahdi is our Imam'
(Courtesy of the Trustees of the British Museum)

Islam.[72] Both the ʿAbd al-Wadids at Tlemcen and the Marinids at Fes were nomadic Zanāta in origin, tribal warriors without the inspiration of religion, taking power in the wake of the empire-builders as they had done before the coming of the Almoravids. They were the beneficiaries of the Almohad practice of relying on such tribesmen for military service, who now seized the strategic cities abandoned to them by a failing regime. While Tunis emerged as the capital of Ifrīqiya and one of the great cities of the Mediterranean, Tlemcen, the capital of the Berber chieftain Yaghmurāsan, continued to thrive at the crossroads of trade routes running east and west between Ifrīqiya and Morocco, and north and south from the Sahara to the Mediterranean. Ruled by the Zanāta in the tenth and eleventh centuries, it now reverted to a profitable independence under its new warlord as a principal supplier of West African gold to Europe.[73] Fes had grown under the patronage of the Almoravids and the Almohads into the obvious capital of northern Morocco. Under the Marinids it took the place of Marrakesh as the capital of the whole country.

Marrakesh, however, remained a major city, the capital of a southern region now thoroughly incorporated into the civilization of the Maghrib.[74] Morocco itself survived as a political unit, ruled from Fes, albeit with some difficulty, by the Marinids, who found the High Atlas a barrier to their effective control of the Sous. Here in the fragmentation of the Almohad empire lay the genesis of modern Morocco, whose present borders roughly correspond to the Marinid domain in the thirteenth and fourteenth centuries. Such an entity was naturally meaningless to the Marinids themselves, whose ambition was at the very least to recreate the greater Morocco of the Almoravids by the capture of Tlemcen from the 'Abd al-Wadids. At the most it was to recreate the Almohad empire in the West. After their occupation of Tlemcen in 1337, their resounding defeat and expulsion from Spain in 1340–44, and their conquest of Ifrīqiya in 1347, their grand project only finally ended with the palace murder of their last great sultan, Abū 'Inān, in 1358. This century-long attempt to don the mantle of their predecessors meant that the empire of the past effectively survived as a theatre of conflict between rivals who all, at one time or another, aspired to suzerainty over the whole. Out of the three revolutions came the three Berber dynasties who ruled over North Africa down to the end of the fifteenth century as enemy brothers in a single political community.[75]

Underpinning that community was not only the fading sense of an imperial mission to unite the Muslims against the infidel, nor yet the circulation of the ruling elite of princes and princesses, ministers and secretaries from court to court in the quest for allies, patrons and clients. A common political culture extended downwards and outwards to the towns and the tribes. It was expressed in the ceremony which, in the aftermath of the disaster of Las Navas de Tolosa, accompanied the accession of the new Caliph Mustanṣir. As the delegations of nobles and commoners presented themselves in order of rank over a period of days, they swore to keep, through thick and thin, the oath of homage to the man who held power from God as the keeper of His flock:

> And this is the admonition, to the Caliph and to his officers and to the Muslim folk, which binds you to him and him to you, that he shall not keep your contingents too long abroad in enemy territory, nor withhold any of the booty from you, but give you your pay, and remain approachable by all. May God help you to fulfil your duty, and help him in the charge of your affairs.[76]

Administered against the background of Las Navas de Tolosa, where those same contingents had been slaughtered in battle, the oath, which was couched in terms dating back to the origins of Islam, may have had the ring of irony. Administered within two years of the Magna Carta, it may have been a similar reminder of the rights of the subject as well as an affirmation of the authority of the monarch. The parallel is not quite as far-fetched as it may seem.

A curious entry by the highly reputable Matthew Paris into the chronicle of Roger of Wendover describes how in 1213, the year before the installation of the new Caliph al-Mustanṣir, 'He Who Asks God for Victory', King John sent an embassy to his father the Caliph al-Nāṣir, 'Giver of Victory', offering the Commander of the Faithful his conversion to Islam and his homage as a vassal, in return for aid against his own rebellious barons and the impending invasion of England by the King of France. The offer was treated with the contempt it deserved by the Caliph, who commented that no free man should willingly become a slave, and no man should ever abjure the faith into which he had been born.[77] The contrast between the virtuous unbeliever and the vicious Christian is an early example of a well-worn satirical theme, and is not to be taken as a matter of fact: it is inconceivable that King John could have made such an approach to the broken-hearted monarch whose defeat at Las Navas de Tolosa in the previous year gladdened Christendom. The portrait in the anecdote of the wise and studious Caliph nevertheless agrees with the Arabic descriptions of a quiet, reserved and obsessively conscientious man who took every decision upon himself, and made up his mind only after long thought.[78] These echo in their turn the less flattering accounts of the pious Almoravid ʿAlī ibn Yūsuf, in which we should probably see an element of hostile parody. The ideal of the ruler as scholar and saint, although it might conflict with the image of a conquering hero, was in principle one and the same.

Ibn Khaldūn and the Kitāb al-ʿIbar

Despite the efforts of Ibn Tūmart to instruct his tribal followers in their own Berber language, his works have survived only in Arabic, the language of Islam and its civilization in the Maghreb, in which this political and religious culture was expressed and epitomized. Far removed from the simple stories of the faith and faithlessness of the Berbers put into the mouth of the Prophet at the time of the Kharijite rebellion in the eighth century, the *Kitāb al-ʿIbar*, or Book of Exemplary Information, was the work of a typical product of the political system that had evolved by the end of the fourteenth. Ibn Khaldūn was of Spanish Arab descent, but had been born and brought up at Tunis until the Marinid invasion of 1347 opened the way to Fes, Granada, Tlemcen and Tunis once again. For thirty years he moved from court to court and dynasty to dynasty as a minister in search of employment, at a time when they were ceaselessly, and inconclusively, at war. Betraying each patron in turn, like the calculating politician he was, in the course of the 1370s he prudently went almost literally to ground for four years in the troglodytic cliff village of the Qalʿa of the Banū Salāma near Frenda in western Algeria, to write the *Muqaddima* or theoretical preface to his so-called 'Universal History'. There, at a period when all sense of historical direction seemed lost, he set out to celebrate the achievements of the Berbers in the deeds of their dynasties.[79]

Judging the veracity of historical information by its conformity to the fundamental rules of human behaviour, Ibn Khaldūn found his basic subject in the nation, the human group which had been produced by these rules, and whose deeds had generated the stories he had gathered from books, oral tradition and eye-witnesses. This nation had first been created physically in the form of an extended family, by descent; then economically, by the territory it inhabited and the way of life which this imposed; and finally politically, by government and the pursuit of power. From the pursuit of power came the dominant nations which provided the *Kitāb al-ʿIbar* with its structure: its account of peoples past and present is written around the story of those who had attained to empire, since only their deeds could supply the information on which the historian depended. Those whom they conquered fell back into oblivion, for without such deeds they ceased effectively to exist. The *Muqaddima*, penned in some remote cave in the Algerian highlands, thus provided the justification for a work which began and ended with the doings of the Berbers as the master race of the Maghreb.[80]

The work itself is encyclopaedic. Ibn Khaldūn took the various genres of Arabic literature with which he was familiar – genealogical, geographical, nationalist, dynastic, and so on – and twisted them together into a profound reflection upon civilization in general and civilization in North Africa in particular. We find a stark contrast between the affluent industry of the town and the laborious poverty of the countryside matched by an equally sharp difference between the dependence of the townsmen on their rulers and the self-reliance of the bedouin, that is, the country people in their tribal societies. Equally, however, we find it is the tribesmen who have created the state, for only they have the necessary fierce *'aṣabiyya* or solidarity to win power, and thus provide the conditions for the cities to develop. Since in its most extreme form among the nomads of the desert the tribal way of life is wholly alien to civilization and totally destructive of its fruits, there must nevertheless be some mediating influence to mobilize its innate ferocity for a constructive purpose. That influence is most readily provided by religion in the form of the prophet come to appeal to the simple hearts of the tribesmen to fight for God as well as themselves. There were some obvious exceptions to these basic rules of which Ibn Khaldūn was well aware and which he endeavoured to explain, such as the continued existence of a city like Fes irrespective of the conquerors who came and went, or the rise of the Marinids, a dynasty which took up the cause of religion only after it had come to power. But in his theory of the rise of empire, drawn in large measure from his own North African background and most conspicuously developed in his history of the region, we find a triumphant account of its unification by Islam through the appeal of the faith to the unlikely force of Berber tribalism.

The *Kitāb al-'Ibar* is itself a monument to that unification. Written by a man whose political career took him from one end of the Maghreb to the other, it stepped from the stage of the dynastic theatre in which the imperialism of the past was playing itself out towards the end of the fourteenth century. Written by a scholar in full command of the knowledge of his age, it gave expression to the civilization that had come into being in North Africa over the past 700 years. Written, finally, on the narrower subject of the state in which the Berber nation was fully realized, it was a treatise on the type of government which had grown up in North Africa under Islam – dynastic and elitist in its constitution; populist in its appeal to the Muslim community; and Shakespearean in the instability of power.

Not until the sixteenth century were the lines of battle redrawn in a more constructive conflict for control of the Maghreb. Meanwhile in the fifteenth century, the Ḥafṣid dynasty came near to disproving the rule. It did so, ironically, from the moment the *Kitāb al-'Ibar* came to an end in North Africa. Ibn Khaldūn left his Berber village refuge in 1378 to resume his political career at

Tunis, only to find that his reputation for unreliability had not deserted him. In 1382 he left with the pilgrimage to settle in Egypt where he remained until his death in 1406, a politician to the end, but simultaneously at work upon the oriental sections of the *'Ibar*, which transformed what had initially been a book about the Maghreb into a universal compendium. Information was added to the North African section down to the 1390s; but it stopped before the new sultan Abū Fāris took Tripoli in 1398 at the beginning of a campaign which reunited the Hafṣid dominion under the central control of the dynasty at Tunis.

This unity was maintained by the longevity of Abū Fāris and his successor Abū 'Amr 'Uthmān, who ruled between them for over ninety years. Ifrīqiya settled into a routine of patronage in which the central government grew down into provincial society in a regime of largely uninterrupted peace. Such strength was in marked contrast to the enfeeblement of Tlemcen and Fes, where the last of the Marinids was executed in 1465 and the Wattasids who succeeded them ruled only in the north. But it continued to hang upon the unity of the dynasty, and in the succession dispute which broke out on 'Uthmān's death in 1488, the Hafṣids followed their fellows into terminal decline. The boasts of the Berbers were almost at an end, and their fate as a nation was in the balance.

4

The Arabization of North Africa

Language and Religion

The Arabs in Barbary, to translate the title of Georges Marçais' work,[1] raise questions of a different kind from the Berbers in Arabic literature. In Norris's book it is a question of seeing the native population of North Africa through the language of its invaders, which eventually became the language of its civilization. With the Arabs in Barbary, it is a question of explaining how the language of those invaders eventually became the speech of the majority of the population of the region, transforming the Berber speakers, and thus in effect the Berbers, into a minority in their own country.

Such Arabization is certainly not the same as Islamization. Berbers became increasingly Muslim without speaking Arabic; indeed, Ibn Tūmart, the Mahdi of the Almohads, not only preached but wrote in Berber in his effort to bring the people to the faith.[2] The same, of course, holds true in Iran, Turkey and all other non-Arab Muslim countries. On the other hand, the Coptic language of Egypt at the time of the Arab conquest is now dead except for liturgical purposes, and the Coptic Christian minority speaks Arabic. If Arabic only came to North Africa in conjunction with Islam, its spread within the Muslim context was largely independent of the faith. Beneath the political surface of the unification of North Africa by the new religion lurks a different kind of history, in which the tribalism which gave rise to the great Berber dynasties was instrumental in the retreat of their native tongue.

It is all the more strange that this should be so, because Berber had successfully resisted the advance of both Punic and Latin for a thousand years, and with the retreat of Classical civilization appears to have regained much of the ground it had lost in Numidia and Mauretania.[3] On the strength of their language, indeed, the Berbers had been elevated by the Arabs to the status of the great nation extolled by Ibn Khaldūn. Nevertheless, it was Arabic rather than Berber which finally put paid to the Latin-speaking community of Ifrīqiya encountered by the Arabs on their arrival in the seventh century. Their treatment of this community was governed by its Christianity, which meant that, like the Copts of Egypt and the Christians of Spain, the Afāriqa or Ifriqiyans (the 'Africans' of 'Africa') were allowed to keep their religion in return for the payment of a poll-tax. Defined and isolated in this way from their conquerors, Christians in all three countries diminished in number to small minorities in Egypt and al-Andalus, and to none at all in North Africa by the end of the twelfth century. Their native languages suffered accordingly. In Egypt, Coptic was restricted to the liturgy, while the Copts themselves turned to Arabic like the Mustaʿribūn or Mozarabes of Muslim Spain, that is, Christians who 'claimed to be Arabs'. Latin, in the form of Spanish, nevertheless survived as a vernacular under Muslim rule in the peninsula, not least because it flourished across the broad and indefinite frontier with the Christian kingdoms in the north. In North Africa there was no such reservoir of support. Minoritarian from the start, Latin survived there in the Latin names inscribed in Latin epitaphs on Christian tombstones in Tripolitania, and as late as the middle of the eleventh century at Qayrawān. As an index of the size of its community, however, the number of African bishoprics tumbled from two hundred under Byzantium to some forty at the beginning of the eighth century, to five in the middle of the eleventh and only two in 1076, the year of the last surviving letter from Rome. The Latin correspondence reveals a community sufficiently literate to produce the figure of Constantine the African, who at Salerno and Monte Cassino was the first of the great translators of Arabic science for the benefit of the Latin West. But native Christianity in Ifrīqiya is likely to have perished a hundred years later at the time of the Almohad conquest, when the Normans of Sicily were expelled from Mahdia in a fury of zeal. It probably lasted longest in the oases of Djerid, where Latin is reported for the last time about 1150. Identified with the religion, the language shared its fate.[4]

Why they should both have vanished in this way says a great deal about the dynamics of the religion and the language which replaced them. Christians were not initially welcomed into the community of the faithful, and the conversion of individuals was probably late in starting and slow to take effect, given the change of loyalties which it supposed. Far more effective in the eclipse of the old by the new is likely to have been the rapid growth in the society of the conquerors as successive armies brought successive waves of immigrants and drew in batch upon batch of male and female slaves, so that the invaders began to reproduce their religion and their language far faster than those they had conquered and subjected. The acquisition of slaves as booty continued into the ninth century as raids across the Mediterranean took the place of raids into the mountains and deserts of North Africa, where a regular slave trade had sprung up with the Bilād al-Sūdān, or Land of the Blacks on the far side of the Sahara, to satisfy the large markets for oasis cultivators and domestic servants. Down to the end of the century, the Arab aristocracy of Ifrīqiya was able to colonize its estates with its captives, cutting away at the native population in the countryside as well as in the towns.[5]

The towns themselves, beginning with Qayrawān, were substantially new: cities of the faith which grew along with their mosques into centres of Islam where Christian immigrants were effectively strangers in their own land. The vigour of the new society was amply demonstrated in the course of the ninth century, when the Aghlabids launched the invasion of Sicily as a distraction from rebelliousness at home. An entire new Muslim community was created as the island was conquered and colonised, the first such creation for over a hundred years. Ifrīqiya itself was far from drained of its resources. Sousse turned from a tiny fortress into a major port for the enterprise, while Tunis resumed the Mediterranean role of Byzantine Carthage.

In such a society, it is not only likely that for most people Islam was the badge of the citizen, but that Arabic, the language of the conquerors, their religion and their administration, was the *lingua franca* which rapidly became a mother tongue. This may have been especially true of the Berbers who immigrated into the community in Ifrīqiya. Although Berbers played an important part in the conquest of Sicily, Arabic was the chief and ultimately the only language of the colony, and is still the language of Malta, which was occupied in 869. At Qayrawān by the end of the eighth century it had already blotted out the ethnic origins of many of its

Plate 4.1   The view over the high plains towards the desert from the troglodytic Qal'a of the Bānū Salāma, where Ibn Khaldūn wrote the Muqaddima *to his great history*
(Photo: Michael Brett)

citizens, as the pious Buhlūl well knew on the day he gave a dinner to celebrate the discovery that he had only Arab blood in his veins, not a drop of Berber.[6] But if the capital was the melting-pot of a flourishing new society, in the aftermath of the Kharijite

rebellion the ancient prejudice against the 'barbarians' of the
countryside had clearly returned to redefine them as rustics beyond the pale of Arabism. Ibn Khaldūn himself, the historian of
the Berbers, reiterates and reformulates the Roman and Byzantine
view of the tribesmen and their language in a pregnant passage:

> Their language is not only foreign but of a special kind, which is
> why they are called Berbers. They say that when Ifrīqish, son of
> Qays, son of Sayfī, one of the Ṭubba's (kings of the Yemen),
> invaded the Maghrib and Ifrīqiya (to which, they say, he gave his
> name), killing Jurjis, the king, and building villages and towns, he
> encountered this strange race with its peculiar tongue, and struck
> with amazement exclaimed: 'What a *barbara* you have!' For this
> reason, they were called the Berbers. The word *barbara* in Arabic
> means a mixture of unintelligible noises, applied for example to the
> roaring of a lion.[7]

Repeated at a time when the Arabization of this rustic race had
spread well beyond its confines in the ninth century, the anecdote
not only establishes its starting-point in the pejorative definition of
the Berbers as primitives, but sets the process firmly in the matrix
of the civilization which excluded them in this categoric fashion.

The process itself was slow to develop. While Islam became
popular and ultimately lower class, descending from the faith of
an aristocratic elite to the religion of a cross-section of the population, and broadening steadily into the creed of the great majority, the evolution of Arabic into a vernacular or mother-tongue of
the North Africans lagged far behind. The further away from the
metropolis to the south and west, the further into Berber territory,
the more Arabic operated solely as the language of the literate. The
Ibāḍī scholars of Tahert and Tripolitania, for example, used it as
well as most in their religious writings, yet their congregations
remained resolutely Berber, to the point at which the scholars
themselves eventually feared for their own ability to dispute in
matters of faith.[8] That is not to say that the Arabic of such
societies was confined to the Qur'ān. The rapidity with which the
tongue of God went on to replace its Classical predecessors as the
written language of North Africa demonstrates not only the will of
the conquerors and the prestige of the Book but the practical value
of the faith.

Having first created an army, that faith went on to create a
society which was defined by far more than the *shahāda*, the
declaration of belief in God and His Prophet, more even than the

remaining four pillars of prayer, fasting, alms and pilgrimage, which reinforced the sense of community. It entailed the government of the community by leaders who claimed divine authority for their decrees. A body of rules and regulations thus came into existence, which by the beginning of the ninth century had been recognized as the Law of God, a heavenly original revealed to humanity as a directive for every kind of human behaviour from the lowest bodily functions to the highest act of worship. The elaboration of these directives by the scholars who studied and transmitted them from generation to generation was inseparable from their application to daily life in the form of practical judgements by the *qāḍī* on behalf of the amir or sultan, the ruler whose duty it was to enforce the Sharīʿa or heavenly Law on earth. The outcome was a large and proliferating literature governing the whole of daily life, including its economic base in property, inheritance, contracts and sales. Many of the rules and regulations were Roman in origin, but under the rubric of Islam they were subsumed into provisions for a distinctively Islamic way of life with a logic of its own. It was these provisions which carried the use of Arabic far beyond the bounds of worship, and far beyond the boundaries of Arabic speech.[9]

The reason was certainly not that Berber tribesmen who claimed to be Muslim substituted the Sharīʿa for their own customs and thereby changed their society out of all recognition. Even the Kharijite Ibāḍīs who colonized the oases of the Mzab in the northern Sahara in the tenth century, establishing their community in accordance with their school of Islamic Law, have preserved or relapsed into tribal structures, tribal ways.[10] ʿUrf or ʿamal, indeed, traditional practice, came gradually to be recognized by the Muslim jurists of the Maghreb as a valid though scarcely respectable alternative to their scriptural doctrines, and was thus given the grudging approval of the holy Law.[11] In the course of the confrontation, however, Arabic became almost universally accepted as the language of learning, not least because it took over from the very beginning as the language of business, the language of trade.

The expansion of Islam beyond the old Roman frontiers was military to the extent that the colonists who established themselves in the new cities of southern Morocco did so if necessary by force of arms in the midst of a pagan population. But their motives were largely commercial, so that Islam was no longer called upon to identify the conquerors in relation to the conquered, so much as the merchants in relation to their clients. When the pagan Vikings appeared on the Spanish and Moroccan coasts in the ninth century, for example, they were called Majūs, that is, Magians or Zoroastrians, in the manner of the Berbers themselves in a few early texts. This was not because they were thought to be Persians, but because as a people recognized by Law, they did not have to be fought, but were eligible for a truce for the purpose of trade.[12]

This use of the categories originally devised by the Arab conquerors to govern their relations with the rest of humanity is even more apparent to the south of the Sahara, where the pagan Hausa are known today as Maguzawa or Majūs to distinguish them from the Muslim majority. In the ninth and tenth centuries the Muslims in the Bilād al-Sūdān were a small minority of immigrants from North Africa, who formed their own colonies living and trading by the Law, under the protection of pagan monarchs, with the approval of the jurists of Qayrawān.[13] The employment of the Sharī'a in this way as an instrument of commerce in lands beyond the pale of the original Arab empire was not only a powerful factor in the growth of an Islamic identity and an Islamic community, but a means to the establishment of Arabic over the whole of North Africa, the Sahara and the Sudan as the language of literacy and civilization.

The Golden Age of Islam

This vast extension of the faith and speech of God is a testimony to what Maurice Lombard has called the Golden Age of Islam.[14] That golden age, from the middle of the eighth century to the middle of the eleventh, saw the Arab empire which had emerged from the Arab conquests turn into a common market stretching from the Atlantic to Central Asia and northern India, and drawing its supplies from tropical Africa, the Far East and northern Europe – almost the whole of the known world.

The creation of this empire and this common market out of the political and economic union of the Mediterranean and Iranian worlds reinvigorated the economic life of both after the recession of late antiquity, nowhere more so than in the Far West. It did so by making a virtue out of necessity, by linking together the relatively small and widely scattered areas of intensive cultivation and urban settlement running the length of the arid belt from the

Plate 4.2   The tombs of the Marinid sultan Abu'l-Ḥasan and his queen, with their beautiful Arabic calligraphy, in the dynastic mausoleum of Chella, Rabat
(Photo: Michael Brett)

borders of China across the Middle East to North Africa, through long-distance routes of invasion, expansion, travel and trade. Areas such as Mesopotamia, Egypt, Tunisia and southern Spain were in effect so many oases separated by mountains, deserts and seas. The annihilation of the immense distances between them by the explosion of the armies out of Arabia was perpetuated by the implosion of the tribute they exacted and sent back over thousands of miles to the Commander of the Faithful at the centre of their web. Not only was local wealth forcibly concentrated in the hands of the invaders, but brought equally forcibly into relationship with similar concentrations elsewhere, as the specialities of each region flowed into an intercontinental network of supply and demand. What began, in St Augustine's famous generalization from the equally spectacular empire of Alexander the Great, as a *magnum latrocinium*, a great robbery, gave rise to a worldwide economy, the greatest prior to the discovery of the Americas and the economic integration of the globe from the sixteenth century onwards.

This economy depended in the first instance upon the knots of settlement in relatively fertile spots such as Tunisia, with its Mediterranean lowlands in the north and east and its Saharan oases in the south. Ibn Khaldūn was at pains to evoke the way in which civilization was rooted in an agricultural economy whose surplus supported a population much larger than necessary for the production of food, which was thus free to engage in other ways of making a living. In a passage reminiscent of Adam Smith and *The Wealth of Nations*, he envisaged the growth of civilization as the growth of cities in which a growing population was gathered together. Prosperity was directly related to the variety of occupations, and these in turn to the number of people. This, he says,

> may be exemplified in the Maghrib, by comparing the situation of Feź with other Maghribi cities such as Bijaya, Tlemcen and Ceuta. A wide difference, both in general and in detail, will be found to exist between them and Fez. The situation of a judge in Fez is better than that of a judge in Tlemcen, and the same is the case with all other population groups. The same difference exists between Tlemcen on the one hand and Oran and Algiers on the other, and between Oran and Algiers and the lesser cities, until one gets down to the hamlets where people have only the necessities of life through their labour, or not even enough of them.[15]

Typically, the peasant has a hard life, as we have seen from the use of slaves as cultivators in Ifrīqiya in the eighth and ninth centuries.[16] But the Tunisian heartland at this time was evidently just such a land of growing numbers, giving rise to new cities of which Qayrawān and then Tunis grew to be very large, with a population of perhaps as many as 100,000 in the case of the capital.[17]

It certainly led to trade, over and above the retail purchase of goods by the consumer from the producer. The feeding of Qayrawān with grain, part of which was brought in by taxation of the Berber countryside for distribution and sale, was a major enterprise. The merchant himself was a specialist in the art of buying cheap and selling dear in the market he elected to supply, most obviously the mass market for medium-priced goods of medium quality.[18] But, as Ibn Khaldūn remarked, it was greatly to his advantage to travel longer rather than shorter distances to obtain higher prices for rare and therefore expensive items. So,

> the merchants who dare to enter the Sudan country are the most prosperous and wealthy of all people. The distance and

the difficulty of the road they travel are great. They have to
cross a difficult desert which is made almost inaccessible by fear of
danger and beset by thirst. Therefore, the goods of the Sudan
country are found only in small quantities among us, and they are
particularly expensive. The same applies to our goods among
them.[19]

In general, therefore,

> merchandise becomes more valuable when merchants transport it
> from one country to another. They get rich quickly. The same
> applies to merchants who travel from our country to the East, also
> because of the great distance to be traversed. On the other hand,
> those who travel back and forth between the cities and countries of
> one particular region earn little and make a very small profit,
> because their goods are available in large quantities and there is a
> great number of merchants who travel with them.[20]

It was through this profitable escalation of commerce from the
short to the long distance that a country like Tunisia was connected with Spain to the west, the Sudan to the south and Egypt to
the east, not to speak of Sicily and Europe to the north, while the
specialities of the one became the imports of the other in proportion to their rarity and value. Thus the export of cloth from
Ifrīqiya converted Tunisia, in Goitein's phrase, into 'the hub of the
Mediterranean' in these first few hundred years after the Arab
conquest,[21] and certainly into a central market for Saharan trade.[22]
The concentration of wealth in the country paid for the conquest
of Egypt by the Fatimids in 969, while the continued recruitment
of the Kutāma cavalry into the armies of the Caliphate at Cairo
created yet another link with the distant East. It was a surprising
return towards the prominence gained for the country by the
Carthaginians in the days before Rome and, unsurprisingly, it did
not last.

The military and commercial competition of a new Rome in the
shape of the Norman kingdom of Sicily began with the conquest of
the island from the Arabs in the second half of the eleventh
century; its initiative was followed and eventually supplanted by
the aggressive enterprise of Pisa, Genoa and Venice, beginning
with the sack of Mahdia in 1087. The pressures which the commercial republics brought to bear upon North Africa reflected the
growing strength of the Western European economy in the later

middle ages, in which the maritime supremacy of the Italians in the Mediterranean played a vital part. By the fifteenth century, the economy of Islam as a whole was being drawn into dependence upon its north-western neighbour. Ifrīqiya under the Ḥafṣids had become, with few exceptions, an exporter of primary products in exchange for manufactures, most notably the products of the pastoral economy, wool, skins and leather.

The beeswax of the Berber mountains of Kabylia, exported through the port of Bijaya or Bougie, gave the French their word *bougie* for a wax candle. But the ṣūrat al-arḍ or picture of the world established in the Muslim West by this vast infrastructure of travel and trade was more than a technical matter of language. Geographers like Ibn Ḥawqal, the tenth-century author of the *Ṣūrat al-arḍ*, compiling their descriptions of the globe with encyclopaedic zeal, were the scientific exponents of an image taking shape in the mind of the most illiterate, as the most remote and savage populations, judged by the standards of Ibn Khaldūn, were drawn into the network of his *'umrān* or civilization. At the centre of the image was Mecca, to which the annual pilgrimage drew so much of the traffic it encouraged along the highways of the Muslim world, and from which the faithful travelled back to the far horizons of their physical and mental universe.

Behind the sense of this implosion, however, this returning to God through space and time, was the idea of previous explosions: of humanity out of the Ark and the Arabs out of Arabia. The colonization of the world by the sons of Noah provided the Berbers with the Canaanite genealogy ascribed to them by Ibn Khaldūn. At the same time he repeats the legend of the Yemeni conqueror Ifrīqish, who would have left behind him in the Maghreb, in the midst of the Berbers with their *barbara*, the ancestors of the major Berber tribes of his day.[23] The story is held up to ridicule in the *Muqaddima* as a complete impossibility.[24] Ibn Khaldūn himself, the champion of the Berber nation, was nevertheless obliged to concede that some at least of the tribes may have been descended from these Arabs of the Yemen, who in the days before Islam had prefigured its conquest of the world with their own heroic exploits. This claim to Arab ancestry, advanced on behalf of quintessentially Berber peoples, induced a sense of Arabism in a nation which the Arabs of the conquest had raised up in sharp contrast to themselves; and it undoubtedly contributed to its eventual Arabization.

The Sons of the Crescent Moon

It was an odd form of treason to the concept of a Berber race which ran from the time of the Arab conquest through to Ibn Khaldūn. The idea that the Berbers originated in Palestine among the sons of Canaan gave genealogical precision to the perception of the Arab conquerors that the Berbers were not only a nation, but were divided into two distinct groups, the Butr and the Barānis. The original meaning of these terms is obscure: one suggestion is that the Barānis (sing. Burnus) wore the burnous, a long garment, while the Butr wore a brief tunic, *abtar*, 'cut short'. E.-F. Gautier supposed that the Butr were nomads and the Barānis peasants. All we know is that the Arabs appear to have taken most of their recruits from the Butr, while some of the Barānis were Christian, and thus liable to the poll-tax. By the tenth or eleventh century they had been converted into the descendants of eponymous ancestors, Abtar and Burnus, the sons of Barr, the grandson of Canaan and father of the race. Ibn Khaldūn lists the major tribes in each moiety, giving particular prominence to the Zanāta among the Butr and the Ṣanhāja and Maṣmūda among the Barānis, since these were the peoples who had founded the great Berber dynasties, and thus led the nation on to the stage of history. Whereas Butr and Barānis have faded away as historical actors, therefore, Zanāta and Ṣanhāja have come to dominate the literature as eternal enemies in everlasting conflict.[25]

Today a linguistic distinction is made between two families of Berber dialects represented by Zanāta on the one hand and Ṣanhāja on the other; but its historical significance remains unclear, since Ṣanhāja in particular is scattered across mountain and desert. What is important for the present purpose is the fact that from the tenth century onwards, the Ṣanhāja and their fellows the Kutāma claimed to have originated as Arabs from the Yemen who had 'gone native' among the Berbers of North Africa. The claim, reluctantly admitted by Ibn Khaldūn, was undoubtedly political in origin. The Kutāma were the chosen people of the Fatimids, the instruments of their revolution at the beginning of the tenth century. From the Ṣanhāja of the central Maghrib came the Zirids, the viceroys of the Fatimids in the West, who affirmed their descent from the kings of the Yemen in order to assert their independence of the Fatimids in Egypt. From the Ṣanhāja of the western Sahara came the Lamtūna, who in the shape of the Almoravids took over from the Zirids the task of building a Sunni Muslim empire in the West and, in so doing, declared themselves to be ultimately Arab. It is clear that in two out of the three great revolutions which called upon Berber tribesmen to establish a universal dominion in the name of Islam, the conquerors felt the need to appeal not only to the faith but to a myth of Arab origin to justify their mission and their assumption of power.

Out of the same political history of Fatimids, Zirids and Almoravids grew the most potent myth of all. The critical event was the appearance of the Banū Hilāl or 'Sons of the Crescent Moon', a collection of some half-dozen bedouin Arab tribes allegedly dispatched from Egypt in 1051 by the Fatimid Caliph, to punish his Zirid vassal at Qayrawān for his change of allegiance to the 'Abbasid Caliph at Baghdad. In 1052 they would have accomplished this mission with the defeat of the Zirid sultan Mu'izz at the battle of Ḥaydarān, and proceeded to overrun the country. They are celebrated from their epic, or romance: a vast cycle of heroic legend describing their adventures in the Middle East, their *taghriba* or journey to the West, and finally their conquest of the Maghrib. They are notorious for the devastation ascribed to them by authors such as the fourteenth-century travel writer al-Tijānī.[26] They are famous above all for their treatment by Ibn Khaldūn, who described them as 'a swarm of locusts',[27] and held them up as an example of the savage so remote from civilization that he can

Plate 4.3   Arab tents on the high plains of eastern Algeria
(Photo: Michael Brett)

only destroy what he comes across in search of basic necessities like pasture and fuel.[28] On the other hand, he elevated them into a race second only to the Berbers in the Maghreb on the strength of the popular oral narrative of their exploits, the literary historical tradition of their misdeeds, and above all his perception of their nomadic way of life as one which led inevitably to nationhood through the ferocious *'aṣabiyya* or loyalty to kith and kin which was required by the terrible need to survive at the limits of human life in the desert.[29] In consequence, their invasion looms large as a major event in the history of North Africa.

The romance of the Banū Hilāl, which so fascinated Ibn Khaldūn,[30] is an echo of history rather than an historical account.[31] From that day to this, the legend has been the vehicle for endless topical retellings to suit the circumstances of the moment.[32] But the literary tradition of the sending of the Hilālīs from Egypt is itself a legend, designed to blame the downfall of the Zirid sultan on a disgraced Egyptian vizier.[33] Ibn Khaldūn's own account moves from the romance into the fiction as the tribes come to light in Ifrīqiya in the middle of the eleventh century. Not until the Almohad conquest of North Africa in the middle of the twelfth does his information develop into a more detailed account of the tribes, fractions and lineages which claimed Hilālī descent; and not until the Almohad empire itself disintegrates in the middle of the thirteenth does it accumulate to the point at which Ibn Khaldūn is telling the story of his contemporaries, many of whom he knew.

The nation he reveals in this manner hardly meets the criterion of nationhood so amply satisfied by the Berbers: the dynasties it produced to justify its treatment by the historian were petty in the extreme by comparison with those of the Almoravids, the Almohads and their successors – tribal chieftaincies, ephemeral lordships. Lacking the call of faith which had set the Berber tribesmen on the road to empire, the motive for their *taghriba*, their drive to the West, was not so much dominion as opportunism. The fact remains that by the twelfth century these Arabs in Barbary had spread across the whole of Ifrīqiya, from the lowlands of Tunisia to the highlands of eastern Algeria, where they presented the chief internal opposition to the conquest of the country by 'Abd al-Mu'min. By the thirteenth century they were across western Algeria into central Morocco, having been introduced by the Almohads as auxiliaries for the wars in Spain. By the fourteenth, under the name of the Banū Ma'qil, they had overrun southern Morocco to the south of the Atlas, and by the fifteenth were spreading into the western Sahara as the warrior tribes of the Banū Ḥassān. Further north, the weakening of the dynasties of Fes and Tlemcen in the fifteenth century left them free to lord it over yet more of the land. In the process, their Arabic became the vernacular of an increasing number of North Africans, while their genealogies proliferated from end to end of the Maghreb.

Running from east to west, in the opposite direction to the conquest of North Africa by the Moroccans, this vast evolution is the story of the Arabs in Barbary.[34] Georges Marçais' retelling of the tale of the *Kitāb al-ʿIbar* was for the benefit of a modern European audience which found in the Hilalian invasion the explanation for the poverty of the country perceived by the French when they conquered Algeria in the nineteenth century. In a celebrated attempt to explain the explanation, E.-F. Gautier related the phenomenal expansion of the Hilālīs to the fraternal antagonism between Zanāta and Ṣanhāja which Ibn Khaldūn ascribed to race, but which Gautier saw as a reflection of the perpetual opposition of nomads and peasants, of a kind familiar from the biblical story of Cain and Abel, and much in evidence in Ibn Khaldūn's own thinking.[35] Zanāta nomads would have competed on more or less equal terms with Ṣanhāja peasants, until the arrival of the Arab bedouin tipped the balance in favour of the pastoralists. Paradoxically, the Zanāta themselves would then have disappeared, absorbed by the new immigrants after a long period of conflict into an Arab tribal structure and an Arabic dialect. By the fifteenth century, therefore, the Berbers, in the sense of Berber speakers, would largely have vanished from the lowlands and level uplands of the Maghreb, their place taken by Arabic speakers claiming Arab descent. Apart from the Tuareg and other nomads deep in the Sahara to the south, the Berbers who remained would have been almost entirely identified with the tribal peasant population, and concentrated in the more rugged and inaccessible mountain massifs, such as the Djurdjura to the east of Algiers, which appears to have been settled for the first time in the thirteenth and fourteenth centuries.

The difficulty with this theory, as explained by Marçais, is that the division between Butr and Barānis, Zanāta and Ṣanhāja, may correspond to distinctions between Berber dialects, but not between nomads and sedentaries: the names and the speeches cut across the ways of life.[36] Moreover, the distinction between nomads and sedentaries itself is not clear, since many North African peoples have traditionally been transhumant, that is, seasonal migrants from their fields to their pastures, and many of the more nomadic have been to a lesser extent cultivators. Ironically, the first reliable information we have on the Banū Hilāl themselves depicts them in the desert to the west of the Nile in the late tenth century as nomads who wander with their flocks and herds, but who return in summer to the oases of Kharga and Dakhla at the time of the harvest for their provisions.[37] In seizing upon the nations, the objects of Ibn Khaldūn's concern, Gautier has certainly followed the master in relating them to the material conditions of their existence. But by distinguishing so sharply between their ways of life, he has equally certainly overdetermined their history.

The Conflict of Arab and Berber

Racial conflict there certainly was, based upon racial perceptions that came down to physical appearance. The garb of the Berber tribesman had long distinguished him from the Arabized townsman. The Berber troops of the Caliphate at Cordoba wore turbans as distinct from coloured bonnets;[38] the Saharans wore their veils. Ibn Khaldūn described the Berbers of North Africa itself as wearing a woollen plaid, with one end thrown over the left shoulder, beneath a black burnous or hooded cape. Otherwise they went bare and shaven-headed.[39] Many of those same heads, however, were distinguished by the long hanging scalplock of frizzy hair which identified the wearer's clan, a custom which survived into the twentieth century in the Rif, where Abdelkrim in the 1920s had them all cut off as a mark of national unity in his 'country with a government and a flag'.[40] Plaid and scalplock, together with frizzy hair, had characterized the Berber as an enemy alien in the legendary statue erected as a talisman to warn the folk of al-Andalus of the approach of predators from across the Straits.[41] On their entry into Ifrīqiya, the Hilalians seemed equally foreign to the folk of Qayrawān whom they attacked and massacred. Quite what it was is unclear, but each advancing chieftain claimed lordship over the villages through which he passed by leaving his *qalansuwwa* or bonnet, headdress, as a sign of possession.[42] Their Zirid opponents, on the other hand, most probably wore the kind

of turban which had gone with the Kutāma to Egypt and the
Berbers to Spain as a military and official uniform. With two long
ends wound down around the neck, it bandaged the head in such
a way that only the face showed. By the fourteenth century, this
turban had been adopted by the Arabs themselves.[43]

Hostile perceptions like these were translated into words drawn
from the vast repertoire of racial imagery in Arabic literature. 'Oh
king', said the poet of the sultan Muʿizz ibn Bādīs in his lament for
the battle of Ḥaydarān:

> In the end he was beaten by envious fate,
>   Qaḥṭān overthrown by Nizār;
>   Without fortune to help him, Maʿadd would have failed,
>   Abu Dhirr would have won, and Ghafār.[44]

Nizār and Maʿadd were ancestral heroes of the Arab tribes of
Northern Arabia, including the Banū Hilāl; Qaḥṭān, Abu Dhirr
and Ghafār were founders and champions of the tribes of the
Yemen, from whom the Zirids claimed descent. Less personally,
the bedouin were compared to the flood caused by the breaking of
the great Maʾrib dam, which had destroyed the prosperity of the
Yemen at some time before Islam and driven its king and people to
emigrate; it was an appropriate analogy for the abandonment of
the great city of Qayrawān by the modern offspring of the South
Arabian race.[45] With their own tale of a great journey to the West,
the Banū Hilāl flowed naturally into the same stream of thought
which populated the earth with emigrants from some central
breeding-ground in and around the Arabian peninsula. As the
Kitāb al-ʿIbar demonstrates, they powerfully reinforced the concern with Arab ancestry in the Maghrib, greatly extending the
genealogical repertoire while popularizing its appeal. This concern
is clearly visible at the level of oral tradition, where myths and
metaphors of ancestry, emigration and conquest became the for-
mat for the famous romance of the Banū Hilāl.

The romance carries the theme of combat between adventurous
immigrants and indigenous inhabitants into the realm of fiction,
where familiar heroes and heroines offer themselves to the imagination of the audience. At its climax, the Arab hero Dhiyāb slays his
mortal enemy and great rival al-Khalīfa al-Zanātī, the Zanāta
Caliph, the father of the heroine Saʿāda or Suʿdā. At its simplest, in
a version collected in southern Tunisia in 1927, it tells how:

Plate 4.4 *The Hilālī champion Dhiyāb slays the Berber champion Zanātī Khalīfa*
(Modern print from Tunisia)

Zanātī Khalīfa pranced in the field, taunting the Hilālī women: 'Where is your little Dhiyāb? Is the little wolf coming out or lying low?' They were in front of him while the Zanāta women were on the hilltops behind. Suddenly Dhiyāb galloped down into the arena. 'Here I am, Zanātī Khalīfa! I've had to round up the horses you startled with your warcry!' The battle commenced, the dust rose, the sun was hidden, the din rose to the sky. In each camp the tension rose, the guesses multiplied. Then Saʿāda, daughter of Khalīfa Zanātī, saw at a distance one rider down. She thought her father must have won, and ran as usual to catch the horse of the vanquished and bring it to their tent as a prize. But the closer she got the more she was afraid, and her knees trembled. When she arrived and saw what had happened, her heart froze, and in vast grief she cried: 'I clutch my heart, I tear my cheeks, I think my lord has won, I know he's lost. You have broken my back, Dhiyāb ibn Ghānim; may God pay you out the day the earth of the grave covers your corpse!' Dhiyāb simply said: 'Your lord came to meet me, and I came to meet him. We had two fiery horses, and we were two lions. He threw a deadly spear which tore my coat. I threw one

back, and left his blood to dry on the hill. My daughter, I dis-
mounted to say farewell, but saw that my blow was fatal. Don't
cry, Saʿāda, think of me from now on as your father. Tomorrow, if
God wills, you shall marry my son ʿAmr, and live pure and
honoured in our tents.' He lifted her up behind him and married her
to his son.[46]

In the *Kitāb al-ʿIbar*, Zanātī Khalīfa appears as Abū Suʿdā,
'Father of Suʿdā/Saʿāda', the vizier of the Banū Yaʿlā who ruled at
Tlemcen before the Almoravid conquest, appointed to lead the
Zanāta against the Arabs who had driven them back from
Ifrīqiya.[47] What is important about the romance, however, is that
the conflict at its heart is not simply a fiction, but a fiction with a
purpose which serves in this case to sanction alliance and miscege-
nation (even if the sequel to this particular tale is that young ʿAmr
neglected his bride to the point at which Dhiyāb killed his own
son, and returned Saʿāda to her own people – honour is all!). The
legends might cover all kinds of actual compromise; the outstand-
ing example may be the adoption of a Yemeni genealogy by the
Banū Maʿqil as they penetrated southern Morocco. In the guise of
the Banū Ḥassān, they turned into the Blue Men of the western
Sahara, taking the place of the 'Yemeni' Ṣanhāja as the warrior
tribes who ruled the desert as speakers of Arabic rather than
Berber.[48] It is the underlying reality which requires explanation.

The crucial factor remains political. The Banū Hilāl first appear
in Ifrīqiya, not as invaders sent from Egypt, but as warrior tribes
in Tripolitania who were employed by the Zirid sultan Muʿizz as
a check upon the Berbers in the south; he may well have supplied
them with horses, their essential armament.[49] Following his defeat
they overran the countryside, not so much as nomads but as
armies in alliance with the petty dynasties which sprang up in the
cities, and living off tributes and taxes quite as much as flocks and
herds. The story was repeated on the high plains to the west,
where the tribes were recruited by the ambitious Ḥammadids of
the Qalʿa and Bijaya. By the time of the Almohad invasion of
Ifrīqiya, the Hilālīs were a formidable fighting force in both eastern Algeria and Tunisia which required two pitched battles to
defeat.[50] Far from annihilating the Arabs, however, ʿAbd al-
Muʾmin enlisted them for his invasion of Spain. Under the Ḥafṣids
the tribes of the Banū Sulaym, who had taken the place of the Banū
Hilāl in Tripolitania and Tunisia, became the arbiters of power in
the endless quarrels over the succession to the throne at Tunis and

Bijaya. They were the effective representatives of the state away from the towns, while their chiefs acquired large properties in city and countryside.[51]

By the time of Ibn Khaldūn in the late fourteenth century, the chiefs of the Arab Dawāwida were hand-in-glove with the petty dynasty of the Banū Muznī at Biskra to divide the taxes of the Zab between them. Collected in the name of the Ḥafṣid prince at Bijaya, those taxes in turn paid for the military expeditions of the tribes when summoned by the sultan.[52] In the fifteenth century, the renewal of Ḥafṣid power and authority simply confirmed the Arab tribes in their position as an estate of the realm.[53] To the west around Tlemcen, they forced themselves upon the ruling dynasty; Ibn Khaldūn accused the ʿAbd al-Wadids of abdicating in their favour.[54] Only in central Morocco were the tribes severely restricted; there the Arabs depended absolutely upon the monarchy for their existence as warriors in its service. To the south and east of the Atlas, the Banū Maʿqil exploited the rivalries between Marrakesh, Tlemcen and Fes to establish their overlordship in the absence of the state.

The conflict between the nomad and the peasant perceived by Ibn Khaldūn and seized upon by Gautier is much better understood in the light of this military and political career which began under the Zirids, but continued under the Almohads and their successors. Bedouin, says Ibn Khaldūn, are what they are only in relation to the presence or absence, strength or weakness, of royal authority, which dominates them, patronizes them, conciliates them, or leaves them alone in the wilderness.[55] They are in any case creatures of the flat and open land, which they will plunder repeatedly when the dynasty is weak, to the ruin of its inhabitants.[56] Mountains and strongholds they will leave alone; but those places that succumb to the bedouin are quickly ruined, since 'their sustenance lies wherever the shadow of their lances falls'. They take what they want without payment, either as loot or as tribute, without caring whether it is more than the victim can pay. With no proper reward for its labour, the sedentary population disperses and its civilization decays, all the more because the bedouin, as overlords responsible for justice, have no concern for the rule of law, the only defence against anarchy and chaos. The Yemen, Iraq, Syria and all the land between the country of the Blacks and the Mediterranean has been wasted in this way, leaving the monuments to their ancient civilization in ruins in the desert.[57] Around

*Plate 4.5   The minaret of the mosque of the Qal'a of the Banū Ḥammād,
deserted under pressure from the Banū Hilāl
(Photo: Michael Brett)*

the decay of their colossal wrecks, the lone and level sands stretch
far away; but Ibn Khaldūn was thinking in the first place of North
Africa under the auspices of the Berber dynasties. He echoes the
accusations levelled at the Arabs by al-Tijānī, one of his main

sources, at the beginning of the fourteenth century.[58] Both writers, however, were on excellent terms with the bedouin chieftains who gave them hospitality on their missions as representatives of central government, a fact which renders their attitude and their denunciations highly ambiguous.[59]

The ambiguity was to be found in the bedouin themselves. The Banū Hilāl represented what Ibn Khaldūn calls the Arabs of the fourth race, that is, the Arabs who had relapsed into savagery in the wilderness after their fellows had gone out to conquer the world for Islam. Consumed in the holocaust of empire, these heroes had vanished into the servile masses of the Muslim world beneath the level of deeds and therefore history. Their place as an Arab nation has been taken by those they had left behind, but who have now risen from the desert above the horizon of human knowledge. Their ascent into this particular heaven contrasts with the fate of their predecessors, and still more with nations such as the Persians of Iran and the Copts of Egypt, who have dwindled and died under the rule of Islam, simply because 'a nation that has been defeated and come under the rule of another will quickly perish'.[60] Hopelessness leads to apathy and extinction; on the other hand, 'the vanquished always want to imitate the victor', and go to swell his ranks.[61] Beneath the surface of events, Ibn Khaldūn is aware of genesis as well as death.

Genesis and death are equally apparent at every stage in the Hilalian saga. Under the anthropological rubric of 'fission and fusion', they were intrinsic to the tribal society which the Arabs shared with the Berbers. The Banū Hilāl were addicted to the genealogical fiction of descent from a common ancestor, under whose umbrella extended families or clans might break up into fractions, or unite to form new tribes. Al-Tijānī, once again, provides the best example when he describes the Aṣābi'a or 'Fingers', a collection of tribal 'digits' claiming descent from a man with six fingers ostracized by his family; they are a fraction of a clan called the Sons of Yazīd because it has been formed by *ziyāda*, 'augmentation'.[62]

It is entirely possible, indeed very likely, that the Banū Hilāl to the west of the Nile in the tenth century were the product of such a process, creating them out of a mixture of races in the Libyan desert, where Berber peoples like the Lawāta and Ḥawwāra continued to flourish on the borders of Egypt down to the eleventh century or later. What Tijānī's examples make even clearer is that the process in the Maghreb was fiercely inegalitarian, despite the equality which Ibn Khaldūn considers the fundamental feature of nomad society. The warrior clans who served the Ḥafṣids were an aristocratic elite of horsemen headed by great noblemen; the mass of camel-herding bedouin were the impoverished nomads of the *Muqaddima*. Many had simply been forced out of the competition for power by stronger rivals; others were no doubt aspiring to rise to the ranks of the military, where they might enjoy the patronage of the state. In between the winners and the losers were those who had elected to step aside from the struggle into prestige and wealth of a different kind. These were the holy men or marabouts, whose appearance in North Africa from the Almohad period onwards is the most significant development of these centuries. Certainly they were deeply implicated in social change.

The Role of the Marabout

Marabout is colloquial for *murābiṭ*, 'man of the *ribāṭ*', 'Almoravid'. The Almoravids, the holy warriors of the Sahara in the eleventh century, were called after the *ribāṭs* or frontier fortresses built in the eighth and ninth centuries whose name was synonymous with the duty to fight for the faith against the infidel. These survive today at Sousse and Monastir in Tunisia, while one of them, rebuilt by the Almohads, is the original Rabat, the capital of Morocco. But by the tenth century, those who garrisoned them in Ifrīqiya were more likely to be hermits whose flight from the world eventually drove them out into the wilderness to starve themselves into sanctity.[63] *Murābiṭ* thus became a common term for the holy man who placed himself apart from society, even while it continued to evolve in the opposite, Almoravid sense of the militant zealot determined to impose the Law of God upon the people.

In the course of the twelfth century, under the aegis of the Almohad empire, both of these types were embraced by a novel form of Islam introduced from the East into the Muslim West, where it spread back from al-Andalus and Morocco in the direction of Ifrīqiya. This was Ṣufism or Islamic mysticism, a merging of philosophical contemplation with devotional practices which at this time, throughout the Muslim world, began to develop in the manner of the schools of Islamic law into a series of pious *ṭarīqas* or 'ways' to the knowledge and experience of God. These ways were handed down from masters to pupils just like the doctrines of the jurists, and came to supplement the five basic pillars of the faith with meditations and rituals leading to some form of ecstasy. At one extreme of this mysticism was the Andalusian Ibn al-ʿArabī, whose sublime vision of the universe resembled that of Dante in the *Divine Comedy*. At the other was the practical piety of ʿAbd al-Jalīl al-Dukkālī, a devout from the High Atlas whose Islam remained close to the basic legalism of the Almoravids. In between were the great saints of Fes and Marrakesh, Ḥarzihum and Abū Yaʿzā, the one a scholar and ascetic concerned with right and wrong, the other a man of profound piety, who spoke only Berber. Ḥarzihum became Sidi Harazem, the patron of a spring in the valley close to Fes, an ironic example of the persistence of pagan beliefs in the divinity of nature in both Christianity and Islam. Equally paradoxically, the reclusive Abu Yaʿzā became the inspiration for the following generation of Ṣūfīs in North Africa.[64]

What all of them had in common was *baraka*, the blessing they enjoyed as *awliya'* or friends of God, which passed through them to their followers and the populace at large. It was associated with miraculous power, and especially with the gift of second sight, and was held in awe despite the vein of scepticism which regarded many of its manifestations as *shaʿūdha* or trickery. Many indeed feared it as wizardry, for which the Berber saints of Morocco acquired so black a reputation in the curious story of Aladdin, a late addition to the Thousand and One Nights, of uncertain origin:

> This darwish (holy man, marabout), who came from the far interior of Morocco, was a powerful magician, deeply learned in astrology and the reading of faces . . . born and bred in that hotbed of evil sorcerers . . . From his earliest youth he had avidly studied sorcery and spells, geomancy and alchemy, astrology, fumigation and enchantment; so that, after thirty years of wizardry, he had learnt the existence of a magic lamp . . . [65]

The hero's finding of this Grail-like treasure beyond caves of ever more precious jewels is the storyteller's travesty of the mystic quest for the ultimate truth. In Morocco itself, however, the *baraka* or holiness which was generated by such familiarity with the supernatural was more likely to be the power to bring the other world of God and His angels to bear upon the problems of this. Drawn into the public domain to settle its disputes and cure its ills, the *murābiṭ* who renounced society or sought to reform it became the

*Plate 4.6   The Bou Inaniya or Madrasa of the Marinid sultan Abū 'Inān
at Fes
(Photo: Michael Brett)*

marabout who maintained its equilibrium, a priest-like figure who approved rather than abhorred the life of the people. In the aftermath of the three great revolutions, this saintly Islam coloured the whole of the faith in North Africa, and became dominant in the tribal countryside.

At the beginning of the fourteenth century, in the Ifrīqiya of al-Tijānī, the transition from militant righteousness to social control was dramatically illustrated by the movement of the holy man Qāsim ibn Marā, who formed the poorer Arab bedouin of central Tunisia into the Jannāda or Warriors, a roving band dedicated to clearing the routes of brigands. He was murdered for this subversion of the established order by the chiefs of the Arabs in collusion with the sultan at Tunis; but his call was repeated further to the west in the Zab, where the holy man Saʿāda formed a similar band of *murābiṭūn* called the Sunniyya or Men of the Holy Law. His movement was more complicated and long-lasting than that of Qāsim since on the one hand it aimed to liberate the bedouin around the oases from the tyranny of the lords of Biskra, the Banū Muznī, while on the other it divided the leaders of the Dawāwida, the Arab allies of the Banū Muznī, and perished only with the eventual reconciliation of the rival chiefs. The failure of both these revolts of the poorer bedouin against the rich and powerful was highly significant, but no more so than the lasting achievement of the Sunniyya. The *zāwiya* or 'niche', the residence of Saʿāda at Tolga, survived his killing to become, in the hands of his descendants, a centre of religious authority for the nomads, who respected the safe-conducts it granted to travellers on the routes of the region.[66]

Saʿāda had sat at the feet of a Berber saint at Taza in Morocco, and his return eastwards to his people in Ifrīqiya is typical not only of the spread of maraboutism out of the west, but also of the way in which its spread into the eastern Maghreb was associated with the Arabs of Hilāl and Sulaym. Somewhere near the beginning of his journey from Tunis to Tripoli in 1306–7, al-Tijānī tells the story of the Arab who was hired by evil villagers to kill the holy man at the nearby *masjid* or chapel, but in the presence of the saint was so overcome that he slipped from his horse and repented his wickedness. Almost a scene out of a Western, the importance of the story is that the holy man was himself an Arab, none other than al-Dahmānī, the epitome of the noble warrior turned man of God, the founder of Ṣufism at Qayrawān at the beginning of the

thirteenth century. Al-Dahmānī's own master had been the celebrated Andalusian Abū Madyān (from whom the late President
of Algeria, Houari Boumedienne, deliberately took his name), who
had come to Bijaya in the central Maghreb, not from his homeland
in Spain, but from Fes and Marrakesh. The association of Berber
mysticism in Morocco with the bedouin tribesmen of Tunisia was
clearly established from the outset.[67]

It was very apparent a hundred years later to al-Tijānī, as he
travelled along the route from Gabes to Tripoli escorted by the
Arabs of the Banū Sulaym who controlled it on behalf of the sultan
at Tunis. The bedouin went in fear of the Berber marabout Abū
Ghurāra, who had so impressed them with his conjuring tricks
that at his command they would restore to travellers all that they
had stolen. The two *zāwiya*s he visited, however, had each been
founded by Arab holy men who, like al-Dahmānī, belonged to the
ruling lineages of the tribes, but had renounced the life of the
warrior for that of the saint. Their descendants were holy families
who specialized in godliness rather than arms and, by standing
aside from the tribal conflict, kept the peace on their own doorstep
and increasingly for miles around. To travellers they offered both
hospitality and assurances of safety for the journey. The *zāwiya* of
Saʿāda at Tolga was evidently not alone, but part of an extensive
network of wayside refuges created by Arab holy men as a defence
against the lawlessness of their bedouin kinsmen in the open
countryside.[68]

The *zāwiya*s they established went back to the origins of Ṣufism
in the Near East, where itinerant 'brothers' had wandered the
highways meeting for prayer in hostelries or inns. The notion of
wayside hospitality remained fundamental as the *zāwiya* spread
into the Maghreb among the Arabs in Ifrīqiya, and went on to
rival the great mosque as a focus of Islam in the West. Typically it
grew from the dwelling into the tomb of the founder, forming a
shrine, a place of pilgrimage and prayer around which a kind of
family monastery came into existence, a community of his descendants whose shaykh 'spread a table' at which all might eat,
physically and spiritually – his sons and brothers, his disciples and
his guests.[69] Outside there might well be a market place for buying
and selling on neutral ground under the protection of the holy
man. That same protection would be extended to his visitors right
across the territory where he was renowned. Ideally such a *zāwiya*
would live from hand to mouth off the pious gifts of its clients; but

since such gifts were often gifts of property, it easily became the centre of a domain like those which al-Tijānī visited, perhaps a great estate continually collecting around the holiness at its heart. Such centres of affluence could not escape the patronage of the state, and by the fifteenth century in Ifrīqiya the more important *zāwiya*s were performing many of the functions of government in settling disputes, distributing food and maintaining order. At the same time they had become focal points of learning, helping to educate the scholarly elite upon which the dynasty depended as much as it did upon its armies. Underpinning the Ḥafṣid regime with their wealth, prestige and religious scholarship, these *zāwiyas* were a far cry from the rebellions of the Jannāda and the Sunniyya.[70]

They remained nevertheless very close to the foundations of a society divided between rich and poor, weak and strong, even more than between Arabs and Berbers, nomads and peasants, cultural categories of race and way of life which were only meaningful in terms of power, prestige and wealth. Thus al-Tijānī tells the tale of Khalaf Allah, yet another holy man of Arab bedouin extraction, who had left his Arab *zāwiya* along the way to Tripoli

Plate 4.7   Fortified granaries in southern Tunisia
(Photo: Michael Brett)

to build a mosque and 'bring a dead land to life' by irrigation. But
the bedouin themselves had treated his cultivation as pasture, and
made it impossible for him to survive.[71] The story, with which Ibn
Khaldūn was certainly familiar, since al-Tijānī was one of his
sources, well illustrates the theme of the *Muqaddima*, that 'places
that succumb to the bedouin are quickly ruined'. But it shows the
holy man himself, the marabout, in quite a different light as a
settler, a colonist literally at the grass roots, and an agent of a
different kind from the protector of travel and trade. In the social
changes of the post-Almohad period, this was perhaps his most
important role.

In central Tunisia, al-Tijānī encountered two settlements of
Berber refugees from the south, driven from their lands by the
Arabs, much as Ibn Khaldūn supposed. Ibn Khaldūn himself describes another class of refugee at Biskra. The Banū Muznī, the
lords of the oasis, were originally Hilālīs whose tribe, the Athbaj,
had been forced off the steppe by their rivals, the Riyāḥ, and
driven ignominiously into the palm groves as peasants. Reclassi-
fied in this way, they had then risen to power through the political
structures of the oasis, only to be challenged by the impoverished
bedouin of the Sunniyya, who were sufficiently close to settling at
Biskra to fall foul of the Banū Muznī's tax collectors.[72] We are
looking at a population in constant flux, at Arab bedouin tribes
which form and reform around the twin poles of warfare and
sanctity, but also at a mixture of displaced peasants and nomads
continually settling and resettling as cultivators around the
alternative poles of independence and subjection. In the midst of
that flux the marabout and his *zāwiya*, despite the experience of
Khalaf Allah, stands out as the pioneer whose settlement offered
the best security for the landless and the homeless in a dangerous
world. The *zāwiya* made its fortune not simply as a station for
travellers, but because it afforded its protection to those who lived
and worked in its vicinity, and came from miles around to do so.
It was a major factor in the repopulation of the North African
countryside by a new generation of North Africans too humble to
be described by Ibn Khaldūn as a race.

Ibn Khaldūn makes nothing of maraboutism, despite his description of the *murābiṭ*ism of the Jannāda and the Sunniyya, and
despite the fact that he himself took refuge in the Qalʿa of the Banū
Salāma to begin work upon the *Kitāb al-ʿIbar*. A troglodytic
Berber village cut into the scarp of the high plains of western

Algeria where they fall away in great steps towards the desert in the south, the Qal'a or 'fortress' was named after the maraboutic family which presided over it and gave this particular refugee political asylum. We are left to wonder what Ibn Khaldūn would have made of the formation of whole new peoples, like the Zwāyā of the western Sahara, whole new tribes, like the Awlād Sīdī Shaykh of western Algeria,[73] new dynasties even, like the Shābbiyya of Kairouan in the sixteenth century,[74] on the basis of descent from some holy man. These so-called maraboutic tribes are only the more conspicuous products of the social reformation that included the progressive replacement of Berber by Arab nomads, and more generally involved the replacement of Berber by Arabic as the speech of a growing proportion of the population. William Marçais, the critic of Gautier's racial theory of nomads and peasants, was clear on linguistic grounds that the Arabic introduced at the time of the conquest in the eighth century had developed into the urban dialects of today. Its extension into the countryside as the vernacular Arabic of North Africa, however, had been overtaken by the subsequent spread of the bedouin speech of the Hilālīs[75] – a progressive repopulation of the Maghreb with Arabic speakers against a background of radical economic, social and political change of which these Arabs were as much the victims as the Berbers. Precisely how or why the linguistic change should have occurred under these conditions is not clear: unwritten speech leaves few traces of its passing.[76] But in at least two regions Islam itself was at stake; and for these there is some written evidence.

Berberism and Islam

Travelling with a prince of the Ḥafṣid dynasty at the beginning of what was to have been a pilgrimage to Mecca, al-Tijānī stayed at least twice in the midst of a Berber population. Approaching Tripoli, he lodged in the oasis of Zanzūr, whose Berber inhabitants had been reduced from warlike freemen to servile tenants of their own palm groves by the Arab chieftain who hosted the royal party as it passed through his territory.[77] Previously, however, he had stayed for several months (such was the leisureliness of the journey) at the Berber hill village of Ghoumrassen, yet another troglodytic fortress built into the cliffs of the Jabal Nafusa. There again he was the guest of the Arab chieftain in whose territory it lay, but who in this case simply had a pact of non-aggression with the villagers, from whom his secretary or letter-writer came.[78] Between Ghoumrassen and Zanzūr, on the other hand, Arab nomads and Berber peasants were intermittently at war as the Arab warriors attempted to impose their domination in the name of the sultan. Al-Tijānī, the man of learning and letters from the metropolis, found both sides alien and exotic, but the Berbers especially so, since they were Ibāḍī Kharijites who had, in his opinion, almost no religion at all: they appeared not to pray, and buried their dead in a sitting position instead of lying on the left side.[79]

He did them something of an injustice. The fact that Abū Jabbāra al-Warghammī, a man from the village, could act as secretary to the probably illiterate Arab chief Yaʿqūb ibn ʿAtiyya, reveals the existence of a Kharijite elite of scholars learned in their own law, invisible to al-Tijānī, but well documented in their own traditions. These scholars, who in the ninth and tenth centuries offered the earliest example of the colonization of the North African countryside by the Muslim holy man, had become increasingly isolated over the years, with the triumph of Malikism followed by the spread of Ṣufism, to the point at which they had grown anxious over their own education and their ability to comprehend the Arabic which was the key to their faith. From the thirteenth century onwards they came under heavy pressure in one of their erstwhile strongholds, the oases of the Djerid to the west of the Jabal Nafusa, from zealous Malikites who won over the majority of the population to orthodox Sunni Islam. The success of these missionaries was apparent in the rise of the Berber Muḥammad ibn ʿArafa al-Warghammī to be the imam of the Great Mosque of Tunis and the acknowledged head of the Malikite school in Ifrīqiya.[80] Meanwhile, in his homeland in the south, the abandonment of Ibāḍism prepared the way for the abandonment of the Berber language itself.[81] The linguistic change may have been accomplished at Ghoumrassen at some time in the fifteenth century, and would have been largely completed with the arrival of holy men or marabouts from southern Morocco, who in the sixteenth century were instrumental in establishing a mode of peaceful coexistence between nomads and peasants in the Warghamma confederation.[82] Only isolated Berber villages have remained in the region down to the present day.

Further to the east in Tripolitania, however, as well as on the
island of Djerba to the north, the survival of Ibāḍī Islam has
helped to ensure the survival of Berber by locking its speakers into
separate religious communities. The clearest example is undoubtedly the Mzab to the west in the Algerian Sahara, where the Ibāḍīs
who fled from Tahert in the tenth century eventually took refuge,
and where they created their own republic out of the five little
cities they built in the oases of the valley under the strict rule of
their ʿazzābas, their jurists. So strict was their rule in accordance
with Islamic law and Berber custom that the women have never
been allowed to leave the valley or to marry outside the community, and the men have always returned to it to wed and
ultimately to die. Faith, custom and language have in consequence
remained intact in the midst of a desert population otherwise
wholly Arabized, the people themselves a last heroic remnant of
the original attempt to transform the Islam of the Berbers into the
Islam of the world.[83]

Despite their Berberism, which extends to a tribal structure
much like that of non-Ibāḍī populations, the Islam of the Mzabis
has nevertheless remained learned, literate and therefore Arabic.
Much further away in the desert, a similar identification with
religious scholarship led to the similar survival of a Berber population faced with the threat of Arabization and consequent extinction. By the fifteenth or sixteenth century, *zawāyā* or *zwāyā* (the
plural of *zāwiya*) became the name commonly given to those
descendants of the Almoravids, the Berbers of the western Sahara,
who yielded their status of warriors to the incoming Arabs of the
Banū Ḥassān, and preferred instead the pursuit of Islam. Out of
the original genealogies of the Zanaga or Znaga (the Berber form
of Ṣanhāja), many of which appear to have been matrilineal,
developed the lineages of religious scholars who traced their ancestry back to the Prophet and his companions, just as the
Almoravids had claimed descent from the kings of the Yemen.[84]

In this way they established themselves and their clansmen as
maraboutic tribes in a hierarchical Saharan society of Arab warriors, Berber clerics and servile cultivators.[85] Religious tribes such
as the Kunta were no doubt the artificial products of fission and
fusion under the same kind of pressures upon the nomadic way of
life as those on the northern borders of the desert which were
described by al-Tijānī and Ibn Khaldūn.[86] But the scholarly rather
than saintly Islam for which they were famous was no mere

Page

consolation for defeat and dispossession, but a means to wealth
and therefore power as controllers of the trans-Saharan trade from
Morocco to Timbuktu. Timbuktu, which was in but not wholly of
the great Sudanic empire of Songhay in the sixteenth century, was
largely in the hands of their resident merchants and clerics down
to the nineteenth century, despite their lack of military force to
rule the city. From it, they exerted an enormous influence upon the
development of Islam in West Africa.[87]

In the process, despite their claims to Arab ancestry and their
pride in their Arabic learning, which distinguished them from the
illiterate warriors of the Banū Ḥassān with their Arabic dialect, the
Zwāyā of the western Sahara preserved their Berber language[88]
and the memory of their heroic Berber past,[89] in a mirror image of
the Arabization associated with maraboutism in southern Tunisia.
Further to the east, in the vast upland triangle from the Hoggar
mountains to those of Air and the Adrar n-Ifoghas, the past in
question survived into the present. The Tuareg were a people like
the Ṣanhāja of old, warlike Berber nomads dominating a population of cultivators in the oases, lording it from time to time over
cities like Timbuktu, and going on to establish their own sultanate
at Agades from the fifteenth down to the twentieth century. They
too had their marabouts, their *ineslemen* or 'men of peace', not so
clearly separated as the Zwāyā from the Banū Ḥassān, though
equally influential. Once again, however, the long-standing concern with Arab ancestry is in evidence, the mental picture of the
world and its history which so undermined the sense of Berber
identity elsewhere. Locked into that world picture, the Tuareg
stand out all the more clearly as a fraction of the previous dominion of their nation over the great desert as a whole.[90]

The situation of the Tuareg in the wider context of the Sahara
and its peoples is symptomatic of the profound changes affecting
the Berbers even as Ibn Khaldūn was celebrating their grandeur as
a great nation.[91] With the disappearance of so many old identities
and the formation of so many new, we are moving forward, out of
the world of the *Kitāb al-'Ibar* into the modern history of North
Africa, in which the story of the Berbers is no longer the history of
their great dynasties but of their retreat into relative isolation as
they lost, in effect, their monopoly of tribal society in the Maghrib.
The linguistic distinction marked a division of the population at
large, not simply between the rural majority and the urban minority. Its significance, however, remained to be determined. Trib-

alism itself had had its day as a force for revolution, conquest and empire, reverting instead to a mechanism for social change. As a product of its workings, Arabs and Berbers were sharply differentiated. 'You cannot ignore something as conspicuous as that a man speaks an unintelligible language.'[92] But that did not necessarily mean conflict in the manner envisaged by Gautier. The Arabs thus constituted by language out of a melting-pot of people were no longer, if they ever had been, the primitives of the fourth race, united by blood and thirsting for destruction, but a steadily growing cross-section of the native population. The unification of North Africa by Islam ensured that the factors which divided them from those who remained Berber were offset by others which brought them together. Foremost among these was the state.

5

The Wheel of State

The Circle of Equity

No justice without the army; no army without taxes; no taxes without wealth; no wealth without justice.

The political wisdom summarized in this circular maxim had surfaced in the Islamic world by the tenth century. In the Mirrors for Princes, a whole genre of writing which described the ideal monarch in contrast to the tyrant, the concept of the state as a wheel turned by the ruler for good or ill emerged ever more clearly as the model of political thought. For Ibn Khaldūn this wheel became the vehicle whose annual rotation carried the dynasty onwards from cradle to grave. 'Oh King', said the old Persian priest into whose mouth he put the wisdom:

the might of royal authority materializes only through the religious law, obedience toward God, and compliance with His commands and prohibitions. The religious law, on the other hand, persists only through royal authority. Mighty royal authority is achieved only through men. Men persist only with the help of property. The only way to property is through cultivation. The only way to cultivation is through justice. Justice is a balance set up among mankind. The Lord set it up and appointed an overseer of it, and that is the ruler. You, oh King, went after the farms and took them away from their owners and cultivators. They are the people who pay the land tax and from whom one gets money. You gave their farms as fiefs to your entourage and servants and to sluggards. They did not cultivate the farms, nor were they asked to pay the land tax, because they were close to the king. The remaining landowners who did pay the land tax and cultivated their farms had to carry an unjust burden. Therefore they left their farms and abandoned their settlements. They took refuge in farms that were far away or difficult of access. Thus, cultivation slackened, and the farms were ruined. There was little money, and soldiers and subjects perished. Neighbouring rulers coveted the realm, because they knew that its foundations were undermined.[1]

For the Ottomans, in the centuries following the composition of the *Kitāb al-'Ibar*, the wheel became the Circle of Equity, the commonplace description of their empire and its administration.[2] Their *'askar* or army comprised all the servants of the monarch, domestics, secretaries and soldiers alike. Its military might represented the *shawka* or 'thorn' of the prince, fear of whom kept his subjects, and therefore society, in order. At the height of the Ottoman empire in the sixteenth century, the maxim epitomized the government of half the world, as the saying went. Certainly it extended into North Africa as far as the borders of Morocco. There, in the Moorish empire of the Maghrib al-Aqṣā or Furthest West, the same wisdom applied to the notion of *makhzan*.

*Plate 5.1   The courtroom of the palace at Meknes, overlooking the underground dungeons
(Photo: Michael Brett)*

Makhzan is 'magazine' in the old sense of a storehouse, not in this case of gunpowder but of treasure. The use of 'the Makhzen' or Treasury as a term for the government of Morocco nicely describes a regime which lived to tax and taxed to live, and in the process provided a measure of order in the Muslim commonwealth. The wealth at which it aimed was more problematic. The *ra'iyya* or flock of subjects was not always shorn to its advantage: the wheel of state, as Ibn Khaldūn foresaw, was likely to be oppressive. Predictable as the routine and its effects may have been, however, the consequences were not so much the rise and fall of dynasties as the evolution of the modern states of North Africa. The establishment of these states determined the character of social change in the Maghrib in the age which opened with the arrival of the *Reconquista* on the southern bank of the Mediterranean.

The Ottoman Conquest

The *Reconquista*, the 'reconquest' of the Iberian peninsula from the Moors by the Christian kingdoms of the north, arrived in North Africa with the capture of Ceuta by the Portuguese in 1415. A hundred years later, almost the whole of the coast from Agadir in southern Morocco to Tripoli was in the hands of the Portuguese and Spaniards; Tunis itself was famously conquered by the emperor Charles V in 1535, and only Algiers held out equally famously against him in 1541. The Portuguese on the Atlantic were crusaders with an eye to the kingdom of Morocco, but another to the development of their newfound trade with West Africa, where Moroccan blankets were much in demand. The Spaniards on the Mediterranean were also crusaders, but their occupation of Oran failed to develop into a war of conquest, and the main purpose of their seizure of so many ports was to deter the corsairs, the North African pirates whose raids on the coast of Spain were a poor revenge for the fall of Granada in 1492 and the end of Moorish rule on the 'far bank' of the Muslim West. Their piracy, and the aura of holy war which surrounded it, rapidly attracted fellow marauders from the Ottoman Aegean, whose intervention resulted in the Turkish conquest of Algeria, Tunisia and Libya; the spectacular growth of the Ottoman navy into a challenger for mastery of the Mediterranean; and the confrontation of the two great powers of the sixteenth century, the

Habsburgs and the Turks, in 'the Age of Philip II' so memorably evoked by Fernand Braudel.[3]

In this confrontation, the enfeebled dynasties of the mediaeval Maghreb were swept aside, even the Ḥafṣids, who at the death of their long-lived sultan 'Uthmān in 1488 lapsed into a succession dispute from which they never recovered. Their lightly armed troops were virtually 'naked in battle' in the eyes of the heavily armed and armoured Spaniards.[4] Above all, they lacked the essential weapons of the time: the cannon and the musket, the firearms of the modern age. These came to their aid only with the Turks, whose expertise in their use had conquered the Middle East from the Byzantines, the Iranians and the Mamluks of Egypt, and brought them repeatedly to the walls of Vienna.

Gunpowder in North Africa drove the Spaniards back to Oran, but meanwhile blew away the fragile political structures of Tunis and Tlemcen to impose a new and durable framework of government on the Maghreb. By the end of the sixteenth century North Africa had been converted into a series of Ottoman provinces corresponding to the modern states of Libya, Tunisia and Algeria, which confined Morocco north of the Sahara more or less within its present boundaries. Ifrīqiya, that ancient political entity, had ceased to exist. Tripoli had become the capital of a new dominion comprising Tripolitania and Cyrenaica, and eventually the Fezzan. To the west, an equally unprecedented union between Numidia and Mauretania, between Bijaya and Constantine on the one hand and Tlemcen on the other, had created a new and powerful state in the central Maghreb with its capital at the hitherto modest port of Algiers. Tunis in between was left at the head of a mere torso. With this drastic recarving of the body politic, the Maghreb was set upon its modern destiny.

Algeria, the keystone of the new edifice, was created out of the vacuum of the central Maghreb into which the Turks were drawn in the absence of any effective political control by the Ḥafṣids and Ziyanids. Algiers itself became the capital largely by chance, after it was occupied in 1516 by the brothers Barbarossa at the invitation of its people and their protector, the shaykh of the Arab Tha'āliba tribe of the hinterland. Seadogs from the Ottoman Aegean, who like the Spanish *conquistadores* in the Americas were out to build themselves an empire, these adventurers seized upon the city as the bridgehead of their invasion. But only one of the three, Khayr al-Dīn or Hayreddin, survived the battle with the Spaniards and the tribal groups of the interior, including the 'sultans' of the mountains of Kabylia. These Berbers, the 'king' of Kouko and the Banū 'Abbās respectively, will have emerged out of their tribal society in the manner described by Masqueray in the nineteenth century, by an accumulation of riches, respect and success in warfare, to the point at which they possessed their own armies and fortresses, and ruled over their feuding peoples with a mixture of patronage, diplomacy and force.[5] Islam was a powerful ingredient; Aḥmad ibn al-Qāḍī of Kouko, the hill village which served as his capital, was a marabout, a holy man whose political and military authority was sanctioned by God. As the battle for Algiers developed into a war for the whole of Algeria, he was briefly in control of the city; the massif of the Djurdjura, so recently colonized, was now populous enough to dominate the entire region.

In the event, however, the Berbers of the mountains failed to withstand the alliance between the corsairs, including the large population of Spanish Muslims who had taken refuge on the coast, and the janissaries or regular troops dispatched from Istanbul. The victorious combination was effected by Khayr al-Dīn in the name of the Ottoman Sultan, by whom he was appointed Pasha, or governor, and Beylerbey, or commander-in-chief of the ambitious enterprise in the West. Under his aggressive leadership, the Turks finally won control of Algiers in 1525, and under his successors proceeded to the conquest of eastern and western Algeria within the next thirty to forty years. Algiers was confirmed as their capital by their failure to capture and keep the great city of Tunis until 1574, by which time there was little left of Ifrīqiya for the old metropolis to administer. Tripoli had been taken in 1551 by the corsair Dragut, and became the capital of the new Libya. All three cities initially were under the control of the Beylerbeys, the greatest of whom served as Grand Admirals of the Ottoman fleet. With the death of the last Beylerbey, 'Ilj 'Alī, in 1587, however, they became the capitals of separate provinces of the empire, lining the Barbary coast from Morocco to the borders of Ottoman Egypt.[6]

Turks and Berbers

As the Barbary states, the home of the Barbary corsairs or pirates, the notoriety of the regencies of Algiers, Tunis and Tripoli spread throughout Europe. The Barbary legend of Christians captured and cruelly enslaved for the harem, the galleys, hard labour and eventual ransom flourished on the basis of a highly profitable commercial enterprise. Corsair captains and janissaries alike put their money into piratical voyages whose proceeds they divided between them in proportion to their investment, just as the Elizabethans financed the privateering expeditions of Hawkins and Drake against the Spaniards in the New World. The holy war upon the infidel turned into good business as well as great romance.[7] Ironically, while the name of Barbary won fame and fortune in the languages of Europe,[8] the Berbers themselves, from whom the name derived, were largely lost to view.

By their spectacular intervention in the affairs of the Maghrib, the Turks had effectively captured the enthusiasm for the holy war upon the Spaniards, which at the beginning of the sixteenth century had promised to turn marabouts such as Aḥmad ibn al-Qāḍī, the 'king' of Kouko, into home-grown *mahdīs* for the defence of the faith,[9] The eclipse of such native initiatives by the super-power of the Ottomans meant that no new Almoravids or Almohads emerged from the mountains, and the Berbers of Kabylia who served in the armies of Algiers and Tunis under the name of Zwāwa or Zouaves did so simply as mercenaries. The place of the tribesmen in the new order was established in the course of the Ottoman conquest. In 1542, says Joseph Morgan,

Hassan Aga (Khayr al-Dīn's successor at Algiers) set out from Algiers with a Camp of 3,000 Turks, 1,000 Moorish Foot, all Fire-Arms, with 2,000 Arab Cavalry, and 12 small Field-Pieces. His march was directed against Aben al Cadhi, King of Cucco, or Sheikh of the Zwouwa, whose strongly situated Capital, named Cucco, lies from Algiers, Eastward, about three Days Journey distant, to requite that unmanageable Prince for coming down from his Mountains, at the head of so many thousands of bold, sturdy Highlanders, Horse and Foot, in Favour of the Emperor (Charles V, who had unsuccessfully attacked Algiers in 1541); the Result of which Campain was, that those Highlanders prevailed upon their Sheikh to strike up a Peace with the Turks, nay, even to purchase it with a considerable Sum of Money, besides a great number of Cattle, and to acknowledge the Algerines in some guise their Sovereigns, by remitting them a certain annual Tribute; for the due Performance whereof, the said Prince gave in Hostage his Son and Heir apparent. By way of equivalent for this unexpected Condescension and Compliance in those scarce-come-at-able Mountain-

eers, the Turks granted them a free Commerce at Algiers and
throughout their whole Dominion; the which the Algerines have
since found by Experience to have proved far more detrimental to
their Affairs, than all the Tribute they ever received could ever
counterpoise: For it has so furnished those martial Nations with
Fire-Arms, to which they were till then utter Strangers, that the
Turks have, ever since, less cared to meddle with them than before:
And the Encouragement there given to fugitive Slaves and
Renegadoes, has stood that ingenious and industrious People in so
good Stead, that they now make excellent Arms, and large Quantities of Powder, nothing inferior to some made at Algiers. They are
as nice Marks-men as any other People whatever; all which Contin-
gencies have rendered them really very formidable; and they might
attempt great things were they but unanimous: But their unaccountable intestine Dissensions surpass even Credulity.[10]

Elsewhere, Morgan attributes the commercial concession to
Hassan Pasha, the son of Khayr al-Dīn Barbarossa, who had
married the daughter of the King of Kouko about 1560. As a
result, he adds, among the tribesmen 'it would be a difficult Matter
for a young Fellow to get even a Wife, worth having, before he is
master of a Fuzil'.[11] Its advantages evidently induced the men of
Kouko to join the Turks against the Banū 'Abbās, their neighbours
and inveterate enemies to the east, who controlled the Iron Gates,
the gorge through which passes the direct route from Algiers to
Constantine. Their power, as they too recruited Christians and
renegades as musketeers, was all the more menacing for being
insulting: 'all the Turks that fell alive into [their] Hands, the
Punishment inflicted on them, was cutting off their Genitals in the
Middle, and turning them loose, with their Hands bound behind,
so to bleed to Death in the Roads'.[12] But they too came to terms
when their Sultan was hit by a musketball, and

the new Prince struck up a Peace with the Turks, entering into a
League with the State of Algiers; but without the least tincture of
Vassalage or Dependence. – 'Tho', adds Haedo, at the arrival of a
new Basha, the Abbassi sends him a Compliment, accompanied
with a Present; in Return to which, the Vice-Roy of Algiers presents
him with a rich Sabre and a Turkish Garment. They are still upon
the like footing: Nor have the Algerines had any very considerable
Falling-out with Beni-Abbas for many Years. But upon the least
Dispute, even the whole Eastward Camp dares not attempt passing
by the Damir Capi, or Al Beban (the Iron Gates); but is obliged to
take a tedious Circumference round the Mountains, and come out
by Mesila, upon the Borders of the Numidian Desarts.[13]

The Regime of Algiers

On such a basis, the relationship between the Turks and the Berber tribesmen came to rest. By the beginning of the eighteenth century, when Morgan was writing, it had endured for well over a hundred years. Despite his remarks, the Ottomans were firmly in control. From the seat of power in all three regencies, Arabs and Berbers were conspicuously absent. Turks formed the regular army, and held most of the offices of government. Nor had they, like the Arabs of the original conquest, begun to assimilate. Far from absorbing North Africans into their ranks, they had excluded their own offspring by their native wives, preferring to rely on the intake of fresh recruits from Anatolia. Thus the army remained not only Turkish but foreign, a corps of musketeers who maintained their military efficiency in the Maghreb long after their fellow janissaries at Istanbul had degenerated into an hereditary militia. Their children meanwhile constituted yet another caste, the *kuloghulları*, the kouloughlis or 'sons of the slaves of the Sultan'. Outside the ranks of the *ojak*, as the Turkish army was called, the kouloughlis remained almost equally distinct from the native population, even as they became inevitably Arabized; instead they formed a second army of spahis or cavalrymen, and a rival elite. Government itself was in the hands of the great title-holders, the Pashas, Aghas, Beys and Deys, with specific appointments such as treasurer and chief of police. These officers, together with the heads of the *ṭā'ifa* or corporation of the corsairs, composed the Divan or Council, whose weekly meetings conducted the affairs of state. The structure was a replica of procedure at Istanbul, which had survived the inevitable deformations of the past 200 years.

Foremost among these was independence. In the course of the seventeenth century all three regencies ceased to be ruled by governors sent out from Istanbul, though they remained within the Ottoman empire. By the eighteenth century both Tripoli and Tunis were hereditary monarchies of kouloughli origin, which had reduced the numbers and powers of the Turkish *ojak* to a minimum. At Algiers the opposite was true. In contrast to the Karamanli Pashas of Tripoli and the Ḥusaynid Beys of Tunis, the Deys of Algiers were the captains of the janissaries, several thousand strong, who had taken effective control of the state, so that the Deys themselves were made and unmade at will, often by assassi-

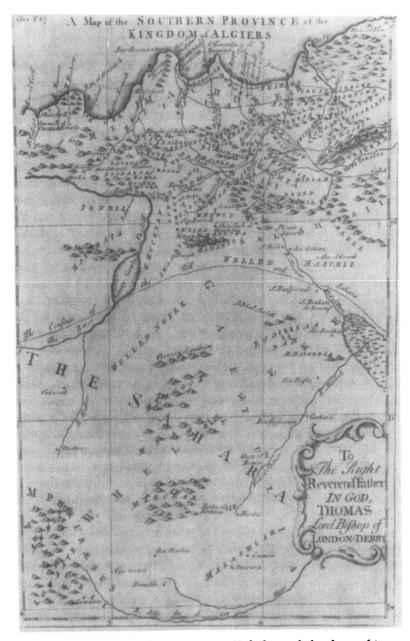

Map 5.1 Map of Algiers, western Kabylia and the desert fringe
(*From Thomas Shaw*, Travels, London, 1738)

nation. Their grip on the country nevertheless remained unbroken although, with the exception of the Mitidja, the coastal plain behind the capital, power was exercised on their behalf by the Beys of the East at Constantine, those of the South (the Titteri) at Medea, and those of the West at Mascara and eventually Oran. Likewise drawn from the *ojak* at Algiers, the Beys administered their beyliks with detachments of janissaries and local auxiliaries in garrisons or mobile camps, whose *qā'ids* or commanders supervised the tribal population. The Beys themselves were restrained by the obligation to send a substantial tribute every six months to the capital, and to bring it to Algiers in person once every three years. As a result they were as liable as the Deys to dismissal and execution.[14]

The racial exclusiveness of the Turks, the complete licence and total immunity enjoyed by the janissaries as 'slaves of the Sultan' in their dealings with his native subjects, heightened the distinction between rulers and ruled in the Ottoman provinces of North Africa, and emphasized the fiscal character of their relationship. The former were exempted from the burden of tax which fell on the city and the countryside; so too were their native auxiliaries and the so-called *makhzan* tribes, the warrior Arab nomads of the past who were now charged to 'eat' those belonging to the common herd by collecting their tribute. Such tribes were most conspicuous in the regency of Algiers, where they collaborated with the *mahalla* or 'camp', the regular tax-collecting tours of the three Beyliks which were conducted by the soldiery. This old Ḥafṣid practice formed the annual routine of central government at Tunis and at Tripoli, where it gave the Beys who commanded the winter and summer expeditions the military force to dispossess the janissaries of their monopoly of power, and to establish their own dynasties. The wheel of state was all too obviously represented by these circular campaigns of the army, beginning and ending at the capital, which kept the peace and gathered the wealth from leading subjects who handed it over on behalf of their communities to the forces of law and order. Year in, year out, they carried each regime, each society, forward into the future.

Like the Romans and the Arabs before them, the Turks did not establish the same kind of control over the mountain massifs of Algeria, and only a fluctuating overlordship over the desert fringe and the oases of the northern Sahara apart from Biskra and the

Djerid. The history of Algiers in particular was punctuated by tribal rebellions against the demands of the regime and its allies, until by the beginning of the nineteenth century the Beylik of the West was actually facing defeat. *Vis-à-vis* the *bilād al-bārūd*, 'the land of gunpowder', or the *bilād al-khalā*, 'the empty land', the *bilād al-Turk* or land under the routine control of the Turks was less than half of the whole. Part of the reason lay in that word *bārūd*; as Morgan observed, the acquisition of firearms by a rural population in which a musket was inseparable from manhood had deprived the regular army of much of its original advantage. Nevertheless, the quality of the *ojak*, and the authority of its commanders in the name of the Sultan, were sufficient to prevent any challenge to the regimes themselves from tribesmen whose 'unaccountable intestine Dissensions' inhibited the development of that unity and purpose which once upon a time had carried the great mediaeval dynasties to power.

Instead, in his capacity as vice-consul at Algiers in the early years of the eighteenth century, Joseph Morgan was witness to the dissolution of the very idea of a Berber nation identified by the Arabs and celebrated by Ibn Khaldūn. Even as a name for the speakers of their language, the word itself was fast fading from the minds of natives and foreigners alike:

This Highland Nation whose present name I absolutely take to have been their original Appellation; I mean the Zwouwa. These people are actually dispersed throughout Barbary, and for ought I know there may be of them not only in South-Numidia, but even in Libya. They are a sturdy Race, behaving like such wherever they are, but, like most of the other African Mountaineers, are dangerous enemies to be attacked in their scarce accessible Fastnesses, as the Algerines, and, I doubt not, all who have gone before them, have often found to their Cost. Leo Africanus, Marmol, and from them many other moderns, erroneously call this tough Highland Nation Azuaga, whereas the true Name is, as I said, Zwouwa. North-Westard of Costantina there is a People named Zwaga; but they are a very small Tribe in Competition with those I treat of, dwelling all in Tents, and using no Language but Arabick; whereas all the Mountaineers who bear the general Denomination of Kabeyls (of which Number are the aforesaid Zwouwa and Beni-Abbas, with an Infinity of others,) inhabit Villages, and speak the African Tongue, Multitudes of them being incapable of making themselves understood in Arabick. It must be observed, that all the Barbary Highlanders, at least those within the Compass of the

Algerine Dominion, are distinguished by the general Names *Kabeyl* and *Jibeylia*, which last Word has no other Signification than Mountaineers, from *Jibil* a Mountain, in the Plural *Jibeyl*, and so *Jibeylia*. As for *Kabeyl*, it is no other than the Plural of *Kabela*, which implies a Tribe, or Family, who live and keep together, just like the Clans in our North-British Highlands. The *Kabeyls* value themselves excessively upon their Antiquity, Purity of Blood, and Invincibility.[15]

But of Berber there is not a trace in this miscellany of proper names and descriptive terms, only a general distinction between Arabs who live in tents, and 'clansmen' who live in houses in the hills. From Morgan's report that 'Kabeyl' was said to have come from 'hanna kabelna' or *nahnū qabilnā*, 'we have accepted' Islam from the Arab conquerors, and his remark that the Arabs never boasted of having conquered the 'Zwouwa' in the seventh and eighth centuries, as they were wont to do with every nation under the sun, it would seem that Barbar, the original term, had become a largely literary word, divorced from the descendants of the peoples it had once designated.[16]

The Dominion of the Algerines

Morgan's work is for the most part a compilation of the two great sixteenth-century Spanish authors, Haedo and Marmol, and others. That of Dr Thomas Shaw is wholly original. Chaplain to the British Consulate at Algiers from 1720 to 1732, he travelled extensively in the Ottoman provinces as far as Egypt and Palestine. His monumental *Travels or Observations relating to Several Parts of Barbary and the Levant* was published in 1738, with a posthumous second edition in 1756. A Classical scholar who went on to become Regius Professor of Greek at Oxford, he was concerned to plot the topography of the country from the descriptions of the Greek and Roman geographers. A Doctor of Theology, he interpreted the life of the people with reference to the Bible. A European of the Enlightenment, he described what he found with scientific enthusiasm and considerable sympathy. But in his work he confirms Morgan's broad distinction between Arabs and Berbers, and makes clear that the Kabyles were by and large left to themselves by the traveller, who wisely followed the main routes across the open country of the bedouin:

In the Inland Towns and Villages of *Barbary*, there is, for the most Part, a House set apart for the Reception of Strangers, with a proper Officer to attend it. Here Persons are lodged and entertained, for one Night, in the best Manner the Place will afford, at the Expence of the Community. Except at these and the Places above-mentioned (the maritime towns), I met with no *Khanns* or Houses of Entertainment throughout the whole Course of my Travels. If therefore we did not fall in with the Hovels of the *Kabyles*, or the Encampments of the *Arabs*, we had nothing to protect us from the Inclemency either of the Heat of the Day, or the Cold of the Night. [But] when we are so fortunate, in travelling in *Barbary*, to find out the Encampments of the *Arabs*, (for we are not fond of visiting the *Kabyles*, who are not so easily managed,) we are entertained, for one Night, upon free Cost: the *Arabs*, either by long Custom, the particular Tenure of their Lands, or rather perhaps from Fear and Compulsion, being obliged to give the *Spahees*, and those who are with them, the *Mounah*, as they call it, which is a sufficient Quantity of Provisions for themselves and their Horses. When our Company was at any Time entertained in a courteous Manner, I used to give the Master of the Tent a Knife, a Couple of Flints, or a small Quantity of English Gunpowder; which, being much stronger than their own, they have in great Esteem, and keep for the priming only of their Fire-Arms. If the *Lallah* (or Lady) his Wife had been obliging also in her Way, by making our *Cuscasowe* savoury and with Expedition, She would return a thousand Thanks for a Skean of Thread; a large Needle; or a Pair of Scissars; all of them great Rarities. Our constant Practice was, to rise at Break of Day, set forward with the Sun, and travel till the Middle of the Afernoon; at which Time, we began to look out for the Encampments of the *Arabs*; who, to prevent such Parties as Ours from living upon them, take Care to pitch in Places the least Conspicuous. And indeed sometimes, unless we discovered the Smoke of their Tents, observed some of their Flocks, or heard the barking of their Dogs, it was with Difficulty (if at all) that we were able to find them.[17]

Journeys like these were made safe by the subjection of these 'roving Herdsmen' to the Turks, although one could never be too sure:

I rarely carried along with me more than three *Spahees*, and a Servant; all of us well armed: though we were sometimes obliged to augment our Numbers, particularly when we travelled among the independent *Arabs*, upon the frontiers of the neighbouring Kingdoms, or where two contiguous Clans were at Variance. These, and such like *Harammees*,[18] as the Free-booters are usually called, must be, I conjecture, what the Europeans mean by *Wild Arabs*; notwith-standing there is no such Name peculiar to any one Body of them; they being all of them the same, and have all the like Inclinations, (whenever a proper Opportunity or Temptation offers itself,) of robbing, stripping, and murthering, not Strangers only, but also one another. However, to prevent as much as possible the falling into their Hands, the greatest safety for a Traveller, at all Times, is to be disguised in the habit of the Country, or dressed like one of his *Spahees*. For the *Arabs* are very jealous and inquisitive; suspecting all Strangers to be Spies, and sent to take a Survey of those Lands, which, at one Time or other, (as they have been taught to fear,) are to be restored to the *Christians*.[19]

As an illustration of the workings of the wheel of state, Shaw's experience as a traveller in the 'Country of the Algerines' conforms to his general description of the southern borderlands of the Regency:

> The Dominion which the *Algerines* have beyond the Tell (Land proper for Tillage) or the more advanced Parts of the Mountains of *Atlas*, is very uncertain and precarious: for which Reason I have fixed the proper Boundaries and Limits of this Kingdom that Way, upon the northern Skirts of the *Sahara*. Some of the Villages indeed of *Zaab*, and others likewise, that have a more distant Situation from the Capital, pay regularly their annual Taxes, or at least give some Token of their Submission to the *Turks*: but the other Com-munities are independent; and the *Bedoween Arabs* of these parts are seldom to be brought under Contribution; taking always a particular Care to be upon their Guard, or at a Distance, when the *Turkish* Armies are abroad.[20]

The Kabyles or Africans, meanwhile, remain equally on the margin of Shaw's narrative. Their mountain haunts, 'that remark-able Chain of Hills', are invoked in the pastoral mode of the eighteenth century:

> If we conceive of a Number of Hills, usually with a perpendicular Height of four, five or six hundred yards, with an easy Ascent, and several Groves of Fruit and Forrest-Trees, rising up in a succession of Ranges one behind another; and if to this Prospect, we here and there add a rocky Precipice of a superior Eminence and difficult Access, and place upon the Side, or Summit of it, a mud-walled *Dashkrah* or village of the *Kabyles*; we shall then have a just and lively *Idea* of these Mountains . . .[21]

The Kabyles themselves, however, are variously described as 'numerous', 'powerful' and 'troublesome'. More scattered in the western part of the Regency, they came together in the east, where the mountains of Kabylia were altogether grander, with their 'naked Rocks and Precipices':

> The whole Tract of This (Eastern) Province, from the Sea Coast to the Parallels of *Seteef* and *Constantina*, is little else besides a continued Chain of exceeding high Mountains. Very few of the Inhabitants to the Westward of the *Wed el Ajebby* (the Soumman, dividing Greater from Lesser Kabylia)[22] pay any Tribute to the *Viceroy*; Their rugged and impracticable Situation being too difficult for the whole Strength of *Algiers* to penetrate. But among those to the Eastward, except near the Sea Shore, the *Turks* pass every Summer with a flying Camp, and receive some Tokens of Homage and Submission from Their respective *Kabyles*; who notwithstanding are all of Them so obstinate and tenacious of Their Liberty, that They give Nothing, 'till They are compelled to it by Fire and Sword.[23]

'Those to the westward' were most notably the *Zwowah* or Zwawa, under their Shaykh or Sultan at Kouko. Across the Soummam in the ranges of the Biban to the south-east, their old rivals the Banū 'Abbās were still formidable, being capable of fielding over 3,000 foot and 1,500 cavalry. But since, unlike the Zwawa, they lay 'directly in the great Road to *Constantina*' through the Iron Gates, they had over the years been forced into submission.[24] Across the high plains beyond Constantine, in the far south-east of the Regency, lay the Aures mountains, where Shaw visited the ruins of Timgad. Of this second major Berber region, however, he has little to say except that

> the Inhabitants have a quite different Mein and Aspect from their Neighbours. For their Complections are so far from being swarthy, that They are fair and ruddy; and Their Hair, which, among the other *Kabyles*, is of a dark Colour, is, with Them, of a deep Yellow. These Circumstances, (notwithstanding they are *Mahometans*, and speak the common Language only of the *Kabyles*) may induce us to take Them, if not for the [yellow-haired] Tribe mentioned by *Procopius*, yet at least for some Remnant or other of the *Vandals*, who notwithstanding they were dispossessed in His Time, of these strong Holds, and dispersed among the *African* Families, might have had several Opportunities afterwards of collecting Themselves into Bodies, and reinstating Themselves.[25]

After the genealogical theories of the Arabs, and their apparent fall into disuse, a whole new set of speculations regarding the Berbers and their origins was evidently beginning to emerge from the point of view of the European observer. As perceived by Shaw in the 1720s, their present situation was meanwhile as quiet as possible. A mere 2,000 Zwawa joined no more than 4,500 Turks and kouloughlis to form the regular army whose garrisons and expeditions kept the peace and raised the taxes throughout the Regency of Algiers with as much diplomacy as force.[26] Every market day the Kabyles who, in spite of the presence of the troops, 'lay [Bijaya] under a perpetual Blockade', came into the city with the ironware they manufactured, and large quantities of oil and wax for export to Europe and the Levant, doing good business till the market closed, when they fell to rioting.[27] Out of the Sahara came the *Beni Mezzab*, the Ibāḍites of the Mzab, who, 'notwithstanding they pay no Tribute, have been, from Time immemorial, the only Persons employed in the Slaughterhouses of *Algiers*; but as they are of the Sect of the *Melaki*, they are not permitted to enter the *Mosques of the Algerines*'.[28] On terms such as these, society and state circled each other in apparent equilibrium.

The Descendants of the Prophet

Shaw's travels along the coast by sea took him as far west as the mouth of the Moulouya in the land of the Tingitanians or western Moors, in other words the Moroccans. The picture of government there was much the same, with garrisons of troops in well-built fortresses aweing the tribal population to such good effect that

> during the long Reign of the late *Muley Ishmael, These,* as well as the Parts of It more immediately influenced by the *Capital*, were under so strict a Government and Regulation, that, notwithstanding the Numbers of *Arabs* who are every where in the Way, intent, every one of them, upon Plunder and Rapine; yet *a Child,* (according to Their Manner of speaking) *might safely carry a Piece of Money upon his Hand from one End of the Kingdom to another,* whilst the Merchant travelled from *Salee* to *Woojeda,* and from *Tanger* to *Taffilett,* without Danger, or Molestation.[29]

The past tense is significant, since upon the death of the Sultan Mawlāy Ismā'īl in 1727, a disputed succession brought disorder for the next thirty years. The commonplace about the child, or woman, in complete safety on the road, which dated at least from the days of ʿAbd al-Muʾmin and the Almohad empire, nevertheless places the Moroccan empire, its achievements and its pretensions, on a par with the Ottoman provinces at the beginning of the eighteenth century, despite the difference in their histories over the past 200 years.

The occupation of most of the coastal cities of Morocco by the Portuguese began with the capture of Ceuta in 1415, and ended as far south as Agadir a hundred years later. The Marinids, that Zanāta Berber dynasty which had conquered the country from the Almohads in the thirteenth century, were in terminal decline, and neither they nor their cousins the Waṭṭasids, who came to power in 1472, could halt this trespass of the infidel on Muslim soil. As their kingdom shrank to the region of Fes, this dereliction of their supreme duty to defend the lands of Islam opened the way for others to lead the community of the faithful in the holy war. No longer, however, was that a straightforward question of a new prophet for a new community of new tribesmen. The Berbers were still a substantial majority of the Moroccan population, not yet eliminated or isolated as in Tunisia and Algeria by the progress of Arabization. But their divine simplicity, extolled by the Kharijites, admired by Ibn Khaldūn, and touched by the preaching of the Faṭimids, the Almoravids and the Almohads, was in the hands of the marabout rather than the *murābiṭ*, the saint whose authority stemmed from his innate holiness rather than his call to righteousness. His sanctity had created the *zāwiya* or monastery as a centre of power, prestige and wealth. At the same time it had produced a class of holy men who traced their spiritual descent from a founding father such as al-Shādhilī, and handed their charisma, their 'gift of God', down to their offspring. This proliferation of maraboutic families was only matched by that of the *shurafāʾ* or *sharīf*s, the 'nobles' who claimed descent from the Prophet himself.

In principle the descendants of Muḥammad had lived in Morocco since the foundation of the Idrisid dynasty at Fes in the eighth century by a great-great-great-grandson of the Prophet, but they became prominent in the city only under the Marinids, and only strong with the decline of the dynasty in the fifteenth century. In 1437 they celebrated the repulse of a Portuguese attack upon Tangier with the discovery of the tomb of their ancestor Idrīs II

*Plate 5.2   The seventeenth-century sharifian city of Moulay Idris from
the ruins of Volubilis or Walila
(Photo: Michael Brett)*

close to the great Qarawiyyīn mosque, and in 1465 deposed and
executed the last of the Marinids. In 1472 the city was retaken by
the Waṭṭasids, but meanwhile other *shurafā*, claiming to have
come from Mecca and Medina in the thirteenth and fourteenth
centuries, had established themselves in the oases to the south of
the High Atlas, and the phenomenon of sharifianism was widespread in Morocco and western Algeria. It was the latest example
of that passion for Arab descent which had led good Berbers like
the Zirids and the Almoravids to claim an Arab origin in the
Yemen, and to the popularity of the Hilālī legend. To belong to
the lineage of the Prophet himself became the ultimate distinction,
beautifully illustrated by the tale of the Berber scholar and saint al-
Yūsī in the seventeenth century, who defied the tyrannical Sultan
Mawlāy Ismāʿīl, miraculously halted the charge of the enraged
monarch to kill him, then pardoned his sovereign in return for his
own recognition as a *sharīf*.[30]

The story shows the way in which it was possible for a wholly
new class of person to come into existence in the Maghrib after six
or seven hundred years of Islamization and Arabization of the

Berber population. On the basis of their ancestry, the *shurafā'* rose
to be a prestigious elite whose status was officially recognized in
the sixteenth and seventeenth centuries when they became the
pensioners of the Moroccan state. Their achievement of this privileged position as beneficiaries of rather than contributors to the
coffers of the Makhzen was the result of the political success of a
sharifian family from the canyon of the Draa in southern
Morocco, which in the sixteenth century revived the Moroccan
empire under a new dynasty whose descent from the Prophet was
its title to the throne.

The Sa'dīs or Saadians combined the roles of *sharīf* and
marabout to set on foot a revolutionary movement which arose in
the cradle-land of the Almoravids and Almohads, and like theirs
swept to power from a capital at Marrakesh. Like the Almohads
they invoked the figure of the Qā'im or Mahdi, the Messiah sent to
deliver the land from injustice and oppression. But unlike either
the Almoravids or the Almohads, they had no specific doctrine,
trading upon their victories to vindicate their claim to rule the
community as Commanders of the Faithful or Caliphs. Their
armies, moreover, were not so much tribal as professional, relying
upon expertise with cannon and musket which came for the most
part from outside their society, from Spanish Muslims, Europeans
and European renegades, and Turks. Champions of the *jihād*
against the infidel, they were the most intermittent enemies of
the Portuguese on the coast, and their celebrated defeat of the
Portuguese invasion in 1578 at the battle of Alcazarquivir (al-Qaṣr
al-Kabīr) came about as a result of Portuguese aggression, not
theirs.

Their real enemies were the Turks at Algiers, who briefly occupied Fes in 1554, and assassinated the first Sa'dī ruler, Muḥammad
al-Shaykh, in 1557. If the Beylerbeys feared the charismatic appeal
of a rival to the Ottoman Sultan in Morocco, the Moroccans
themselves were still more anxious to keep the Turks at bay
by imitating the power and prestige of Istanbul. Their greatest
monarch, therefore, Aḥmad al-Manṣūr al-Dhahabī, 'the Golden
Conqueror' from his victory over the Portuguese, not only built
himself an amazingly extravagant palace at Marrakesh, but created for himself an army on the Ottoman model. Its troops were
janissary-style musketeers, and its administration in the hands of
ministers and secretaries who met in regular sessions of the royal
Diwan or Council; a city of tents took this government around the

country in the wake of the Sultan, a vast *mahalla* which the Moroccans preferred to call *haraka* or harka, 'expedition'.

In 1591 Ahmad's efforts were spectacularly rewarded with the destruction of the Sudanese empire of Songhay by a force of musketeers who marched across the Sahara to establish themselves in Timbuktu. But unlike the Spaniards in Mexico and Peru, his men did not succeed in laying their hands upon the gold mines of West Africa, and the cost of Ahmad's ambition fell heavily upon the Moroccan subject. Protests merely elicited, we are told, a parody of the maxim of justice, that Moroccans were mad, and must therefore be treated to the chains of the madhouse.[31]

The impressive structure, however, was fragile, and crumbled within a few year of the great Conqueror's death in 1603. A despotism not yet firmly rooted in a society divided between flocks of townsmen and packs of tribesmen, it lacked the institutional strength to survive the subsequent squabbles of the royal house. By the middle of the seventeenth century, the Moroccan empire had effectively ceased to exist. It was recreated only in the 1660s by Mawlāy (My Master) Rashīd, a *sharīf* from the Tafilelt in south-eastern Morocco who was enlisted along with his musketeers as the protector of Fes. The wholly exceptional length of his brother Ismā'īl's reign ensured the final triumph of sharifianism as the dynastic principle of the Moroccan state. The Black Sunrise of Mawlāy Ismā'īl set the seal upon the achievement of Ahmad al-Mansūr in establishing a government over the heads of the people which combined both power and authority, might and right.

Black Sunrise, the title of Wilfrid Blunt's book, evokes the legend of a Moroccan Sun King seen through the romantic eyes of Europe.[32] For fifty-five years from 1672 to 1727, Ismā'īl did indeed seek to rival his contemporary Louis XIV, building his vast Versailles at Meknes just as his Saadian predecessor Ahmad had built the Badī' at Marrakesh, to outshine the world. Meknes, however, represented a very different style of government from that of Ahmad the Golden. Unlike his great precursor, whose regime had been modelled upon that of the Ottoman Sultan, Ismā'īl dispensed with central administration. The wheel that was turned from his great palace was driven by the simple expectation of the monarch that he and his army would be provided for by the gifts of his loyal and obedient subjects. 'The gobbling palace economy'[33] ate up the revenues and services delivered by the *qā'id*s or governors, to whom were delegated the tasks of building, feeding, clothing, arming and generally supplying the vast household complex. This they did out of the tribute they extracted from their charges, most of which they kept for themselves. It was left to the tributary communities, towns, villages and tribes, to calculate how much each person should pay; central government in particular had largely renounced the effort of accounting.

The justice of the system consisted in the awe in which the Sultan was held by his servants as well as his subjects, as a master without compunction in the punishment of offenders by his own hand. The image of a madhouse ascribed to Aḥmad al-Manṣūr was realized in the underground dungeons below the yard before the courtroom at Meknes. The requisite force was provided by the regiments of *'abīd* or black slave troops and the Udaya or tribal cavalry who garrisoned the country. The result, as in Algeria, was a country only half under control; the Berbers of the Middle Atlas, for example, were 'locked up' rather than subdued by the detachments of *'abīd* in the castles newly built at the foot of the mountains. The *bilād al-makhzan* or 'government land' contrasted with the *bilād al-sība* or 'land running to waste'; the legend echoed by Shaw, of a realm so secure that a woman could travel across it alone and without fear, applied only to the main routes between the main cities.[34] The eclectic elite of *qāid*s or commanders, a general title for those who rose to prominence in the Sultan's service, had by the end of the reign produced a series of provincial dynasties on which the Makhzen was forced to rely.[35] At Ismāʿīl's death, however, the ʿAlawī dynasty was universally acknowledged on the strength of its claim to lead the Muslim community of the country in defence of the land of Islam against the infidel.[36] The dynasty, which took its name from ʿAlī, the son-in-law of the Prophet and second father of the *shurafā*, was not destroyed as the Saadians had been, by the quarrels of Ismāʿīl's sons over the succession. Its survival into the reign of the next great Sultan, Sīdī Muḥammad, in the second half of the eighteenth century, perpetuated both the monarchy and the state.

The Highlanders of Morocco

As in the Ottoman regencies, the creation of this Moroccan empire was at the expense of the Berbers. Like the 'kings' or 'sultans' of Kouko a hundred years previously, the great Berber marabouts of the Moroccan Atlas, whom the Sa'dīs had vigorously repressed but never exterminated, had mobilized their tribal followers at the death of Aḥmad the Conqueror in 1603 to take control of the Sous, Marrakesh and Fes. Al-Simlālī at Iligh in the Anti-Atlas, al-Ḥāḥī in the High Atlas, and above all Muḥammad al-Ḥajj at Dilā' in the Middle Atlas, challenged the Saadian *shurafā* for the government of the country. Their *zāwiya*s, developing in the course of the sixteenth century, had turned from centres of holiness into centres of power. Great scholars and great saints, the rulers of Dilā' claimed descent from the Almoravids and thus ultimately from Qaḥṭān. Between 1640 and 1660 their Berber forces occupied all the major cities of northern Morocco. But neither the charisma of sanctity nor that of old-fashioned ancestry were sufficient to establish their dynasty. Muḥammad al-Ḥajj lost his hold on Fes to the 'Alawī prince Rashīd. In 1668 Dilā' itself was captured and destroyed by the new monarch, and his family went quietly back to a life of scholarship at Fes.[37] The triumph of the *shurafā* put an end to any prospect of a maraboutic revolution leading to a Berber empire in the manner of the past.

Confronted by the power and authority of the 'Alawī Sultan, descendant of the Prophet and Commander of the Faithful, the Berbers of the Atlas and the Rif assumed instead the role of highlanders ascribed by Morgan and Shaw to the Kabyles. As Berbers, moreover, they suffered a similar eclipse. In the second half of the eighteenth century, the Sultan Sīdī (My Lord) Muḥammad opened the port of Essaouira or Mogador for trade with Europe after a century in which all contact with the infidel had been kept to a minimum. With the development of trade came the development of diplomatic relations, and the arrival in Morocco of men like Morgan and Shaw, full of historical and scientific curiosity. At a time when the African Association had been founded to promote the exploration of the interior of the Dark Continent, James Grey Jackson published *An Account of the Empire of Morocco*,[38] in which the name Berber is given, but only for the peoples of the Middle Atlas. Those of the High Atlas appear as the Shelluh:

The inhabitants of the Emperor of Morocco's dominions may be divided into four classes, namely, Moors, Arabs, Berebbers, (which latter are probably the aborigines,) and Shelluhs. The *Moors* are the descendants of those who were driven out of Spain; they inhabit the

cities of Marocco, Fas, Mequinas, and all the coast towns . . . The
Arabs have their original stock in Sahara, from whence they emigrate to the plains of Marocco . . . These Arabs live in tents, inhabiting the fertile and extensive plains, and indeed the whole
territory west of Atlas, as far south as Mogodor . . . These populous
tribes travel over the whole of Africa; and are the agriculturalists of
Barbary . . . The *Berebbers* inhabit the mountains of Atlas north of
the city of Marocco, living generally in tents; they are a robust,
nervous and warlike people, having a language peculiar to themselves, which . . . is probably a dialect of the ancient Carthaginian
. . . The general occupation of these people is husbandry, and the
rearing of bees for honey and wax. They possess much cunning and
duplicity, and are never outwitted by the Moors, or entirely
worsted by the troops of the Emperor, with whom they have had
very frequent encounters, but have never been permanently
subdued . . . The *Shelluhs* inhabit the Atlas mountains, and their
various branches south of Marocco; they live generally in walled
habitations, or in towns, and are, for the most part, occupied in
husbandry like the Berebbers, though differing from them in their
language, dress and manners . . . The term Kabyle applies to all
cultivators of land, and to those who rear the cattle and flocks.
Sometimes we discover . . . an encampment of Bedouin Arabs,
who, in their migrations to far distant countries, pitch their tents
wherever they find the country productive and unoccupied; here
they sojourn till their flocks have consumed all the pasture, when
they strike their tents and proceed on their long journey. These
people live, for the most part, on camel's milk; they are an indolent
race, and neither cultivate the earth, nor do any kind of work,
attacking and plundering caravans whenever they can do it with
impunity.[39]

This is an illuminating text, even though the Berbers of the Rif are
labelled Arabs on Jackson's map, and the Moors of the major
cities were not simply immigrants from Spain, but the traditional
bourgeoisie. It describes a Moroccan nation defined by its allegiance to the Sultan, but divided between town and country,
community and race. The Berbers themselves, identified as mountain peoples like the Kabyles of the Regency, are clearly distinguished, as were the inhabitants of Kabylia and the Aures, as
two separate populations whose languages are doubtfully the
same. While acknowledging the authority of 'the Emperor', they
remain opposed to his Makhzen or state, and largely beyond his
control. Because of their propinquity to Meknes and Fes, where
they inhabited the rolling uplands as *barābir al-waṭā* or Berbers of

the Plain, as distinct from the *barābir al-jabal*, the Berbers of the Middle Atlas,[40] they nevertheless bulked much larger in the politics of the dynasty. At the time of Jackson's writing in the first decade of the nineteenth century, the campaigns of the Sultan Mawlāy Sulaymān had brought them all, from the Sahara to the Rif, as much under his government as possible:

> Their allegiance to the Emperor has often been secured by retaining their chiefs at court, conferring favours on them, appointing them to offices of state, and to seats in the Diwan; thus making them hostages, as it were, for the peaceable conduct of their respective Kabyles.[41]

Ten years later, in 1819, Sulaymān had been disastrously defeated and captured by the tribesmen at the battle of Zaian in the Middle Atlas. But he was returned to Meknes with all due respect, while his tent was cut to pieces and distributed among the tribesmen as talismans of his *baraka* or spiritual power.[42] So great, in fact, was

*Plate 5.3 Horsemen of the Aït 'Atta of the Anti-Atlas, the last Moroccans to be conquered by the French in 1934
(From W.B. Harris, Tafilet, London, 1895)*

the prestige, as distinct from the variable power of the monarch, that Sulaymān survived the subsequent rebellion of Fes, leaving his nephew ʿAbd al-Raḥmān to restore the equilibrium of society and state.

The Entry to Modernity

In continuing the endless game of tribal politics, of setting one tribe against another, however, the ʿAlawī dynasty did more than merely survive. Under its leadership, Morocco joined Algeria, Tunisia and even Libya in the course of national development.[43] The appearance of changelessness was in fact deceptive. In Algeria the great chiefs of the *makhzan* tribes had come to form a warrior nobility known as the *ajwad* or *djouad*, 'the best', ruling over vast tracts of land occupied by their clients or cultivated by their sharecroppers. The *ajwād* were strongest in the old stamping-grounds of the Banū Hilāl in the east of the country, where the Turks came closest to marrying into them, and where in 1826 Aḥmad Bey became the first kouloughli or child of such a union to hold power at Constantine. When Algiers fell to the French in 1830 he put himself forward as the rightful successor to the Deys, and when Constantine itself was captured in 1837, he maintained a stubborn resistance for the next ten years. He had the makings of a national monarch.[44]

National is certainly an adjective which can be applied to the regency of Tunis to describe a much smaller country whose population was increasingly drawn together by a provincial administration of *qāïd*s, shaykhs and tax-farmers, a ruling class increasingly dependent upon the native monarchy of the Ḥusaynid Beys. Ḥusayn himself, the founder of the dynasty, was a kouloughli, a Tunisian born and bred, who came to power by appealing to the population at large, townsmen and tribesmen, Arabs, Berbers and Turks, to resist the invasion of the Algerians in 1705. When the enemy had been defeated, he called upon the country as a whole to oust the Dey, the commander of the janissaries who had seized control of Tunis. On the strength of this broad appeal, the Ottoman regime was transformed into the despotism of a royal family increasingly identified with the country. In the struggle over the succession which broke out in 1728, the tribes divided into two factions which endured long after the dispute was finally settled in 1756, part of a Tunisian society modelled by its *makhzan*, its central government, into a Tunisian whole.[45] On this basis, the Bey and his subjects faced the challenge of Europe in the nineteenth century.

The epic conflict of the age of Philip II, provoked by the Portuguese and Spanish invasions of North Africa, had resulted in victory for the Turks and the Moroccans, whose corsairs flourished in the seventeenth century out of the safe havens they had built on the Barbary coast. But in the eighteenth century, the presence of consular officials like Morgan, Shaw and Jackson in the capitals and ports of Algiers, Tunis, Tripoli and Mogador was a sign that the heyday of the Barbary corsairs was a thing of the past. Their highly profitable operations were being killed off: by government monopoly; by government diplomacy, which exacted an annual tribute in exchange for safe-conducts for the various European flags; and finally by the naval force of the French and English fleets. During the Napoleonic wars, when these fleets were hostile to each other, the corsairs enjoyed a last summer; but in 1816 Lord Exmouth bombarded Algiers into submission, and from then on official piracy out of the North African ports was virtually dead.

The death of piracy is frequently represented as the effective death of the regencies, in that it deprived the Pasha of Tripoli, the Bey of Tunis and the Dey of Algiers of the revenue they could not hope to obtain from their own impoverished hinterlands. In fact, it had long since ceased to be the foundation of their maritime prosperity, giving way in the course of the eighteenth century to a reliance upon the export of grain, skins, wool, leather and wax, the staple exports of North Africa to Europe in the later middle ages. Again in the course of the Napoleonic wars, these were in unusual demand, the grain for revolutionary France, and cattle for the British fleet at Malta. The grain was largely the product of taxation and its export to Europe was an important source of revenue which Sīdī Muḥammad was anxious to exploit when he opened the port of Essaouira in 1765. Handled on behalf of the princes of the Maghreb by Jewish merchants and bankers,[46] such exports brought North Africa back towards the position it had enjoyed in antiquity as 'the granary of Rome', that is, as an important supplier of basic foodstuffs and commodities for Mediterranean trade. Tunisia, indeed, repeated its classical history when in the nineteenth century it switched from grain to olive oil as its main export.[47] It was on the basis of such overseas trade that the rulers of the Maghreb at the beginning of the nineteenth century set out to modernize their regimes.

They did so in the manner of Muḥammad ʿAlī in Egypt, by monopolizing exports to pay for the military reforms which were required to bring their armies up to European standards, and thereby turn the wheel of the traditional state into the mechanism of a new monarchy. Only Tunisia, however, succeeded in keeping pace with the Khedives, not because the Ḥusaynid dynasty achieved its goal of military efficiency, but because in the process it brought the population under ever more centralized control with a combination of conscription and taxation. Moreover, it produced a generation of more liberal reformers headed by the prime minister Khayr al-Dīn or Kheireddine, which briefly introduced the first constitution in an Arab country, and sought to apply the principles of Eúropean government to the European purpose of government for, and even by, the people. In Morocco, the ʿAlawīs were painfully slow to extend the *bilād al-makhzan* at the expense of the *bilād al-sība*, approaching the ideal of a regular provincial and fiscal administration very gradually and very imperfectly;

Plate 5.4 Casbah country
(From W.B. Harris, Tafilet, London, 1895)

central government meanwhile remained rudimentary, with only the ministry for foreign affairs, created to deal with the European powers, beginning to develop into a department of state. Late in the nineteenth century it was necessary for the Sultan himself to cross the High Atlas at the head of the traditional grand expedition to bring southern Morocco back into the fold.

Tripoli and Algiers, on the other hand, were allowed no time to succeed or fail. At Tripoli, the long reign of the ambitious Karamanli ruler Yūsuf Pasha, who sought like Muḥammad ʿAlī to create an empire for himself in the Sahara and the Sudan, ended in foreign debt and internal rebellion; in 1835 the Ottoman Sultan intervened to repossess the country as a province of the empire, where it remained under minimal Turkish administration for the rest of the century. Algiers in 1830 was taken by the French, who went on to annex the whole of the regency to France.[48]

Trade with Europe, by which the rulers of the Maghreb set such store, proved in fact to be the Trojan horse of European conquest and colonization.[49] The whole of North Africa was overshadowed by the political as well as the economic supremacy of Europe, although it was not until 1881 that the Scramble for Africa imposed a French Protectorate on Tunis, and not until 1911–12 that Italy invaded Libya, and France and Spain divided Morocco between them. The motives for the conquest were political rather than economic, despite the contemporary pressures of the business community and the subsequent theories of Marxist-Leninism; nevertheless the European colonization of all four countries had profound economic and social consequences. 'The army' of the old Turkish and Moroccan Makhzen was effectively replaced by an army of soldiers and settlers who kept themselves as aloof from the native population as ever the *ojak* had done.

Their presence, however, was far more pervasive, not only because of the destruction wrought by the various wars of occupation, but because the new rulers introduced the kind of administration which their predecessors had merely coveted; they did so, moreover, not simply for the sake of taxation, but for the purpose of production. The creation of wealth was no longer the prime responsibility of the tributary subject but that of the colonist whom the government encouraged with access to land, finance and technology. Far from introducing the North Africans themselves to the economic and social benefits of modernity, the wheel of the colonial state devalued their traditional livelihood while providing only limited employment in the new European sector. Exposed to the market forces so ruthlessly at work upon the populations of nineteenth-century Europe, they were meanwhile denied any effective political voice. Unsurprisingly, North Africans revolted against a system which lacked the sanction of Islam to excuse its oppression, and failed to substitute its own ideals of equal rights.

The Rediscovery of the Berbers

Conquest itself was not easy. Despite attempts at modernization, the *makhzan* state was no match for the armies of France, Spain and Italy. With the exception of Aḥmad Bey at Constantine and the Turks in Libya, who withdrew in 1912 only in the face of international pressure on Istanbul, the existing rulers of the Maghreb all capitulated on terms which included the abdication and exile of the Dey of Algiers and the Sultan of Morocco, and the survival of the ʿAlawīs and the Beys of Tunis as mere puppets of the French. With their removal from power, however, the invaders were confronted by the forces of the *bilād al-bārūd*, the *bilād al-khalāʾ* or the *bilād al-sība*, which engaged the French, the Spanish and the Italians in a long and frequently devastating contest for possession of the land. It was a contest shot through with religion, for the end of the eighteenth century and the beginning of the nineteenth had witnessed what amounted to a revolution in Islam in the form of popular piety and political concern.

Right across the Muslim world these had produced an explosion of Ṣūfī brotherhoods, followers of the holy men who sprang up to preach a gamut of godliness, from ecstatic poverty, like the Darqawiyya, to intellectual severity, like the Tijāniyya. Both of these were Moroccan in origin, but both spread far beyond its borders, the former to Arabia and the latter into the Sudan. They were typical of a new internationalism, for want of a better word, which crossed political boundaries to confront the rulers of Islam with what amounted to an effective public opinion. In Arabia the Wahhabis launched their militant campaign against the Europeanizing policies of Istanbul, and founded their own state. West Africa was swept by the holy wars waged by the brotherhoods upon infidelity. In Morocco the Sultan Sīdī Muḥammad was driven to claim supreme religious authority for himself in an attempt to take control of the revolution he foresaw and feared.[50] In Algeria the Qādiriyya led the revolt against the Turks in Oran.[51]

When Oran was occupied by the French in 1831, Muḥyī al-Dīn, 'Reviver of the Faith' in the form of the Qādiriyya order in the Maghreb, proposed his son 'Abd al-Qādir to the anti-Turkish tribes of the Beylik as the *sharīf* destined to lead the holy war against the new enemy. For the next sixteen years until his final surrender in 1847, Abdelkader, as he was known to the French, seized the opportunity presented by the sudden demise of the Turkish state and the slow growth of the French to create one of his own, which at its greatest extent stretched from the borders of Morocco into the old Beylik of Constantine. He failed because of the need to justify his demands upon his tribal subjects with success in the *jihād*, committing him to a war he could not ultimately win. His defeat nevertheless required the devastation of the countryside, a tale of frightful atrocity, and immense loss of life among the French as well as the populations they set out to subdue. The conquest itself dragged on for a further twenty-five years, during which time all the forces of the indigenous society, brotherhoods, marabouts, tribes and even the warrior aristocracy, which had been the first to transfer its allegiance from the Turks, were progressively arrayed against the foreign foe.[52]

Reflecting their long-standing isolation, the Kabyles were the last to be subdued by expeditions in the 1850s. The final campaign of 1857 cost the French 1,500 casualties, but ended with the submission of Greater Kabylia, its clans and its marabouts. In the heart of the mountains the invaders built their Fort National to be 'the thorn in the eye of Kabylia', and the conquest of the old Ottoman regency was apparently complete.[53] Warfare receded into the Sahara and, with the opening of regular passenger services from Marseilles, Algeria in the 1860s began to develop as a tourist resort. But the defeat of France by Prussia in 1870 revealed the depth of hostility to the conquerors and the continued ability of the population to rebel. In 1871 the whole of eastern Algeria was engulfed in a revolt that was begun by the *djouad*, the warrior nobles, but was taken over by the Kabyles under the leadership of the marabout al-Ḥaddād and his son Sī 'Azīz. Al-Ḥaddād, the Berber son of a Berber blacksmith, lived in the Soummam valley on the border between the former territories of the Zwāwa and the Banū 'Abbās, the head of the Raḥmāniyya brotherhood which had taken over the religious leadership of Kabylia since the defeat of its rivals by the French in 1857. On 8 April 1871 he came out into the market place of Seddouk to proclaim the holy war to an enthusiastic crowd.[54]

As in the sixteenth century, so in the nineteenth, Islam filled the space vacated by central government with a call for unity under a new commander. The call was answered as far south as the Sahara by peoples traditionally subject to the state but traditionally largely independent. Traditional leadership, however, was no longer sufficient for revolution. The great revolt was little more than an ill-armed, unco-ordinated peasants' rebellion which by the end of the year had been effectively suppressed. The massive confiscation of land which followed put an end to the possibility of further resistance along traditional lines. If the Kabyles remained isolated within the colonial framework, it was simply to bring them under special control.

They were allowed, for example, to keep their customary law, which went under the name of *qānūn* or canon law. *Qānūn* was an Ottoman term for non-Islamic law, and in recognizing the customs of the Kabyles, the French were deliberately distinguishing them from the bulk of the Muslim population, which was officially subject to the Sharīʿa or Islamic law.[55] Codified and entrusted to the *jamāʿa* or village council instead of to the *qāḍī* or Muslim judge, Kabyle custom was a means of building on pre-colonial divisions in order to prevent the development of Islamic unity into nationalism. This translation into administrative practice of the long-established differences between Arabs and Kabyles perceived by Morgan, Shaw and other observers, however, was more than merely precautionary. It reflected a much wider interest in the people concerned.

In the first place, it represented a rediscovery of the Berbers as a nation in their own right, thanks largely to the discovery of Ibn Khaldūn. In the general zest for publication of the major Arabic sources for the history of North Africa, books VI and VII of the *Kitāb al-ʿIbar*, which deal with the Arabs and Berbers in the Maghrib, were edited and translated by Baron MacGuckin de Slane in the 1840s and 1850s under the significant title of the *Histoire des Berbères*.[56] Ibn Khaldūn's identification and description of the Berbers as a race put an end to the speculations of the previous century on the subject of the Kabyles, and enabled French scholarship to place them, as the Arabs themselves had done, securely within a framework of universal history and culture. As it had been for Shaw, that framework was constructed out of the

Bible, the Classics and natural philosophy, with the further addition of elements from the repertoire of Arabic science. Transferred in this way from an Arabic to a European context of
thought, the Berbers were now studied with particular emphasis
upon the world of antiquity. Emile Masqueray, for example,
not only described the way in which the sedentary Berber
populations of Algeria, from Kabylia to the Aures to the Mzab,
constructed their villages and tiny cities out of families and clans,
but argued that they did so in the manner of the ancient Romans,
preserving the world of Romulus and Remus down to the present
day.[57] Stephane Gsell was interested in their history in the
Carthaginian and Roman empires, Charles Diehl in the Byzantine
period.[58]

The world of Ibn Khaldūn, on the other hand, to which the
Berbers had originally belonged in thought, word and deed, was
translated into the middle ages of European historiography, and
prolonged down to the nineteenth century as a time when North
Africa and its inhabitants had been appropriated by the Orient. As
to the character of this long period, the fact that North Africa had
been Christian before it became Muslim suggested to many that
the Berbers celebrated in the *Kitāb al-'Ibar* had been the victims of
Islamization quite as much as Arabization, and that it should be
the aim of French policy to recover them for Rome and the West.
The White Fathers of Cardinal Lavigerie, the Archbishop of
Algiers, thus singled out Kabylia for conversion, ignoring the
opinion of Morgan, 'that there is not one natural *African*, on this
Side the *Niger*, who if asked, of what Religion he is, will not, with
Indignation in his Countenance, on account of so dubious and
affronting a Question, immediately reply, "I am, God be praised,
a *Mussulman*"'.[59] Despite their lack of success, the thesis of a
country and its people wrenched away from Europe by waves of
invaders from the East pervaded the whole French outlook on
North Africa. As a justification for French colonialism, it found its
final expression on the eve of North African independence in a
work by Eugene Guernier, editor-in-chief of the *Encyclopédie
coloniale et maritime*, significantly entitled *La Berbérie, l'Islam, et
la France*, in which he argued that North Africa's best hope for the
future lay in preferring the progressive French to the stultifying
Arab connection.[60]

The reality of colonialism for the Berbers themselves was very
different. The photographs taken in 1900 by Randall-McIver and

Wilkin to illustrate their investigation of the links between the
ancient Libyans and the Berbers of today are displayed in the
context of a scientific study of the distant past, but reveal a peasant
people in the Aures and Kabylia apparently untouched by modernity.[61] Economically, these Berbers shared the general fate of the
rural population of Algeria, with less and less land, decreasing
yields and diminishing livestock per household.[62] The Shawiya or
Chaouia Berbers of the remote Aures came nearest to surviving in
traditional isolation, but the Kabyles had lost most of their best
land to colonization, and could only divide what remained into
smaller and smaller parcels as the population recovered from the
wars and famines of the mid-nineteenth century, and their numbers began relentlessly to grow. Inhabiting what the French called
the Auvergne of the Maghreb, they turned instead to the strategy
already adopted by the peasants of the Massif Central of France,
seeking seasonal work in the winter in the new towns and cities.
Out of this migration there had developed by the time of the First
World War the nucleus of an emigrant North African labour force
in France, predominantly Berber in character, whose remittances
were increasingly needed to keep the mountains alive. A population which had once turned Greater Kabylia into a self-sufficient
and comparatively affluent homeland was driven to pay itself to
remain in the region with money from abroad.[63]

The Berber Policy

Not all Berbers were so badly affected. In Tunisia, where the
Berbers had dwindled to a small minority in the centre and south,
the Ibāḍīs of Djerba preserved their community in their island
oasis. Those of the Mzab, finally annexed to Algeria in the 1880s,
seized the opportunity to become prosperous cloth merchants
in the cities of the north. Even before the occupation of Morocco
in 1912, the Berbers of the Sous were beginning to do the same in
Casablanca, and making their way to Europe, often as circus
acrobats. Within a few years of the establishment of the French
and Spanish Protectorate, they were to be found as traders in
Tlemcen and in Paris, even though they came from a region which
was not completely subdued until 1934.[64] Since the middle of the
nineteenth century, a heavy European presence had built up along
the Moroccan coast from Essaouira to Tangier, breaking the

Sultan's old monopoly of trade, and weaning away his subjects from their traditional obedience long before the actual conquest began in 1900. Defeat by the French at the battle of Isly in 1844, in the course of the war against Abdelkader, had shattered the illusion of his military might and destroyed the equilibrium of his Makhzen. In an attempt to bring the interior of the country under greater control, the Sultan Mawlāy Ḥasan succeeded in imposing the presence of his caids or *qāïd*s, his governors, beyond the High Atlas, but only at the cost of his life and his absolute authority. He died in 1894 from the rigours of a journey back across the mountains in the midst of winter, in the course of which he had appointed the greatest chieftain of the High Atlas, Madanī el-Glaoui, as his *khalīfa* or caliph, his lieutenant over the lands to the south.

From his fortress at Telouet, provided by the Sultan with arms and artillery, El Glaoui commanded the route over the Tizi N'Tichka, the main pass from the Tafilelt and the Draa to Marrakesh, just as his rival El Goundafi commanded the way over the Tizi N'Test from Marrakesh to Taroudant, and El-Mtouggi the passes still further west. Between them these three Great Caids,

Plate 5.5   Telouet in its precolonial grandeur
(From W.B. Harris, Tafilet, *London, 1895)*

the Lords of the Atlas in Gavin Maxwell's phrase, were raised through the favour of the dynasty from *amghars* or tribal warlords into the rulers of the south.[65]

With the rise of the Great Caids of southern Morocco, the Berbers of the Moroccan highlands returned to the centre of the political stage in the great revolution that began with the death of Hasan in 1894, came to a head with the creation of the French and Spanish Protectorate in 1912, and ended only with the French occupation of the Anti-Atlas in 1934. The Great Caids themselves were instrumental in the overthrow of the Sultan 'Abd al-'Azīz by his brother 'Abd al-Hafīz in 1908,[66] and after a brief taste of power at Fes, passed smoothly into the service of the French, who left them to rule over the south. By 1925 T'hami el Glaoui, appointed Pasha of Marrakesh, had eclipsed all his rivals, and lorded it with legendary tyranny over the High Atlas as a partner rather than a servant of the Résident in Rabat.[67]

The Berbers of the Middle Atlas, on the other hand, not only opposed the efforts of 'Abd al-Hafīz and his Glaoui ministers to levy high taxes, but offered fierce resistance to the French occupation of Fes in 1911 and again in 1912. Lyautey, the French commander and first French Resident, was dismayed by 'an almost completely united army, with one flag and one spirit, whose various members willingly accepted a single discipline and risked death for the same cause'.[68] By the end of 1912 this astonishing unity had evaporated, and over the next ten years the French proceeded to 'eat' the Middle Atlas slowly, 'like an artichoke', tribal leaf by tribal leaf,[69] until there too they were able to install chiefs like Hasan ou Moha of the Zaian as pashas and caids who enjoyed almost as much power as the Glaoui. Before the Berbers of the Rif could be consumed in this way, however, they had created for themselves 'a country with a government and a flag'.

The Rif war lasted from 1920 to 1927, spilling out of the Spanish into the French zone of the Moroccan Protectorate. The rout of the Spanish army at Anwal in 1921 gave the Rifi leader Muhammad ibn 'Abd al-Karīm al-Khaṭṭābī, or Abdelkrim, the time and the opportunity to impose upon the disparate tribes of the mountains the elements of a modern state in which administrative decrees overrode customary law. Like that of Abdelkader almost a century before, this state was eventually destroyed by the need to keep its tribal following by waging war successfully upon a more powerful enemy, when what was required was peace to

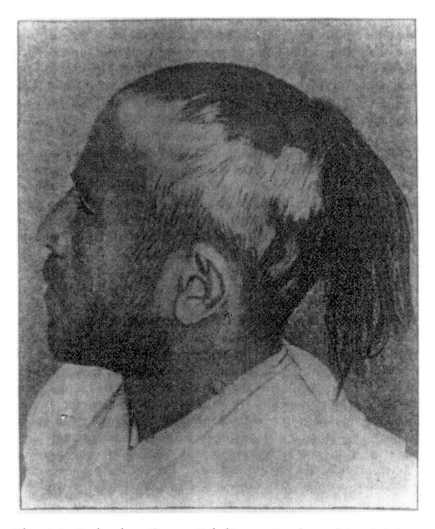

Plate 5.6 Berber from Greater Kabylia, wearing the traditional distinctive scalplock forbidden by Abdelkrim in the Rif
(From D. Randall McIver and A. Wilkin, Libyan Notes, *London and New York, 1901)*

consolidate the new regime; although once again it required the full weight of a major modern army, French as well as Spanish, and equipped with tanks and aeroplanes, to overwhelm it in 1927.[70] When the war was over, the old *bilād al-sība* had virtually disappeared after its final spectacular throw. In the heyday of

European empire, Abdelkrim's appeal for international recognition was simply ignored, and without him the Rif reverted to its tribal structure, becoming a reservoir of recruits for Franco's army in the Spanish civil war. With the defeat of the Aït 'Atta and the occupation of the Jebel Saghro in the Anti-Atlas by the French in 1934, the last vestige of traditional Berber independence was eliminated.

It seemed a triumph for the French anthropologist Robert Montagne. As the expert on 'the relatively simple mechanisms of traditional Moroccan society', he analysed the underlying structure of the 'country with a government and a flag', and successfully advised the military on their strategy.[71] His classic explanation of the rise of the Great Caids in the High Atlas, *Les Berbères et le Makhzen au sud du Maroc*,[72] went on to become the bible of the French regime in its dealings with the tribes.[73] In Hermassi's phrase, the conqueror-ethnologist, armed with his ethnographic maps and index cards, first divided and then ruled the Berber population for the political ends of the Protectorate.[74]

From the viewpoint of the Moroccan state, it was a historic achievement: for the first time the Berbers had been brought within the cycle of its regular administration. Their rediscovery as a nation, moreover, was complete. Just as the Berbers had been invented by the Arabs for the purpose of the Arab conquest and the Arab empire, so now they were finally resurrected by the French as a subject race to be kept apart from their Arab neighbours in the interest of French hegemony. A hundred years after the process began in Algeria, it was brought to conclusion in Morocco with the creation of what Berque called a national Berber park whose inhabitants were so many sequoias, a protected species on which the French hoped to rely in their dealings with the untrustworthy Arabs of the plains and cities.[75] Far more than in Algeria, they turned ironically to the old Kabyles, those ancient enemies of direct rule, to buttress their government of the country as a whole.[76]

In the Second World War, the Berber policy paid off. Recruited into the French forces as *goums* or native soldiers (from Arabic *qawm*, sc. 'nation', 'people', 'tribe'), Moroccan Berbers fought with legendary ferocity in Tunisia and Italy, where they were invaluable in the mountains at Monte Cassino; as Montgomery said laconically, 'Dark men, dark night. Very hard to see coming.'[77] They accounted for over half the French troops who invaded France in August 1944, while 80,000 of them served in Korea and Indo-China.[78] But long before heavy losses in Vietnam made recruitment unpopular, the Berber policy itself was undermined by the success of the state in uniting the country. As modern communications broke down long-standing barriers between peoples and regions, the use of Arabic became increasingly common, and traditional distinctions between the speakers of the two languages became less clear and less important. For the growing number of immigrants into the towns, their ethnic identity was only one of many factors in their new life. Nor was it especially divisive, entering positively into their friendships and relations with their neighbours rather than negatively into the identification of aliens and enemies in some urban jungle.[79] Certainly it failed to obstruct the rise of Moroccan nationalism.

In 1930, the year of publication of *Les Berberes et le Makhzen*, the promulgation of the Dahir Berbère, or the decree which would have placed the Berbers in their intended reservations firmly under customary rather than Islamic law, reawakened the sense of Moroccan solidarity against the dominion of the infidel. The indignation it aroused began in the student population of Salé, as far as could be from the subjects of the decree,[80] but proved nevertheless to be a major step towards the creation of a national movement for independence. Politically, the administrative segregation of the Berber population was unable to prevent the spread of the nationalist appeal into the countryside, especially after the Second World War and the foundation of the Istiqlal or Independence Party. ·

By the early 1950s, as the constitutional crisis mounted towards the deposition of the Sultan by the French in 1953, the rural Berber population was sliding rapidly towards armed insurrection. The march of the tribesmen on Rabat in 1951 and 1953 organized by the French authorities to demonstrate against the monarchy and its support for the Istiqlal was a weapon that turned in their hands. The encouragement given to the peoples of the mountains to show their strength simply boosted the formation of the largely Berber army of liberation, whose guerrilla warfare was instrumental in the return of the Sultan Sidi Mohammed in 1955, and the achievement of Moroccan independence in 1956. T'hami el Glaoui, the Pasha of Marrakesh to whom the French had turned to lead the Berbers on behalf of the Protectorate, was exposed as a man of straw, his empire in the south a hollow mockery of his power in the past. The ancestral fortress of Telouet was left to crumble by the rulers of the new Morocco as a monument to the failure of the French as well as of the Glaoui family enterprise.[81]

The Independence of the Maghreb

Morocco achieved its independence at the same time as Tunisia, five years later than Libya and six years before Algeria. In little more than a decade, the administrations created by European colonialism passed into the hands of the colonized, little more than twenty years after the conquest of North Africa was completed with the occupation of the Jebel Saghro in 1934. It was a capitulation on the part of the conquerors to the demands of self-appointed leaders such as Habib Bourguiba in Tunisia, Messali Hadj in Algeria and Allal el-Fassi in Morocco, who employed European methods of party political agitation and organization to appeal to their public in the name of Europe's own political values: liberty, equality and self-determination.

In *L'Afrique du Nord en marche*, Charles-André Julien spelt out the writing on the colonial wall.[82] Frantz Fanon declared that the time had come for a population which had retreated into its traditional culture in the face of European aggression, to turn its old faith from a refuge into a revolution.[83] In *Le Maghreb entre deux guerres* Jacques Berque supposed that by 1934 the Depression had brought such a mass of unemployed into largely European cities like Algiers, that for the first time the street lent its force to the call of the nationalist elites for independence.[84] But in a vigorous attack upon the *bien pensant* liberalism which condemned the French rather than the terrorists who fought the Algerian war, Elie Kedourie called in question the national character of the nationalist leadership.[85] Controversy as well as irony surrounds the judgement of Berque, that 'the downfall of the system was immanent in its apogee . . . the Maghribi nation arose out of the colonial triumph'.[86]

The Marxist dialectic underlying Berque's conclusion is central to the controversy, not simply because it emphasizes the extent to which the Maghreb was transformed by colonization, but because it has been integral to the argument over the future. Where Tunisia and Morocco aligned themselves with capitalism, first Algeria and then Libya preferred state socialism. However it has been pursued, the creation and distribution of wealth has become the prime concern of government. The accent on wealth has not displaced either justice or the army from their place in the political cycle, but rather given them new life in the form of ideologies and bureaucracies. Hermassi's *Leadership and National Development* is a celebration of the system as it settled into place in the 1960s, with authoritarian kings and presidents to direct the revolution as it moved beyond independence to the reconstruction of national societies and economies. Between the practice and the principles of these regimes, the Berbers have been effectively squeezed.

The Fight for Survival

It is ironic that the Berbers should have been reappointed to the pantheon of nations at a time when they are threatened with extinction. Few Berbers in the sense of native Berber speakers remain in Tunisia, a mere 1 per cent of the population. In Libya the Ibāḍī villagers of the Jabal Nafusa may account for little more than 5 per cent.[87] Early in the twentieth century, they played an active part in the resistance to the Italian conquest under Sulaymān Bārūnī, a Berber deputy for Tripolitania to the Turkish parliament from 1909 to 1911.[88] But the country today is officially Arab, Muslim and Libyan, a threefold definition of the nation by territory, language and religion which ignores the sectarian Berber identity of this particular hill region, and leaves it to survive as best it may below the surface of national society. These three criteria of the nation are not confined to Libya; they are of the essence of Arabic thought in the liberal age, to quote the title of Albert Hourani's classic work,[89] and in the Maghreb at large they amount to a formidable denial of any other identity. Affirmed in the slogan of the Algerian Muslim reformers of the 1930s: 'Islam is our religion, Algeria our country and Arabic our language',[90] they are enshrined in the constitution of independent Algeria, and are close to the heart of Moroccan nationalism. In Tunisia, where religion and language receive rather less emphasis, the stress upon the unity of the country and its people stands out all the more clearly as the overriding justification for the state. Against this deliberate modern twist to the tale of Arabization, turning the culture of the majority into the standard expected of the whole, Berberism is the name for a separate Berber identity suspected of disloyalty to the ideal of national unity. In both Morocco and Algeria, where Berbers are still a substantial minority, Berberism has been identified as an actual or potential threat, even if in Morocco at least it has been politically exploited by the government.

Since independence in 1956, Morocco has continued to move towards national integration under a monarchy which received from the French the gift of that modern administration it had struggled and failed to create for itself before the imposition of the Protectorate in 1912. As Telouet crumbles, the apparatus of modernity has been systematically employed to transform the Sultan into the King, a change of title which reflects his newfound power as head of state and head of government. The Istiqlal or Independence Party, which claimed to speak on behalf of the nation, was rapidly driven into permanent opposition as a potential rival to the dynasty. In its place as the political instrument of government, a royalist majority in parliament and the country has been constructed by the judicious use of patronage at the local as well as the national level.[91] Such a policy has divided the Berbers of Morocco into their local communities under their local leaders. At the same time it has drawn them into the royalist camp, where the rural

Plate 5.7   Telouet today
(Photo: Michael Brett)

constituencies are ranged against the city-based opposition.[92] In this way the *Mouvement populaire*, the largely Berber political party led by Mahjoubi Ahardane, has been effectively conscripted into the King's parliamentary majority.[93] This prudent patronage of the Berber constituency has refrained from encouraging, or permitting, the conscious development of Berberism at the cultural level, but has benefited from the pronounced anti-Berberism of the Istiqlal. The ardent champion of Moroccan nationalism, the Istiqlal has welcomed Berbers only to the extent that they have put aside their Berber identity as a relic of the colonial past. Berbers have, as a result, been much less prominent in the party than in the government coalition, where their aspirations have been contained within the overall strategy of the regime.[94]

The ideological purism of modern nationalism, however, has gained the upper hand in Algeria, where the nationalist movement of the FLN, the *Front de Liberation Nationale*, came to power in 1962 as the undisputed victor in the struggle for national liberation, only to drive the Berbers into opposition as enemies of the people. Throughout the long and bloody history of the Algerian war, the *Front* had held out consistently for a definition of the Algerian nation which included all native residents of the country, Arab, Berber and European alike, irrespective of race or religion. The principle was established in the Evian Agreements with France which brought the war to an end, and it was not the fault of the FLN that the flight of the entire European population in 1962 left Algeria almost wholly Muslim. It was, nevertheless, the fault of the FLN that in the summer of 1962 warfare broke out between the commanders of its forces, and especially between those of Algiers and Greater Kabylia and the army command at Tlemcen. This was to a very large extent a conflict between Berbers and Arabs, which not only revealed the way in which the war had divided the nation in spite of the unity which had led it to victory, but presaged the trouble to come.

Long before the outbreak of the Algerian war in 1954, the largely Berber workforce of Algerian emigrants in France had been mobilized by Messali Hadj in support of his demand for Algerian independence. Taken from France into Algeria in the years of the Great Depression, Messali's *Etoile nord-africaine* or North African Star offered as great a challenge to the Muslim leadership as to the French, to the constitutional reformers and the reformers of Islam who kept their opposition to the colonial regime within the legal limits of French Algeria. To the French his organization was treasonable and was accordingly banned, along with its successor, the Algerian People's Party. But as the Movement for the Triumph of Democratic Liberties it resurfaced at the end of the Second World War as the most radical, and the most popular, Muslim political party in Algeria. The Berber element in its composition was reinforced by French army veterans such as Belkacem Krim, while it attracted recruits from the fluent French-speaking minority of Berbers who had received a good French education, most notably Hocine Ait Ahmed. Berbers in France might protest at their lack of recognition by the party,[95] but both its membership and its ideology remained resolutely national, as did the programme of the National Liberation Front which broke away from Messali's leadership to take up arms in 1954. From beginning to end of the war, the aim of national independence led to the 'extraordinarily rigid consistency of the F.L.N.'s demands',[96] to which eventually the French gave way.

This rigidity, however, was required by the personal character of the collective leadership, in which individuals counted for more than the embryonic institutions they were unable to develop into constitutional structures under the severe pressures of guerrilla war. Four of the principal leaders, including Hocine Ait Ahmed, the intellectual founder of the movement, were captured by the French and interned. The remainder divided between those who established a government in exile in Cairo, Tunis and Tripoli, and created an army in waiting in Tunisia and Morocco, and those who conducted the war inside Algeria, increasingly isolated and systematically hunted down. Kabylia was an especially important base for their operations, and it was in the Soummam valley, where al-Ḥaddād had proclaimed the holy war in 1871, that the internal leaders met in 1956 to create the skeleton of an organization for the *Front* as a whole. The skeleton survived as the minimum structure required by the movement, but the Soummam Congress opposed the internal leaders, headed by the Berbers Ramdane Abane and Belkacem Krim, to those abroad.

Abane himself was murdered by his colleagues in 1958.[97] However, by the end of the war in 1962, as the predominantly Arab forces under the command of the external leadership moved into Algeria, the opposition to this takeover of power from the men who had borne the brunt of the fighting in the country took on a strongly Berber character. This character was enhanced by the leadership struggle which at once took place between Ben Bella, newly released from imprisonment in France, and his rivals from the Provisional Government which had negotiated the Evian Agreements. These established themselves at Tizi Ouzou, the capital of Greater Kabylia, where Belkacem Krim called upon the Berber colonel Mohand Ou El Hadj to defy Ben Bella and his ally, the Arab colonel Boumedienne, at Tlemcen. Ben Bella duly came to power, and Krim retired from the fray, to be murdered in exile some years later. His place, however, was taken by Ben Bella's fellow-prisoner in France, Hocine Ait Ahmed, who in 1963 and 1964 mounted an unsuccessful rebellion in Kabylia before his capture, imprisonment and eventual escape abroad.

As far as the Berbers of Algeria were concerned, the upshot of this struggle for power was to identify them as potential if not actual opponents of the revolutionary ideal of national unity for which the war of independence had been fought. In the one-party state created by Ben Bella there was no room for Aït Ahmed's FFS or Front des Forces Socialistes, either as a nationwide or as a largely Kabyle party of opposition. Nor was there a place for a separate Berber identity in the Arab nation which Ben Bella declared the new Algeria to be. The suppression of Berber studies at the University of Algiers in 1962 was the first sign of official disfavour. At the time there was little protest: the *élan* of the national revolution carried all before it, as Aït Ahmed, its original ideologue, found to his cost. Ben Bella himself was removed by Boumedienne in 1965, when the army finally took power from the politicians. The army has remained in power ever since, ruling through the apparatus of the single party to which Ben Bella gave the old name of FLN. As the new President, Boumedienne carried the revolution still further with a Stalinist drive for industrialization financed by the oil and gas revenues of the country, to the acclamation of the world and the expectations of the people. But at his death in 1978, the failure of this programme to achieve the necessary results revived all the old quarrels of 1962, magnified by the disillusion and dissatisfaction of a rapidly growing population. Ten years later popular frustration boiled over in the riots of 1988 against a regime discredited by corruption and austerity. The riots marked the beginning of a second Algerian revolution, which is still in progress. The introduction of multiparty democracy was halted when the army cancelled the elections of 1991. Deprived of electoral victory, the FIS (the Front Islamique du Salut or Islamic

Plate 5.8   *The Djurdjura from Beni Yeni, home of the guerrilla leader*
Amirouche in the Algerian war of independence
(Photo: Michael Brett)

Salvation Front) resorted to terrorism, claiming the legitimacy of
the freedom-fighters of the war of independence in the name of
Islam. Thousands have since perished in the conflict with the
military.

In this conflict, the Berbers of Algeria stand somewhat apart, opposed not only to the Islamists who seek to affirm the Islamic identity of the nation, but also to the creed of the army and the FLN. Nevertheless, in the troubled years since 1978, Algerian Berbers have not only become politically and culturally self-conscious (in ways which were merely embryonic in 1962), but they have appeared on the stage to demand recognition as a separate element in the life of the nation. As will be seen in chapter 8, the growth of this self-consciousness has opened up a prospect of the future which is quite new. As the wheel of state turns into a wheel of fortune for governments and peoples alike, this recent Berberism is the principal hope of survival for the subjects of this book, in danger of complete elision by the forces of the modern world.

6

Pastoral Berbers:
Nomads, Slaves and Saints

The People of the Veil

The five peoples of whom we have spoken, that is to say the Zanaga, the Guenziga, the Terga, the Lemta and the Berdeua are all called Numidians by the Latins. They all live in the same way, without law or reason ...

From birth to death these nomads pass their time hunting or stealing the camels of their enemies. They never stop for more than three or four days, time for their camels to graze ...

The nobles of these people wear, as I have said, a black veil on their heads, of which a part is used for covering the face all but for the eyes. They never leave it: when they want to eat they have to uncover their mouths each time they take a bite, and quickly cover them up again ...

I went by there some years ago in a caravan with other travelers. When we arrived in the plain of Araoan, the prince of the Zanaga met us with five hundred men, all on camels. After having made us pay a tax, he invited all the caravan to come to his tents and to rest for two or three days. As the camp was around eighty miles off our route, and as our camels were heavily laden, the merchants did not want to accept the invitation so as not to lengthen their journey. To keep us, the prince decided to let the camel drivers continue their voyage with the animals and to bring the merchants with him.

When we arrived at the camp the excellent fellow immediately gave the order to kill a number of camels, old and young, as many sheep and some ostriches which had been captured along the way. The merchants explained to the prince that the camels should not be killed, as they weren't accustomed to eating anything but sheep. He responded that it was not done to have a banquet with only small animals, especially given that we were not only strangers but also guests of the camp.

We thus ate what we were given. The bulk of the repast was composed of roast meat and soups. The meats were brought to the table in slices seasoned with herbs and a good quantity of spices from the land of the Blacks. The bread was made of a very fine flour and of millet. At the end of the meal dates were brought in abundance, and great jars full of milk. The lord wished to honour the banquet with the presence of himself, the most noble of his entourage, and members of his family, but he ate apart from us. He called to his side some religious and educated men who were to be found there. During the meal none of the Numidians would touch the bread, taking only meat and milk. The prince, noticing our surprise, amiably explained by saying that he was born in the desert where no grain grows and that their people ate only what the land produced. He said that they acquired enough grain to honour passing strangers. However, to tell the truth, they eat bread at the great festivals such as the *aid es-seghir* and the *aid el-kebir*.

The prince kept us another two days in his camp, treating us with great solicitude and honour. The third day he let us go and accompanied us to the caravan himself. It must be said that the animals he killed were worth ten times what we paid for the right of passage. From both his acts and his words we saw that he was a noble and courteous lord, even though we understood nothing of his language, nor he of ours, so that we had to speak through an interpreter.[1]

This passage, written around 1550, introduces the Berber groups which have always aroused the most interest for outsiders, the 'People of the Veil'. Found between Morocco and Libya, their veiled faces, hierarchical society and warrior ethos made them the perfect subject not only for western ethnography, but also for film treatment and romantic novels. This 'hard primitivist' imagery, like that of the pastoral Masai in Kenya, perfectly satisfied a certain vision of the noble and free. Although, as Leo Africanus says, the People of the Veil are divided into several distinct groups, we shall concentrate on the Terga or Tuareg (sing. Targui), the modern name for the warrior Berber nomads of the Sahara, who came to fame in 1881 by wiping out a French expedition. Since then, the Tuareg have been studied by generations of ethnographers and anthropologists: Anglo-Saxons in the Sahel and French in the Sahara itself. This is an extremely rich and complex body of material; consequently, much of what will be said here should carry the caveat 'not necessarily true of all Tuareg groups'. However, a number of traits are – or were – common to the majority of groups, and it is these similarities which will be treated here. Even

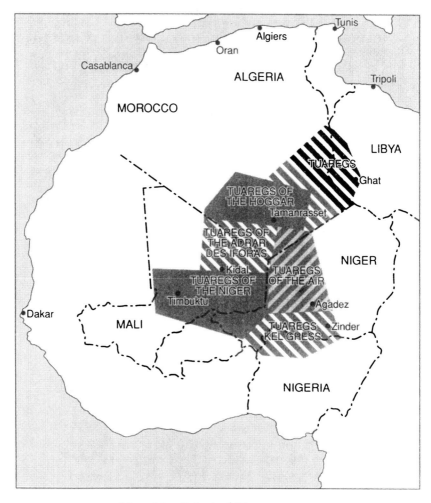

Map 6.1   Principal Tuareg groups

more than in the Berber highlands, the violent changes of the last thirty years have to some extent invalidated the ethnography: these will be briefly touched on at the end of this account.

Nomadic Pastoralism and African History

'Pure' nomadism implies full mobility for the whole society and its flocks, and an economy in which agriculture plays no part. Always a *topos* among historians of the Maghreb, the existence of fully nomadic pastoralism in antiquity is usually now denied, even for the Roman period. It has for many years been a dogma of European prehistory that nomadic pastoralism is a late and specialized economic system, operating, as Renfrew says, 'either where farming economies are not very successful or (more often) on the margins of such economies... Nomad pastoralism is always dependent on the existence of agriculturalists. It is clear that nomad pastoralism normally develops out of mixed farming and herding.'[2] The basis for this argument is that no society really lives without cultivated grain. Therefore in order to move from transhumance (where cattle are moved away from a settled village to winter or summer pastures) to full nomadism (where the whole community travels together away from its winter base) there must first exist a settled society of agriculturalists from whom the nomads acquire their grain – by fair means or foul. This argument is supported in the Near East by the fact that domestication of cereal grains there antedated the domestication of sheep and goats. However, as we have seen in the first chapter, this primacy of agriculture is by no means sure in the Saharan neolithic, where the first species certainly domesticated was cattle, and where we have no certain evidence for the domestication of millet until one or two millenia later.

The Tuareg, at least in Leo Africanus' account, certainly did not depend on cultivated cereals. It could, of course, be argued that his informant was giving a noble male's point of view, and that women and slaves regularly consumed cultivated cereals; but there is no evidence for this. Any need for cereal grains could be met at least in part by wild grains, which were regularly collected and ground by the slaves of the Tuareg. Millet was evidently available, but rarely used. Furthermore, although the supply of milk is seasonal for each species, mixed herds, and the production of cheese, will tend to mitigate the periodic milk shortages.[3] It is thus possible that fully nomadic groups occupied the Sahara from the neolithic onwards, depending only marginally on resources from cultivated oases such as Augila, south of the Great Syrtis between Tripolitania and Cyrenaica, or Tozeur, in southern Tunisia.

This is hard to demonstrate archaeologically, for nomadic sites are notoriously difficult to identify and date.[4] While we are able in many areas to perceive the gradual expansion of settled agriculture, it is harder to see nomadic pastoralism. We have, once again, to depend on ancient sources which are not always entirely trustworthy.

Herodotus, for example, tells us that nomads lived between Egypt and the Djerid,[5] subsisting on meat and milk, with very little of the former – a classic Tuareg diet. Three hundred years later Polybius states that 'many African tribes do not use cultivated crops, and are nourished by and live with their flocks'.[6] Strabo, whose information was probably first-hand, tells of the Pharusii, who lived near the Ethiopians, and 'occasionally meet with the Moors, coming through the desert with sacks of water slung under their horses' stomachs; occasionally they come to Cirta through a region of marsh and lakes.'[7] The Gaetulians, operating along the whole of the pre-desert fringe, were certainly pastoralists to some extent, even though the horses and cattle they raised could never have tolerated life in the Sahara proper.

We can supplement these texts with some archaeological material. The cemeteries of the pre-desert consist of groups of large tumuli or cairns, sometimes comprising hundreds of graves. This suggests that they were used by a substantial population, but contemporary settlements are extremely rare in these areas. The archaeologist Gabriel Camps has shown that many of these tombs contained skeletons which had evidently been reburied after exposure elsewhere, suggesting they were the communal cemeteries of widely dispersed nomadic groups.[8]

There is thus reasonable evidence for pastoralism in the classical period along the desert fringes and into the Sahara. The spread of settled agriculture may have pushed the pastoralists further into the desert, leading to a more intensive and wider-ranging nomadism. It remains unclear, however, whether the pastoralists also cultivated the oases. Certainly some did. In Herodotus' time the Nasamones 'in summer leave their flocks behind by the sea, and go up to a place called Augila to collect dates, for there grow numerous tall palm trees, every one of them fruitful'.[9] As we have seen, the valleys of the Fezzan are filled with the settlements of the Garamantes, and the foggaras and dry stone walls which ensured their cultivation. The textual evidence points to nomadic pastoralism, while the archaeological evidence suggests oasis cultivation. The best explanation seems to be that the economy was mixed, although whether the cultivation was actually carried out by the nomads themselves is unclear: in modern Tuareg society agriculture is scorned as an occupation for slaves and the lower classes.

Even today, no noble will willingly take up a hoe. This may have been true in the past as well, although we have no direct evidence for it. Generally the nomads live to a certain extent in symbiosis with the oases, and often acquire – or claim – rights over their surplus.

The first characteristic of nomads is their mobility. In Africa they travelled with their flocks, though they also maintained links of one kind or another to the desert oases. Nomadic mobility over long distances is contingent on the animals they ride, as well as the animals they drive. The horse and the cow, for example, are inappropriate for long-distance travel in the waterless desert. The change-over from the horse to the camel thus had a significant effect on nomadic mobility. This effect was so marked that its introduction into North Africa has had an almost mythical value in modern historiography. E. F. Gautier, and more recently G. Camps, imagined waves of camel-riding nomads sweeping in from the east, conquering and absorbing earlier groups.[10] There is, however, little evidence for this invasion, and the diffusion of the camel throughout North Africa may well have occurred by far more peaceable means.[11]

The camel was certainly present in Tripolitania and Byzacena at an early date: Caesar captured twenty-two camels at the battle of Thapsus, and by the fourth century the city of Leptis Magna was able to give up 4,000 camels at the demand of Count Romanus.[12] Traces of the camel in Africa Proconsularis and Numidia are rare, however: it is absent from the customs tarifs of Zarai and Lambaesis, and no camel bones are found at Carthage or Sitifis before the fifth century.[13]

It would seem that although camels were available, until late antiquity the status of the horse was unassailable. Common both to nomadic and settled North African groups, it was both the only means of travel and a major source of prestige. Camels were used as draught animals in agriculture,[14] and only slowly began to be used as pack animals. The use of the new 'technology' for long-distance pastoralism and trade was probably introduced from the south: indeed, the first obvious instance of a people moving with their camels is found in Corippus' account of the battle between the Austuriani (southerners) and the Byzantines: although the battle was fought on horseback, Corippus relates that a ring of camels was drawn up around the women and baggage of the nomads.

Tuareg Origins

We cannot establish with any certainty the relationship between the desert tribes described by Corippus and the modern Tuareg, but even allowing for the changes which have no doubt taken place over the last 1,500 years a substantial continuity seems likely. The physical anthropology of the skeletons recovered from the tombs of the Garamantes in the Fezzan and protohistoric tombs in the Ahaggar compares well with the modern Tuareg.[15] The name of the Fezzan in Tamachek, the Tuareg language, is

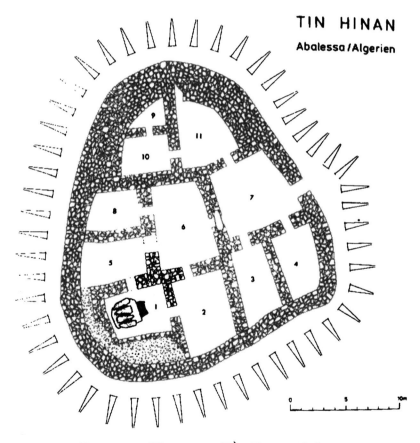

Figure 6.1   The grave of Tin Hinan, Abalessa
(From R. Horn and C. Rüger, Die Numider: Reiter und Könige nördlich der Sahara, Bonn, 1979)

Plate 6.1   The skeletal remains of Queen Tin Hinan
(From B.K. de Prorok, Mysterious Sahara, *London, 1930)*

Teraga, which suggests that Tuareg means 'people of the Fezzan'. The Tuareg themselves are in no doubt: they claim that in the whole of the desert there is no trace of human activity they do not recognize as their own.

Another link between antiquity and the modern Tuareg is provided by the most famous archaeological site of the desert, the tomb of Tin Hinan, at Abalessa. The Jesuit missionary and linguist Père Charles de Foucauld discovered an oral tradition concerning the history of the Ihaggaren, the Tuareg inhabitants of the Ahaggar, or Hoggar. In this story two Berber women from the oasis of Tafilet in Morocco journeyed to the Ahaggar. 'The first, Tin Hinan, was noble, the other, Takama, was her servant. They found the country empty, although there were traces of previous settlers. . . . Tin Hinan established herself at Abalessa: here she had a daughter, Kella, from whom descend the Kel Rela. Takama had two daughters; from one descend the secondary tribe of the Ihadanaren; while from the other descend the plebeian tribes of the Dag Rali and Ait Loaien. Tin Hinan gave the oases of Silet and Ennedid to the two daughters of Takama, to whose descendants they still belong.' In another version of the story Tin Hinan arrived on a white camel, charged with dates and millet and accompanied by numerous slaves as well as by her servant.

When it was excavated, the monument known as the tomb of Tin Hinan at Abalessa revealed the remains of an unusually tall woman, about forty years of age (plate 6.1). She lay on a leather-covered wooden bed, with seven gold bracelets on her right arm and eight silver bracelets on her left. Beside her lay a Roman glass cup, as well as a wooden cup with a Constantinian monogram. A radiocarbon date of 1,480 ±130 BP, along with the Roman finds, suggests that the structure was constructed in the second half of the fifth century: its original purpose may have been simply that of a dwelling like the qsar of the pre-desert, subsequently converted to a tomb.[16] Who she was and what she was doing remains a mystery, but the continuity of the tradition is evident.

Alphabet and Language

Another element of continuity with the classical period is the modern Tuareg alphabet, Tifinagh, which is certainly related to the Libyan alphabet of the early years of Roman occupation. Although the morphological relationship between the two is clear, the historical relationship is less obvious. Possibly the alphabet arrived with the first Mediterraneans in the desert, the Garamantes, around the middle of the second millennium BC. Certainly it is associated with paintings showing horses in the Fezzan, and elsewhere. This is a very early date, however, and it is more likely that it was developed in the Tell at a later stage, and learned there by the Garamantes. From then on, however, it clearly followed a separate development. Roman period inscriptions from Gholaia and Ghirza in the Libyan desert are already quite distinct from those of the Tell.[17] Little can be said of the fragmentary inscription used in the construction of the tomb of Tin Hinan, but it shows that the alphabet was already in use in the central Sahara by the fifth century. The Tuareg language, Tamachek, is also distinctly different from the Berber languages of the Tell, with a more elaborate grammar and fewer loan-words from Arabic.

Just as Tamachek seems to represent a purer, less Arabized form of the Berber languages than those of the Tell, the culture of the modern Tuareg may give us some hope of recovering some of the earlier Berber cultural forms, less influenced by the intensive Arabization of the north. The Tuareg are not only peculiarly interesting in themselves, but also for the light they shed on early Berber society. Naturally they are no more exempt from the effects of history than anyone else, except in so far as they seem to have vigorously resisted changes imposed from outside. However, a number of cultural traits which form an integral part of Tuareg society can be found embedded in relict form in the more highly Arabized societies of the north; this seems to show that they were common to Berber peoples before the first invasions separated the destinies of the settled populations from those of the nomads.

The Household and its Reproduction

The Tuareg occupy a huge area extending from the oasis of Ghat in Libya through the mountains of Ahaggar to the Niger River and Timbuktu in Mali. They may conveniently be divided into two groups. The northern, or Saharan, Tuareg comprise the Kel Ahaggar of the Ahaggar and the Kel Ajjer, who are found in the

Fezzan and Tassili. The southern groups are far more numerous; the Nigerian and Malian Tuareg comprise the Ifoghas, the Iwillimeden, the Kel Air and the Tingeregif, once the lords of Timbuktu. Although never politically united, the Tuareg have always been conscious of themselves as one people. Those still occupying the original Tuareg area number perhaps 300,000 individuals, of whom the vast majority are found in the south: the Saharan Tuareg in all are fewer than 10,000–15,000.

The material culture of the Tuareg is as limited as one might expect from a people who are perpetually on the move. The property of any family consists of a few mats or, more rarely, rugs, a tent made of hides or palm-leaf mats, some leather and wooden vessels, blankets and cushions, gear for the camels, and the jewellery worn by the women. Their diet is equally simple, based, as we have seen, on meat and milk products and, more recently, millet. The essential wealth of a Tuareg family lies in its herds alone. In contrast to their extremely simple material culture, however, the Tuareg possess a social culture of great complexity. This is both highly articulated and very rigid, defining the relationships between men and women, between classes and between Tuareg and associated groups. We shall start by looking at the former.

One aspect of the story of Tin Hinan which is immediately striking is the fact that both the noble and the vassal groups of the Ahaggar claim women for their ancestors. This is not accidental: although Tuareg inheritance runs through both the matriline and the patriline, matriliny is perceived as the dominant form, and is certainly the rule for the inheritance of political power. Members of each Tuareg sub-group, or *tawsit*, define themselves as the uterine descendants of a single eponymous ancestress.[18] With this matriliny goes a relationship between men and women which for its equilibrium is unique in North Africa. Women control their own property, own the family tent, and can choose, and divorce, their husbands. Islam has had no effect on the monogamy of Tuareg marriage. The woman's freedom to own and dispose of her property does not, of course, mean that women shared in the political leadership of the tribe. This was largely left in male hands. Still, a Tuareg woman's freedom amounts to something more than just freedom in the domestic sphere.

The tent is the basic unit of Tuareg society, for the tent defines a family. The tent is not only a woman's space, but it is also a

Figure 6.2   Pectoral pendant in silver
(From H. Lhote, Les Touaregs du Hoggar, *Paris, 1984)*

woman's property. Beside her jewellery, the most important objects owned by a woman are her marriage bed and her tent, which is constructed from a portion of her mother's tent cut out at the time of her marriage, and reconstructed by the artisans or slaves. The new husband joins his wife in her tent, and this will be their home as long as their marriage lasts. The interior is divided into halves by gender, the men's to the east and the women's to the west. Although the men's objects, such as saddles and arms, are stored in their half, the men themselves normally spend almost all of their time outside the tent, sleeping outside it from puberty onwards. In the woman's half are kept the stores, musical instruments and the marriage bed, which serves during the day as a sofa for her and her children. Although boys and girls are raised together, the boys' exit from the tent at puberty means that the girls spend more time with their mothers, and thus learn much more of the abundant folklore: fairy tales, but also long epics with some historical content. The transmission and conservation of Tuareg culture is, once again, in the hands of the women.

Tifinagh is taught by the mother to all her children, but the decoration of household objects with short Tifinagh inscriptions with magical significance is the work of the women alone; this aspect of Tifinagh is worth stressing. Although like all writing it conveys language, in fact its use is intimate and symbolic, rather than generalized and public. It is an alphabet for love letters, for secrets and for charms, but not for proclamations and literature. The alphabet carries with it a private discourse, closer to (but not exclusively for) the women's world and the home than to the external contacts of the men.

Within the nuclear family the relationships are clear: the man occupies his wife's tent, and leaves it in the case of divorce. However, the smallest residential unit in Tuareg society is the group which camps together, and this is effectively patrilocal – a father and his sons, with their families. At the head of the camp is the *amghar*, typically the eldest male in the patriline (an instance of the Berber tendency towards gerontocracy). This structure is, of course, diametrically opposed to the first. The resolution of this apparent conflict is highly symbolic: after a year of marriage, during which the husband lives with his wife's camping group, his own family arrives in a surprise 'raid' on the camp. After a feast, they remove the tent and the young couple, and carry them off to their own camp. Order is restored, and the essentially female household is removed to its new patrilineal enclave.

The Tuareg women have little in common with other North Africans. They are not veiled or sheltered, may invite guests into their tents, and have a surprising freedom of behaviour. Their

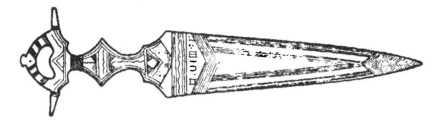

Figure 6.3   Small hairdressing knife, with maker's name inscribed in tifinagh
(From H. Lhote, Les Touaregs du Hoggar, *Paris, 1984)*

*Figure 6.4   Amzad, single-stringed violin played by Tuareg women
(From H. Lhote,* Les Touaregs du Hoggar, *Paris, 1984)*

good name is based as much on their wit as on their beauty and the status of their family. Leo Africanus relates that women are 'very amiable in conversation, and freely give you their hands. They are sometimes so kind as to allow themselves to be kissed. But it would be dangerous to go beyond this, for the men will kill without quarter for this sort of offence.'[19] This does not exclude a significant freedom of action before marriage. From puberty on-wards both men and women attend the *ahal* outside of the camp, in a place chosen for its charm. Accompanied by the music of the local one-stringed violin, which is played by the women, the men improvise poetry, using it to exchange insults, boasts, gallantry and the occasional epic tale. This is one of the defining moments in Tuareg society, in which reputations are established and assig-nations agreed. It is marked as well by a simple friendliness be-tween the sexes, a friendliness which is inconceivable in the north. It is not surprising that a woman is always consulted on the choice of a husband, and though the rigid endogamy of the society leaves her with a very limited choice the final decision rests with her.

Hierarchy and Status

Until recently, Tuareg society contained three main classes: nobles (*imajaghen*), vassals (*imghad*) and slaves (*eklan*, legally servants).

With the exception of the slaves, these groups are highly endogamous, creating family groups which are almost impermeable to
new members.[20] The relationship between the nobles and vassals
was, up to the beginning of the twentieth century, effectively
'feudal': the nobles provided protection for the vassals in return
for dues in the form of livestock and milk. This is the only
systematic form of surplus extraction by one Berber group from
another that we can find after antiquity. The *imghad*, vassal tribes
such as the Kel Ulli in the Ahaggar, might themselves have sub-
vassals, although this was not a very common phenomenon. Each
dependent tribe was attached to a noble tribe, who in theory was
the owner of the flocks and could take from them what they
wanted.[21] Attached to these groups were also found small, pacifist
tribes of marabouts, called *ineslemen*, or 'those of Islam'. These
claim to descend from companions of the Prophet and may have
originated in Morocco: as we have seen, Leo Africanus encountered some of these in the entourage of the prince of the
Zanaga. Finally, there were a number of artisans, principally
blacksmiths, who accompanied the tribes but formed an endogamous group apart.[22]

The largest tribal groupings were ruled by a chief called the
Amenukal, a post which was inherited in the matriline, from uncle
to nephew. The Amenukal's symbol of office was the war
drum. This was a wooden drum covered with white calf skin, with
gold pellets and amulets inside to augment its protective potency.
So important was this object that all the tribes under the chief were
referred to as a 'drum group'.[23] Like all Berber leaders, however,
the chief's powers were largely external: he was responsible for
war and diplomacy, but did not interfere too closely with the
lives of his subjects. His power also varied from group to group: in
the Ahaggar the Amenukal of the dominant Kel Rela also
commanded the loyalty of the other drum groups of the region,[24]
while in the south the Amenukal might be the leader of a single
sub-group.

The origin of the Tuareg divisions into classes along 'feudal'
lines is obscure. Whenever the subject has been touched upon it is
generally argued that the divisions arose as the result of conquest.
Thus the noble Kel Rela, supposedly arriving from the East with
their camels, are said to have conquered the Kel Ulli, who were a
tribe of herders. This supposedly explains their subsequent re-

lation as lords and vassals. In reality, there is no evidence to support this explanation. It fits, moreover, into the all-too-recognizable *topos* of nomads arriving from the East.[25] The Tuareg's own origin myths are always western, however. Indeed, the same class divisions are ascribed to the eleventh-century Almoravids, whose leader Abū Bakr is said to have divided his people into warriors, herders and religious scholars.[26] This, of course, may easily be a myth as well, associating both the Tuareg and their social structure with the most prestigious of the 'People of the Veil', the Almoravids. What is certain is that the attribution of supposed genetic differences between the nobles and the vassals reinforces the distinction between them.[27]

Although there is no *a priori* reason for a nomadic people to adopt a quasi-feudal class structure – and most do not – some clues to its origins can be found in the Tuareg economy as a whole. This was closely bound up with the class divisions. At the beginning of the eighteenth century it was deceptively simple: on the one hand, they raised flocks; and on the other, they hunted and raided their neighbours. The division of labour was equally straightforward: the vassals did most of the herding, and the nobles did most of the hunting and raiding. In the Ahaggar the vassal Kel Ulli ('goat people') kept goats, while the nobles only owned camels – naturally the distinction in status between the two animals reflected that of their owners. This neat division did not hold true everywhere. The Iwillimeden vassals, for instance, had mixed flocks, and took part in some of the raiding expeditions. But the perceived distinction between the two groups remains that between warriors and herders. The nobles protected the vassals and depended on them for their food.

A complex set of behaviour underlay this distinction, particularly in the case of the nobles. For example, a noble should never butcher an animal. This is a general prohibition, and holds true to modern times. Indeed, a Targui anthropologist relates that in the course of a marriage between nobles the camels for the feast are killed with spears and swords – *hunted*, rather than butchered. This attitude is perceived as extremely ancient among the Berbers. The same anthropologist tells that the real offence caused by the Arab conqueror 'Uqba ibn Nāf'i to the sons of the Kāhina lay in obliging them to sacrifice, or butcher, a sheep.[28] Echoes of a similar prohibition are found in Kabylia as well, where certain families refuse to butcher the sheep for the major festivals, and pay others to do it for them. In Kabylia, butchers tend to form a caste apart, and to live outside of town centres.

Other noble behaviour was more subtle: the face might be covered with the *litham* to a greater extent, especially when talking to a vassal;[29] only the nobles were permitted to wear the short sword, or *takouba*;[30] the language they used was purer, with fewer words derived from Arabic, and, in a generally endogamous society, their emphasis on racial purity was almost obsessive. The economic distinctions were thus embedded in a highly complex web of social distinctions which were only tangentially related to actual wealth. The herds constituted the only measurable source of wealth, but they were not by any means the only measure of prestige; and it is prestige, or status, which seems to be the guiding principle of all noble behaviour. A noble was known for his bearing, his prowess in war, his ability to extemporize poetry at the *ahal*, and his generosity – a generosity that was a function of his herds, and one of the main reasons for their accumulation. Wealth enabled a noble to have – and to feed – a numerous entourage, and the number of his followers, like that of the herds they lived on, increased his prestige. We cannot untangle the economic aspects of wealth from the rest of the Tuareg context, and it is in this way that we must look at the raids that were endemic in Tuareg society until this century.

Brigandage, raids on caravans, on other encampments or on the settled farmers of the south was the only activity appropriate for noblemen. Raids were far more frequent than all-out war, and involved their own rules and code of honour. They were aimed at property – herds, food and jewellery – rather than at people. Pacifist groups could not be raided. Black slaves, *eklan*, were taken like cattle, but other Tuareg or Arabs were not touched. Unless they defended themselves the victims of a raid were generally left alive to mount a counter-raid another day. Although their jewellery was fair game, women were always respected: indeed, the French army was surprised to find that defeated Tuareg would abandon their women and children to the conquerors.[31] In general, a raid would not be answered by much of a defence: the victims would simply await a chance to get their own back and even the score. Alternatively, they could complain to the Amenukal and apply for the restoration of their goods – less honourable but perhaps more effective. It is obvious that within Tuareg society as a whole the objects of raiding – herds, slaves and jewellery – circulated between the different groups, in an aggressive counterpart to the circulation of the same goods through marriage. Raiding in this context brought prestige as much as wealth.

We have thus come full circle: the class structure of Tuareg society, manifested in the different prestige accorded to different occupations and their behaviour, can be interpreted as a reflection of their economic structure, which is in turn conditioned by the need for prestige. Clearly, to consider one element of this interlocking structure as more important than the others would be arbitrary in the extreme.

Raiding the South: Gold and Slaves

There is one facet of the Tuareg economy which has not yet been mentioned, and which may suggest a different origin for the class structure. Raids on their southern neighbours were altogether different from raids on other Tuareg tribes, for here new wealth could be created, particularly in slaves. The pursuit of black slaves seems to be a constant in the history of the Saharan nomads. The Garamantes were certainly involved in the slave trade in antiquity. The famous passage in which Herodotus describes them as hunting the Ethiopian Troglodytes from four-horsed chariots[32] clearly suggests slaving. Even more suggestive is a scurrilous poem of the fourth century, addressing a black slave in Hadrumetum (Sousse) as the 'dregs of the Garamantes'.[33] It seems not unlikely that the Garamantes were one of the principal sources of black African slaves in the classical world, and that much of their wealth derived from the slave trade. Indeed, close contacts with Nubia are suggested by the contents of the tombs of the Garamantes, which contain large amounts of material from Upper Egypt and Nubia.[34] Much has been made of the gold routes across the desert in antiquity and the middle ages, but it seems likely that the most valuable cargo of the caravans was human.[35]

The arrival of the Golden Age of Islam meant a qualitative leap in this traffic between the ninth and the eleventh centuries. As nomadic Berber tribes moved towards the Niger – perhaps in response to temporary droughts or to pressure from the north – their contacts with sub-Saharan Africa increased, as did the possibilities of enrichment from raiding and trading. Increasing inter-

Figure 6.5   Tuareg padlock and key
(From H. Lhote, Les Touaregs du Hoggar, *Paris, 1984)*

tribal warfare may also have played a part in the development of
specialized warrior groups.[36] The new needs and the vast distances
required far greater mobility, and thus the possibility of abandoning the slow-moving herds in the hands of dependent, 'protected'
groups. The new wealth which could be produced from slaves,
gold and salt thus both generated and strengthened the class
divisions.

In the middle ages the Zanāga supplied Morocco with black
slaves through the emporium in the southern oasis of Sijilmāsa,
from which a route ran through the desert to the rich town of
Awdaghust, which they controlled. Here a man might have up to
a thousand slaves.[37] Other routes ran up through the Ahaggar to
Ifrīqiya, and from Lake Chad through the Fezzan to Tripoli and
Djerba. The profits from this trade – either direct, or deriving from
the protection money charged to other traders – were most probably transformed into jewellery, metals and luxury goods – and
ever-increasing prestige.

The predatory relationship with sub-Saharan Africa thus became an increasingly important factor in the structures of Tuareg society, as well as the more peaceful trading relationships which developed in order to ensure the supply of gold and salt, and meet the need for the cotton cloth, millet and spices mentioned by Leo Africanus. Caravans were also organized by the vassals, trading in dates and millet. Warfare was never absent, however, either in the form of ritualized raids or as genuine inter-tribal conflict.

Of course, some of the slaves remained in the camps of the Tuareg nobles, caring for their camels and performing other menial tasks such as butchering. A large number of slaves enabled the noble to own a large number of herds, keep a large number of clients, and increase his wealth by trade. In this context it is interesting to find relics of slavery in Kabylia as well. The word for a black man in Kabylia is the Tuareg word for slave, *akli*, and one village is referred to as the village of the *eklan* – not because its inhabitants are black, but because they are primarily butchers.

Transforming Tuareg Society

By the mid-nineteenth century the pattern of Tuareg life described above had already begun to break down, and with French colonies both to the north and to the south of the desert an almost purely predatory economy was no longer possible. New needs arose as well, particularly the need for tea which then began to occupy the peculiar place in Tuareg society which it does today: elaborately prepared and serving as the focal point in rituals of hospitality or in simple conversations between friends. This increased the need for goods to trade, gradually transforming the economy. Without loosening their hold on their society, the Tuareg nobles found new ways of exploiting their vassals and slaves.

The first of these involved the salt trade. Salt deposits exist in the western Sahara, and salt mined from these deposits has long been traded to the lands of the Sudan where salt is scarce. This salt trade of the western Sahara had been big business for centuries; now the Tuareg of the Ahaggar joined in more systematically. The desert mines were worked by the vassals and slaves, the salt transported to the south by the caravans, which traded salt for

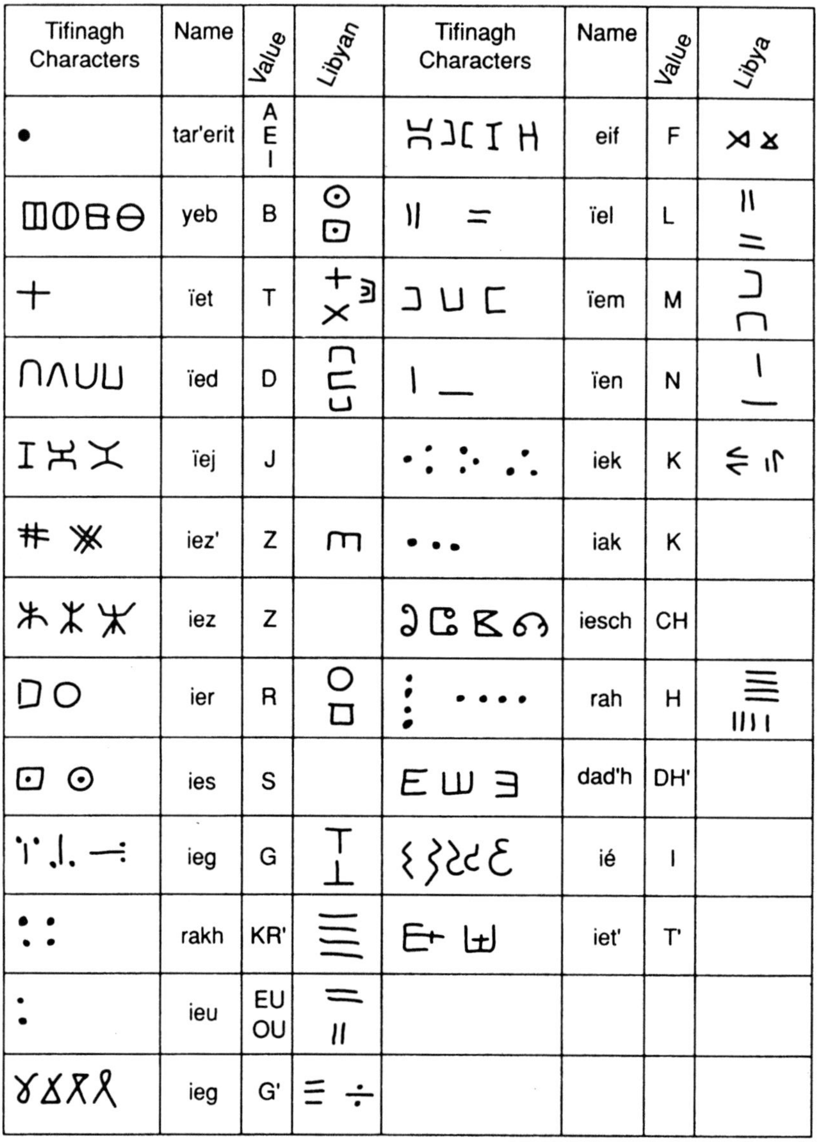

Tifinagh Characters	Name	Value	Libyan	Tifinagh Characters	Name	Value	Libya
●	tar'erit	A E I		ⴴ ⵎ ⵛ I ⵀ	eif	F	ⴰ ⴶ
ⴱ ⵔ ⴴ ⴵ	yeb	B	⊙ ▫	ⵏ ═	ïel	L	ⵊ = =
+	ïet	T	+ × ⵈ	ⵎ ⵓ ⵛ	ïem	M	ⵈ ⵐ ⵐ
ⴶ ⴷ ⵓ ⵑ	ïed	D	ⵌ ⵌ ⵌ	ⵏ —	ïen	N	ⵊ ⵊ
ⵣ ⵛ ⵄ	ïej	J		•⦂ ⦂• ⦂⦂	iek	K	ⵛ ⵏ
ⵤ ⵙ	iez'	Z	ⵍ	• ••	iak	K	
⵿ ⵿ ⵿	iez	Z	ⵌ	ⵌ ⵌ ⵙ ⵩	iesch	CH	
ⵏ ⵔ	ier	R	ⵔ ▫	⦂ ••••	rah	H	≡ ⵊⵊⵊⵊ
ⵔ ⵚ	ies	S		ⵜ �hⵝ ⵟ	dad'h	DH'	
ⵯ ⵑ ⵗ	ieg	G	ⵟ ⵜ	ⵛ ⵛⵛⵛ ⵛ	ié	I	
ⵯ ⵗ	rakh	KR'	≡	ⵝⵜ ⵛⵜ	iet'	T'	
ⵗ	ieu	EU OU	= ⵊ				
ⵖ ⵄ ⵄ ⵄ	ieg	G'	≡ ÷				

Figure 6.6 Tifinagh and Libyan alphabets
(From H. Lhote, Les Touaregs du Hoggar, *Paris, 1984)*

millet and cloth.[38] These slaves and vassals also played an important role in the development of agriculture, both in the oases of the
Sahara and further to the south, where many Tuareg groups now
gravitated. South of the Sahara whole groups of slaves were given
land to farm under various share-cropping arrangements with the
nobles. In the Ahaggar, which had never been farmed, sedentary
groups of black, dependent share-croppers or '*haratin*' from the
old oases of Tuat and Tidikelt were brought in to establish oasis
plantations.[39]

In time, many of the Tuareg systems of dependency became
impossible to enforce, and the process was accelerated by the
conquest of the Ahaggar by the French in 1902. The abolition of
raiding dealt a major blow to the Tuareg class relationships, for
the protection offered by the nobles against other Tuareg was no
longer an excuse for the exploitation of the vassals. The abolition
of the slave trade cut off another source of Tuareg wealth, although slavery has continued in an attenuated form throughout
much of this century. Two examples of these transformations are
worth retelling.

The first example illustrates the continuing importance of traditional Tuareg gender relationships in a changing economic context. It comes from Niger,[40] where slavery was abolished in 1905.
However, although they were no longer legally bound to their
masters, many descendants of ex-slaves remained with the camp as
herders, receiving payment in kind rather than salaries. They are
still referred to by the old term for slaves, *eklan* in the local dialect.
The camp studied by Oxby in the 1970s contained several households, each one of whom included *eklan*. The economy of the
group was almost exclusively pastoral. Grain and other supplies
for a households were bought from the proceeds of the herds, and
stored and distributed by the mistress of the tent.

The inheritance patterns are complex: Islamic, patrilineal rules
applied to most of the transmission of goods on death, but much
property was passed on to the next generation before the death
of the parents, as we have seen in the case of the tent. Women
usually left their herds to their children in relatively equal
proportions, but men tended to favour their sons, so that in
general most of the herds were owned by, and inherited through,
men. The reverse applied to the *eklan*, however, most of whom
were (symbolically) owned by, and inherited through, the women.
The female servants, or *taklaten*, were generally passed on from

mother to daughter, and the children of a *taklit* 'belonged' to her owner, and helped with the owner's children. As Oxby shows, this parallel inheritance was functional. In order to keep the *eklan* with the camp without any legal claim on them, it was important to nurture material and affective ties: the children of the nobles grew up with those of their *eklan*. For the group, the labour of the *eklan* was fundamental for maintaining their herds and managing their caravans. In this way the growth of the master's herds (and prestige) depended on the *eklan*, who were tied materially and affectively, but not legally, to the mistress of the tent. 'In this way we came to understand that women play a crucial role in Tuareg society: it is they who reproduce the herding labour and it is through them that men, who care for the herds, get access to this labour.'[41]

The second example is less encouraging. For the vast majority of Tuareg, the late twentieth century has brought far more disastrous transformations.[42] Tuareg self-sufficiency came to an end almost simultaneously with the departure of the French, and with that self-sufficiency disappeared much of their former way of life. Black cattle-raising tribes in the south were encouraged to move into Tuareg territory, and they over-grazed the delicate pasture. The long Sahel drought of the late 1970s brought to an abrupt end the growth of the southern herds, as well as any attempt to convert to sedentary farming.

While this plight has long been perceived internationally, the more fundamental problems of Tuareg nationality have gone un-recognized. Many Tuareg are refugees: the first revolt of the Adrar in Mali was bloodily crushed by the army in 1963, and many of the survivors fled to Algeria. The periodic welcome afforded by Ghadafi to the Tuareg alternates with moments of repression which drive them away from Libya. It is thus commonplace for the countries where they are found to deny nationality to Tuareg children, on the grounds that they cannot prove their place of origin. Children with no papers, however, have no rights to edu-cation or health care nor, indeed, the right of residence in a country. An understandable resentment on the part of those who were for centuries enslaved by the Tuareg has given rise to periodic persecutions, particularly in Mali and Niger. While Algeria has not engaged in any direct persecution, and has indeed attempted to provide for the refugees, they are encouraged as far as possible to break from any trace of their former way of life.

The loss of herds, slaves, nationality and *raison d'être* has produced in the last ten years a reaction on the part of the young Tuareg. These are known as *ishumar*, from the French word '*chomeurs*', the unemployed.[43] A new, impoverished form of nomadism has exploited the possibilities offered by black market exchange rates, and the desirability of Algerian olive oil for her southern neighbours. Small bands of smugglers, on foot or on ancient camels, use their knowledge of the desert to avoid the border guards, carrying plastic jerry-cans and dreaming of Toyotas and Ghadafi's Kalashnikov rifles. Somewhere between outlaws and organized guerrillas, they have more or less 'liberated' the wastes of the northern Adrar, which has become a no-go area both for the Malian army and the various international aid organizations. Along the way they have evolved a typically Tuareg philosophy stressing freedom and movement, and created a body of poetry composed in the desert or at the *ahal*. They are intensely conscious of the traditions of their people, and when they return to the campsites spend much time recording epics and poetry on the cassette recorders which are the first objects they acquire with the profits from their activities.[44] Their rejection of the miserable *bidonvilles* at the outskirts of the cities is coupled with the demand for a Tuareg state in the deserts crossed by the arbitrary colonial boundaries: the viability of such a state may be questioned, but not the untenable nature of the current situation.

Transhumants and Hagiarchy

If the Tuareg are the most famous, they are hardly the only group of Berber pastoralists. The large majority, however, are not full nomads, but transhumants moving along well-established routes between summer and winter pasture. Transhumance is a rational way of exploiting the resources of the pre-desert area, which range from the winter pasture of the south through to the high mountain pastures of the Atlas or the Aures, where large flocks could not survive the winters, but find abundant pasture and water in the hottest months. The transhumant tribes such as the Ait 'Atta who range from the high Atlas well into the Sahara are predominantly pastoralists, though in the autumn and winter they live in fixed settlements and practise some agriculture. In the summer, a part of the community goes north with the sheep to high pastures in the

Atlas. Although their settlements and tenting groups are limited to one or two clans, several related clans may share the summer pasture.[45] Like the Tuareg, the Ait 'Atta and other Moroccan transhumants have protection arrangements with settled groups of *haratin* cultivators.

The Ait 'Atta are composed of a highly articulated set of lineage segments, each nesting into the next order of segmentation. Together a number of these sections form a single 'fifth', of which there are five. These group together to form the 'supertribe' of the Ait 'Atta, which is administered by a top chief elected annually by the 'fifths'. Each fifth provides the chief in turn, although on the turn of a given fifth its own members are excluded from the vote, and the members of the fifths which are not providing the chief

Plate 6.2 Picture of Tuareg man, Algeria
(Photo: J. Harding King; © Royal Geographical Society)

designate the next leader. The same sort of rotation also holds good for the lower levels of segmentation. This prevents the emergence of a dominant group, for the rival fifths would never vote in a threat to the equilibrium.[46] This is a more elaborate system than is found in the villages of the Aures and Kabylia where, except in exceptional circumstances, political systems are limited to a single village and the larger groupings have no administrative structures. It reflects the size and cohesion of the Ait 'Atta as a unit, although it reduplicates on a grand scale the essentially segmentary political structures of Berber society.

The Mediation of the Saints

The transhumant tribes are not alone in the area they range, and their own political structures are not sufficient to deal with the outside world. The mountains are permanently inhabited by other groups, whose presence would be a permanent source of conflict without some form of higher authority to mediate between them. As we have seen (above, p. 142) this authority is constituted by a group of people peculiar to North African society, the hereditary saints – in Arabic, *marabouts*, and in Moroccan Berber *igurramen* (sing. *agurram*). In a classic study of this situation, E. Gellner has shown how the communities of saints, established at the points of intersection between the mountains and the plains, mitigate and stabilize the potential disorder of the pre-desert world.[47]

The idea of hereditary sainthood is a curious one for Europeans, who believe at best in the concept of individual saints. Like that of European saints, the status of *agurram* is based on the popular belief in his saintliness, blessedness or *bāraka*. His transcendental qualities bestow on him the ability to perform magical acts and to bless others. But there is more to it than that. An *agurram* will only be accepted in the role if his descent is believed to be noble, from a companion of the Prophet, which establishes him as a *sharīf*. Closer in time, the family of *igurramen* to which he belongs will have had a saintly ancestor who established the original lodge, or *zāwiya*, in a new territory. Thus the groups studied by Gellner all claimed descent from one Sidi Said Ahansal, who arrived in the area at the end of the fourteenth century AD. Not all of the descendants of this saint became *igurramen*, but within each generation a few did, and it is their lines which have the greatest chance of the gift of *bāraka*.

How this gift is perceived is complicated and, as Gellner says, largely circular. A man is accepted as an *agurram* if he is generally acknowledged to have *bāraka*, while those with *bāraka* are also perceived as being peaceful, generous, uncalculating and wise. Those whose *bāraka* is accepted become pivotal figures in the whole of the tribal community, mediating in disputes and controlling the flow of knowledge, providing sanctuary and protection for traders from outside the tribal area, organizing religious festivals and the election of chiefs, and dispensing blessings and magic. They are not themselves political leaders, but their prestige affects political decisions. In legal cases, they are not judges but arbitrators, in that their verdict is unenforceable, but must be accepted by all the parties concerned. The verdict is theoretically based on *Sharīʿa* or Islamic law, but we can legitimately doubt just how much Qurʾanic learning the largely illiterate saints possess. They give, in any case, a veil of Islamic legitimacy to the proceedings of the community.

In return, the community and travellers provide the saint and his household with donations. A successful saint, with much *bāraka*, will thus accumulate riches with which to increase his reputation for generosity and thus for even more *bāraka* – and, of course, donations. Avarice would never be perceived as a motivation for his behaviour, either by the saint or by his clients: as with the Tuareg raids, the only conscious object of accumulation is prestige.

A key element in the role of the saint is his habitation in the *zāwiya*, which contains one or more shrines at the tombs of his holy ancestors. Although many lay members of the family inhabit the lodge, the group as a whole remains separate from the surrounding tribes, and thus physically on neutral territory. When more *igurramen* are present in a lodge than can be supported without excessive rivalry, they tend to split off to form other lodges further away. This process cannot be continued *ad infinitum*, however, as each of the new lodges has rather less holiness and prestige than the original *zāwiya*. Nor are old lodges guaranteed the continuance of *bāraka*: in the *zāwiya* studied by Paul Rabinow the members of the holy family commented on a particularly disastrous festival by saying 'that they know very little about their saint, except that his *bāraka* and learning made even the greatest of Sultans tremble', but that *bāraka* has been lost over the years: 'we are nothing but withered grapes on the great vine of Sidi Lahcen'.[48]

The niche occupied by the saints and their lodges in thus a complex and important one. Mediating the difficult relationships between the transhumant and sedentary tribes, and serving as the spiritual authority for the tribes themselves, they are also a manifestation of Islam and Islamic law within the tribal society. As Gellner says, it is in revering the saints that the Berber manifests his identification with Islam.[49] This is a function which is as important as any of those mentioned above, in that it substantiates the Islamic legitimacy of the Berber tribes and, in the process, mediates their relationships with the Arabic speakers. The essentially urban nature of Islam compounds the difficulties faced by the mountain-dwellers in adapting their more relaxed customs to its strictures. Their devotion to the saints is thus a spiritual defence against any accusation of laxity in religious observance.

Not surprisingly, the phenomenon of maraboutism is very widespread among Berbers. In one form or another groups of marabouts with similar roles can be found in all walks of Berber society. In the Rif, communities of *imrabdhen* (the Berberized form of Arabic *mrabtin* or *murābiṭūn*) form major sections of the tribe of the Aith Waryaghar, and although they are territorially discontinuous and dispersed they constitute an integral 'fifth' of the tribe. In Kabylia and Aures villages there is almost always a family of marabouts, while maraboutic tribes nomadize with the Tuareg, and may even intermarry with the nobles. In Morocco they are more likely to live grouped in separate lodges in transitional territories between tribes or between sections of tribes, but their geographical position in the Berber villages of Algeria is equally liminal, usually on the road leading into or out of the village. In the case of the Aures village of Beni Souik studied by Jemma-Gouzon,[50] the *zāwiya* of the maraboutic group was situated towards the south, on the road by which any transhumant groups would approach the village territory.

The Coming of the Saints

As we have seen (above, p. 142), the history of these groups, and their diffusion through the Maghreb, is complex. In almost all

cases their origin is traced to Morocco, but their lineage is uni-
formly sharifian, or believed to be so. This origin myth is similar,
in miniature, to that of the Almoravids, who combined an origin
on the furthest frontiers of the faith with a supposed Yemenite
descent. It is as if the most distant conquests of Islam generated a
returning, missionary wave which served to cement the Berber
tribes to the established religion. There is no doubt, however, that
Islam was Berberized in the process. The word *agurram* is defi-
nitely Berber in origin, which may suggest that the saints were
associated with their pre-Islamic counterparts.[51] This is indeed
what is suggested by all that we have seen of the ambiguous
relationships in the classical period between powerful families and
the sacred, whose central focus is control over communication
with ancestors. Whatever the pre-Islamic background, however,
the spread of the saints throughout the Maghreb is an Islamic
phenomenon, and seems to have started in reaction to the growing
number of Arab nomads, the bulk of the movement into the Aures
occurring in the sixteenth century. Where the origin of a saint is
known, it is often possible to link his establishment to specific
historical circumstances. It is thus a mistake to treat the saints as
part of a timeless, ahistoric 'Berberism'.[52]

The case of the saints belonging to the family of Sidi Said
Ahansal is one of the most studied. The original saint, Sidi Said
Ahansal, is depicted as a missionary of sharifian descent founding
his lodge in the wilds of the Atlas. Several generations later, one of
the direct heirs of Sidi Said Ahansal left the Atlas for Algeria,
where he founded a religious order called the Hansalia. This may
be traced to the end of the seventeenth century by contemporary
North African chronicles.[53] It is a clear example of the eastward
movement which may have been the origin of many of the
Algerian maraboutic families – although the fact that these claim
Moroccan descent may, like the claim to sharifian descent, be an
adoption of the appropriate saintly characteristics. The saints
themselves may simply have come from villages on the other side
of the mountain.

The saints were sacred, as was their home, and thus all who
lived near them benefited from their immunity to a certain extent.
Sometimes the installation of a marabout and the foundation of a
zāwiya occurred in direct response to an actual threat. This was
the case at Beni Souik, in the Aures, where the arrival of the
founding saint towards the end of the sixteenth century coincided

with the arrival in the area of a group of Arab nomads claiming Hilalian descent.[54] The founding saints were integrated into the tribe, given land on its southern borders and established as a lodge. In response to the threat posed by the Arab tribes, the Beni Souik set the most prestigious and influential person they could find on their southern frontier, thus ensuring their own immunity from attack. They thus created an Islamic, Arab shield against the Arab nomads. On another level, of course, the 'shield' mediated between and allied the two populations: the protection they assured at the market place permitted trading relations between them, while nomadic cemeteries were established around the shrines of the saints. Like the Ait 'Atta in the Atlas, the Hilalian tribes were allowed to travel up the Aures valleys in the spring, towards the high plains. The marabouts also acted for the nomads in according their protection to granaries built near their lodge.

Elsewhere, the presence of the saints was perhaps due less to a direct threat to the village than to considerations of status. In one Kabyle village it is told that the saintly family was given land on their arrival from Morocco by the main family of the village. This welcome, which would surely not have been offered to an ordinary newcomer in a land-poor region, shows just how important an asset an *agurram* was perceived to be in terms of the status of the village. Such a family would have been a visible demonstration of the attachment of the village to Islam, and a means of communicating, if need be, with the Arab (or Turkish) authorities of the plain.

As this particular function has faded, the ambiguity of the marabouts' position, and their lack of integration into village life, has become more visible. In the village in question the maraboutic family has even been excommunicated by the town's council for antisocial behaviour, and serious doubt is cast, not only on their own *bāraka*, but on that of their ancestor. Even at Beni Souik, the quarter inhabited by the marabouts is situated on the other side of the main road from the original nucleus of the village.

The hereditary saints in north Africa thus form the seams of the complex patchwork of the society. As such, they perform the valuable function of integrating Arabs and Berbers, but at the cost of being neither one nor the other. The lodges were despised by the socialist government of Algeria until recently, and their status has only recently been artificially revived to combat the newer

Islamicist movements. In this way, the secular North African state is following an old tradition, using the marabouts as a fragile, Islamic protection against a more powerful and all-embracing form of the religion. The reaction of the Islamicist movement has been correspondingly swift, and the tombs of the saints have been frequent targets of the terrorists.

7

The Society and its Habitat

Ethnographic and anthropological studies of the Berbers are almost unanimous in their insistence on one overwhelming characteristic of Berber society: its segmentary organization.[1] By this is meant a principle of symmetry in which a Berber 'tribe' splits into sub-groups, which are in turn divided into further sub-groups, down to the very small fraction of the agnatic nuclear family. All that effectively defines any such tribe as an actual social unit is the belief in a common ancestor, whatever the actual genetic reality might be. Indeed, many segmentary tribes derive from more heterogeneous groups or clans, whose union is based on the fact that they simply occupy the same piece of territory. Thus the idea of a tribe is a very fluid one, and a 'tribal' name may in fact apply to anything from a group of two or three clans to a huge group occupying a vast territory.

A major aspect of the system is that of balance and opposition at the various levels of segmentation, a principle which, in the words of David Hart:

> parallels on a very much smaller scale the 'balance of power' concept of political science. It may be put this way; although the descendants of two brothers, A and B, may fight against each other they join together if attacked by the descendants of those brothers' cousin C, because although A, B and C all go back to the same agnatic ancestor D, none the less A and B are more closely related to each other than either one of them is to C. In other words, the same principle which separates segments at a lower level joins them at a higher one.[2]

The segmentary social universe is a Newtonian one. Although units are, in fact, always embedded in larger units, each individual unit tends to act as if it were fully autonomous. What prevents this from degenerating into chaos is the principle that for every action there is usually an equal and nullifying reaction from an opposing unit. It is for this reason that Hart, in the company of other anthropologists, employs the image of 'balance of power'. Berber society is thus characteristically acephalous: larger, regional groupings of tribes have little in the way of established political structures and hierarchies. Berber society is, at least nominally, egalitarian; indeed, what often unites Berber groups is a common resistance to the imposition of centralized authority. The fascination that Berber society holds for many anthropologists seems precisely in this combination: egalitarianism and the absence of overarching political structures on the one hand, with political stability on the other.

Of course, the egalitarianism does not apply to women, who in general do most of the work and exercise none of the power. The basic parameters of the system are thus that it is agnatic, patriarchal and segmentary. However, the image of Berber society as an acute form of patriarchy, exclusively generated by the balance between segments of the agnatic lineage, is suspiciously like that of Arab bedouin society, which is always an ideal type. Without denying the importance of the segmentary system, the form it takes among the mountain Berbers is fundamentally different from that of many pastoral and mountain societies.[3] They display a degree of political sophistication which is at odds with this essentially primitivist, Islamicist, view. Factions, whose formation is only distantly related to lineage, may call up loyalties which are equally strong. Further, as we shall see, hierarchical stratification cuts across the segmentary structure.

Finally, the apparent anarchic stability of this sort of system seems to have led many historians to a view of Berber society as static, a view which is in no way supported by our knowledge of Berber history. Indeed, from what we have seen so far there is good evidence that the 'egalitarian' structures of settled Berber society are the process of a long historical development in which the effects of the Arab conquest and Islamization are extremely important.

The Hellenistic Berber kings exercised immense, relatively stable political power in the dual theatre of African society and the

Mediterranean world. After the disappearance of the kings the system of chiefdoms, principalities and a high level of hereditary, personal power persisted at the margins of the empire, and re-emerged with the late Roman nobles. This pattern is explicit with the Tuareg, where it is found in the endogamous hereditary classes of nobles and vassals. Even among the Ait 'Atta of southern Morocco distinctions exist between the (superior) herders and the (inferior) artisans and farmers.[4] In the Atlas mountains until recently tribal leaders could command vast, if ephemeral power – as we have seen, the Glaoui is a striking example of this.

In the Aures and Kabylia, however, hereditary personal power, or the domination of one tribe by another, seems to have disappeared, even though the history of the area during the late Roman empire leaves us in no doubt that they existed. The exercise of coercive power by individual tribes re-emerged periodically: the Kutama, shock troops of the Fatimids, are one example; while during the Turkish period the Ait Kaci acted as marcher lords for the Turks, redeeming themselves in the eyes of their Kabyle neighbours only by their glorious defence against the French conquest.[5] This evolution away from the various forms of domination is often perceived as resulting in a truly egalitarian society, each of whose individual cells – the nuclear families – is as good as another.

However, even today in Kabylia the self-image as an egalitarian and patriarchal society remains a myth. Although in theory all village males have a right to a voice in the village assembly, in practice the assemblies are dominated by the 'notables', or families whose status is more or less hereditary, in spite of the lack of any outward manifestations of wealth. Emile Masqueray, writing in the 1880s, pointed out that the identical houses and level of material culture mask a real difference in power between the notable families and the rest.[6] Like *bāraka* or membership in the Roman senate, power passes to individuals not only through their families but also through their personal qualities: notables are both born and made.

A second problem with the 'Islamicist' view of Berber society is the too easy assumption that the position of women is the same as in the Arab society of the towns. The silence of women in our texts is significant: the Kāhina is almost the only Berber woman who acts as a protagonist. But closer examination shows that even in the most primitive villages the Berber woman is more free than her Arab counterpart. As the study of Tuareg society leads us to expect, Berber women play a relatively important role in their communities, and have far more influence in decisions at all levels than the standard view suggests. It is thus a corrective to an essentially text-based history to look more closely at the material aspects of Berber life, and their relation to social structures.

The Village

The organization of Berber society in any given period or place is inextricably linked to its setting – the house, the village, the landscape – which in turn has been created by the group. Further, much of the material culture has been created by women or is used principally by them. This perception we owe in particular to Pierre Bourdieu, whose studies of the society of a village in Kabylia had as its central focus the relation between the Kabyle house and its ideological and symbolic correlates.[7] This study has given rise to others, dealing with villages in the Aures, the Mzab and to a lesser extent the Saharan Atlas and Southern Tunisia. While not all these works explicitly link ideology and social organization to material culture, the connections are there to find. These connections are harder to decipher for earlier periods, for even though we know in some detail what indigenous houses were like in some areas of Roman North Africa, and even possess a few village plans, there is no corresponding source for village life, so our deductions will be more hazardous. The built environment is embedded in the culture, but we cannot deduce the whole from the part.[8] As we have seen, close examination of Berber history leaves little basis for extrapolating from the present to elucidate the past: at best we can use the physical remains to imagine what Berber society might have been like.

From the third century BC onwards there have been four basic types of habitat used by Berber peoples. First, the fragile, moveable shelters of transhumant or nomadic groups, from the *mapalia* described by Pliny[9] (plate 7.1) to the tents of the Tuareg. Secondly, the isolated, rural habitat characteristic of the Moroccan Rif or much of the Algerian–Tunisian border, where houses are scattered a minimum of 300–500 metres apart. Thirdly, the village, probably the most common Berber habitat in any period. Fourthly, the city: this is the most problematic, in that throughout this period the city was usually a manifestation of another, hegemonic cul-

Plate 7.1 Mapalia today
(Photo: E. Fentress)

ture, which determined its form. Successful Berbers could and did live in and use the cities, or create new cities whose nature was subtly transformed, but these transformations are difficult, if not impossible, to read.[10]

We shall concentrate on the habitat which we know best, the village, looking first at its houses, then at the relationships between the houses and the people in a village, and finally at the relationships between villages – trade, markets, and warfare.[11] The perspective must be diachronic: there is nothing rigid or preordained about the characteristics of a Berber village. Rather, a series of traits recombine in infinite variations according to the time and the place which it occupies.

Women's space: the house

Village houses in the Roman period have hardly been studied at all. Indeed, the only buildings we do know are isolated houses, which were the standard rural habitat in much of Libya and southern Numidia. One excavated example from Tripolitania had a series of three rooms, of which only the first communicated with

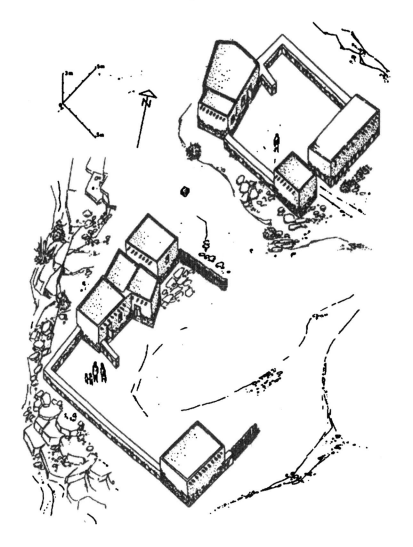

Figure 7.1   Roman farms in the Libyan pre-desert
(From R. Rebuffat, 'Les fermiers du desert', L'Àfrica romana, 5 (1987):
33–68)

the exterior by a door, thus ensuring the increasing privacy of the
second and third rooms.[12] This emphasis on privacy is characteristic of all North African housing at all times: windows are generally absent on the ground floor, and rare in upper storeys when

these exist. The fortified farmhouse characteristic of the late Roman pre-desert took this principle to an extreme: a single door led in to an inner courtyard, above which rose two or three storeys of rooms.[13] The rooms gave on to the courtyard via narrow windows or wooden balconies, but the external walls were innocent of any other apertures. Of course, this was also a response to environmental constraints: the heavy walls insulated the internal rooms, and the reduction of light was probably beneficial throughout most of the year. All these farmhouses had various dependencies – pressing rooms, stables and barns – which remained quite separate from the main building.

The only excavated example of an early medieval rural settlement comes from Spain. In Valencia, the castle, or *ḥiṣn*, of Uxó shows a number of extremely simple dwellings, one- or two-room houses clustered but not touching, and backed against the hillside where possible. In front, a terraced open space took over the functions of a courtyard. That this was a Berber settlement is, of course, only an hypothesis, but the difference between these houses and contemporary, twelfth- and thirteenth-century Arab buildings on urban sites is striking.[14]

Modern Berber houses, while far more complex, maintain the dominance of one room over all the other spaces of the house, and all the subsidiary spaces are clustered within the same four walls. In the houses of Kabylia analysed by Bourdieu all family activities take place in the main room, and the only subsidiary spaces are a loft for storage, sleeping quarters for some family members, and the stables which adjoin the main room below the loft.[15] This space is carefully articulated by activities – weaving, food preparation, sleeping – but this articulation is expressed by relatively few articles of furniture: the loom, the hearth and a single bench against the wall used for sleeping by the head of the household.

The traditional house in the Aures is more elaborately articulated, but the central room, or *tgorfat n-ilmas*, still predominates.[16] Again, the house is a self-contained unit, housing the nuclear family and all its livestock and possessions. The two or three storeys of these houses are stepped back against the hillside, with terraces on the roofs. In contrast to the traditional Arab houses, courtyards are rare and subsidiary to the main building. The lowest storey generally houses animals, along with storage for wood, fodder and farming equipment. On the first storey is found the main room, and on mezzanine levels there are further storage

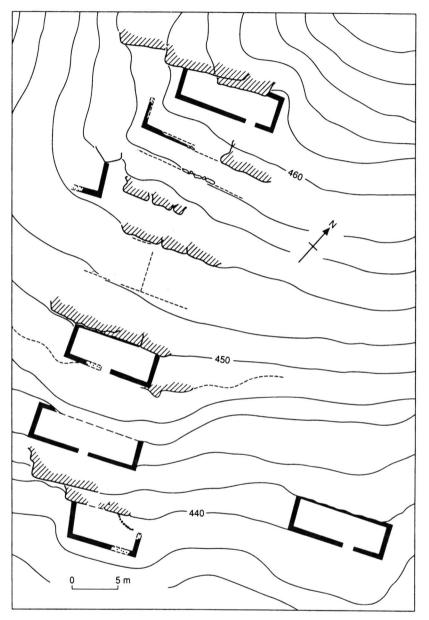

Figure 7.2   Medieval houses from a Berber village at Uxó, in Spain (From A. Bazzana, P. Cressier and P. Guichard, Les Châteaux ruraux d'al-Andalus. Histoire et archéologie des husun du sud-est d'Espagne, Madrid, 1988)

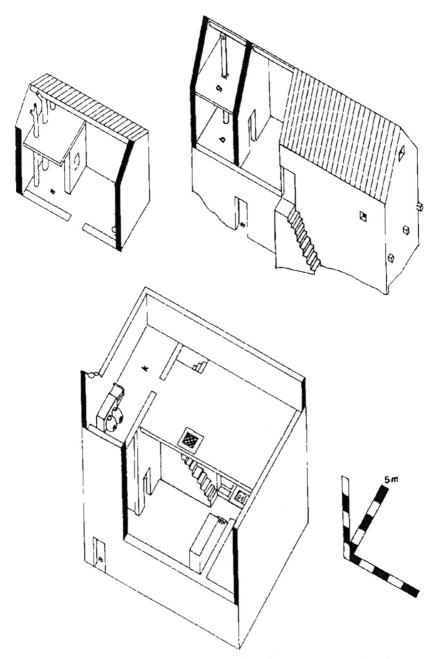

Figure 7.3   Berber houses in Kabylia, the Moroccan Rif and at
Ghadames in Libya

rooms. On the final storey, if it exists, are found drying rooms for perishable substances such as fruit and grain, and above these a terrace. Entrances for humans and for beasts are separate; immediately inside that for humans is found a vestibule, or *sqiffa*. This is a transitional space, more public than the rest of the house and cooler on hot days. Here the women of the neighbourhood may gather to use a hand-mill to grind their grain or to gossip. A guest room, if one exists, would give on to this space, which thus serves as a kind of buffer zone between the outside world and the inner room. The central room itself is a vast space of up to 50 square metres on the first storey, with the roof supported on tall pillars. It is lit by small, high windows and some skylights in the roof. Within it, the hearth is the most important area, often defined by a raised semicircular step in the corner of the room opposite the door. A second raised area is for the loom. As in Kabylia, this is always placed along the wall opposite the door, the 'wall of light'.

Figure 7.4 House in the Aures
(From S. Adjali, Encyclopédie berbère, vol. VI, Paris, 1988)

Weaving is the women's activity which carries the greatest symbolic importance, signifying both the prosperity of a house whose flocks have produced sufficient wool to mount the loom, and the skill and application of the women in it. Cooking and weaving are thus the primary activities which take place within the space: in comparison, sleeping and storage are entirely secondary, occupying spaces which are either temporary (bedding is stored during the day) or inferior (the darkest corners).

In the Mzab, the *sqiffa* gives directly on to a large, gloomy room lit only by a central light-well covered by a grille. Off this room open storage spaces and sometimes a separate kitchen, but in general the space is used much as in Kabylia and the Aures. On the first storey is found an arched portico, which takes over some of the functions of the main room during the winter. An elaborate apartment for guests may also exist upstairs but this would, as usual, be reached only from the *sqiffa*.[17]

Most splendid of all is the central room in the houses of Ghadames. This is found on the first floor, above the stables, and is regularly very high and is lit, like the houses of the Mzab, through a central grille, and beautifully decorated with geometric patterns on a white ground. The kitchen is removed to the roof, and the central room is thus reserved for weaving and eating.[18]

The centralized largely female space is thus a constant in Berber architecture, although the external aspect of the houses varies widely. Bourdieu's study of the Kabyle house underlines the symbolic and ritual significance of these arrangements, a significance which could never be deduced from the empty or ruined remains of the house itself. Each division of the room has its own rituals, according to a balanced division between dry and damp, light and dark, high and low – divisions which reflect a division of the world into male and female spaces. The rites which take place in the house are carried out almost entirely by women: just as they are the principal users of the space, so they also control its magic.[19] Indeed, men leave the house in the early morning and pass the day elsewhere, returning only to eat and sleep. While their presumptive power over the women's activities is absolute, their effective power within the house is very small indeed. The dominance of the central room thus signifies the dominance of women within the household.

The importance of this reservation of the house for women's

activities becomes evident when we contrast it with the traditional
Arab house, the structure of which is quite different and can be
demonstrated to have derived from eastern prototypes.[20] Normally, it consists of a large courtyard off which open a series of
long, narrow rooms. These are in effect dependencies of the courtyard, whose dominance over the rest of the building is the principal characteristic of Arab houses. Rather than being enclosed by
the building, or adjoining it on the outside, the courtyard seems to
contain the rooms. Their relatively equal size and the fact that they
communicate only with the courtyard rather than internally em-
phasize this dominance of the central space. Even those activities
which take place within the rooms can be kept under surveillance
from the courtyard.

As in the Berber house, access to the courtyard is limited by the
single right-angled entrance, which serves as a visual screen as well
as a space where men might sit and chat. This highly restricted
entrance is counterbalanced by the relative ease of entrance into
the rooms around it: even the storage rooms, tucked away upstairs
in the Aures or Ghadames, are easily accessible. All activity in the
house can be controlled from the courtyard, and the separate cells
do not communicate with each other. The highly centralized structure of the Arab house, with equal cells surrounding the central
space, appears to reflect the structure of the family within it. The
patriarchal Islamic family, controlled to a large extent by a single
individual, corresponds closely to this pattern: the other individuals – wives and children – who comprise the family are relatively
equal to each other but entirely subordinate to the male head of
the household.

By contrast, the Berber household is effectively ruled by the wife
or mother of the eldest male. Considered the 'pillar of the house',
it is she who is entirely responsible for the household economy and
the behaviour of the younger women living with her – daughters
and daughters-in-law. Monogamy, which is general in Berber
areas in spite of legal and religious customs permitting up to four
wives, reinforces the unity of the household. In his autobiographic
novel, *Le Fils du pauvre*, Mouloud Feraoun describes the organization of his household like this:

> It was my grandmother who was in charge of our subsistence. She
> alone could open and close the *ikoufan* [the storage jars]. She had
> her own way of moving each of these, her secrets for lifting and

replacing its cover; imperceptible clues could put her on the alert. Her daughters-in-law knew what was forbidden. The loft was her domain, she alone had access to it. She would climb up for a ration of figs, to fill a sieve with barley or to measure out oil and fat. She had her own measures, a personal arithmetic, a sure memory. Her vigilance could not be duped. All the women prepared the meal, but once the couscous was ready it was she who dished it out. She allowed only the meat to be cut by her eldest son: men's work. As we only bought this for festivals it was, in sum, my grandmother who nourished the family.[21]

Womens' circuits are separate, inside rather than outside, dark rather than light, private rather than public, but they constitute an autonomous sphere which touches the men's sphere only at specific times and in specific places. Again, Ghadames and the Mzab provide the extreme examples. In the former, a desert city, the streets are covered with vaults, and are frequented almost exclusively by men, who may while away the day on the benches which line them. Above, the vaults form a network of communications for the women in the different households, who thus may move about in an airy, feminine space (plate 7.2). In the Mzab, women may also move about via the roofs, but when they are forced to walk along the streets convention demands that a man does not appear to notice a woman's existence: clothed from head to toe in a heavy white *haik*, with only one eye showing, she is structurally, if not actually, invisible. The example of the Mzab points out the limits of this autonomy: it is not exactly an enviable one. Before the revolution pre-pubescent girls were regularly married to much older men, and women are in fact never permitted to leave the oasis, although their husbands spend much of their lives away from it. They can be repudiated at will, and any transgression is severely punished. Their lives spin out in unrelieved drudgery, their every gesture controlled.

Yet in the early part of the century the Mzab was the only North African society, besides that of the Tuareg, where women could regularly read and write. Then, as now, social control over women was in the hands of a unique group co-opted from the most learned women of the community. Although the nominal function of this group is to lay out the bodies of the dead, in fact they act as a sort of police force, hearing anonymous denunciations, controlling public and private behaviour, and meting out penances and punishments. Much of their work is more positive, however:

*Plate 7.2   The men below, the women above: festival, Ghardaia
(From M. Roche, Le M'zab, Paris, 1973)*

they give counsel and can, on occasion, change by fiat the customs
of the community – the ban on expensive gifts at Ramadan is an
example cited by Goichon.[22]

It appears that the greater the strictures which separate men
from women, the greater the possibilities of the creation of an
autonomous women's culture. When repression gives way, this
culture is quick to take advantage of its opportunities. Today, a far
greater percentage of women in Kabylia complete high school
and university than their counterparts in an area whose culture is
more traditionally Arab. It is from Kabylia, too, that we have an
example of women's poetry unique in North Africa. These are love

poems, *izlan*, six verses of seven syllables each, infinitely varied, with elaborate and expressive metaphors. Characteristically they are anonymous, almost a collective product, opposing sentimental, universal values to those of order and reason:

> Boy, brother, boy
> of the golden talismans,
>
> When you cross the square
> They swear they'll kill you
>
> This satanic village
> Doesn't want two lovers.[23]

Male space: the village

> Tizi is an agglomeration of 2,000 inhabitants. Its houses cling one behind the other along a ridge like the gigantic vertebrae of some prehistoric monster: two hundred metres long, a main street which is nothing but a stretch of a tribal path linking many villages to the highway, and from there to the cities.[24]

Berber villages, or *Thuddar* (sing. *Thaddart*), are regularly found on an almost inaccessible summit dominating a valley. Even in the lower relief of the pre-Saharan oases, older and abandoned villages are found in the most difficult positions. Perched villages certainly characterized much of the Mediterranean during the middle ages, but villages in the mountainous zones of North Africa carry the principle to extremes. The usual accessory explanations will not hold here. Neither the necessity to leave good soils free for cultivation nor the desire to isolate the village from a malarial plain justify placing a village in the frozen discomfort of a peak in the high Kabylia. Defence and the desire for isolation from their neighbours must have predominated in the choice of site.[25] This was probably conditioned by the influx into the mountains during the middle ages – every village has its mythical memory of the happy times spent on the plains with waving fields of grain.[26] The migration into the mountains resulted from an acute sense of threat, from neighbours as well as from predatory nomadic tribes, and created an extremely high population density.

The closely knit form of the pre-modern village, with its tightly packed houses linked by tortuous alleys and, in the south, its

fortified granary, or *guelaa*, all form a defensive unit. In the
Moroccan pre-desert the fortification is even more explicit: houses
are grouped to form a rectangular fortress with high walls and
corner towers. The strong architectural unity of these constructions, decorated with elaborate brickwork, gives an altogether
bellicose appearance which exaggerates the real strength of the
dozen households grouped within them. In many cases the castle
of a local strong man is included within the fortifications, guarding
the entrance or the highest part of the site.[27] An inner fortification
is also present in the early mediaeval castles of Al Andalus. These
are redoubts occupying the summit of the hill, walled, but often
empty of constructions, which served as refuges for the whole
community.[28]

The villages of the Mzab each occupy conical hills whose verti-

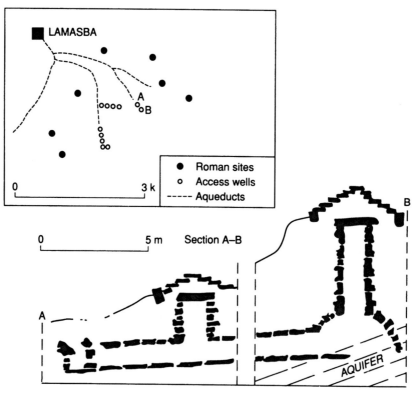

Figure 7.5   Foggara
(From J. Birebent, Aquae Romanae, Paris, 1962)

cal axis is emphasized by the tall spire of the minaret at the top, tapering slowly to a pyramidal point. The mosque is not only the central focus of the spiritual life of the village, it is also its ultimate line of defence if the walls are breached. Down from the mosque at Ghardaia twist a few narrow alleys, which emerge at a first circumferential street some 50 metres below. This forms an inner defence and probably marks the limits of the original village. A second circuit is found outside this one with, again, traces of defensive walls. The modern ramparts surround the whole of the city, market and peripheral quarters included, but the original, defensive heart of the city is still clearly visible from its plan.

The Berber village as a whole is a complex imbrication of spaces used collectively by patrilineal descent groups. The segmentary nature of the settlement is traditionally expressed by its division into two or more *soff*, or halves, which are opposed to each other and composed in their turn of wards, *kharoubas* in Arabic or *thakherroubt* in Kabylia: the word means the pod of a carob tree, with the individual houses the seeds.[29] The smallest unit is that of the agnatic family: in Kabylia, three or four houses – of brothers, or of a father and his sons, cluster around a courtyard with a single entrance from the street. The wards in turn contain the houses of related groups, including newcomers protected by the group. In the Aures, a ward has its own cemetery, grouped around the tomb of an ancestor or holy man, and a collective threshing floor.[30] The wards may be arranged in the order in which groups joined the village, or according to other structural principles. Heterogeneous groups – Jews or Arabs, if they exist – are found on the periphery, along with any group involved in butchering. The lineage structure naturally finds the wards in balanced opposition to each other, and while the whole village may present a fortified front to the outside world, within it the wards huddle in their own compact masses, penetrated by passages off which open the houses of a single lineage. Even in the troglodyte villages of south-eastern Tunisia the individual cell of each nuclear family is dug separately into the rock, but each one opens on to the communal space of the agnatic group. The pattern reflects in a solid way the fluid arrangements of the Tuareg: the individual units, with their feminine centres, are clustered into groups along patrilineal principles.

Between these groupings other relationships result from the layout of the village. Its concentric structure, with the oldest groups at the top and the newer arrivals towards the bottom, implies that the transverse, horizontal axes link allied wards, whereas the vertical axes cut between opposed wards. Relationships between wards are thus both a cause and an effect of their topographical position.[31]

Each ward may have its own council, composed of representatives of the individual families or lineages, which meets in a dedicated space inside the ward – usually a simple series of benches – called by the Arabic term *jamāʿa*, Berber *thajmaʿth*. The village as a whole is also governed by *thajmaʿth*, a term which refers both to the council and to the space in which it meets. In Kabylia there is usually a building specifically dedicated to it, giving on to an open space which recalls in miniature the central piazza of an Italian village. It can also be located at the entrance to the village, where it may take the form of an extended gateway with benches on either side. In general, the *thajmaʿth* is an isolated building with high benches or platforms running down two sides and a corridor a metre wide between them. Openings at one or both ends permit the participation at the meeting of more people than can fit into its restricted space. Elsewhere, the *thajmaʿth* meets in what is simply an open space, without any particular architectural definition but which usually occupies the centre of the village, at the boundary between the various wards.

The *thajmaʿth* is the quintessentially male space of the village, and when it is not used for a formal meeting it is occupied by the men of the village in the same way that a café in a Spanish village square might be. To quote Feraoun:

> The jamāʿa is for men. For all the men. An inalienable right . . . One goes to the jamāʿa to act like a man, talk like a man, look at others in the face. One goes to listen to the old or to teach the young. One goes to show oneself, to keep one's place on the bench. Nothing is more beautiful than a full jamāʿa, like a large family: united, determined, and strong.[32]

Formally, all adult males are represented in the meetings and must attend them or else pay a fine (plate 7.3). These meetings thus correspond exactly to Marx's primitive democracy – or a New England town meeting. They are presided over by an elected official, the *amīn*; he is aided in his activities by an inner circle of elders from the leading families, who perpetuate the gerontocracy we have seen within the household. This more restricted group, related to the *seniores* which we have found on Roman inscrip-

Plate 7.3   The men at the independence celebration, Ghardaia
(Photo: J. Fentress)

tions, is in fact very powerful, and its decisions are rarely
contradicted.[33] During the meetings decisions are taken on communal life, judgments are passed and fines levied. Each village has
its own body of customary law, fixing fines for various infractions.
These refer particularly to behaviour in the streets – loud talk,
insulting behaviour towards women, brawling – as well as various
misdemeanours such as trespassing and petty theft.[34] Money raised
from these fines and, occasionally, some form of taxation form the
bulk of the village treasury, which may be spent on public works
such as streets and pumps. A more valuable asset is the corvée
labour which can be expected of the men in the village for projects
agreed by the whole *thajmáth*: its authority is rarely, if ever,
questioned.[35]

It is hard to overestimate the degree of social control exercised
by a Berber community. Refusal to pay a fine, obey a decision or
a consistently negative attitude on the part of a family may result
in excommunication, a sanction particularly feared in a com-

Figure 7.6 Berber fibulae: (a) from Roman Timgad; (b) from modern Kabylia
(From H. Camps-Fabrer, 'L'origine des fibules berbères', Revue de l'Occident musulman et de la Méditerranée, 1973)

munity whose social fabric is so closely knit. On the collective decision of the *thajma'th* the offender is literally excluded from all communication with the rest of the village: no one will speak to him, do business with him or give their daughters in marriage to his sons. His honour, or public esteem, is permanently damaged.

This public esteem, or *nif* as it is called in Kabylia, is one of the essential characteristics of Berber male society, closely correspond- ing to male honour in other Mediterranean societies such as Sicily or rural Greece.[36] It demands a high degree of conventionally correct behaviour, which extends from one's (solemn) expression to one's response to an insult. The respect for a family's *nif* is equivalent to the speed and efficacy with which it will repay an injury. The word *nif* means nose in Arabic, which as Bourdieu remarks, is very closely associated with virility, and the idea of facing up to, or outfacing, other men.[37] Honour can be expressed negatively by vendetta, or positively by generosity in the giving of gifts – which, of course, put the receiver at a disadvantage. But the *locus* of all this display is public: the street or the *thajma'th*, and the judgement on it is equally public, the respect in which an individual male is held. It is interesting that as women emerge increasingly in public they take an ever greater part in the family's *nif* – not only, as before, by not dishonouring it by a sexual transgression, but also by a public bearing (erect) and expression (proud) which partakes of a series of traditionally male characteristics, appropriate to the public space in which they are displayed.[38]

This notion of honour applied to more than the individual male and his family. The community also possessed its *nif*, and this was closely associated with that of the *thajma'th* as a whole. So absolute was the identification of a village with its *thajma'th* that Christian texts written in Spain after the reconquest refer to rural fortified sites as *aljamas*.[39] When one village was pitted against another in local rivalry, it was the honour of the *thajma'th* which appeared to be at stake. This led in the past to continuous petty warfare between villages. Raiding the neighbours was accepted as a manly activity and those who undertook such raids were heroes in the eyes of their community. Of course, the communities they victimized considered such raids unprovoked attacks and the work of scoundrels that demanded, of course, prompt retribution.

There was little chance for one village to dominate its neighbours, for the system of alliances served to block the rise of any one group. The constant necessity to be on the alert against raids or other offences was, of course, a constant drain on the village society, and no village was eternal. Men's poetry in Kabylia dwells not only on the heroic deeds which warfare might produce, but also on its destruction. A poet of the eighteenth century wrote of one such struggle, which lasted several years:

> The cause of the conflict
> its pretext, I believe,
> Was the unjust claims of the enemies –
> Between Taourirt-el Hadjadj and the enemy's village
> Was a day's march, and this they covered.
>
> So struggles became a daily thing,
> But then they were defeated,
> The village was destroyed from top to bottom,
> Its walls knocked down, and each,
> Leaving his house, took off to new adventures.[40]

Agricultural space

The segmentary structure of the society is reflected not only in its fortification and position, but also in the distribution of the villages: each occupies a relatively equal piece of territory, with clearly demarcated boundaries between them. A group of villages – from two to eight or more – within a given area form a tribe, or *'arsh*, while in some cases tribes would join together to form a confederation, or *thaqbilt*.[41]

Ideally, each village would have a certain quantity of arable land near a stream, as well as terraced land for trees, and mountain pasture. It is commonly remarked that the agricultural land of a Berber village is never sufficient for even the most basic level of subsistence. Nevertheless, intensive gardening, arboriculture and oasis agriculture are essential correlates of the village wherever it is located.

Like the village itself, agricultural space reflects the nested, segmentary structure of the society. Within the territory of a given village we can find individual private property, clan property and tribal property.[42] The existence of these different forms is directly related to the use of the land in question. Most trees and all vegetables are grown on irrigated plots, which are found on terraces near the village or in the oasis. Here boundaries are precise, and individual ownership clearly defined. On the higher slopes, fields on rather ill-defined clan land will be cleared and ploughed only if rain falls early enough to ensure a reasonable grain crop. Finally, the tribe as a whole may own a considerable tract of pasture land.

The recreation of the structure of the village in its fields is something we can trace back as far as the Roman period. Evidence comes from a well-known third-century inscription from Lamasba, a small Roman town just east of the Aures mountains. On it are specified the water rights of each individual farmer in the village, water rights which appear to owe far more to customary law than to Roman practice.[43] The water itself came from a group of *foggarat*, or underground channels, which ran from an aquifer to a central collecting basin and from there to a central channel, (in Latin the *matrix riganda*). Each plot was allotted the water from the main channel for a specific number of hours on a specific day, probably twice each winter. The ration seems to have been based on the amount of land in a given plot. The units are given with the abbreviation K, which probably refers to the area of a single tree, or perhaps 25 square metres.[44]

Much of the structure of the community emerges from this inscription. First, although generally Romanized it was primarily composed of indigenous farmers, with a few veterans, of which two came from outside the community. The plots lay on several systems of terraces, described as *scalae*, or stairs, which were watered in rotation. The distribution of landholdings was very unequal: of the fifty-four known owners, twenty-two owned between 100 and 700K (0.25–1.75 ha.), while three owned between 2,000 and 5,000K (5–12.5 ha.). The social pyramid was evidently steep, although the very richest were hardly wealthy by contemporary African standards. The plots, however, were generally small and the larger properties were composed of multiple plots. Families tended to have adjoining plots, probably resulting from the division of inherited property, but heirs of some estates held land in common. Finally, unlike some modern Berber societies, women were able to inherit and to own land.[45]

The extreme fractioning of irrigated property is a constant characteristic of Berber villages, where ownership of a single tree may be vested in two or three individuals. Equal inheritance and large families prevent the formation of large properties or significant capital accumulation – indeed, the example from Lamasba shows a property structure significantly different from that of the modern village. In the oases of the Mzab, however, there exists a partial remedy to the problem of fragmentation. The gardens are treated as the common property of an agnatic lineage and are thus undivided. While the city house usually holds no more than a single family, the oasis house is occupied in the summer by several families in a clan, who collectively cultivate the gardens. Maintaining and cultivating these gardens is in fact so costly that their cultivation is more a symbolic display of wealth than a means of creating it, and as such interests the whole lineage rather than any given individual.

Agricultural land comes on the market only infrequently, and then at times when a family is under severe financial stress. Once sold, every effort will made to recover a lost parcel, closely related to a family's *nif* and self-esteem. This is one of the few financial transactions which takes place within a village, and the reluctance with which it is undertaken is significant.

The Lamasba inscription also points to another social aspect of Berber agriculture. The creation and maintenance of an irrigated terraced system is a communal activity, perhaps the most important of all for the creation of social cohesion. The Libyan Valley surveys have demonstrated the intense collective effort which went into the elaborate networks of walls built to hold runoff and valuable silts from the rare storms and wadi floods, or to channel water into cisterns.[46]

Of modern systems, the most elaborate are those known from the Mzab, where although most of the water for the gardens in the oasis is derived from individual artesian wells, the rare wadi floods are channelled through infinite numbers of *seguias* (plate 7.4), running through the oasis on raised mud walls. The Ibadite communities of Djerba have a very similar system, with flat fields

Plate 7.4   A seguia in the Mzab
(From M. Roche, Le M'zab, Paris, 1973)

terraced one above another and served by tiny *seguias*. These channels, in one form or another, are a feature of all oasis agriculture, while in the mountains they combine with terraces to distribute the water from springs.

With these systems comes the necessity for mechanisms to resolve disputes over the distribution of water; these are, again, important factors in cohesion. The Lamasba inscription was evidently set up to resolve some sort of dispute over water entitlement, a dispute which was resolved, Roman fashion, by an official and a permanent inscription. In a modern village this sort of precise division would be the responsibility of the *thajma'th*, representing the whole community for whom the irrigation is a resource. However, in cases where one irrigation system is used by a whole tribe, or set of villages, we find officials appointed to ensure the equitable distribution of water. This is the case in the Mzab when the rare wadi floods occur, as it is in the far west at Massat, south of Agadir on the Moroccan coast. Here, a string of villages uses the same canal. Each village has a right to a certain number of days of water, over a forty-day cycle. Surveillance in the early part of this century was the responsibility of a group of men, the *inflas*, whose services were paid for in kind by the farmers. At Massat, as at Roman Lamasba, it is clear that water is not divisible from the land: each parcel of land is entitled to a proportionate share of water, and the water itself cannot be sold.[47]

Like the house and the village the agricultural space is divided between men and women: women, with some help from the men, look after vegetable plots and fruit trees in the fields closest to the village, while men carry out most of the activities connected with grain in the more distant fields. The one public space which is used by women, and which corresponds to the meeting place at the *thajma'th* for men, is the fountain, which is usually found outside the village, in the first ring of fields. The fountain, or *tala*, is often carefully constructed and enclosed to protect the privacy of its users. As Tassadit Yacine points out, this position is transitional between the built space and the cultivated, between culture and nature.[48] Its position outside the town protects the town from the danger which might be produced by the women, but it remains close enough for at least symbolic control. In fact, the paths that lead to the fountain are avoided by men and constitute another privileged female route. Feraoun writes that women have no jamā' as like men; the fountain takes their place. There they can chat, have fun and laugh while waiting for the amphora to fill. They go in bands, group together according to their interests, exchange news and gossip, make friends . . .

Men never go to the fountain. That's the rule. A rule that's never expressed, which is handed down from generation to generation. An indisputable question of decency, or of respect if you prefer. We find the curiosity of those who insist on visiting our fountains out of place. . . . It's certainly the happiest place in the village, the pleasant spot which we pretend to despise and which we're secretly proud of.[49]

Of course, this is perhaps closer to an ideal than to reality: Berber poetry is full of amorous encounters near the fountains, and the branches of olive trees are said to provide the ideal cover for clandestine trysts. In fact, the freedom of Berber women to move about their fields strongly contrasts with the enclosed life of their Arab counterparts.[50]

Just as the fountain is a sort of outpost of the town in its fields, so the fortified granary – *ghorfa* in Tunisia, *guelaa* in the Aures, and *agadir* in Morocco – is a manifestation of agricultural life inside it. Indeed, the word for village in the Aures, *tagliht*, derives from that for granary.[51] They served a semi-sedentary or transhumant population: collective granaries are all but absent in Kabylia, but they occupy a key place in the southern towns, and evidently predate the Arab conquest. Their principal function is, of course, to protect the crop from predators of any sort, and as such they tend to constitute the last redoubt of the village. This was especially necessary with transhumant groups, who would leave the village for high pastures throughout most of the summer or abandon it in the autumn for the desert steppes.

The earliest known examples are from late Roman villages north of the Aures. These are large buildings with numerous equal compartments, walled and defended from predators by doors formed of massive stone wheels that require two men to move them. Again, these are collective constructions, with rigorously equal cells, but destined for individual ownership and use.[52] The same plan is generally followed in the pre-modern examples. In Morocco, they resemble the castles and fortified hamlets, with a regular, modular plan and a central corridor. In Southern Tunisia, the individual module is based on the local troglodyte house, and the *ghorfa* presents a double or triple series of arched entries into the rock face. Larger groups are built free-standing and may, like the Moroccan examples, be built around a courtyard, presenting externally the appearance of a fortress. I know of none in use today, but most of the pre-modern granaries still stand, testaments to the variety of Berber architecture. Their enclosed, inward-looking space with its equal compartments forms a perfect architectural diagram of the society as a whole: independent, egalitarian, endogamous. Characteristically, only men had access to them, and they could be used to 'protect the stores from an extravagant wife'. Male storage in a collective space is thus in direct contrast to domestic storage, which is entirely controlled by women. It may, indeed, have competed with it. It is significant that the granary was often a substitute for the *thajma'th*, and served as a meeting place for men even after it had gone out of use. Like the irrigation systems, the granaries formed a collective structure which held together the often feuding divisions of the village.

Economic space

The difference between Berber and Arab settlements is best measured by the position of their markets. In Arab cities artisans and merchants are grouped in concentric circles around the Friday mosque at the centre of the town, with the most precious products – perfumes, jewellery and spices – closest to the mosque itself. In the Mozabite towns, by contrast, the market is either placed beyond the gate or just inside it. Only at Ghardaia does the market take any part in the political life of the town, or constitute a planned, architectural space.[53]

In the older villages of Kabylia or the Aures, markets do not exist at all. There is more than one reason for this. First, markets imply commerce with foreigners, which goes against the principle of the inviolability of the Berber settlement. The principles of privacy and exclusion combine here to keep traders away from the interior, into which only the occasional travelling peddler, selling jewels or cosmetics to the women, would penetrate. In fact, commerce seems antithetical to the town's ethos of autarchy. Even today, it would be shameful to buy milk, for 'someone always has extra to give away'. Craft production until recently was for the household or for exchange. Potters, usually women, either kept all their pots or exchanged them for enough barley to fill them – the bigger the pot, the greater the quantity.[54] Surplus could be given away, creating good relationships and prestige. Generosity in a good year will be repaid if fortunes change. This applies to labour as well – extra hands at harvest; putting the roof on a house.[55] This sort of help is freely given, but a rough mental accounting is kept and a man with too many excuses for not helping to build his neighbour's houses would end up having to hire labour for his own – not only costly but also shameful. In some villages raising a roof was a corvée, and refusal to participate could result in a fine.[56] Thus all economic exchange within the village itself is, to use Polanyi's term, embedded, with an almost obsessive desire to keep vulgar financial transactions away from it.

The ethos of self-sufficiency notwithstanding, even before the French conquest cash was occasionally needed: for tea, for sugar, for arms if none were produced in the village, for taxes, and most of all for the cereals which there was not enough space to grow. Self-sufficiency has always been an unobtainable ideal for Berber communities, and while commerce and financial transactions were kept away from the village they were nevertheless still necessary.

Markets thus arose outside the village, usually at the territorial boundaries between a number of villages, preferably on a major line of communication followed by traders from other regions. These markets are periodic, usually weekly, operating on a rotating basis within a region. Once again, the sexual division of roles is apparent, for the market is almost exclusively a male space:

> Markets are for men, not women! You've got to be courageous, know when to risk. You've got to look at people without turning a hair, without fear, without blushing, frankly and honestly. Perfectly. You've got to save face. It seems that once upon a time the women got permission to hold a market. They held it once, and it went on for seven days and seven nights. No business got done. So it was broken up, and from then on they just had the fountain.[57]

The possibility of dispute between opposed villages was always high, and thus it was important to ensure peace by rendering market day in some way sacred, by placing it near the tomb of a holy man, and by appointing officials to control its smooth functioning.[58] In the Rif, a stiff fine payable to the council was added to the customary sanctions for murder if it was committed in the market. The consequences of a failure to keep peace in the markets could be disastrous. An eighteenth-century account by the poet Youcef-ou-Kaci starts:

> Some merchants of the Ait Ouaghlis who had come to the market of the Ait Jennat to buy wheat were robbed by them. The Ait Ouaghlis swore to put to death anyone of the Ait Jennad who adventured onto their territory ...[59]

Ideally, a market would ensure exchange between two economic zones – say, a predominantly pastoral area and an agricultural one – but in practice similar villages would have little to exchange with each other. This seems to have led to some degree of specialization in village production, and a transformation of women's domestic production into marketable resources. The most obvious examples are the carpets of the Mozabites, which are produced by the daily labour of the women of the family and sold throughout the Maghreb. In Kabylia various tribes and villages were renowned for their crafts. In particular the Ait Yenni of the villages of Ait Larbaa and Ait Lahsen were known for their metalwork, arms and jewels. Youcef-ou-Kaci writes of them:

> Their hands know how to create
> An abundance of tools
> They are expert armourers –
> One might be in Algiers itself.[60]

This specialization thus dates from well before the French conquest. In 1842 Carette observed that 'There are villages and even entire tribes which have specialized in arms, and have acquired celebrity and fortune.' At Iflissen, in Kabylia, there were eighty forges in 1838, producing sabres known as *iflissa*.[61] In 1900 at Ighil-Ali, in the Little Kabylia, 'The women, from spring to autumn, wove burnous; they or their husbands sold these and the money was reserved for the house.'[62] Again, however, the entry into commerce of these products was only effective after they left the village and were sold at one of the markets.

Pottery was another constant necessity throughout North African history, and as such its production deserves closer examination here. Camps has shown to what degree the painted motifs from pre-historic times are faithfully repeated on pots produced in Kabylia today: the similarity is, in fact, the most common argument for proving that Berbers are immobile.[63] But on closer examination the situation appears more complex: ceramic production provides an excellent example of the dual nature of the village economy.

Archaeology has shown that as early as the first century AD there appear to have been two distinct modes of ceramic production. On the one hand, we find wheel-thrown pots of an almost industrial standardization, produced in workshops, fired in well-constructed kilns and exported throughout the Roman world. On the other, there are the hand-made, coarse-grained cooking wares,

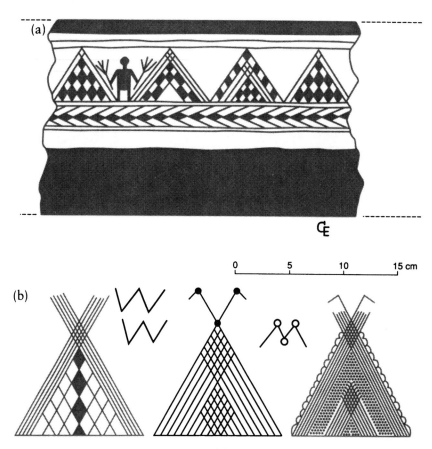

Figure 7.7 (a) *Decorative motif from prehistoric pottery, Tiddis* (From G. Camps, Aux origines de la Berbérie: monuments et rites funéraires protohistorique, *Paris, 1961*)

(b) *Motifs representing soldiers* (From D. Grüner, Die Berber-Keramik, *Berlin, 1973*) produced at home, decorated with painted motifs, fired in bonfire kilns and traded no further afield than the local market town, if there. These productions are complementary, as the wheel-thrown pots with their minimal temper are useless for cooking, and the handmade pots are usually too fragile and heavy for carrying water. Modern ethnography suggests that the wheel-thrown pots were produced by men, and the handmade pots by women.[64] On our model, the first would have been intended for trade and the second for domestic use or barter. Now, it is only the women's pottery which shows the striking consistency of decorative tradition remarked on by Camps. Today, as in the Roman period, a dense symbolic language is conveyed in the traditional geometric patterns.[65] This decorative symbolism is not limited to pottery but occurs on everything which forms part of the women's world – mural paintings inside the main room of the house, the *ikoufan* storage jars, rugs, jewellery and tattoos.

The mass-produced, standardized productions of specialized Berber villages shown no such immobility, but reflect the demands of a changing market. Thus the red-slipped pottery of the Roman North Africa which was produced over five or six hundred years can be closely dated on the basis of its style. It was produced on large estates, but also in specialized villages such as Tiddis, an old Numidian town north of Constantine, where evidence for a large potters' quarter comes from both before and after the Arab conquest.[66] This specialization at the village level is still characteristic. At Tamegrout in Morocco the potters occupy a large rectangular square, of which two sides are taken up by workshops, one by

Figure 7.8 Decoration of ikoufan
(From G. Laoust-Chantreaux, Kabylie côtes femmes: la vie féminine à Aït Hichem, 1937–1939, *Paris, 1990)*

Figure 7.9 Tattooed necklace motifs
(From G. Laoust-Chantreaux, Kabylie côtes femmes: la vie féminine à
Aït Hichem, 1937–1939, *Paris, 1990)*

stalls selling pottery, while at the far end are found the large kilns
shared by all the workshops. The central space is used for drying
the newly thrown pots. But production is only co-operative up to
a point, for each workshop produces and markets its own pottery.
Marketing may take place by way of the periodic markets or, as in
the case of Djerba, through the extensive trading networks of the
Ibadites of the island.

Thus pottery provides a classic example of the complementary
structures of Berber society. On the one hand, women's production maintains a closed symbolic tradition which may reach,
but is not designed for, the wider market. It remains domestic and,
as such, conservative. On the other hand, men's pottery, produced
with a high degree of co-operation, is designed for sale in a wider
market, and takes part in general stylistic changes.

Emigration and the missing men

This complementarity in the roles of the sexes is also seen in the
patterns of emigration. Even taking into account a village's artisan
production, its resources are usually inadequate to keep its

population from starvation. Since the Roman period, the solution for a Berber man has been to find work elsewhere – as a peddler; in the fields, like the harvester of Mactar (above, p. 61); in the cities; and, in the last hundred years, in France. This has never been an easy solution. Depending on the strength of the community the women are left at home, or follow the men once they are established elsewhere. The village tends to reproduce itself abroad, and Parisian suburbs are filled with little communities whose inhabitants all originate in the same village. The theme of exile is a constant in Kabyle poetry, for instance in this little *izli*:

> The boy with the beautiful eyes is gone
> Wearing a beret
>
> Here with me yesterday
> In Paris today.[67]

The habit of emigration is most entrenched and stable among the Ibadites, for whom the native town can best be described as a summer home or retirement community. Throughout the whole of the Maghreb groceries and textiles are handled by Ibadite shops. A boy will leave his home in Djerba, the Mzab or the Jabel Nafousa and follow his father to the town in which his father's shop is found. There he will learn the trade, and until he is past forty will see his home only rarely. This commerce, based on widespread Ibadite networks, has always been the only way in which the extremely expensive life of the Mzab could continue to flourish. In the past, their position in the desert allowed the Ibadites to control much of the slave trade from the south, and even today many of the inhabitants of the Mzab are the descendants of slaves. Not everything could be traded, however, and even commerce is hedged about, for the Ibadites, with religious proscriptions. They are not allowed to deal in precious metals or raw meat, and thus in the Mzab itself these commodities are dealt with by other communities.[68]

The importance of emigration as an economic resource has tended to obscure another of its possible social effects. The autonomous 'republican' villages of Kabylia or the Aures have in the last few centuries managed to avoid any form of state formation. In spite of the continuous friction between them no one village has managed to acquire more than ephemeral ascendancy. This is in contrast to the recent history of the Atlas mountains, where the predatory expansion of groups such as the Glawa could, and did, establish dominance over whole regions. Now, it may be that emigration has served as a safety valve for the village communities, keeping their population growth in check and, particularly, keeping down the number of resident males of an age to make war. The possibility of emigration will have varied according to the geographical and economic context of a region and the availability of work. The auxiliary units of the Roman army would have had a similar function, keeping down the population of villages whose poor lands could not support too many people.

On a deeper level, however, emigration created a society in which the women, left at home, assumed the role of guardians of traditional cultural forms, while the men were free (or forced) to adapt to the hegemonic culture. The 'immobility' of Berber society is a man's view of the women's culture, not an organic view of the society as a whole.

Sacred space

All Berber societies follow Islam, at least nominally, although some recent ethnography ignores or plays this down.[69] In some areas, such as the Moroccan Rif, where Islam came early, orthodoxy is strict and acceptance is total. It is true, however, that the Islamic political parties of the modern Maghreb are extremely unpopular in the Berber areas. Minarets are rare even when a mosque exists, and in the Aures and the Atlas mountains most of the mosques are of very recent date. Observance, even of the Ramadan fast, is sometimes lax, and wild boar is consumed in the coastal mountains; but Islamic festivals such as the Mouloud and the Aid el Kebir are always celebrated. On the whole, the village elders are the most devout: religion, like power, is an attribute of age.

The great exceptions are the Mzab and the other Ibadite communities, whose very foundation was based on a fundamentalist Islamic sect. It is interesting to observe how in the Mzab Berber society has adapted to a highly religious structure. First, as we have seen, it is the mosque, rather than the *guelaa*, which forms the focal point of the village. It is the centre of both cultural and religious life and as such is normally the only mosque in the town. The exception is the oldest village in the valley, El Atteuf, where there were originally two mosques. These immediately became the centres of two opposed *soffs*, or rival factions, and a source of schism. The mosque also serves as the meeting place for the council of clerics, or *tolba* (*ṭulabā'*), which is the supreme authority of the town, combining both legislative and judicial power in addition to its religious role. However, unlike the *thajma'th*, the *tolba* lack executive function. Their council makes its decisions known to a second, lay council of elders, which meets in the market. This resembles the *thajma'th* in the normal Berber village, except that it is presided over by an official called the *ḥākim* who is also responsible for the market. Although in principle a lay group, the council until recently held its deliberations around a raised prayer platform in the middle of the square. Such a prayer platform clearly alluded to the presence of the sacred in the centre of what, otherwise, was the heart of the most profane area of the town.

The Berber ideal of privacy and exclusion of outsiders is taken to extremes in the villages of the Mzab: at Beni Izguen, the 'holy' city, no one foreign to the village may pass the night there. Marriage between a man and a non-Mozabite woman is frowned on, while that between a Mozabite woman and an outsider forbidden.

Even within this extremely rigorous observance of a sectarian Islam, however, there exists among the women a remnant of the magical practices common elsewhere in North Africa. These are all the more striking for being found here, in this most exacting of Islamic communities. Wise women are tolerated, if they are discreet and not perceived as having the evil eye. They concoct philtres and potions – typically, love potions, brews to make a travelling husband return or to maintain his affections, or else to bring harm to an enemy.[70] A more curious form of magic was practised with the slaves of the family: to bring rain, a male slave was almost smothered in a pile of grain. However, songs and chants to bring rain – possibly because they were sung by groups of women – were considered pagan and were outlawed.

A more acceptable form of women's rites are those which, in the Mzab and everywhere else in North Africa, link the women through the sanctuaries built over the tombs of holy men and women. In order to understand the importance of these sanctuaries, however, we must turn back to a humbler form of religion, the worship of the *genius loci*, or tutelary spirit of place. In the Roman period these were worshipped in caves, on mountain tops or at springs, but also in the cities themselves, each of which would have its own tutelary genius. By others they were collectively known as the *Dii Mauri*, though their adepts knew them by name – Baldir, Canapphare or Ingirozoglezim.[71]

Traces of these cults are found in caves such as that on the Djebel Taya, where the local god Bacax received a dedication every year from the magistrates of the nearby towns. These spirits remain important today – not only the domestic spirits, which may be saluted and offered the first taste of the family dinner,[72] but also the tutelary spirits of particular trees, which can be seen in the countryside, hung with white rags to mark a pact with the spirit (plate 7.5). Typically, a village will have a single such tree, which will be visited occasionally by the women. Caves may be inhabited by spirits, who receive *ex votos* and offerings of bread or of lamps. The sense, of course, is that a cave is a space which gives access to the world of chthonic deities.

If the presence of maraboutic groups in Kabylia is a fairly recent phenomenon, dating back not much further than the sixteenth century, the tombs of saints occupy a traditional place in the sacred landscape. As places of worship they are more legitimate than caves, but they are part of the same landscape. Rather than

Plate 7.5   Saint's shrine and sacred tree, southern Morocco
(Photo: J. Fentress)

being in some way related to the *genii*, however, they show clear continuity with the importance of the tombs of important ancestors in antiquity. Since the time of Herodotus, the rite of incubation, or sleeping on the tomb of an ancestor to receive guidance from him, has been practised by African people. The Hellenistic kings, as we have seen, appropriated this relationship with the ancestors to enhance their control over their subjects, and their example was pursued during the Roman period by peripheral groups such as the tribunes at Ghirza (above, p. 27, 66). The schismatic African church of the Donatists – whose puritan spirit recalls that of the Kharijites – glorified martyrdom, and sanctified the tombs of its many martyrs. Thus the town of Nova Petra, in Southern Numidia, became an important sanctuary because of the Donatists who were thrown from its overhanging cliff. St Augustine, who preached innumerable sermons against the Donatists, relates that they danced around their martyrs' tombs, which seem to have been almost as important as the churches.[73]

With the medieval phenomenon of maraboutic groups, the cult of the saints and of the ancestors who were assimilated to them gathered strength. The confusion between the two is sometimes complete: just as a holy man may be appropriated as an ancestor, so an ancestor may acquire sainthood, simply because he *is* an ancestor. The tomb of the saint thus took the place of the ancestor's tomb (plate 7.6). The Nasamones' use of tombs for oaths or incubation is mirrored in contemporary practice at the sanctuaries of saints.[74]

Further, as the Hellenistic sanctuary of Slonta demonstrates (above, p. 35), there is a strong association between the cult of the dead and various forms of fertility cult, and this association did not disappear with Islam. It goes some way towards explaining the importance of these sanctuaries for women. A typical example is taken, again, from the Aures village of Beni Souik.[75] As we have seen, each ward has its own sanctuary, built in honour of the founding ancestor of the group. These are visited regularly by all the women in the ward. They are also the sites of occasional gatherings of all the women in the village, who prepare and consume meals at the sanctuary. One sanctuary was the object of a pilgrimage made by a bride on the seventh day after her marriage, accompanied by a cortège of her relatives. They carried seven skin bags of water, each representing one of her future children. These were poured on to a hollowed stone to ensure the

Plate 7.6   Tomb of a Marabout with offerings – Menaa'
(From D. Randall-MacIver and A. Wilkin, Libyan Notes, London and
New York, 1901)

protection of the saint for the issue of the marriage. However, as
one ward became socially ascendant, its sanctuary became more
important and was then frequented by males as well, gradually
acquiring the status of mosque – and losing its role among the
women.

Some sanctuaries, however, retain their importance for women
even though they have attained regional status. The sanctuary of
Sidi Gennaou between Gabes and Kebili, on the Tunisian coast,
was especially important to the women of Matmata for its efficacy
in granting wishes. But wishes could only be granted to unmarried
women. Thus women making the pilgrimage in the spring would
be repudiated by their husbands, and remarried on their return. It
was not considered legitimate to thwart one's wife from making a
pilgrimage – although it was forbidden to approach women on the
pilgrimage.[76]

Thus, while no woman would dream of denying taking part in
the official religion, in fact her participation is tangential to it,

occupying a different space and taking different forms. This is easy to understand if we look briefly at the history of North African religion. The first 'official' religion of North Africa was certainly eastern, the Punic cult of the goddess Tanit, combined with that of Baal, Egyptianized as Baal Hammon, who was worshipped from the oasis of Siwa to Gibraltar. The interest of this religion, whose subsidiary gods were insignificant compared to the chief deities, one male and one female, is its dualism, which neatly matches the dual character of Berber society, in which public and private, male and female, external political behaviour and internal traditional culture remain distinct but not opposed. The cult of Baal Hammon was carried over into the Roman period by the worship of Saturn,[77] but although the goddess Caelestis took over some of Tanit's attributes she did not assume the same importance. Already, the woman's part in the official religion was diminishing. Nor did the cult of the Virgin Mary assume the same role in the African Church which it was later to achieve in the northern Mediterranean. With the coming of Islam, any female pole in the official religion disappeared altogether. This must be one of the reasons why women's devotions have remained tied to the private, domestic and family spheres of magic, tutelary geniuses and the ancestor saints. The similarity between Sicilian churches, almost exclusively occupied by women except on feast days, and the sanctuaries of the saints, is striking. Both are decorated with precious stuffs, hung with lamps, resplendent with murky glitter. It is the sanctuary, and not the mosque, which is the woman's sacred space.

A Dual Society

The duality of religious expression – women/magic/sanctuary – men/Islam/mosque – reflects the duality which is so often felt by Berbers themselves about their culture, although this duality is usually expressed as the necessary response of a subaltern people to the hegemonic culture. Jean Amrouche, in a famous article written just after the war, used Jugurtha as a metaphor for all Berbers. This is remembered as a description of the Berber as an eternal rebel, but in fact he wrote as well of the Numidian's ability to 'wear the livery of the Other, to mime to perfection his language and customs'. But this double soul goes deeper than that. He finishes with a hope that 'Jugurtha' will interest himself in the world as more than an object for aesthetic contemplation or as an inexhaustible source of pleasure and ephemeral pain. He must learn to consider it as his field of action, on which to assemble all his forces . . . only then will he have moved away from the age of theology and of magic.[79]

In other words, for Berber society to emerge into the (male) world stage it would have to suppress its (female) characteristics – introversion, traditions and magic. The duality was not perceived as a strength, for no stable identity myth could be constructed on it.

8

Berbers and Berberism

Recognize what is yours
Make sure you never forget it!
Kabyle, our language
One who loves you
Is ready to sacrifice his life for you
Venerate you
And keep his head high for you
It's thanks to your children
That Algeria exists.

                                   Lounis Ait Menguellet[1]

The cancellation of Mouloud Mammeri's 1980 lecture on Berber poetry at Tizi Ouzou touched off not only a series of demonstrations, but also the beginning of a process which had not been foreseen: the creation of a Berber movement in Algeria. Indeed, in the 1970s the received wisdom among Western scholars was that no such movement was possible. Berberism was not only absent, it was ideologically impossible. The most obvious empirical demonstration that Berbers were Moroccans or Algerians first, and Rifians or Kabyles second, was the abject failure of the French to create a Berber fifth column to oppose Algerian or Moroccan Arabs in the independence movement.

Charles Micaud, concluding an important volume on Arabs and Berbers, stated: 'There is a remarkable consensus concerning the absence of a Berber problem.' Of the Tuareg, Maurice Gast said: 'the problem of the ethnic diversity of these populations and of the old social classes is not even posed any more.'[2] In the new orthodoxy most of the divisions between Berbers and Arabs could be seen as the products of French politics, if not pure imagination. The new, rational nation states could bypass ethnic identification, and class interest would soon overcome ethnic interest. Ethnicity, in sum, was a thing of the past. The one caveat was expressed by William Quandt in the same volume: with some prescience he warned that the only conditions which would lead to Berberism in Algeria would be an abrupt Arabization of the country, or the feeling on the part of the Berbers that they were the victims of economic and political as well as cultural discrimination.[3]

The situation in the 1970s seemed to justify this position. The Berber population was insignificant in Tunisia, while in Algeria and Morocco Berbers had no immediate reason to rock the boat. This was due in part to French policy, which had emphasized the importance of education in French rather than Arabic for the Berber areas. Since the early part of the century the Berber areas had had far more than their share of French schools, and while these had been refused in the Mzab for religious reasons and ignored in the Aures for economic ones, they had slowly taken hold in Kabylia.[4]

But an increasing literacy in French did not carry with it an increasing loyalty to France. Around a third of the founders of the Front for the Liberation of Algeria were Kabyle, while a French effort to create counter-insurgency guerrillas in the supposedly loyal village of Iflissen, an operation charmingly named '*Oiseau Bleu*', ended in a spectacular double-cross and the death of perhaps 264 French soldiers.[5] The FLN held firm, and if there were internal disputes they were not along Arab–Berber lines. After the war there was no trace of a specifically 'Berber' discourse, and even Hocine Ait Ahmed's short-lived insurrection in Kabylia of 1963–4 was in large part a move in a struggle internal to the elite, which was rejected by half of the Kabyle delegation in the national parliament (above, p. 196f.).[6] With the exile of Ait Ahmed and the abolition of his party, the FFS (*Front des Forces Socialistes*), there was no political group which represented the Berbers. The Kabyles provided a disproportionate amount of the national leadership, and if most of them were old war heroes without any particularly important portfolios, there was no apparent reason for political protest. French remained the dominant administrative and academic language, and Kabyle entry into the administration and the universities was helped as much by their command of French as by their superior education.[7]

In Morocco the situation was rather different. There, the French had pursued a policy of co-option hardly different from that of the Romans: the 'use of influential notables to assist in the process of pacification'.[8] Despite their use by the French against the monarchy in the struggle for independence in 1956 this policy of favouring the Berber notables was maintained after the death of Mohammed V in 1961 by his son King Hassan II to counterbalance the political opposition in the cities: their alliance with the king protected the tribesmen of the Atlas and the Rif against the political dominance of the urban bourgeoisie. By reinforcing the role of the Berber sheikhs, he preserved traditional forms of social control. A by-product of such policies was a strong over-representation of Berbers among army officers. But, even though the failed coup against Hassan II of 1971 was led by Berber officers, it was hardly a Berberist coup: if it had not been for these recruiting practices 'they could easily have been Arab'.[9] Both Morocco and Algeria continued to court their Berber populations, the former by favouring the traditional elites, and the latter by serious investment in the infrastructure and industries of Berber regions.

As the Arabization of education in Algeria, set in motion as far back as independence in 1962–3, spread upwards through the school and university system, however, the situation began to change. In 1962, proficiency in written Arabic as distinct from the spoken, dialectal forms of Algerian Arabic was restricted to a small number whose education had usually been religious. Twenty years later, the growing use of the written form as the national language of literacy and educated speech in place of French had begun to threaten those Berbers who, for years, had enjoyed an advantage from their proficiency in French, but for whom standard Arabic was a third or even fourth language. This was especially so in the cultural field, where traditional intellectuals who taught such subjects as classics or sociology were no longer needed and were slowly discarded.

This blow to the bilingual culture built up over the previous sixty years was the beginning of a radical revision of the Berber position in the country. Most badly hit were the Kabyles: in the Aures, the Arabizing and Islamizing work of the Islamic fraternities had taken a greater hold, and a number of groups in the northern Aures had dropped their Shawi dialect after the 1930s.[10] As we have seen, French had never taken a particularly strong hold in the Aures, or the Mzab. In Kabylia, however, the generation born just after the war, whose parents had gradually risen to a reasonable prosperity and whose education was still largely francophone found themselves in a dangerous position: possibly better educated than their Arab-speaking contemporaries, they were unable to compete with them. Nor was it politically possible to lead a popular battle for French: Arabic is the language of Islam, and French remains that of the colonizer. The battle lines had thus to be drawn between the natural languages of the country – Berber and Algerian Arabic – and standard, classical Arabic.

Proponents of the latter added a new touch: English, rather than French, as a second language. Since liberation, an increasing number of intellectuals had received their higher education in Britain and the US. Among these were many of the Islamic fundamentalist leaders, whose ideas were formed in London in contact with other founders of the movement. The shift to English was promoted as part of a new economic rationality, but was also a slap in the face for the francophones. It was, moreover, a gift to other enemies of Berberism. Arabization thus politicized Berber ethnicity. Once the state moved from 'Algerian' to 'Arab' the ethnic question could not be avoided.

It would, of course, be absurd to reduce Berberism to a hidden conflict between French and Arabic, or its motivation to simple economics. Direct cultural repression was a phenomenon that started as early as the mid-1960s, when the transmissions of the one Berber radio station became limited to four hours a day, and it became illegal to give children Berber names. Systematic repression of festivals, of musical groups, and finally the abolition of Mammeri's course in Berber at the University of Algiers were all aimed at establishing the linguistic and cultural unity of the country, and preventing the growth of Berberism into a political force.

The reaction has had just the reverse effect, accentuating the destabilization of the national sentiment which was still so strong at the beginning of the 1970s. Just as in Arab-speaking areas opposition to the FLN throughout the 1980s created a strong Islamist party (the FIS), the Berber areas have seen an incredible growth in the following of the Berberist parties: Ait Ahmed's revived FFS, and Said Sadi's Assembly for Culture and Democracy (RCD), which grew out of the Berber Cultural Movement. Led initially from exile by Ait Ahmed, the party has based its policy on the premiss that 'Berber exists, and is entitled to participate fully in the life of the nation'.[11] The corollary of the statement, in political terms, is a demand for freedom for the whole of Algeria, for multiparty democracy in place of the one-party system created by Ben Bella and Boumedienne. Berberism, in other words, has become identified with the growing demand for political liberalization which has since shaken the grip of the FLN, if not the army, on the government of the country. What Ait Ahmed called '*la braise berbère*', the smouldering of Berber consciousness against the time when it would burst into flame, is less luridly, but no less significantly, evaluated from this point of view by Salem Chaker in the authoritative *Annuaire de l'Afrique du Nord*:

> For a whole set of reasons, social and cultural, it seems clear that no national proposal for democracy in Algeria can seriously be contemplated without significant support from the Kabyles and other Berbers.[12]

Berberism in Algeria nevertheless remains on the defensive. The very name of the 'Kabyle question' under which Hugh Roberts treats the 'Berber Spring' is a reminder of the historic limitations of his subject.[13] Moreover, Berber championship of democracy in the nation at large has been overtaken by less liberal demands in the name of Islam. Despite what has been construed as a local majority for Berberism in Kabylia, the FIS or Islamic Salvation Front collected the national protest vote against the government in 1989; and the threat which it seemed to pose to the new democracy and the old values of the FLN in the national elections of 1991 provoked the return to a presidential regime dominated as before by the army.[14] Kabyles have divided on the issue, and Berberism is not their sole concern.

Nevertheless, at the time of writing, the FFS has been encouraged by the descent of Algeria into a murderous cycle of Islamist terrorism and government counter-terrorism costing tens of thousands of lives, to call successfully for strikes and marches to demand the political and cultural recognition of the Berbers of Kabylia in particular. The wave of indignation at the kidnapping by Islamist extremists of the popular Berber singer and member of the MCB, Matoub Lounès, in September 1994, may have prompted his release in October, and demonstrates the strength of Berberism on the political scene. The risk of civil war is plain, for any government compromise with the Islamists may provoke further hardening of the Berber positions. An anti-government alliance between the FFS and the FIS, proposed in Rome in 1995, may offer some hope, but at the time of writing the outcome remains unclear.

In Morocco, where Berber-speakers constitute up to 40 per cent of the population, a similar hostility on the part of the regime to the cultural expression of Berberism has not provoked a similar reaction. The country has no Kabylia; its Berber mountains, the High and Middle Atlas and the Rif, are more like the Aures in terms of their remoteness from the capital and its concerns. Their traditional society has not suffered the extensive transformations of society in Algeria. The regime, moreover, is different. The Arabizing nationalists who have held power in Algeria are in opposition in Morocco, while the Islamist opposition finds it hard to challenge the authority of the King in his capacity as Commander of the Faithful. The ruling ideology is that of the monarchy, insistent upon loyalty, suspicious of the Berber identity encouraged by the French, and resistant to Berberist claims, but nevertheless wholly pragmatic in its approach to the Berber question, aiming to incorporate rather than repress. Parties with a Berber appeal find themselves in the royalist majority in parliament. Culturally, the measures taken to dilute the sense of Berber identity, such as the widespread substitution of neutral Arabic names like Tawfiq as surnames in place of Berber clan names, have not aroused the same antagonism: the people themselves know the name of the people to which they belong. The government, moreover, has recently shown itself more favourable to the Berber cultural movement than in the past. In the summer of 1994 the Berber language was introduced both in schools and in news broadcasts. No doubt the Moroccan monarchy has its eye upon Algeria, seeking to avoid the mistakes of Algiers in provoking a wave of Berber opposition at a time when Islamism offers a more radical challenge to the direction of the state. But it appears as yet another judicious move on the part of the King to hold the political balance of the country steady.

The Prospect for the Future

As Chaker states in his title, 'La voie étroite', the Berber path to survival is a narrow one. Berber speakers are everywhere in a dwindling minority, as younger generations are universally educated in other languages, and leave the homelands for a wider world. The round figures of 40 per cent in Morocco and 20 per cent in Algeria are decades out of date.[15] Berber identities are correspondingly in danger of dilution. Meanwhile the North African population as a whole, and especially in Algeria and Morocco, is growing faster than almost anywhere else in the world. By the year 2000 that population will have risen to about 80 million, two-and-a-half times as large as it was at the time of independence in the middle of the century, when it was already three times higher than the estimate of 12 million in 1900.[16]

An increase of this magnitude, associated as it is with the growth of the urban population, is capable of swamping any section of the community which fails to keep pace with the rate of reproduction. At the same time it generates new problems and new opportunities in place of the preoccupations of the past. The evolution of the North African population in France, for example, has witnessed a predominantly Algerian, predominantly Kabyle, predominantly male community in the earlier part of the century become approximately half Moroccan and Tunisian, and increasingly feminine, as it has grown from about 300,000 in 1954 to over 1,500,000 at the present day.[17] Increases and alterations of this order may fortuitously preserve or fortuitously eliminate cultural traits irrespective of the efforts of those who seek to defend them against erosion. Berber seems unlikely to be lucky in this respect, and will have to rely upon self-conscious cultural chauvinism if it is not finally to dissolve into Arabic and French in the flow of the demographic tide.

Kabylia itself, and the Aures, together with their local particularisms, will clearly survive whatever language their inhabitants speak. But their Berber character has lacked not only political but also economic value. In this respect it contrasts with the south of Morocco, where tourism has placed a premium on Berber arts and crafts as the distinctive attractions of an attractive region. The requirement for a Berber identity to seduce the visitor leads to the designation of the Blue Men of the desert as Tuareg rather than Hassani, a modest reversal of the long process of Arabization along the familiar lines of the previous chapter. Such image construction might well create the Berbers of the future even as the Berbers of the past are transformed by continuous modernization.

The Tuareg themselves are in danger of becoming the most striking emblem of the change. Their romantic image as the veiled aristocracy of the desert is well established for the visitor to Tamanrasset in the Hoggar mountains of the Algerian Sahara. The nomadic way of life on which that image depends, however, has more enemies than friends. Successive droughts over the past twenty years have weakened it; still more have the policies of the Algerian state. These have destroyed the traditional hierarchy of nomads and cultivators in the oases in the name of equality, turning the Tuareg into survivors on the margins of civilization, in danger of becoming the 'towrags' of English slang. Right along the southern border of the Sahara, from Mauritania to Tchad, where the states of the former French West Africal ballon up into the desert from their anchors in the Sudan – the old 'Land of the Blacks' – the danger is still more alarming, as racial tensions threaten the ancient symbiosis of desert and savannah. Conflict in Mauritania and open warfare in Tchad have been echoed by violence and confrontation between the Tuareg and the peoples to the south in both Mali and Niger, the two republics which share with Algeria the territories of the nomads. War in the desert has already transformed the lives of the Blue Men who fight under the banner of the Polisario at Tindouf in western Algeria against the occupation of the old Spanish Sahara by Morocco. It would surely convert the Tuareg, the last of the great Berber nomads, from an image to an illusion as insubstantial as any pursued by Alexander the Great in his legendary search in the Sahara for the Water of Life.[18]

What then is the prospect for the future? Unlike European minorities, the Berberist parties have never made serious claims for separatism (although radical Tuareg groups are an exception to this rule). Kabylia would hardly be a viable economic unit, and the geographical separation of the principal Berber groups in Algeria makes the idea of any greater Berber area unthinkable. Instead, the battleground is linguistic and cultural. Much use is made of symbols: liberalizing the laws on naming children has resulted in a whole generation of Jubas, Masinissas and Jugurthas; while the 'decolonized' history of the Maghreb is periodically rewritten by Berber historians to include Arabs among the colonizers. Kabyle university students flock to ancient history and archaeology, but there is a corresponding lack of interest in the more Arabic middle ages.

If the linguistic question is central, the cultural and historical aspects are no less important. The roots of this reaction can be traced much further back, to the period just after the war when the first steps were taken by Kabyles to transcribe their own oral culture. Pioneers such as Fatima Ait Mansour and her children, Jean and Taos Amrouche, collected, collated and, in the case of Taos, sang the tales of Kabylia. Mouloud Feraoun, a Kabyle schoolteacher killed by the OAS just before the end of the war of liberation, wrote a number of short essays on his village and, like Mammeri, a series of novels centred on the mountains he came from.[19] More recently, Mammeri's monumental study of Berber poetry has been joined by the work of Tassadit Yacine.[20] Together, with the support of the *Maison des Sciences de l'Homme* in Paris, they founded the review of Berber studies *Awal*, which ranges between linguistic and ethnographic studies to translations of Molière into Kabyle. This interest in the transcription and study of oral literature is not limited to academics. As we have seen, when the young *ishumar* Tuareg, engaged in petty smuggling and occasional banditry in the Sahara, scrape together enough money they buy tape recorders and return to their family's camp to record the women's tales.[21] Illiterate scribes, their tape recorders provide a link with the past and an illusion of its preservation.

Of course, the strength of the culture is not measured by the extent to which it is recorded, but to what extent it continues to grow. The central position of poetry in Berber life has developed into a passionate interest in the songs of the new Berber musicians, of whom the best known is Lounis Aït Menguellet. His concerts attract huge crowds both in Algeria and in France, and his lyrics have already been collected and studied. He is perhaps the most prominent symbol of the Berber revival and, like other Berber singers such as Idir and Ferhat, many of his lyrics are overtly political.[22]

In Paris, where second-generation immigrants search for their roots in Kabyle, Aït Menguellet is wildly popular, and has been an important stimulus for those who no longer speak Kabyle to learn it. The language is now accepted as a subject for the baccalaureate examination, is taught at the cultural associations and heard all day on a number of radio stations.

Language remains the key to the movement, and much stress has been put on its academic position. A department of Berber languages has been opened at the University of Tizi Ouzou in Kabylia, while linguistics has become one of the favourite topics

Plate 8.1   Aït Menguellet
(Photo courtesy of the subject)

for post-graduate research, particularly in the Berber department of the University of Paris (VIII).

As a written language, Berber can be used for education, and there is a new industry producing school texts in Kabyle. An '*Académie berbère*' studies neologisms and scientific terms, and has agreed on a standard transliteration of Berber consonants.[23] The importance of the change from oral expression is underlined by the attempt to introduce the Tuareg Tifinagh alphabet as a universal Berber means of expression. This has immense semiological importance: like Arabic and European languages, Berber languages can now be expressed in their own alphabet, not only moving from oral to written, but also presenting their own characteristic letter forms which have to be learned to be understood. The success of this move is not yet apparent, and most Berber texts continue to be transcribed in modified Latin characters. However, a new word-processing program allows the user to write a Berber text in modified Latin characters, and then to change them to Tifinagh at the touch of a function key.[24] The general effect is rather like encoding and is reminiscent of the magic and symbolic power of Libyan inscriptions in the pre-Roman Maghreb.

In the end we return to the paradox that runs through the pages of this book. Whether restrained in Morocco, defiant in Algeria or flourishing in Paris, Berber culture has been apparent to its users only when they themselves are bilingual and bicultural. Ibn Khaldūn in Arabic, writing for the Berber dynasties of Fes, Tlemcen and Tunis, and Mouloud Mammeri in French, both described Berber culture and history in the language of the conquerors, which was also their own. Such a perspective, from such a distance, has been necessary to the definition of the Berbers as a people, and especially as a self-conscious people aware of their difference from others in the world. The difference from the past is that the new Berber consciousness has seized upon Berber itself as a written language to rival both French and Arabic for this purpose.

Now, at the end of the twentieth century, the emergence of this new Berberism is an emergence under threat. The threat is on the one hand impersonal. As in the Roman period, the individual has been lured away from a closed, endogamous village society with its traditional culture, by the possibilities of economic and social promotion. Awareness of the consequent loss of identity on the part of the emigrant by those with the education and ability to express themselves has created a more studied, less instinctive defence of traditional Berber society and culture. That in turn has provoked a more direct threat from those others within the North African world who perceive in the new Berberism a challenge to their own politics and religion. The challenge is felt the more keenly since the Arabism which they favour is by no means secure. Despite its long history in the Maghreb, Arabic as the language of mass education and mass consciousness has preceded the cultivation of Berber as a written language by less than twenty years. Faced by the hostility of those who have yet to realize their nation-building programme, the vigorous promotion of Berber languages as part of a newly literate culture might be transformed into political nationalism, with a separatist political programme calling for a greater or lesser degree of recognition within the state system of the Maghreb. Severe provocation by the Islamists of Algeria, for example, might in the interim lead to an armed confrontation, and the kind of scenario which has followed the collapse of the central governments of Eastern Europe. Such a possibility is both extreme and may for the moment be remote. Nevertheless, the re-emergence of Berber culture in its new guise, just at the moment when, in its traditional form, it was scheduled to enter the museums of folklore, is a remarkable tribute to the subject of this book. The final adoption of the language as a means of expression in all the modern media of communication is the culmination of four thousand years of history. While we cannot be sure it will not follow the Berber sermons of Ibn Tumārt into disuse, for the moment it has placed the Berbers themselves firmly back among the nations of the world where Ibn Khaldūn located them. It is a final justification for tracing their evolution under the title of *The Berbers*.

Notes

Introduction

1 Felicity Barringer, personal communication.
2 L. Cavalli Sforza, P. Menozzi and A. Piazza, *History and Geography of Human Genes* (Princeton, N.J., 1994), pp. 158ff.
3 Ibn Khaldūn, *Kitāb al-'Ibar*, tr. A. Cheddadi (Paris, 1986), vol. II, p. 464.
4 For example, G.H. Bousquet, *Les Berbères*, 2nd edn (Paris, 1974), p. 20.
5 The term is first recorded in Arab authors. Traditionally it derives from the Greek *Barbaroi*, Latin *barbarus*. S. Gsell, *Histoire ancienne de l'Afrique du Nord*, vol. V (Paris, 1927), p. 115, observes that in a third-century grammar written at Carthage the use of '*barbar*' instead of '*barbarus*' was condemned. However, G. Camps, 'Les Bavares', *Revue africaine*, **99** (1955), 241–88, notes that the word appears frequently in Semitic names, and a tribe such as the *Bavares* of the early empire could have given their name to the whole, just as the term *Mauri*, our Moor, derives from what was in origin a specific group.
6 Gsell, *Histoire ancienne*, pp. 115f, citing the cosmography of Ethicus (ed. Riece) which talks of *gentes Mazices multas*; G. Camps, *Les Berbères: mémoire et identité* (Paris, 1987), pp. 66–7.
7 Leo Africanus, *Description de l'Afrique* (Paris, 1981), p. 15.
8 S. Chaker, *Encyclopédie berbère*, 1987, *s.v.* Amazig.
9 Al-Qāḍī al-Nuʿmān, 'Kitāb iftitāḥ al-daʿwa wa ibtidāʾ al-dawla', in F. Dachraoui (ed.), *Les Commencements du Califat fatimide au Maghreb* (Tunis, 1975), pp. 37–8, describing the preparation for the Faṭimid revolution in 910: see chapter 3, below.
10 M. Benabou, *La Résistance africaine à la Romanisation* (Paris, 1976).
11 A French Marxist scholar recently observed to one of us that the Berbers were a French invention.

12 Exceptions include the rather thin G.H. Bousquet, *Les Berbères*, 2nd edn (Paris, 1974), and W. Neumann, *Die Berber: Vielfalt und Einheit einer alten nordafrikanischen Kultur* (Cologne, 1983).

13 M. Mammeri, *Poèmes kabyles anciens* (Algiers, 1988), p. 9; H. Roberts, 'The unforeseen development of the Kabylie question in contemporary Algeria', *Government and Opposition*, 17 (1982), 312–25.

Chapter 1 Berbers in Antiquity

1 P.E. Smith, 'The late palaeolithic and epi-palaeolithic of northern Africa', *The Cambridge History of Africa* (Cambridge, 1982), vol. I, p. 404. The name 'Mekta-Afalou' is composite, deriving from the original type site, 'Mekta el-Arbi', and a site with much skeletal and cultural material at Afalou bou Rhummel, near Constantine in Algeria.

2 H. Camps-Fabrer, *Matière et art mobilier dans le préhistoire nord-africaine et saharienne* (Paris, 1986); idem, 'Le Sahara neolithique, centre d'art mobilier', in *Archéologie africaine et sciences de la nature* (Bordeaux, 1966). For the two rams' heads from Afalou, which remains largely unpublished, *Encyclopédie berbère* (Paris, 1984), vol. I, *s.v.* Afalou; L. Cavalli-Sforza, P. Menozzi and A. Piazza, *History and Geography of Human Genes* (Princeton, N.J., 1994), pp. 158f.

3 G. Camps, 'Avertissement', in *Encyclopédie berbère* (Paris, 1984), vol. I, p. 19; 'Beginnings of pastoralism and cultivation in north-west Africa and the Sahara: origins of the Berbers', in *Cambridge History of Africa*, vol. I, p. 616.

4 F. Wendorf and R. Schild, *Prehistory of the Eastern Sahara* (New York, 1980), pp. 267f; F. Wendorf, A. Close and R. Schild, 'Early domestic cattle and scientific methodology', in L. Krzyzaniak and M. Kobusiewicz (eds), *Environmental Change and Human Culture in the Nile Basin and Northeast Africa* (Poznan, 1989).

5 F. Marmier and G. Trécolle, 'La céramique néolithique du type "Hassi Mouillah", charactéristiques, diffusion, datation', *Archéologie africaine et sciences de la nature* (1986), 235–44. The increasing use of domesticated animals may be somewhat later, coinciding with the drying out of the Sahara: see, for example, B. Barich, *Archaeology and Environment in the Libyan Sahara* (Oxford, 1987). However, Wendorf, Close and Schild, 'Early domestic cattle', K. Banks, 'The appearance and spread of cattle-keeping in the Saharan North Africa', in Krzyzaniak and Kobusiewicz (eds), *Environmental Change*, pp. 57–67, and others, have produced strong arguments for the domestication of cattle – rather than sheep and goats as in the Near East – as early as 7,500BC. For the lack of links with the Near East, see A. Smith, 'The Near Eastern connection', in Krzyzaniak and Kobusiewicz (eds), *Environmental Change*. Skeletal material associated with an early neolithic site in the Fayum is of 'negroid' type: M. Henneberg, M. Kobusiewicz,

R. Schild and F. Wendorf, 'The early neolithic burial from the northern Fayum desert (Egypt)', in Krzyzaniak and Kobusiewicz (eds), *Environmental Change*, pp. 181–96.

6   C. McBurney, *The Hawa Fteah (Cyrenaica) and the Stone Age of the South East Mediterranean* (Cambridge, 1967).

7   C. Roubet, *Economie pastorale préagricole en Algérie orientale. Le Néolithique de tradition capsienne* (Paris, 1979). Here the idea that the neolithic in North Africa developed everywhere from the Capsian tradition is successfully dismantled.

8   C. Renfrew, *Archaeology and Language: The Puzzle of Indo-European Origins* (London, 1987), pp. 145f. The idea that it was farmers, and not simply farming, that moved from the Middle East is found in A. Ammerman and L. Cavalli-Sforza, *The Neolithic Transition in Europe* (Princeton, N.J., 1984).

9   The 'wave of advance' model for this diffusion is based, like Renfrew's, on the work of A. Ammerman and L. Cavalli-Sforza, 'The wave of advance model for the spread of agriculture in Europe', in C. Renfrew and K.L. Cooke (eds), *Transformations: Mathematical Approaches to Culture Change* (New York, 1979), pp. 175–294.

10   On climatic change, see B.D. Shaw, 'Climate, environment and history: the case of Roman North Africa', *World Archaeology*, 8 (1976), 379–403; J.A. Allan (ed.), *Sahara: Ecological Change and Early Economic History* (London, 1981); A. Muzzolini, *L'Art rupestre préhistorique des massifs centraux sahariens* (Oxford, 1986; BAR no. 318), pp. 49f.

11   A good and sceptical summary of the problem of the Berber languages is J. Bynon, 'The contribution of linguistics to history in the field of Berber studies', in D. Dalby (ed.), *Language and History in Africa* (London, 1970). For Afro-Asiatic languages, see M. Diakanoff, *Semito-Hamitic Languages: An Essay in Classification* (Moscow, 1965). On Berber, see L. Galand, *Langue et littérature berbères (vingt-cinq ans d'études)* (Paris, 1979); S. Chaker, *Textes en linguistique berbère. Introduction au domaine berbère* (Paris, 1984); idem, 'Les bases de l'apparentement chamito-sémitique du berbère: un faisceau d'indices convergents', *Etudes et documents berbères*, 7 (1990), 28–57.

12   The one experiment in glottochronology which has been carried out on Berber languages is David Hart's study of the three Berber languages of Morocco, which gave a rough date for the 'separation' of the language of the Sus from that of the Rif of around 1000 BC (*The Aith Waryaghar of the Moroccan Rif* (Tucson, Ariz., 1976), p. 339) – but no work has been done on the other languages, and we may suppose that the difference between the Rif, Kabylia and the Tuareg are much greater.

13   G. Souville, 'Témoignages sur l'Age du Bronze au Maghreb occidental', *Comptes rendues de l'Académie des Inscriptions* (1986), 97–114. The working of bronze is only found in Southern Morocco:

D. Grébénart, 'Le cuivre d'Agadez. Principaux types de fourneaux', *Archéologie africaine et sciences de la nature* (Bordeaux, 1986), pp. 473–87.

14   G. Camps, 'Beginnings of pastoralism and cultivation in north-west Africa and the Sahara: origins of the Berbers', in *Cambridge History of Africa*, vol. I, p. 616, although in his contemporary introduction to the *Encyclopédie berbère* he leans towards the view that the Berbers are entirely autochthonous. The political implications of these positions are interesting, and recall the debates in the 1930s on the origins of the Etruscans.

15   The major work is that of H. Lhote, *Les Gravures de l'Oued Djerat (Tassili-n-Ajjer)*, *Mémoires du Centre de recherches anthropologiques, préhistoriques et ethnographiques*, 25 (Algiers, 1976); see also idem, *A la découverte des fresques du Tassili* (Paris, 1958; reprinted 1973). Lhote, with his school, produced the basic classification of the frescos, which has been called into question by Muzzolini, *L'Art rupestre*; see also M. Hechd, 'Le chronologie relative des gravures rupestres de l'Atlas Saharien (Algérie) et le région de Djelfa', *Libyca* (1983), 30–1, 59–142. More recently A. Smith, 'New approaches to Saharan rock art of the "Bovidian" period', in Krzyzaniak and Kobusiewicz (eds), *Environmental Change*, and others have begun to investigate the social significance of the frescos.

16   M.C. Chamla, *Les Populations anciennes du Sahara et des régions limitrophes* (Paris, 1968).

17   G. Camps, 'Les Chars Sahariens. Images d'une société aristocratique', *Antiquités africaines*, 25 (1989), 11–42.

18   A. Smith, 'New approaches'.

19   P. Huard, J. Leclant and C. Allard-Huard, *La Culture des chasseurs du Nil et du Sahara*, *Mémoires du centre de recherches anthropologiques, préhistoriques et ethnographiques*, 29 (Paris, 1980). L. Allard-Huard and P. Huard, 'La femme au Sahara avant le désert', *Etudes scientifiques* (Sept. 1986), 1–36.

20   O. Bates, *The Eastern Libyans* (London, 1914); D. O'Connor, 'Egypt, 1552–664BC' in *Cambridge History of Africa*, vol. I, pp. 830–925.

21   Herodotus, *Histories*, 4.183.

22   G. Caputo, 'Parte seconda', in B. Pace, G. Caputo and S. Sergi, 'Scavi Sahariani: Ricerche nell'Uadi el Agial e nell'Oasi di Gat della missione Pace–Sergi–Caputo', *Monumenti Antichi, Accademia Nazionale dei Lincei*, XLI (1951), 151–551, esp. p. 211; C.M. Daniels, 'Fieldwork amongst the Garamantes', *Libyan Studies*, 20 (1988), 45–61, suggests that this figure could be safely doubled.

23   C.M. Daniels, *The Garamantes of Southern Libya* (Michigan, 1970, 1988); idem., 'Fieldwork among the Garamantes', *Libyan Studies*, 20 (1989), 45–61.

24   Pace et al., 'Scavi Sahariani'. For the palaeo-botanical evidence from Zinchecra, see M. Van der Veen, 'Garamantian agriculture', *Libyan Studies*, 23 (1992), 7–40.

25 Ptolemy, *Geography*, 1.8.4.

26 Livy, *History of Rome*, 34.62.12.

27 M. Fantar, *Kerkouane: cité punique du Cap Bon, Tunisie* (Tunis, 1986). On Punic North Africo, see M. Sznyier, 'Carthage et la civilization punique', in C. Nicolet (ed.), *Rome et la conquête du monde méditerranéen* (Paris, 1978); S. Lancel, *Carthage* (Paris, 1992).

28 Justin, *Historiae Philippicae*, 21.4.6; Diodorus Siculus, *Bibliotheca historica*, 20.8.4.

29 Hegesianax, *Fragmentum Historicorum Graecorum*, III. 50, no. 11, cited by J. Desanges, 'L'Afrique romaine et libyco-berbère' in C. Nicolet, *Rome et la conquête du monde méditerranéen*, p. 2.

30 On the coins, see H.R. Baldus, 'Die Münzprägung der numidischen Königreiche', in R. Horn and C. Rüger (eds), *Die Numider* (Bonn 1979), pp. 187–208.

31 Sallust, *Bellum Jugurthinum*, 5.4, and the discussion in Gsell, *Histoire ancienne*, vol. v, pp. 101–2. It is possible that the sub-groupings are geographical terms, perhaps meaning east and west.

32 Livy, *History of Rome*, 30.17.13: on gifts to client kings, see D. Braund, *Rome and the Friendly Kings* (London, 1984), pp. 27f.

33 Livy, *History of Rome*, 27.4.

34 F. Coarelli and Y. Thébert, 'Architecture funéraire et pouvoir. Réflexions sur l'hellenisme numide', *Mélanges de l'Ecole Française de Rome*, 100(2), (1988), 761–818. See also Gsell, *Histoire ancienne*, vol. VI, p. 136; G. Camps, 'Nouvelles observations sur l'architecture et l'age du Medracen, mausolée royal de Numidie', *Comptes rendues de l'Académie des Inscriptions* (1973), 470–516.

35 On the royal tombs the best summary is F. Rakob, 'Numidische Königsarchitektur in Nordafrika', in Horn and Rüger (eds), *Die Numider*, pp. 119–71, with all previous bibliography.

36 Caputo, 'Parte seconda', in Pace et al., 'Scavi Sahariani', 251–66.

37 N. Ferchiou, 'L'habitat fortifié pre-impérial en Tunisie antique: aperçus sur le typologie des sites perchés et des sites de versant, illustrés par quelques exemples à Carthage et sa territoire dans l'antiquité', *Antiquités africaines*, 26 (1990), 43–86.

38 Livy, *History of Rome*, 30. 13.

39 R. Rebuffat, 'Les fermiers du desert', *L'Africa romana*, V (1987), 33–68; R.B. Hitchner, 'The Kasserine archaeological survey, 1982–1986', *Antiquités africaines*, 24 (1988), 7–41; and 'The organization of rural settlement in the Cillium-Thelepte region (Kasserine, Central Tunisia)', *L'Africa romana*, VI (1988), 387–402; R.B. Hitchner, 'The Kasserine archaeological survey', *Antiquités africaines*, 26 (1990), 231–58. No early sites have been found on this project.

40 A. Jodin, 'Volubilis avant les Romains. Dix années de recherches dans la cité punique', *Archeologia*, 102 (1977), 6–19.

41 S. Girard, 'Banasa pré-romaine: un état de la question', *Antiquités africaines*, 20 (1984), 11–94.

42 A plan is given in C. Rüger (1979), 'Siga, die Hauptstadt des Syphax', in Horn and Rüger (eds), *Die Numider*, pp. 181–4, esp. p. 183.

43 Personal observation.

44 A. Berthier, 'Un habitat punique à Constantine', *Antiquités africaines*, 16 (1980), 13–26.

45 Diodorus Siculus, *Bibliotheca historica*, 24.

46 Masinissa is said to have left 10,000 *plethra* of land to each of the ten sons who survived him, together with all that was necessary for its cultivation (Diodorus Siculus, *Bibliotheca historica*, 32.16.4). On Varro's figure of 1 *plethra* = 10,000 square feet (*De re rustica*, 1.10) this gives 89.4 square kilometres. All these estates were apparently found in Africa Vetus, in territory that was formerly under Carthaginian control.

47 E. Gellner, *Nations and Nationalism* (Oxford, 1983).

48 Pliny, *Natural History*, 5.1. Tribes named in classical authors have been exhaustively catalogued by J. Desanges, *Catalogue des tribus africaines de l'antiquité classique à l'Ouest du Nil* (Dakar, 1962).

49 M. Sahlins, 'The segmentary lineage: an organization of predatory expansion', *American Anthropologist*, 63 (1961), 322–45.

50 R. Montagne, *The Berbers*, trans. D. Seddon (London, 1973), pp. 45f.

51 For example, C. Renfrew and J. Cherry (eds), *Peer Polity Interaction and Socio-political Change* (Cambridge, 1986); on state formation, see C. Ward Gill and J. Patterson, 'State formation and uneven development', in J. Gledhill et al. (eds), *State and Society: The Emergence and Development of Social Hierarchy and Political Centralization* (Oxford, 1988).

52 Strabo, *Geography*, 17.3.19.

53 Livy, *History of Rome*, 25.11.7; M. Rostovtzeff, 'Numidian horsemen on Canossa vases', *American Journal of Archaeology*, 50 (1946), 265–70; F. Bertrand, 'A propos du cavalier de Simitthus', *Antiquités africaines*, 22 (1986), 57–76.

54 Pomponius Mela, 1.8.45; G. Camps, 'Funerary monuments with attached chapels from the Northern Sahara', *African Archaeological Review*, 4 (1986), 151–64.

55 M. Luni, 'Il santuario rupestre libyco delle immagini a Slonta (Cirenaica)', *Cirene e i Libyi* (Quaderni di Archeologia della Libia), 12 (1987), 415–18, a detailed publication on which this brief analysis is based, although I would suggest a Hellenistic rather than a Roman date for the whole.

56 On this pattern, see J. Friedman and M. Rowlands, 'Notes towards an epigenetic model of the evolution of civilisation', in J. Friedman and M. Rowlands (eds), *The Evolution of Social Systems* (London, 1979), pp. 201–76. On king worship, see Gsell, *Histoire ancienne*, vol. VI, pp. 192f.

57 Translated into English from *Recueil des inscriptions libyques*, no. 2,

with the correction of 'prefect of 50' to prefect in charge of construction' suggested by S. Chaker, 'Une inscription libyique du Musée des Antiquités d'Alger', *Libyca*, xxv (1977), 193–202.

58 M. Benabou, *La Résistance africaine à la romanisation* (Paris, 1976), pp. 479f.

59 Dating is very difficult: the earliest securely dated Tifinagh inscription from the Sahara comes from the fifth century AD tomb of Tin Hinan, where broken pieces of the inscription are reused in the construction of the building.

60 Strabo, *Geography*, 17.3.9; 25.2.

61 Apuleius, *Apologia*, 24.1.

62 The echo of this treachery lives on in the social memory of Kabylia, where a traitor is commonly referred to as 'Bexha', a deformation of the name Bocchus (personal communication, Ali Ait Kaci).

63 Sallust, *Bellum Jugurthinum*, 54f.

64 Pausanius, *Description of Greece*, 1.17.2; quoted in D. Braund, *Rome and the Friendly Kings* (London, 1984), p. 78.

65 P. Leveau, *Caesarea de Mauretanie* (Rome, 1984), pp. 25–80.

66 Ibid., pp. 143–208.

67 Dio Cassius, *History*, 55.28.

68 Tacitus, *Annals*, 2.52.

69 Braund, *Rome and the Friendly Kings*, p. 139.

70 The original rule may have been that the eldest agnate succeeded: at the death of Masinissa's father, Gaia, the kingdom passed to Gaia's brother, Oezalces, and from him to his son, Capussa, who died in combat. Only then did it return to Gaia's line. C. Saumagne, 'Etudes d'histoire social et politique relative à la province romaine d'Afrique de Charles Saumagne', *Cahiers de Tunisie*, 10 (1962), 301–71, p. 366, suggests that Scipio Aemilianus engineered the change in custom.

71 E. Gellner, *Saints of the Atlas* (London, 1969), p. 56.

72 Gsell, *Histoire ancienne*, vol. v, pp. 45–6.

Chapter 2   The Empire and the Other

1 Unfortunately, there is very little in English, and much is out of date. An exception is S. Raven, *Rome in Africa* (London, 1993). For a general history, see P. Romanelli, *Storia delle province romane dell'Africa* (Rome, 1959); for the early empire see M. Benabou, *La Résistance africaine à la romanisation* (Paris, 1976). G.-C. Picard, *La Civilization de l'afrique romaine*, 2nd edn (Paris, 1990); for the late empire, see B. Warmington, *The North African Provinces from Diocletian to the Vandal Conquest* (Cambridge, 1954); C. Courtois, *Les Vandales et l'Afrique* (Paris, 1955); for Byzantine Africa, see C. Diehl, *L'Afrique byzantine* (New York, 1896).

2 *Corpus Inscriptionum Latinarum*, VIII, 16159.

3 Ibid., VIII, 22729; M. Corbier, 'Les familles clarissimes d'Afrique

proconsulaire (Ier–IIIe siècle)', *Epigrafia e ordine senatorio, Tituli* v, 705–78.

4 *Année epigraphique*, 1979, p. 679; J. Desanges, 'Un *princeps gentis* à Sétif', *Bulletin du Comité des travaux historiques*, 12 (1980), 121–7; T. Kotula, '*Principes gentis* et *principes civitatis* en Afrique romaine', *EOS*, 55 (1955), 363–90.

5 Tr. J. Oliver, 'The text of the *Tabula Banasitana*, AD177', *American Journal of Philology*, 93 (1972), 336–40, esp. p. 339. On the *Tabula Banasitana*, see W. Seston and M. Euzennat, 'Un dossier de la Chancellerie romaine: la *Tabula Banasitana*', *CRAI* (1971), 468–90. On the Zegrenses, see M. Euzennat, 'Les Zegrenses', in *Mélanges Seston* (Paris, 1974), pp. 175–81.

6 N. Ferchiou, 'Le paysage funéraire pre-romain dans deux regions céréalières de Tunisie antique (Fahs-Bou Arada et Tebourba Mateur): les tombeaux monumentaux', *Antiquités africaines*, 23 (1987), 13–70.

7 It should be noted that the *Tabula Banasitana*, certainly the property of the family of Julian, was found inside the city and not in some tribal village.

8 To Optatus of Mila, *Corpus Scriptorum Ecclesiasticorum Latinorum*, 26.185, quoted by P.A. Février, 'L'Histoire Auguste et le Maghreb', *Antiquités africaines*, 22 (1986), 115–40, esp. p. 119.

9 Benabou, *Résistance africaine*, pp. 522–5; A.R. Birley, *Septimius Severus the African Emperor* (London, 1971).

10 *Scriptores Historiae Augustae*, Septimus Severus, 19.10; Geta, 2.6.

11 Y. Le Bohec, *La Troisième Légion Auguste* (Etudes d'Antiquités Africaines) (Paris, 1989); E. Fentress, *Numidia and the Roman Army*, BAR 53 (Oxford, 1979) p. 176f.

12 Ferchiou, 'Le paysage funéraire pré-romain'; N. Ferchiou, 'L'habitat fortifié pré-impérial en Tunisie antique: aperçus sur le typologie des sites perchés et des sites de versant, illustrés par quelques exemples à Carthage et sa territoire dans l'Antiquité', *Antiquités africaines*, 24 (1988).

13 Vitruvius, *De Architectura*, 7.3., 24f.

14 Pliny, *Natural History*, 18.51.188.

15 J. Kolendo, *Le Colonat en Afrique sous le Haut-Empire* (Paris, 1976); D. Kehoe, *The Economics of Agriculture on Roman Imperial Estates in North Africa* (Gottingen, 1985).

16 The UNESCO Libyan Valleys survey: the English–Libyan team was directed by G.D.B. Jones and Graeme Barker: G. Barker et al., 'UNESCO Libyan Valleys survey 6: Investigations of a Romano-Libyan farm', *Libyan Studies*, 15 (1984), 1–44; D. Buck, J. Burns and D. Mattingly, 'Archaeological sites of the Bir Scedua Basin: settlements and cemeteries', *Libyan Studies*, 14 (1983), 39–68; D.J. Mattingly, 'New perspectives in the agricultural development of the jebel and pre-desert in Roman Tripolitania', *Revue de l'Occident musulman et de la Méditerranée*, 40–1, 46–65. The French–Libyan team was directed by

R. Rebuffat: see R. Rebuffat, 'Les fermiers du desert', *L'Africa romana*, v (1987), 33–68.

17 On the economics of olive cultivation, see D.J. Mattingly, 'Libyans and the "Limes": culture and society in Roman Tripolitania', *Antiquités africaines*, **23** (1986), 71–94. We learn from Apuleius that his wife, Pudentilla, held estates outside of Oea (Tripoli) which were worked by large numbers of slaves (*Apologia*, 93).

18 G.W.W. Barker and G.D.B. Jones, 'The UNESCO Libyan Valleys Survey VI: Investigations of a Romano-Libyan farm', *Libyan Studies*, **15–16** (1984–5), 1–44; Mattingly, 'Libya and the "Limes"'; Rebuffat, 'Les fermiers du desert'.

19 Rebuffat, 'Les fermiers du desert'.

20 Ibid.

21 O. Brogan and D. Smith, *Ghirza: A Libyan Settlement in the Roman Period* (Tripoli, 1984).

22 The inscriptions from Ghirza are discussed by J. Reynolds in ibid., pp. 260–3.

23 R.B. Hitchner, 'The Kasserine Archaeological Survey, 1982–1986', *Antiquités africaines*, **24** (1988), 7–41; 'The organization of rural settlement in the Cillium–Thelepte region (Kasserine, Central Tunisia)', *L'Africa Romana*, VI (1988), 387–402; 'The Kasserine Archaeological Survey', *Antiquités africaines*, **26** (1990), 231–58.

24 Hitchner, 'Kasserine Archaeological Survey, 1982–1986', 39.

25 P.A. Février, 'Inscriptions inédites relatives aux domaines de la région de Sétif', in *Mélanges Piganiol*, ed. R. Chevallier (Paris, 1966), pp. 217–28. On the economy of the area, see E. Fentress, 'The economy of an inland city: Sétif', in *L'Afrique dans l'Occident romain (Iᵉʳ Siècle av.J.-C.–IVᵉ siècle ap.J.-C.)*, CEFR, **134** (1990), 117–28.

26 P. Leveau, *Caesarea de Maurétanie* (Rome, 1984).

27 These villages may also have been known as *castella*. For discussion, see P. Leveau, 'Un cantonnement de tribu au sud-est de Caesarea de Maurétanie: borne de Sidi-Bouzid', *Revue des études anciennes*, **76** (1974), 293–304.

28 R. Rebuffat, 'Recherches sur le bassin du Sebou', *Comptes rendues de l'Académie des Inscriptions*, 1986, 633–61.

29 *Corpus Inscriptionum Latinarum*, VIII, 11824.

30 The best treatment of this subject is Benabou, *Résistance africaine*.

31 For a comprehensive study of this survey, see P. Trousset, 'Les bornes du Bled Segui, nouveaux aperçus sur la centuriation romaine du Sud tunisien', *Antiquités africaines*, **12** (1978), 165–88.

32 Benabou, *Résistance africaine*, pp. 62–84; E. Fentress, *Numidia and the Roman Army*, BAR 53 (Oxford, 1979), pp. 66–8, 76.

33 S. Gsell, *Histoire ancienne de l'Afrique du Nord* (Paris, 1927), vol. v, pp. 63–6; T.R.S. Broughton, *The Romanization of Africa Proconsularis* (London, 1929), p. 118. For Sicca, see *Corpus Inscriptionum Latinarum*, VIII, 5880; and for *castellum* Tituli, ibid.,

27828. A slightly different system existed in the region of the Aures mountains, where inscriptions generally mention two *magistri* rather than only one.

34 Ibid., VIII, 8379; and below p. 93.

35 Ibid., V, 5267.

36 *Année épigraphique* (1973), 654; P. Leveau, 'L'Aile II des Thraces, Mazices et *Praefecti Gentis*', *Antiquités africaines*, 7 (1973), 153–91.

37 On prefects in the late empire, see C. Lepelley, 'Le préfecture de tribu dans l'Afrique du Bas-Empire', in *Mélanges d'histoire ancienne offerts à William Seston* (Paris, 1974), 175–86.

38 P.A. Février, 'L'art funéraire et les images des chefs indigènes dans la Kabylie antique', in *Actes du premier congrès d'études des cultures Méditerranéennes d'influence arabo-berbère* (Malta, 1972), pp. 152–74. There remains some doubt as to the dating of the stele, which Camps suggests dates to the fifth century BC: Camps art. 'Abizar', *Encyclopédie Berbère*, vol. I (1984).

39 On the Baquates, see E. Frézouls, 'Les *Baquates* et le province romaine de Tingitane', *Bulletin d'archéologie marocaine*, 2 (1957), 65–115; P. Romanelli, 'Le iscrizione Volubilitane dei Baquati e i rapporti di Roma con le tribu indigene dell'Africa', in *Hommages à A. Grenier*, ed. Renard (Paris, 1962), pp. 1347–66; Benabou, *Résistance africaine*, pp. 144f; M. Sigman, 'The Romans and the indigenous tribes of Mauretania Tingitana', *Historia*, 26 (1977), 415–39; B.D. Shaw, 'Autonomy and tribute: mountain and plain in Mauretania Tingitana', *Revue de l'Occident musulman et de la Méditerranée*, 40–1, 66–86. Romanelli, followed by Shaw, is certainly right in seeing these altars as formal renewals of previous treaties, rather than as proof of eleven revolts.

40 The French adopted a similar practice in colonial Algeria, giving a newly appointed Qadi three *burnus*, one red, one white and one blue: B. Etienne, 'Clientelism in Algeria', in E. Gellner and J. Waterbury (eds), *Patrons and Clients* (London, 1977), pp. 291–307, esp. p. 295.

41 Procopius, *Bellum Vandalicum*, xxv. 58.

42 Brogan and Smith, *Ghirza*, pp. 223–4.

43 Many are known from the cemetery of Bir Ed Dreder, on the Tarhuna plateau: see R.G. Goodchild, *Libyan Studies* (London, 1976), pp. 59–71. Goodchild suggests that these had specific military responsibilities on the *limes*, but Smith points out that the word might simply mean 'chief of a tribe' (Brogan and Smith, *Ghirza*, p. 229). See also Lepelley, 'Le préfecture de tribu'.

44 Brogan and Smith, *Ghirza*, pp. 80–8. It is possible that the rite practised here involved severed human heads: ibid., p. 82.

45 Y. Moderan, 'De Bellis Libycis: Berbères et Byzantins en Afrique au VIᵉ siècle', unpublished doctoral thesis, Universite de Paris X, 1990, p. 232.

46 Only two churches are known from the Wadi Sofeggin: see A. Di Vita, 'La diffusione di Cristianesimo nell'interno della Tripolitania attraverso i monumenti, e sua sopravivenza nella Tripolitania araba', *Quaderni di Archeologia della Libya*, 5 (1967), 121–42.

47 R. Marichal, 'Les ostraca de Bu Njem', *Classical Review* (1979), 436–52.

48 P. Trousset, *Recherches sur le limes Tripolitanus du Chott Djerid à la frontière tuniso-libyenne* (Paris, 1974); ibid., 'Les Milliaires de Chebika (Sud tunisien)', *Antiquités africaines*, 15 (1980), 135–54; Fentress, *Numidia and the Roman Army*, pp. 111–20; R. Rebuffat, 'Au-delà des camps romains d'Afrique mineure, renseignement, contrôle, pénétration', *Aufstieg und Niedergang der Römische Welt*, II, *Principat*, 10 (2), 474–513. In a decree of the emperor Anastasius I we read that the soldiers of the fortresses should keep watch over the comings and goings along the roads, but that the Maces, if they had letters from the prefect, were authorized access to the cities of the Pentapolis (cited in Rebuffat, 'Les fermiers du désert', 67).

49 *Corpus Inscriptionum Latinarum*, VIII, 8369.

50 Benabou, *Résistance africaine*, pp. 127f.

51 *Corpus Inscriptionum Latinarum*, VIII, 4508.

52 In a letter of AD418 St Augustine talks of the tribes 'among whom the evangelist has never been preached: we learn of this from those who have been brought here as captives and slaves of the Romans' (Letter 119, *Corpus Scriptorum Ecclesiasticorum Latinorum*, VII, 243–91).

53 *Scriptores Historiae Augustae*, Septimius Severus, 18.3; Aurelius Victor, 20. 19.

54 R. Rebuffat, 'Notes sur le camp romain de Gholaia (Bu Ngem)', *Libyan Studies*, 20 (1989), 155–62.

55 G. Camps, 'Les Bavares', *Revue africaine*, 99 (1955), 241–88; Benabou, *Résistance africaine*, pp. 214f.

56 C. Lepelley, *Les Cités de l'Afrique romaine au Bas-Empire* (Paris, 1979).

57 M. Blanchard-Lemée, *Maisons à mosaiques du quartier central de Djemila (Cuicul)* (Etudes d'antiquités africaines) (Aix-en-Provence, 1976).

58 The names Monnica and Nonnica are found on tombstones in the Libyan language – as such, Monnica is the only Berber name commonly used in English. For the family background of Augustine, see C. Lepelley, 'Spes Saeculi: le milieu social d'Augustin et ses ambitions séculières avant sa conversion', *Studia ephemeridis 'Augustinianum'*, 24 (1987), 99–117.

59 Letter 24*; C. Lepelley, 'Liberté, colonat et esclavage d'après la Lettre 24*: la juridiction épiscopale "de liberali causa"', *Les Lettres de Saint Augustin découvertes par Johannes Divjak* (Paris, 1982), pp. 331–42.

60 A. Ait Kaci, N. Bounssair and E. Fentress, 'Prospections à Zana: rapport préliminaire', *Bulletin d'archéologie algérienne* (1993), supp.

7. Hitchner, 'The Kasserine Archaeological Survey, 1982–1986'; 'Organization of rural settlement'; 'The Kasserine Archaeological Survey'.

61 D. Vera, 'Terra e lavoro nell'Africa Romana', *Studi Storici*, 4 (1988), 967–92.

62 Ammianus Marcellinus, 29.5.2; *Inscriptiones latinae christianae veteres*, 1822.

63 *Comptes Rendus de l'Académie des Inscriptions* (1901) p. 170: *Inscriptiones Latinae Selectae*, 9351; J. F. Matthews, 'Mauritania in Amïanus and the Notitia', in R. Goodburn and P. Bartholomew (eds), *Aspects of the Notitia Dignitatum, BAR* suppl., Series 15 (Oxford, 1976) pp. 157–86, p. 175f.

64 J. Matthews, *The Roman Empire of Ammianus* (London, 1989), pp. 369f.

65 On Gildo, see Y. Moderan, 'Gildon, les Maures et l'Afrique', *Mélanges de l'Ecole française de Rome*, 101 (1989), 821–72, with previous bibliography. On coins, see C. Courtois, *Les Vandales et l'Afrique* (Paris, 1955).

66 Nubel himself sprang from the Iubaleni, and the regal names of the tribe seem to have been in some way emblematic, based on the idea of the appropriation of the royal ancestor by the tribal chief.

67 Ait Kaci et al., 'Prospections à Zana'.

68 A.F. Elmayer, 'The Centenaria of Roman Tripolitania', *Libyan Studies*, 16 (1985), 77–85.

69 A.A. 22.63.

70 Ammianus Marcellinus, 28.6.

71 Herodotus, *History*, 4.172; Moderan, *De Bellis Libycis*, pp. 171f. The following account of the war against the Austuriani owes much to Moderan's work, esp. pp. 226f.

72 *Inscriptions of Roman Tripolitania*, 480; and J. Reynolds, 'The Austuriani and Tripolitania in the early fifth century', *Libyan Studies*, 8 (1977), 13 *(Austurianorum furore repraessa)*.

73 Corippus, *Johannes*, 3.195–6.

74 On Tripolitania, see Moderan, *De Bellis Libycis*, p. 236.

75 Brogan and Smith, *Ghirza*, p. 231; Moderan, *De Bellis Libycis*, p. 239.

76 Procopius, *Bellum Vandalicum*, 55.21.

77 Moderan, *De Bellis Libycis*, p. 248; see also Mattingly, 'Libyans and the "Limes"'.

78 Courtois, *Les Vandales*, pp. 333f.

79 *Corpus Inscriptionum Latinarum* VIII, 9835; *Année Epigraphique* (1945) p. 97. See most recently P. Morizot, 'L'Elogium de Masties', *Antiquités Africaines*, 25 (1989) pp. 263–84.

80 G. Camps, '*Rex Gentium Maurorum et Romanorum*: recherches sur les royaumes de Maurétanie des VI et VII siècles', *Antiquités africaines*, 20 (1984), 183–218.

81 F.K. Kadra, *Les Djedars: monuments funéraires berbères* (Algiers, 1983).

82 Camps, '*Rex gentium*', 202.

83 Procopius, *Bellum Vandalicum*, IV, xiii, 8.

84 Among those in favour of substantial continuity into the Arab period are J. Durliat, *Les Dédicaces d'ouvrage de défense dans l'Afrique byzantine* (Rome, 1981), and Y. Thébert and J.-L. Biget, 'L'Afrique après la disparition de la cité classique: cohérence et ruptures dans l'histoire maghrèbine', *L'Afrique dans l'Occident Romain, Collection de l'Ecole française de Rome*, 134 (Rome, 1990), pp. 575–602.

85 A. Akerraz, 'Note sur l'enceinte tardive de Volubilis', *Bulletin archéologique de Comité des travaux historiques*, N.S. (1983), 429–38.

86 H. Hurst and S. Roskams (eds), *Excavations at Carthage: the British Mission* (Sheffield, 1984), vol. I, 1, pp. 42f. For an argument for substantial continuity between Roman and mediaeval North Africa, see Thébert and Biget, *L'Afrique après la disparition de la cité classique*.

Chapter 3   The Unification of North Africa by Islam

1 H.T. Norris, *The Berbers in Arabic Literature* (London and New York, 1982).

2 Ibn Khaldūn: *Kitāb al-'Ibar*, 7 vols (Būlāq, 1867), variously reprinted; cf. A. Al-Azmeh, *Ibn Khaldūn in Modern Scholarship* (London, 1981), Bibliography.

3 Ibn Khaldūn, *Tārīkh al-duwal al-islamiyya bi 'l-Maghrib*, ed. Baron de Slane, 2 vols (Algiers, 1847); *Histoire des Berbères*, tr. Baron de Slane 4 vols (Paris, 1852 etc.); rev. edn (Paris, 1925 etc.).

4 Ibn 'Idhārī: *Al-Bayān al-mughrib fī akhbār al-Andalus wa 'l-Maghrib*, ed. G.S. Colin and E. Lévi-Provençal, vol. I (Leiden, 1948), p. 27.

5 Camps's suggestion that the term Barbar derives from Bavares is wholly plausible, but only perhaps because this proper tribal name became conflated with the common noun *barbarus* in the minds of the civilized Latins, just as Tatar became Tartar in the minds of mediaeval Europeans, who equated the Mongols with the devils of Hell.

6 Cf. R. Brunschvig, 'Ibn 'Abdalh'akam et la conquête de l'Afrique du Nord par les Arabes', in R. Brunschvig, *Etudes sur l'Islam classique et l'Afrique du Nord* (London, 1986), xi; and M. Brett, 'The Arab conquest and the rise of Islam in North Africa', in *Cambridge History of Africa* (Cambridge, 1978), vol. II, pp. 505–7.

7 E.F. Gautier, *Le Passé de l'Afrique du Nord. Les siècles obscurs* (Paris, 1952), p. 268. Cf. Ch.-A. Julien, *Histoire de l'Afrique du Nord*, 2nd edn (Paris, 1951–2), vol. II, pp. 24–6; Eng. tr., *History of North Africa from the Arab Conquest to 1830* (London, 1970), pp. 10–11, 16–17. M. Talbi, *Encyclopaedia of Islam*, 2nd edn, *s.v.* 'Kusayla', is strongly in favour of a Mauretanian origin at Tlemcen.

8 For the tradition that the *takirwan* was a second foundation a mile or two away from the *qayrawān*, cf. 'Kusayla', ibid.
9 Cf. Talbi, *Encyclopaedia of Islam*, *s.v.* 'Kāhina'. The Jewish legend is discounted by H.Z. Hirschberg, 'The problem of the Judaized Berbers', *Journal of African History*, 4 (1963), 313–39; Brett, 'The Arab conquest', p. 509.
10 Ibn 'Abd al-Hakam, *Kitāb Futūḥ Miṣr*, ed. and tr. C.C. Torrey (New Haven, 1922); rev. edn and French tr. of part dealing with North Africa and Spain by A. Gateau, *Conquête de l'Afrique du Nord et de l'Espagne* (Algiers, 1942); 2nd rev. edn, 1948.
11 Ibn 'Abd al-Ḥakam, *Conquête de l'Afrique du Nord*, pp. 78–9.
12 Ibn 'Idhārī, *Bayān*, vol. I, p. 38.
13 Ibid., p. 42; Ibn 'Abd al-Ḥakam, *Conquête de l'Afrique du Nord*, pp. 88–9.
14 Ibid., p. 43.
15 Cf. R. Collins, *The Arab Conquest of Spain, 710–797* (Oxford, 1989).
16 Despite the attempt of E. Lévi-Provençal, 'Un nouveau récit de la conquête de l'Afrique du Nord par les Arabes', *Arabica*, 1 (1954), 17–52, to substantiate his conquest of the High Atlas. Cf. the fundamental article of Brunschvig, 'Ibn 'Abdalh'akam et la conquête', and the conclusions of Brett, 'The Arab conquests', 505–6.
17 Ibn 'Idhārī, *Bayān*, vol. I, pp. 36–7.
18 Cf., for example, M. Talbi, *L'Emirat Aghlabide* (Paris, 1966), p. 19.
19 Ibn Sallām, *Kitāb Ibn Sallām*, ed. W. Schwartz and Sālim ibn Ya'qūb (Wiesbaden, 1986), pp. 161–5.
20 Brett, 'The Arab conquest', 517.
21 Ibn 'Abd al-Ḥakam, *Conquête de l'Afrique du Nord*, pp. 112–15.
22 Cf. Collins, *Arab Conquest of Spain*, pp. 88–90.
23 Ibn 'Abd al-Ḥakam, *Conquête de l'Afrique du Nord*, pp. 128–9.
24 Cf. G. Marçais, *La Berbérie musulmane et l'Orient au Moyen Age* (Paris, 1946), ch. 2, 'La renaissance du IXᵉ siècle'; despite its age, this work is still the best history of North Africa in the period seventh to thirteenth centuries. See also idem, 'La Berbérie au IXᵉ siècle d'après El-Ya'qoubī', in idem, *Mélanges d'histoire et d'archéologie de l'Occident musulman*, 2 vols (Algiers, 1957).
25 Al-Ya'qubī, *Kitāb al-buldān*, in N. Levtzion and J.F.P. Hopkins (eds and trans.), *Corpus of Early Arabic Sources for West African History* (Cambridge, 1981), p. 22. Cf. M. Brett, 'Ifrīqiya as a market for trans-Saharan trade', *Journal of African History*, 10 (1969), 347–64.
26 Cf. R.I. and S.K. McIntosh, 'The inland Niger Delta before the empire of Mali', *Journal of African History*, 22 (1981), 19–22; E.A. McDougall, 'The view from Awdaghust', *Journal of African History*, 26 (1985), 1–31.
27 Cf. M. Lombard, *The Golden Age of Islam* (Amsterdam, Oxford and New York, 1975); K.N. Chaudhuri, *Trade and Civilisation in the Indian Ocean* (Cambridge, 1985), chs 1 and 2.

28 Cf. R. Bulliet, *The Camel and the Wheel* (Cambridge, Mass., 1975); J. Devisse, 'Trade and trade routes in West Africa', *UNESCO General History of Africa*, vol. III (Paris, London and Berkeley, 1988), ch. 14.

29 Al-Ya'qūbī, *Kitāb al-buldān*, ed. de Goeje, *Bibliotheca geographorum arabicorum*, vol. VII (Leiden, 1892); G. Wiet (trans.), *Les Pays* (Cairo, 1937).

30 Cf. Chaudhuri, *Trade and Civilisation in the Indian Ocean*, ch. 2.

31 Cf. M. Brett, 'The Islamisation of Morocco. From the Arabs to the Almoravids', *Morocco*, 2 (1992), 57–71.

32 Ibid., 63, 65.

33 Al-Bakrī, *Description de l'Afrique septentrionale*, ed. and trans. M. de Slane, 2nd edn (Paris, 1913; reprinted 1965), p. 160, trans. p. 304.

34 Cf. G. Marçais, *Encyclopaedia of Islam*, 1st edn, *s.v.* 'Ribāṭ'.

35 Al-Bakrī, *Description*, p. 161, trans. p. 305.

36 Ibid., pp. 148, 150, trans. pp. 282–3, 286.

37 Ibid., p. 153, trans. pp. 291–2.

38 Cf. M. Brett, 'Islam and trade in the *Bilād al-Sūdān*', *Journal of African History*, 24 (1983), 431–40.

39 Al-Bakrī, *Description*, pp. 134–41, trans. pp. 259–71; Norris, *Berbers in Arabic Literature*, pp. 92–104.

40 Above, p. 63; C. Courtois, *Vandales et l'Afrique* (Paris, 1955), p. 121.

41 For the Fatimid revolution, cf. Qāḍī al-Nu'mān, *Iftitāḥ*; Talbi, *L'Emirat Aghlabide*, pp. 537–692; H. Halm, *Das Reich des Mahdi* (Munich, 1991).

42 Cf. H.R. Idris, *La Berbérie orientale sous les Zirides* (Paris, 1962).

43 Cf. Le général L. de Beylié, *La Kalaa des Beni-Hammad* (Paris, 1909); L. Golvin, *Le Maghreb centrale à l'époque des Zirides* (Paris, 1957).

44 'An example of a secondary cultural frontier': F. Braudel, *The Mediterranean and the Mediterranean World in the Age of Philip II*, 2 vols (London, 1972), pp. 771–3.

45 Cf. M. Brett, 'The Fatimid revolution and its aftermath in North Africa', *Cambridge History of Africa* (Cambridge, 1978), vol. II, ch. 10.

46 Ibn 'Idhārī, *Al-Bayān al-mughrib*, vol. III (Paris, 1930), p. 48.

47 Ibid., p. 276, explains Dhū 'l-Nūn, lit. 'fishman', 'fishy', as a deformation of the normal Berber name Zannūn.

48 For details cf. Idris, *La Berbérie orientale*; E. Lévi-Provençal, *Histoire de l'Espagne musulmane*, vol. I (Cairo, 1944); D. Wasserstein, *The Rise and Fall of the Party-Kings* (Princeton, N.J., 1985).

49 By E. Lourie, 'A society organized for war: medieval Spain', *Past and Present*, 35 (1966), 54–76.

50 For the rise of the Christian kingdoms, cf. J.F. O'Callaghan, *A History of Medieval Spain* (Ithaca, N.Y., 1975).

51 With its extensive quotations, the best description of the Almoravids is Norris, *Berbers in Arabic Literature*, ch. 7; see also his *Saharan Myth*

and Saga (Oxford, 1972); sources for the West African side of the movement are translated in Levtzion and Hopkins, *Corpus of Early Arabic Sources*. For Ibn Yāsīn, cf. H.T. Norris, "'Abdullah ibn Yāsīn et la dynamique conquérante des Almoravides', in Ch.-A. Julien *et al.* (eds), *Les Africains*, 12 vols (Paris, 1977–8), vol. XII, pp. 15–39; idem, 'New evidence on the life of 'Abdullah b. Yāsīn and the origins of the Almoravid movement', *Journal of African History*, 12 (1971), 255–68; Brett, 'Islam and trade'.

52 Levtzion and Hopkins, *Corpus of Early Arabic Sources*, pp. 74–5.

53 Ibn Ḥawqal, in ibid., pp. 46–51; al-Bakrī, ibid., pp. 66–9, 73–4; cf. McDougall, 'View from Awdaghust'.

54 Both the vocalization and the location are unknown: al-Bakrī in Levtzion and Hopkins, *Corpus of Early Arabic Sources*, p. 73; cf. Norris, *Saharan Myth and Saga*, p. 107.

55 Al-Bakrī in Levtzion and Hopkins, *Corpus of Early Arabic Sources*, p. 74: cf. A. Benachenhou, 'Sîdî 'Abdallâh Moul l-Gâra ou 'Abdallâh ibn Yâsîn', *Hespéris*, 33 (1946), 406–13.

56 Disputed on the grounds of lack of evidence by H.J. Fisher and D.C. Conrad, 'The conquest that never was: Ghana and the Almoravids, 1076', *History in Africa*, 9 (1982), 21–59; 10 (1983), 53–78.

57 Cf. E. Lévi-Provençal, 'La fondation de Marrakech (462–1070)', in G. Marçais, *Mélanges d'histoire et d'archéologie de l'Occident musulman*, 2 vols (Algiers, 1957), vol. II, pp. 117–20.

58 M. Brett, *The Moors: Islam in the West* (London, 1980), p. 25; cf. Ibn 'Idhārī in Levtzion and Hopkins, *Corpus of Early Arabic Sources*, pp. 225–8, and ibid., Index, *s.v.* 'Aghmāt'.

59 Al-Idrīsī, *Nuzhat al-mushtāq*, in ibid., p. 128.

60 Cf. A. Launois, 'Influence des docteurs malékites sur le monnayage ziride de type sunnite et sur celui des Almoravides', *Arabica*, 11 (1964), 127–50.

61 Levtzion and Hopkins, *Corpus of Early Arabic Sources*, p. 72.

62 Cf. V. Lagardère, *Le vendredi de Zallaga: 23 octobre 1086* (Paris, 1989); reviewed P. Guichard, 'Pouvoirs et sociétés islamiques dans l'Espagne médiévale', *Annales ESC*, 46 (1991), 1122–6. The developed tactics of the Almoravids are described by the contemporary Andalusian writer al-Ṭurtūshī: *Sirāj al-mulūk*, Cairo (1298H), pp. 298ff; cf. R. Levi, *The Social Structure of Islam* (Cambridge, 1957), pp. 434, 456.

63 Al-Marrākushī, *The History of the Almohades*, ed. R. Dozy, 2nd edn (Leiden, 1881; reprinted Amsterdam, 1968), pp. 122, 127–8; cf. Julien, *History of North Africa*, pp. 87–8.

64 Cf. Norris, *Berbers in Arabic Literature*, pp. 157–83; J.M. Abun-Nasr, *A History of the Maghrib in the Islamic Period* (Cambridge, 1987), pp. 87–103; R. Le Tourneau, *The Almohad Movement in North Africa in the Twelfth and Thirteenth Centuries* (Princeton, N.J., 1969).

65 Cf. A. Bel, *La religion musulmane en Berbérie*, vol. I (Paris, 1938), pp. 233–65, esp. pp. 247–8.

66 Cf. J.F.P. Hopkins, *Medieval Muslim Government in Barbary* (London, 1958), pp. 104–8, in the context of ch. 7, 'The Almohad hierarchy'.

67 Ibid.; Julien, *History of North Africa*, pp. 93–104; R. Brunschvig, *La Berbérie orientale sous les Hafsides*, 2 vols (Paris, 1940, 1947).

68 Cf. V.J. Cornell, 'Understanding is the mother of ability: responsibility and action in the doctrine of Ibn Tūmart', *Studia Islamica*, 66 (1987), 71–103.

69 Cf. Idris, *La Berbérie orientale*, pp. 384–93.

70 Ibn Saʿīd: *El Libro de las Banderas de los Campeones*, ed. and Spanish trans. E. Garcia Gomez (Madrid, 1942), p. 19; Eng. trans. Brett, *The Moors*, p. 82.

71 Cf. O'Callaghan, *History of Medieval Spain*, pp. 234–49.

72 Cf. Brunschvig, *La Berbérie orientale*, esp. vol. ii, pp. 7–82, 286ff.

73 Cf. E. Dufourcq, *L'Espagne catalane et le Maghreb aux XIIIᵉ et XIVᵉ siècles* (Paris, 1966).

74 Cf. G. Deverdun, *Marrakech des origines à 1912*, 2 vols (Rabat, 1959).

75 Cf. Julien, *History of North Africa*, ch. 4; Abun-Nasr, *History of the Maghrib*, pp. 103–43.

76 Al-Marrākushī, *History*, p. 239.

77 J.A. Giles (trans.) *Roger of Wendover's Flowers of History*, 2 vols (London, 1849), vol. ii, pp. 283–7, quoted by P.G. Rogers, *A History of Anglo-Moroccan Relations to 1900* (London; Foreign and Commonwealth Office, n.d. [1972]), pp. 1–5.

78 Al-Marrākushī, *History*, pp. 225–6; Julien, *History of North Africa*, p. 119.

79 Ibn Khaldūn: *Kitāb al-ʿIbar*, vol. i, *The Muqaddimah: an Introduction to History*, trans. F. Rosenthal, 3 vols (Princeton, N.J., 1958, 1967; reprinted London, 1986; abridged N. Dawood, London, 1967); vols vi–vii, dealing with the Berbers and Arabs in North Africa, ed. de Slane (1847), trans. de Slane (1852ff). Cf. Al-Azmeh, *Ibn Khaldūn in Modern Scholarship*.

80 Cf. Ibn Khaldūn, *Peuples et nations du monde*, selected translations by A. Cheddadi, 2 vols (Paris, 1986), Introduction.

Chapter 4   The Arabization of North Africa

1 G. Marçais, *Les Arabes en Berbérie du XIᵉ au XIVᵉ siècle* (Paris, 1913).

2 See above, chapter 3, p. 108.

3 Cf. Bynon, 'Contribution of linguistics' (1970).

4 Cf. C.A. Julien, *Histoire de l'Afrique du Nord*, 2nd edn, 2 vols (Paris, 1951–2), vol. i, pp. 277–9; H.R. Idris, *La Berbérie orientale sous les Zirides* (Paris, 1962), pp. 757–64, 810.

5 Cf. M. Talbi, 'Law and economy in Ifrīqiya (Tunisia) in the third Islamic century', in A.L. Udovitch (ed.), *The Islamic Middle East, 700–1900* (Princeton, N.J., 1981), pp. 209–49.

6 M. Talbi (ed.), *Biographies Aghlabides. Extraites des Madārik du Cadi*

'Iyāḍ (Tunis, 1968), p. 30.

7 Ibn Khaldūn, *Peuples et nations du monde*, selected translations by A.
   Cheddadi, 2 vols (Paris, 1986), p. 464; *Muqaddimah* (1967), vol. I, pp.
   21–2.

8 Cf. R. Brunschvig, *La Berbérie orientale sous les Hafsides* (Paris,
   1940–7), vol. I, p. 333.

9 For the character and history of the Islamic Law, cf. N.J. Coulson, *A
   History of Islamic Law* (Edinburgh, 1964).

10 Cf. P. Cuperly, 'L'Ibāḍisme au XIIᵉ siècle: la ʿAqīda de Abū Sahl
   Yaḥyā', *IBLA* (*Revue de l'Institut des Belles Lettres Arabes*, Tunis), 42
   (143–4) (1979), 67–89, 277–305; idem, 'La cite ibāḍite: urbanisme et
   vie sociale au XIᵉ siècle', *Awal: Cahiers d'Etudes Berbères*, 3 (1987),
   89–114; 4 (1988), 7–14; E. Masqueray, *Formation des cités chez les
   populations sédentaires de l'Algérie* (Paris, 1886; reprinted Aix-en-
   Provence, 1983), pp. 173–221; E.A. Alport, 'The Mzab', in E. Gellner
   and C. Micaud (eds), *Arabs and Berbers* (New York, 1972; London,
   1973), pp. 141–52.

11 Cf. Coulson, *History of Islamic Law*, pp. 143–8.

12 Cf. R. Brunschvig, 'Ibn Abdalh'akam et la conquête de l'Afrique du
   Nord', in his *Etudes sur l'Islam classique et l'Afrique du Nord*
   (London, 1986), vol. XI; reprinted from *AIEO* (*Annales de l'Institut
   des Etudes Orientales*, Algiers), 6 (1942–7), 108–55. esp. pp. 111–13;
   pace A. Melvinger, *Encyclopaedia of Islam*, 2nd edn (Leiden, 1954) 2
   s.v. al-Mādjūs'.

13 Cf. M. Brett, 'Islam and trade in the Bilād al-Sūdān, tenth–eleventh
   century AD', *Journal of African History*, 24 (1983), 431–40.

14 M. Lombard, *The Golden Age of Islam* (Amsterdam, Oxford, New
   York, 1975).

15 Ibn Khaldūn, *Muqaddimah*, vol. II, p. 273; abridged edn (1967),
   p. 274.

16 See above, n. 5.

17 Cairo, a similarly attractive capital city, and undoubtedly the largest in
   the Islamic world after the decline of Baghdad, may have had a
   population as high as 450,000 prior to the Black Death, and at least as
   many as 250,000 thereafter: cf. M. Dols, 'The general mortality of the
   Black Death in the Mamluk empire', and C. Issawi, 'The area and
   population of the Arab empire' (quoting A. Raymond), both in A.
   Udovitch (ed.), *Islamic Middle East, 700–1900* (Princeton, N.J.,
   1981), pp. 397–428; 375–96.

18 Ibn Khaldūn, *Muqaddimah* (1967), vol. II, pp. 336–8; abridged edn
   (1967), pp. 309–10.

19 Ibid.

20 Ibid.

21 S.D. Goitein, 'Medieval Tunisia – the hub of the Mediterranean', in
   idem, *Studies in Islamic History and Institutions* (Leiden, 1966–8),
   vol. XVI.

22 Cf. M. Brett, 'Ifrīqiya as a market for Saharan trade from the tenth to the twelfth century AD', *Journal of African History*, 10 (1969), 347–64.

23 See above, n. 7.

24 Ibn Khaldūn, *Muqaddimah* (1967), vol. I, pp. 21–2; H.T. Norris, *Saharan Myth and Saga* (Oxford, 1972), pp. 26ff.

25 Ibn Khaldūn, *Kitāb al'Ibar*, vols (Būlāq, 1867); reprinted as *Ta'rīkh al-'allāma ibn Khaldūn* (Beirut, 1956), vol. VI, pp. 89–97; *Peuples et nations*, pp. 463–70.

26 Al-Tijānī, *Rihlat al-Tijānī* (Tunis, 1958), pp. 15–22; cf. M. Brett, 'The journey of al-Tijānī to Tripoli at the beginning of the fourteenth century AD/eighth century AH', Society for Libyan Studies, *Seventh Annual Report 1975–6*, pp. 41–51.

27 Ibn Khaldūn, *'Ibar*, vol. VI, pp. 13–16.

28 Ibn Khaldūn, *Muqaddimah* (1967), vol. I, pp. 302–5; abridged edn (1967), pp. 118–19.

29 Ibid., vol. I, pp. 249–58, 282–3, 295–6, 305–8; 91ff.

30 Ibid., vol. III, pp. 415ff.

31 Cf. F.A. Mukhlis, 'Studies and comparison of the cycles of the Banu Hilal romance', PhD thesis, London; L. Saada (ed. and trans.), *La Geste hilalienne* (Paris, 1985); H.T. Norris, *The Adventures of Antar* (Warminster, Wilts., 1980); idem, 'The rediscovery of the ancient sagas of the Banū Hilāl', *Bulletin of the School of Oriental and African Studies*, 51 (1988), 462–81.

32 Cf. A. Ayoub, 'The Hilālī epic: material and memory', *Revue d'histoire maghrébine*, 11 (35–6) (1984), 189–217.

33 Cf. M. Brett, 'Fatimid historiography: a case study – the quarrel with the Zirids, 1048–58', in D.O. Morgan (ed.), *Medieval Historical Writing in the Christian and Islamic Worlds* (London, 1982), pp. 47–59; idem, 'The Zughba at Tripoli, 429H (1037–8AD)', Society for Libyan Studies, *Sixth Annual Report, 1974–5*, pp. 41–7; idem, 'Ibn Khaldūn and the Arabisation of North Africa', *Maghreb Review*, 4 (1979), 9–16; idem, 'The Flood of the Dam and the Sons of the New Moon', in *Mélanges offerts à Mohamed Talbi* (Tunis, 1993), pp. 55–67.

34 See n. 1, above.

35 E.-F. Gautier, *Le Passé de l'Afrique du Nord. Les siècles obscurs* (Paris, 1952); Ibn Khaldūn, *Muqaddimah* (1967), vol. I, pp. 249–52, 302–5; abridged edn (1967), pp. 91–2, 118–19 (though the meaning of 'sedentary' rapidly shifts from 'tribal peasant' to 'city-dweller').

36 Cf. C.A. Julien, *History of North Africa from the Arab Conquest to 1830* (London, 1970), pp. 14–16.

37 Ibn Hawqal: *Sūrat al-ard* (Leiden, 1938–9), p. 155; trans. J.H. Kramers and G. Wiet, *Configuration de la terre* (Paris, 1964), p. 153.

38 See ch. 3, n. 46, above.

39 Ibn Khaldūn, *Peuples et nations*, p. 464.

40 Cf. R. Pennell, *A Country with a Government and a Flag* (Outwell,

Wisbech, 1986).

41   Cf. M. Brett, *The Moors: Islam in the West* (London, 1980), p. 88.
42   Ibn 'Idhārī, *Bayān*, vol. I, p. 290.
43   On costume generally, cf. Idris, *La Berbérie orientale*, pp. 594–600; R. Brunschvig, *La Berbérie orientale sous les Hafsides* (Paris, 1940–7), vol. II, pp. 276–82, esp. p. 279.
44   Ibn Sharaf, quoted in al-'Umarī, *Masālik al-abṣār*, vol. 17, ms. Bibliothèque nationale, Paris, no. 2327, fo 44 vo.
45   Cf. Brett, 'The Sons of the New Moon'.
46   A. Guiga, *La Geste hilalienne* (Tunis, 1968), pp. 81–2.
47   Ibn Khaldūn, *'Ibar*, vol. VI, pp. 16, 19; vol. VII, pp. 50, 61; idem, *Histoire des Berbères*, trans. M. de Slane, 4 vols (Paris, 1852; rev. edn Paris, 1925), vol. I, pp. 37, 45; vol. III, pp. 284, 306–8. Cf. Idris, *La Berbérie orientale*, p. 244.
48   Cf. H.T. Norris, *The Arab Conquest of the Western Sahara* (Harlow, Essex, 1986).
49   Cf. Brett, 'The Zughba at Tripoli' and 'The journey of al-Tijānī'.
50   Cf. Idris, *La Berbérie orientale*, pp. 249–406, passim.
51   Cf. Brett, 'The journey of al-Tijānī'; idem, 'Arabs, Berbers and Holy Men in southern Ifriqiya, 650–750AH/1250–1350AD', *Cahiers de Tunisie*, 39 (117–18) (1981), 533–59.
52   Cf. M. Brett, 'Ibn Khaldūn and the dynastic approach to local history', *Al-Qanṭara*, 12 (1991), 157–80.
53   Cf. Brunschvig, *La Berbérie orientale*, vol. II, pp. 99–104, 161.
54   Ibn Khaldūn, *Berbères*, vol. II, pp. 472–3.
55   Ibn Khaldūn, *Muqaddimah* (1967), vol. I, pp. 308–10; abridged edn (1967), p. 122.
56   Ibid., vol. I, p. 302; abridged edn, p. 118.
57   Ibid., vol. I, pp. 302–5; abridged edn, pp. 118–19.
58   Cf. Brett, 'The journey of al-Tijānī' and 'Arabs, Berbers and Holy Men'.
59   Ibid., and idem, 'Ibn Khaldūn and the dynastic approach'.
60   Ibn Khaldūn, *Muqaddimah* (1967), vol. I, pp. 300–2; abridged edn (1967), p. 117.
61   Ibid., pp. 299–300; abridged edn, p. 116.
62   Cf. Brett, 'The journey of al-Tijānī' and 'Arabs, Berbers and Holy Men'.
63   Ibid.; al-Bakrī, *Description, de l'Afrique septentrionale*, ed. and trans. M. de Slane, 2nd edn, 2 vols (Paris, 1913; reprinted 1965), p. 84, trans., p. 170. For *ribāṭ* cf. G. Marçais, *Encylopaedia of Islam*, 1st edn (Leiden, 1913–38), *s.v.* 'Ribāṭ'.
64   Cf. A.M.M. Mackeen, 'The early history of Ṣūfism in the Maghrib', *Journal of the American Oriental Society*, 91 (1971), 398–408; more generally, M. Brett, 'Islam in North Africa', in S. Sutherland *et al.* (eds), *The World's Religions* (London, 1988), pp. 329–53; reprinted in P. Clarke (ed.), *The World's Religions: Islam* (London, 1990).

65 J.C. Mardrus and P. Mathers, *The Book of a Thousand and One Nights*, 4 vols (London, 1958), vol. III, pp. 369–70, 382; for the apocryphal character of the Aladdin story, cf. R. Irwin, 'There's the rub ... and there too: the elusive meaning of the Aladdin story', *The Times Literary Supplement*, 24 December 1993: 14–15, and more generally, his *Companion to the Arabian Nights* (London, 1994).

66 Cf. Brett, 'Arabs, Berbers and Holy Men' and 'Ibn Khaldūn and the dynastic approach'.

67 Cf. Brett, 'Arabs, Berbers and Holy Men', p. 548; Brunschvig, *La Berbérie orientale*, vol. II, pp. 321, 331–2, 333.

68 Cf. Brett, 'Arabs, Berbers and Holy Men'.

69 On the Scriptural authority of the Qur'ān, see Sura v, 'The Table', 112–15.

70 The activities of the *zāwiya* in late mediaeval Ifrīqiya are illustrated in picturesque detail in the biographies of the scholars and saints of Qayrawan contained in the *Ma'ālim al-īmān* of Ibn Nājī, 4 vols (Tunis, 1320H), for example that of al-Jadīdī, vol. IV, pp. 226–41; cf. Brunschvig, *La Berbérie orientale*, vol. II, pp. 317–51; Brett, 'Arabs, Berbers and Holy Men'.

71 Cf. Brett, 'Arabs, Berbers and Holy Men', p. 553.

72 Cf. Brett, 'Ibn Khaldūn and the dynastic approach'.

73 Cf. P. von Sivers, 'Alms and arms: the combative saintliness of the Awlād Sīdī Shaykh in the Algerian Sahara, sixteenth–nineteenth centuries', *Maghreb Review*, 8 (1983), 113–23.

74 Cf. Brunschvig, *La Berbérie orientale*, vol. II, pp. 350–1.

75 W. Marçais, 'Comment l'Afrique du Nord a été arabisée', *Annales de l'Institut des Etudes Orientales*, Algiers, 4 (1938), 1–22; 14 (1956), 5–17. Cf. Ph. Marçais, *Encyclopaedia of Islam*, 2nd edn (Leiden, 1954) s.v. ''Arabiyya'.

76 Cf. Brunschvig, *La Berbérie orientale*, vol. I, pp. 324ff.

77 Cf. Brett, 'Arabs, Berbers and Holy Men', pp. 539–41.

78 Ibid., pp. 536–7.

79 Cf. Brunschvig, *La Berbérie orientale*, vol. II, p. 313.

80 Ibid., pp. 293–4.

81 Ibid., vol. I, pp. 329–33.

82 Cf. A. Louis, 'Contactes entre culture "berbère" et culture arabe dans le sud tunisien', in *Actes du Premier Congrès d'Etudes des Cultures Méditerrannéenes d'Influence Arabo-Berbère* (Algiers, 1973), pp. 394–405; idem, *Tunisie du Sud: ksars et villages de crêtes* (Paris, 1975); Brett, 'Arabs, Berbers and Holy Men', pp. 534, 555.

83 See n. 10, above.

84 Cf. T. Whitcomb, 'New evidence on the origins of the Kunta', *Bulletin of the School of Oriental and African Studies*, 38 (1975), 103–23, 403–17.

85 Cf., for example, C.C. Stewart, *Islam and Social Order in Mauritania*

(Oxford, 1973).

86 Cf. Norris (1972), pp. 110–16; idem (1986).

87 Cf. E.N. Saad, *Social History of Timbuktu: the role of Muslim scholars and notables, 1400–1900* (Cambridge, 1983).

88 Cf. Norris, *Saharan Myth and Saga*, p. 191.

89 Ibid., pp. 110–217: accounts and translations of three traditional histories.

90 Cf. H.T. Norris, *The Tuaregs: Their Islamic Legacy and its Diffusion in the Sahel* (Warminster, Wilts., 1975).

91 For the situation of the Tuareg in the ethnographic picture of the Sahara in the twentieth century, cf. L.C. Briggs, *Tribes of the Sahara* (Cambridge, Mass., and London, 1960).

92 Gellner and Micaud, *Arabs and Berbers*, p. 13.

Chapter 5 The Wheel of State

1 Adapted from Ibn Khaldūn, *The Muqaddimah: An Introduction to History*, trans. F. Rosenthal, 3 vols (Princeton, N.J., 1958, 1967), vol. II, p. 105. Cf., e.g., A.K.S. Lambton, 'Changing concepts of justice and injustice from the 5th/11th century to the 8th/14th century in Persia', *Studia Islamica*, 68 (1988), 27–60.

2 Cf. C. Fleischer, 'Royal authority, dynastic cyclism, and "Ibn Khaldunism" in sixteenth-century Ottoman letters', in B.B. Lawrence (ed.), *Ibn Khaldūn and Islamic Ideology* (Leiden, 1984), pp. 46–68.

3 F. Braudel, *The Mediterranean and the Mediterranean World in the Age of Philip II*, 2 vols (London, 1972).

4 R. Brunschvig, *La Berbérie orientale sous les Hafsides* (Paris, 1940–7), vol. II, p. 83.

5 E. Masqueray, *Formation des cités chez les populations sédentaires de l'Algérie* (Paris, 1886; reprinted Aix-en-Provence, 1983), pp. 116ff.

6 The history of the Ottoman conquest is best told in A.C. Hess, *The Forgotten Frontier* (Chicago and London, 1978), and in J.M. Abun-Nasr, *A History of the Maghrib in the Islamic Period* (Cambridge, 1987). Cf. M. Brett, 'Morocco and the Ottomans: the sixteenth century in North Africa', *Journal of African History*, 25 (1984) 331–41.

7 Cf. Sir G. Fisher, *Barbary Legend: War, Trade and Piracy in North Africa, 1415–1830* (Oxford, 1957).

8 Cf. *Oxford English Dictionary*, 1st ed, *s.v.* 'Barbary'; Fisher, *Barbary Legend*, pp. 17–18.

9 Cf. J. Berque, 'Un maître de l'heure renoncé', in J. Berque, *L'Intérieur du Maghreb* (Paris, 1978); reviewed M. Brett, 'Jacques Berque and the history of the Maghreb', *Maghreb Review*, 4 (1979), 140–8.

10 J. Morgan, *A Complete History of Algiers* (London, 1731; reprinted New York, 1970), pp. 326–8, abridged.

11 Ibid., p. 417.

12 Ibid., p. 408.

13 Ibid., p. 409 (abridged); cf. pp. 407–16.
14 Ibid.; cf. C.A. Julien, *History of North Africa from the Arab Conquest to 1830* (London, 1970), ch. 6 , and W. Spencer, *Algiers in the Age of the Corsairs* (Norman, Okla, 1976), pp. 40–65.
15 Morgan, *Complete History of Algiers*, pp. 69–70 (abridged). The modern transliteration is *jabal, jabā'il, jabā'iliyya*, for mountain(s), mountaineers; and *qabīla, qabī'il, qabā'iliyya*, for tribe(s), tribesmen, land of the tribes; whence Kabylia, the mountains from east of Algiers to Annaba.
16 Ibid., p. 71.
17 Dr T. Shaw, *Travels or Observations relating to Several Parts of Barbary and the Levant* (Oxford, 1738), pp. ii–vii (abridged).
18 From *haramiyyūn*, 'people of no-man's-land, "no-go" regions'; the *bilād al-khalā'* or 'empty land'.
19 Shaw, *Travels or Observations,* p. viii.
20 Ibid., pp. 4–5.
21 Ibid., p. 7.
22 Ibid., p. 91, for the explanation of the name.
23 Ibid., p. 100.
24 Ibid., p. 102.
25 Ibid., p. 120.
26 Ibid., p. 312.
27 Ibid., p. 90.
28 Ibid., p. 86.
29 Ibid., p. 17.
30 Recounted in C. Geertz, *Islam Observed* (Chicago and London, 1968), pp. 33–5.
31 Al-Ifrānī, *Nuzhat al-hādī*; trans. O. Houdas, as *Nozhet-Elhâdi* (Paris, 1888–9), p. 259.
32 W. Blunt, *Black Sunrise* (London, 1951).
33 The phrase is Patricia Mercer's; cf. P. Mercer, 'Palace and jihād in the early 'Alawī state of Morocco', *Journal of African History,* 18 (1977), 531–53, esp. p. 540. For the comparison with the Saadians, cf. Brett, 'Morocco and the Ottomans'.
34 Al-Nāṣirī: *Kitāb al-istiqsā'*, 9 vols (Casablanca, 1954–6), vol. VII, p. 97.
35 Mercer, 'Palace and jihād', 546.
36 Ibid., 546–53.
37 Cf. Abun-Nasr, *History of the Maghrib*, pp. 219–30; J. Berque, 'Une perspective nationale manquée', in J. Berque, *Ulémas, fondateurs, insurgés du Maghreb: XVIIᵉ siècle* (Paris, 1982), pp. 81–123.
38 J.G. Jackson, *An Account of the Empire of Morocco and the Districts of Suse and Tafilelt*, 3rd edn (London, 1814; reprinted 1968).
39 Ibid., pp. 140–3.
40 Cf. M. El Mansour, *Morocco in the Reign of Mawlay Sulayman* (Outwell, Wisbech, 1990), p. 101.
41 Jackson, *Account of the Empire of Morocco,* p. 142.

42 El Mansour, *Morocco*, p. 189.
43 Cf. E. Hermassi, *Leadership and National Development in North Africa* (Berkeley and Los Angeles, 1973).
44 Cf. M. Emerit, 'Hajj Ahmed Bey', in Ch.-A. Julien et al. (eds), *Les Africains*, 12 vols (Paris, 1977–8), vol. 8, pp. 101–31.
45 Cf. Abun-Nasr, *History of the Maghrib*, pp. 173–83.
46 Cf. H.Z. Hirschberg, *A History of the Jews in North Africa*, 2 vols (Leiden, 1981); D.J. Schroeter, *Merchants of Essaouira* (Cambridge, 1988).
47 Cf. L. Valensi, *On the Eve of Colonialism* (New York and London, 1977), pp. 35–70; idem, *Tunisian Peasants* (Cambridge, 1985).
48 For these various developments, cf. M. Brett, 'Modernisation in 19th-century North Africa', *Maghreb Review*, 7 (1982), 16–22; idem, 'Continuity and change: Egypt and North Africa in the nineteenth century', *Journal of African History*, 27 (1986), 149–62.
49 The expression is Valensi's: *On the Eve of Colonialism*, p. 57.
50 Cf. F. Harrak, 'State and religion in eighteenth-century Morocco. The religious policy of Sīdī Muḥammad b. 'Abd Allah', unpublished PhD thesis, University of London (1989).
51 For these revivalist movements in general, cf. G. Marçais, *Encyclopaedia of Islam*, 1st edn (Leiden, 1913–38), s.v. 'Ṭarīka'; J.S. Trimingham, *The Sufi Orders in Islam* (Oxford, 1971), pp. 105–32.
52 Cf. Ch.-R. Ageron, *Modern Algeria: A History from 1830 to the Present* (London, 1991).
53 Cf. Ch.-A. Julien, *Histoire de l'Algérie contemporaine*, vol. I, *La Conquête et les débuts de la colonisation (1827–1871)* (Paris, 1964), pp. 394–5.
54 Ibid., pp. 473–500; Ageron, *Modern Algeria*, pp. 47–53.
55 Cf. M. Brett, 'Legislating for inequality in Algeria: the Senatus-Consulte of 14 July 1865', *Bulletin of the School of Oriental and African Studies*, 51 (1988), 440–61. Examples of the *qānūns* or *kanouns* in question are provided by Masqueray, *Formation des cités*, pp. 263–324.
56 See ch. 3, n. 3, above.
57 Masqueray, *Formation des cités*, pp. 221–61.
58 S. Gsell, *Histoire ancienne de l'Afrique du Nord* (Paris, 1927); C. Diehl, *L'Afrique byzantine* (New York, 1896).
59 Morgan, *Complete History of Algiers*, p. 71, adding: 'I cannot help surmising, that, even while *Christianity* was at its most flourishing State in Africa, there was scarce one *African* in ten who was not either a professed *Pagan*, or at least a secret Enemy to every Tenet of the Orthodox Church: For, by what I know of these modern *Africans*, they never were a People capable of conforming to a regular and civil Course of Life, such as *Christianity* enjoins: Mahomet allowed a Scope suitable to their Depravity of Genius.
60 E. Guernier, *La Berbérie, l'Islam et la France*, 2 vols (Paris, 1950).
61 D. Randall-McIver and A. Wilkin, *Libyan Notes* (London, 1901).

62   Cf. Ageron, *Modern Algeria*, pp. 65–9.

63   Cf. A. Aron et al., *Les Origines de la guerre d'Algérie* (Paris, 1962), pp. 232–40.

64   Cf. J. Waterbury, *North for the Trade: The Life and Times of a Berber Merchant* (Berkeley and Los Angeles, 1972).

65   Cf. G. Maxwell, *Lords of the Atlas* (London, 1966); W.B. Harris, *Tafilet* (Edinburgh and London, 1895); R. Montagne, *Les Berbères et le Makhzen au sud du Maroc* (Paris, 1930); idem, *The Berbers: Their Social and Political Organisation*, trans. D. Seddon (London, 1973); Masqueray, *Formation des cités*.

66   Cf. E. Burke III, *Prelude to Protectorate in Morocco* (Chicago and London, 1976), pp. 99–152.

67   Cf. R. Bidwell, *Morocco under Colonial Rule* (London, 1973), pp. 98–127.

68   Quoted by Burke, *Prelude to Protectorate*, p. 192.

69   Bidwell, *Morocco under Colonial Rule*, p. 34; the phrase was used by Steeg, Lyautey's successor, in speaking of the Rif.

70   Cf. C.R. Pennell, *A Country with a Government and a Flag* (Outwell, Wisbech, 1986).

71   Cf. R. Montagne, *Révolution au Maroc* (Paris, 1951).

72   See n. 65, above.

73   Cf. Ch.-A. Julien, *Le Maroc face aux impérialismes, 1415–1956* (Paris, 1978), pp. 165ff.

74   E. Hermassi, *Leadership and National Development*, pp. 61–2.

75   J. Berque, *French North Africa* (London, 1967), p. 219.

76   Cf. Bidwell, *Morocco under Colonial Rule*, pp. 48–62; Ageron, 'La politique berbère', pp. 109–48.

77   I am indebted to Dr A. Clayton, Royal Military Academy, Sandhurst, for this reference to R. Trevelyan, *Rome '44* (London, 1981), p. 271; cf. more generally his *France, Soldiers and Africa* (London, 1988).

78   Cf. Bidwell, *Morocco under Colonial Rule*, pp. 293–301.

79   Cf. L. Rosen, 'The social and conceptual framework of Arab–Berber relations in Central Morocco', in E. Gellner and Ch. Micaud (eds), *Arabs and Berbers* (London, 1972), pp. 155–73; idem, *Bargaining for Reality: The Construction of Social Relations in a Muslim Community* (Chicago, 1984).

80   Cf. K.L. Brown, *People of Salé* (Manchester, 1976), pp. 198–202.

81   Cf. Julien, *La Maroc*.

82   Ch.-A. Julien, *L'Afrique du Nord en marche* (Paris, 1952; 3rd edn, 1972).

83   F. Fanon, *A Dying Colonialism* (London, 1970); originally *L'An cinq de la révolution algérienne* (Paris, 1959). The phrase is Berque's: *French North Africa*, p. 72.

84   J. Berque, *Le Maghreb entre deux guerres* (Paris, 1962; 2nd edn, 1970); cf. Berque, *French North Africa*, pp. 104–7.

85   E. Kedourie, 'The retreat from Algeria', in E. Kedourie, *Islam in the Modern World* (London, 1980), pp. 213–32.

86 Berque, *French North Africa*, p. 390.
87 Cf. C. and Y. Lacoste (eds), *L'Etat du Maghreb* (Paris, 1991), p. 276.
88 Cf. J. Wright, *Libya* (London, 1969), pp. 131–2, 143–52, *passim*.
89 A. Hourani, *Arabic Thought in the Liberal Age* (Oxford, 1962; reprinted Cambridge, 1980).
90 Cf. M. Kaddache, *Histoire du nationalisme algérienne*, 2 vols (Algiers, 1980), vol. I, p. 227.
91 Cf. J. Waterbury, *The Commander of the Faithful* (London 1970); R. Leveau, *Le Fellah marocain, défenseur du trone* (Paris, 1976).
92 Leveau, *Le Fellah marocain*, pp. 83–9; 174–9.
93 Cf. S. Chaker, 'La voie étroite: la revendication berbère entre culture et politique', *Annuaire de l'Afrique du Nord*, 28 (1989), 281–96; W. Spencer, *Historical Dictionary of Morocco* (Metuchen, N.J., and London, 1980), pp. 22, 79.
94 Leveau, *Le Fellah Marocain*, p. 84.
95 Cf. B. Stora, *Histoire de l'Algérie coloniale, 1830–1954* (Paris, 1991), p. 111.
96 A. Horne; *A Savage War of Peace*, 2nd edn (London) p. 547.
97 Ibid., p. 229.

Chapter 6   *Pastoral Berbers: Nomads, Slaves and Saints*

1 Leo Africanus, *Description de l'Afrique* (Paris, 1981), pp. 35f.
2 C. Renfrew, *Archaeology and Language: The Puzzle of Indo-European Origins* (London, 1987), p. 98. A good summary of the various theories of nomadic pastoral origins is provided by R. Cribb, *Nomads in Archaeology* (Cambridge, 1991), pp. 12–14.
3 See, for example, the discussion in J. Nicolaisen, *Economy and Culture of the Pastoral Tuareg* (Copenhagen, 1963), pp. 209–13, and the chart for (modern) consumption, p. 216.
4 Although see R. Cribb, *Nomads in Archaeology*, pp. 65f.
5 Lake Triton: Herodotus, *History*, 4.186.
6 *Polybius, History*, 12. 2–3.
7 Strabo, *Geography*, 17.3.7.
8 G. Camps, *Aux origines de la Berbérie. Masinissa ou les débuts de l'histoire* (Algiers, 1961), pp. 481–505: however, reburial is common in tombs of the Tell as well.
9 Herodotus, *History*, 4.172.
10 E.F. Gautier, *Le Passé de l'Afrique du Nord: les siècles obscurs* (Paris, 1942); G. Camps, *Berbères. Aux marges de l'histoire* (Toulouse, 1980), pp. 124–5. On the effects of the 'new technology' which the camel implied, see the interesting study in R. Bulliet, *The Camel and the Wheel* (Cambridge, Mass., 1975).
11 The evidence is summarized in E. Demougeot, 'Le Chameau et l'Afrique du Nord romaine', *Annales: économies, sociétés, civilisations*, 15 (1960), 209–47; see also B. Shaw, 'The camel in Roman

North Africa and the Sahara', *Bulletin de l'Institut française de l'Afrique noire*, **41** (1979), 663–716.

12 Caesar (pseud.), *De Bello Africano, 68.* 4; Ammianus Marcellinus, *Rerum gestarum libri*, 28. 6. 5.

13 Carthage: J. Schwartz, 'The (primarily) mammalian fauna', in H. Hurst and S. Roskams (eds), *Excavations at Carthage: The British Mission* (Sheffield, 1984), vol. ɪ, ch. 1, pp. 229–56; Sétif: A. King, 'Animal bones', in E. Fentress (ed.), *Fouilles de Sétif, 1977–1984* (Algiers, 1991), pp. 7–267.

14 They appear pulling ploughs on the tombs at Ghirza and on a second-century mosaic from Tigi in Tripolitania: O. Brogan and D. Smith, *Ghirza: A Libyan Settlement in the Roman Period* (Tripoli, 1984), fig. 64; O. Brogan, 'Henscir el-Ausaf by Tigi (Tripolitania) and some related tombs in the Tunisian Gefara', *Libya Antiqua*, 2 (1965), 47–56, pl. xɪv. On the introduction of the camels, see particularly Bulliet, *The Camel and the Wheel.*

15 B. Pace, G. Caputo and S. Sergi, 'Scavi Sahariani: Richerche nell'Uadi el Agial e nell'Oasi di Gat della missione Pace–Caputo–Sergi', *Monumenti Antichi, Accademia Nazionale dei Lincei*, 41 (1951), 151–551. M.C. Chamla, *Les Populations anciennes du Sahara et des régions limitrophes* (Paris, 1968), pp. 200f.

16 M. Reygasse, 'Le Monument de Tin Hinan', *Bulletin de la Société Géographique et Archéologique d'Oran* (1940), 148–66; M. Gast, 'Témoignages nouveaux sur Tine Hinane, ancêtre légendaire des Touareg Ahaggar', *Revue de l'Occident Musulman et de la Méditerranée*, 13–14 (1973), 395–400.

17 For these, see R. Rebuffat, 'Graffiti en "Libyque de Bu Njem"', *Libya Antiqua*, 11–12 (1974–5), 165–87; Brogan and Smith, *Ghirza*, pp. 250–8.

18 Tuareg kinship patterns are complex, and more balanced than their matrilineal ideology would suggest; see the articles in S. Bernus, P. Bonte, L. Brock, and C. Clodot (eds), *Le Fils et le neveu. Jeux et enjeux de la parenté touarègue* (Paris, 1986), particularly those of Gast and Claudot.

19 Leo Africanus, *Description de l'Afrique*, p. 37.

20 It should be noted that the children of noble men and slave women (*taklaten*) are generally considered nobles; this is possible in so far as the slaves do not constitute a class in terms of Tuareg society.

21 E. Bernus, 'L'Evolution des relations de dépendance depuis la période pré-coloniale jusqu'à nos jours chez les Iullemeden Kel Dinnik', *Revue de l'Occident musulman et de la Méditerranée*, 21 (1976), 85–99; H. Guillaume, 'Les liens de dépendance à l'époque précoloniale chez les Touaregs de l'Imannen (Niger)', ibid., 111–29.

22 On the artisans, see D. Jemma, 'Les artisans de l'Ahaggar', *Libyca*, 20 (1972), 269–90.

23 Nicholaisen, *Economy and Culture*, pp. 57f; J. Keenan, 'Some theo-

retical considerations on the "Temazlayt" relationship', *Revue de l'Occident musulman et de la Méditerranée*, 21 (1976), 33–46. The symbolic importance of the drum is underlined by the fact that in 1974 the Amenukal's drum was appropriated by the mayor of Tamenrasset and placed in his office to indicate the final transfer of power to the Algerian state: M. Vallet, 'Les Touaregs du Hoggar entre décolonisation et indépendance, 1954–1974', ibid., 54 (1990), 77–90.

24 J. Keenan, 'Social change among the Tuareg of Ahaggar (Algeria)', in E. Gellner and C. Micaud (eds), *Arabs and Berbers: From Tribe to Nation in North Africa* (London, 1973), pp. 345–60: he dates this system to around the sixteenth century.

25 For example Nicolaisen, *Economy and Culture*, p. 479.

26 E.A. McDougall, 'The view from Awdaghust: war, trade and social change in the southwestern Sahara from the eighth to the fifteenth century', *Journal of African History*, 26 (1985), 1–31.

27 See, for a similar point, E. Gellner, *Nations and Nationalism* (Oxford, 1983), p. 10.

28 Dida Badi, personal communication. I'm unable to trace this story, which is a variant of the account on pp. 84–6.

29 The wearing of the veil may have already started in Roman times: Corippus describes some Moors as winding up their heads with a linen cloth, tied with a tight knot (*Iohannis*, 2.135).

30 Keenan, 'Some theoretical considerations'.

31 H. Lhote, *Les Touaregs du Hoggar* (Paris, 1984), p. 227. The French considered this evidence of cowardice. Lhote complacently relates that the Tuareg eventually changed their view of the French because of the honourable behaviour they showed towards the women.

32 Herodotus, *History*, 4.183; see above, p. 22.

33 F. Buecheler and A. Riese (eds), *Anthologia Latina* (Leipzig, 1894), vol. 1, no. 183.

34 Pace, Caputo and Sergi, 'Scavi Sahariani', *passim*; this material has been recently studied by Sergio Fontana (personal communication).

35 For the gold trade, see E.W. Bovill, *The Golden Trade of the Moors* (London, 1958), who has probably exaggerated its importance.

36 This is the view of McDougall, 'View from Awdaghust', 17.

37 al-Bakri, *Description de l'Afrique Septentrionale*, ed. and trans. M. de Slane, 2nd edn, 2 vols (reprinted Paris, 1962); English trans. in *Corpus of Early Arabic Sources for West African History*, ed. and annotated M. Levtzion and J.F.P. Hopkins (Cambridge, 1981).

38 Keenan, 'Social change'; P. Gouletquer and D. Klenmann, 'Structures sociales et commerce du sel', *Revue de l'Occident musulman et de la Méditerranée*, 21 (1976), 131–9.

39 Keenan, 'Social change'.

40 The following is based on the analysis of C. Oxby, 'Women and the allocation of herding labour in a pastoral society: southern Kel Ferwan Twareg, Niger', in Bernus et al., *Le Fils et le neveu*. However, as the

research was done in 1973, before the drought, it is likely that this pattern can no longer be regarded as contemporary.

41 Ibid., p. 124.

42 In spite of Maurice Gast's wildly optimistic assertion that 'sedentarization has been accomplished without serious dislocation': 'La société traditionnelle des Kel Ahaggar face aux problèmes contemporains', in E. Gellner (ed.), *Islam: Société et Communauté* (1980), pp. 107–36.

43 An excellent collection of articles on the *teshumara* is found in H. Claudot-Hawad (ed.), *Touaregs, exil et résistance, Revue du Monde Musulman et de la Méditerranée* 57 (1991), particularly the article by Hawad, 'Le teshumara, antidote de l'Etat', 123–39.

44 Hawad, 'Le teshumara', 130.

45 D. Hart, *Dadda 'Atta and his Forty Grandsons: The Socio-Political Organisation of the Ait 'Atta of Southern Morocco* (Cambridge, 1981).

46 On rotating chieftainships, see E. Gellner, *Saints of the Atlas* (London, 1969), p. 81; on the five fifths, or *khams khmas*, see D.M. Hart, 'Segmentary systems and the role of the "five fifths" in tribal Morocco', *Revue de l'Occident musulman et la Méditerranée*, 12 (1967), 35–95; idem, *Dadda 'Atta and his Forty Grandsons*, pp. 76ff.

47 Gellner, *Saints of the Atlas.*

48 P. Rabinow, *Reflections on Fieldwork in Morocco* (Berkeley, Cal., 1977), p. 141.

49 Gellner, *Saints of the Atlas*, p. 297.

50 D. Jemma-Gouzon, *Villages de l'Aurès: Archives de pierres* (Paris, 1989), p. 47.

51 Gellner, *Saints of the Atlas*, p. 299.

52 The confusion between the various cults of shrines and the saints is total in E. Dermenghem, *Le Culte des saints dans l'islam maghrébin* (Paris, 1954), for example.

53 Gellner, *Saints of the Atlas*, p. 277.

54 Jemma Gouzon, *Villages de l'Aurès*, pp. 48f. On the fourteenth-century relations between Berbers and Arabs in the area of Biskra, see M. Brett, 'Ibn Khaldūn and local history', *Al-Qantara*, 12 (1991), 157–80.

Chapter 7   The Society and its Habitat

1 For instance, R. Montagne, *The Berbers: Their Social and Political Organisation* (London, 1973), p. 27; D.M. Hart, 'Segmentary systems and the role of the "five fifths" in tribal Morocco', *Revue de l'Occident musulman et de la Méditerranée*, 12 (1967), 35–95. On segmentary societies in general, see M. Sahlins, 'The segmentary lineage: an organization of predatory expansion', *American Anthropologist*, 63 (1961), 322–45.

2 D.M. Hart, 'The tribe in modern Morocco: two case studies', in E. Gellner and C. Micaud (eds), *Arabs and Berbers: From Tribe to*

Nation in North Africa (London, 1973), pp. 25–59, esp. p. 30. For territorially based tribes, see idem, *The Aith Waryaghar of the Moroccan Rif* (Tucson, 1976), pp. 11f, who criticizes the too-neat patterning of the segmentary model.

3   Criticism of the segmentary model is growing: see, for example, A. Hammoudi, 'Segmentarité, stratification sociale, pouvoir politique et sainteté', *Hespéris Tamuda*, 15 (1974); H. Munson, 'On the irrelevance of the segmentary lineage model in the Moroccan Rif', *American Anthropologist*, 91 (1989), 386–400, and Hart's reply: D.M. Hart, 'Rejoinder to Henry Munson, Jr., "On the Irrelevance of the Segmentary Lineage Model in the Moroccan Rif"', ibid., 766–9.

4   Hammoudi, 'Segmentarité'; he suggests that these divisions came about by the absorption of allogenic groups by the 'original' Ait ʿAtta.

5   M. Mammeri, *Poèmes kabyles anciens* (Algiers, 1988), poems 99–103.

6   E. Masqueray, *Formation des cités chez les populations sédentaires de l'Algérie* (Paris, 1886; reprinted 1983), pp. 47f.

7   P. Bourdieu, 'The Kabyle house, or the world reversed' (1970) reprinted in P. Bourdieu, *The Logic of Practice* (Paris, 1990), pp. 271–83.

8   A. Rapoport, 'Systems of activities and systems of settings', in S. Kent (ed.), *Domestic Architecture and the Use of Space* (Cambridge, 1990), whose pessimistic view is far more plausible than that of Kent in the same volume, who holds that 'it should be . . . possible to predict the sociopolitical organization of a group by knowing its architecture and the use of space' (p. 7). Apart from the theoretical difficulties here, one is staggered by the sheer impossibility of knowing more than a fraction of the uses that a space was put to from its archaeological remains.

9   Pliny the Elder, *Natural History*, 16.178. All ancient texts on mapalia are collected in Ch. Le Coeur, 'Les "mapalia" numides et leur survivance au Sahara', *Hespéris*, 24 (1937), 29–45.

10 For a discussion of Berbers in cities in an archaeological context, see E. Fentress (ed.), *Fouilles de Sétif, 1977–1984* (Algiers, 1991), p. 282. For integration of Berbers in modern Moroccan cities, see L. Rosen, 'Arab–Berber relations in Central Morocco', in Gellner and Micaud, *Arabs and Berbers*, pp. 155–73; J. Waterbury, 'The coup manqué', in ibid., pp. 397–423; D.M. Hart, 'Notes on the Rifian community of Tangier', *Middle East Journal*, 11(2), (1957), 153–62.

11 Masqueray called the villages of North Africa 'des modèles si parfaits de la vie barbare sédentaire qu'ils sollicitent d'abord l'attention, et la captivent', *Formation des cités*, p. 16.

12 G. Barker et al., 'UNESCO Libyan Valleys Survey 6: investigations of a Romano-Libyan farm', *Libyan Studies*, 15 (1984), 1–44.

13 D. Buck, J. Burns and D. Mattingly, 'Archaeological sites of the Bir Scedua Basin: settlements and cemeteries', *Libyan Studies*, 14 (1983), 39–68.

14 A. Bazzana, P. Cressier and P. Guichard, *Les Châteaux ruraux d'al-Andalus. Histoire et archéologie des husūn du sud-est de l'Espagne*

(Madrid, 1988), pp. 200f. For contemporary Arab houses, see J. Lopez and A. Bazzana (eds), *La Maison hispano-musulmane, apports de l'archéologie* (Granada, 1990).

15 Bourdieu, 'The Kabyle house'; R. Basagana and A. Sayad, *Habitat traditionnel et structures familiales en Kabylie, Mémoires du CRAPE*, **23** (1990).

16 D. Jemma-Gouzon, *Villages de l'Aurès: archives de pierres* (Paris, 1989), pp. 120f.

17 M. Mercier, *La Civilization urbain au Mzab* (Paris, 1922), pp. 177f.

18 J. Martin Evans, 'The traditional house in the oasis of Ghadames', *Libyan Studies*, **7** (1975–6), 31–40.

19 Bourdieu, 'The Kabyle house'; Jemma-Gouzon, *Villages de l'Aurès*, pp. 136f.

20 E. Fentress, 'The house of the Prophet: African Islamic housing', *Archeologia Medievale*, **14** (1987), 47–68. This discussion is necessarily brief, citing only the most obvious examples of Berber houses. With the exception of those in the north-west of the chain, Berber houses in Anti-Atlas appear to derive from Arab prototypes, although their decoration is characteristically Berber (Dj. Jacques-Meunier, *Architectures et habitats du Dadés*, Paris, 1962). The houses of the Mzab are a hybrid: they probably derive from Arab-style houses – that, at least, appears to be the plan of houses at the earlier towns of Sedrata and Tahert – but have been adapted by the closure of the central court to a more typically Berber plan.

21 M. Feraoun, *Le Fils du pauvre* (Algiers, 1950; reprinted 1990), p. 29, translation EF.

22 A. Goichon, *La Vie féminine au Mzab* (Paris, 1931), pp. 228f.

23 See the splendid analysis by Tassadit Yacine which introduces the collection of *izli* from which this example is translated (T. Yacine, *L'Izli ou l'amour chanté en Kabyle* (Paris, 1990), p. 119.

24 M. Feraoun, *Jours de Kabylie* (Algiers 1954; reprinted 1990), p. 14, translation EF.

25 N. Maarouf, *Lecture de l'espace oasien* (Paris, 1980), p. 12, and the discussion in Jemma-Gouzon, *Villages de l'Aurès*, pp. 85f.

26 For example, M. Mammeri, *L'Opium et le bâton* (Paris, 1965; reprinted 1992), p. 79.

27 Dj. Jacques-Meunier, (1951), *Greniers-Citadelles au Maroc*, Paris, pp. 26f.

28 Bazzana et al., *Les Châteaux ruraux, passim*.

29 Masqueray, *Formation des cités*, p. 31.

30 Jemma-Gouzon, *Villages de Aurès*, pp. 63f.

31 Ibid., pp. 98f.

32 Feraoun, *Jours de Kabylie*, p. 27.

33 Masqueray argues that the inner circle is in fact a covert aristocracy, acceded to only by the families of the 'notables' (*Formation des cités*, pp. 45f).

34 Masqueray (ibid.) gives several examples of these *kanoun*, a word

which he suggests derives from the Roman word *canon*.

35 This description applies to the Kabyle village: in Morocco, power is all delegated to councils, at the neighbourhood, clan and tribal level: see Hart, *The Aith Waryaghar*, p. 284.

36 The literature on Mediterranean honour is vast, and the Berber variations few: I shall not dwell on it here, but see, for example, J. Campbell, *Honour, Family and Patronage* (Oxford, 1964); J.G. Peristany, (ed.), *Honour and Shame* (London, 1965).

37 P. Bourdieu, *Outline of a Theory of Practice* (Cambridge, 1977), p. 15. One cannot help being reminded of the old Sicilian definition of a *mafioso* as someone who would not suffer a fly to sit on his nose!

38 Describing the behaviour of his fourteen-year-old sister, a man from a Kabyle village remarked with pride that 'of course she *terrorizes* all the boys in her class at school'.

39 Bazzana et al., *Les Châteaux ruraux*, pp. 287f. The transformation of these sites into seigneurial domains, or standard European mediaeval castles, occurred only *after* the reconquista.

40 Youcef-ou-Kaci. The poet was born around 1680: the poem is taken from a collection of Kabyle poetry: M. Mammeri, *Poèmes Kabyles anciennes* (Algiers, 1988), p. 109 (translation EF).

41 'Arsh in Moroccan Arabic means 'throne', *Thaqbilt* is a Berberization of the Arabic *qabīla*, tribe, from which Kabylia is derived: in Morocco it is applied to all levels of the tribal section.

42 For example, J. Berque, *Structures sociales du Haut Atlas* (Paris 1955), pp. 105f.

43 *Corpus Inscriptionum Latinarum*, VIII. 18,582. The best recent work on this inscription is B.D. Shaw, 'Lamasba, an ancient irrigation community', *Antiquités africaines*, 18 (1982), 61–104, but see also R.P. Duncan-Jones, 'Some configurations of landholding in the Roman Empire', in M.I. Finley (ed.), *Studies in Roman Property* (Cambridge, 1976), pp. 7–34.

44 Shaw, 'Lamasba', 86.

45 Although Islamic law prescribes that women should inherit one-half the share of her brothers, in fact many Berber societies circumvent this: see, for example, Hart, *The Aith Waryaghar*, p. 107. In villages in Kabylia women will inherit land inside the village rather than outside it. If they sell it, they must offer it to their brothers first.

46 R. Rebuffat, 'Les fermiers du désert', *L'Africa romana*, 5 (1987); Barker and Jones, 'The UNESCO Libyan Valleys Survey VI', 31–42; on the Tunisian oases, see P. Trousset, 'Les oasis présahariennes dans l'Antiquité; partage de l'eau et division du temps', *Antiquités africaines*, 22 (1986), 163–93.

47 For Lamasba, see Shaw, 'Lamasba'; for Massat, see R. Montagne, 'Une tribu berbère du sud Marocain: Massat', *Hésperis*, 4 (1924), 357–403. There is a significant difference between these systems and those in the south, where water is owned separately from land: exceptions are also

found in the Rif (Hart, *The Aith Waryaghar*, p. 108). For the foggaras
of Touat, see the excellent study by G. Grandguillaume, 'Régime
économique et structure du pouvoir: le système des foggara du Touat',
Revue de l'Occident musulman et de la Méditerranée, 13–14 (1973),
437–56. Here the water from a foggara is divided by the labour input
of each proprietor – in other words, the number of man-hours his
slaves or employees put into it. It has been calculated that up to 48,000
man-hours are required to dig a foggara 4 km long.
48 Yacine, *L'Izli*, p. 12.
49 Feraoun, *Jours de Kabylie*, p. 111; translation EF.
50 Yacine, *L'Izli*, p. 30. Meetings at the well outside of town are a topos
    in Semitic literature – one thinks of John 4.6–30.
51 Jemma-Gouzon, *Villages de l'Aurès*, p. 85, n. 58. On granaries, see
    Jacques-Meunier, *Grenier-Citadelles*; A. Louis, *Tunisie du Sud. Ksars
    et villages de crêtes* (Paris, 1975).
52 For example, W.H.C. Frend, 'The end of Byzantine North Africa:
    some evidence of transitions', *Bulletin archéologique du Comité des
    Travaux Historiques*, NS (1983), 387–97.
53 On the plan of Ghardaia, see M. Mercier, *La Civilization urbain au
    Mzab* (Paris, 1922), pp. 67f.
54 Feraoun, *Jours de Kabylie*, p. 58f.
55 Bourdieu, *Outline of a Theory of Practice*, pp. 185f; and, for the
    exchange of pottery for grain, the novel by M. Feraoun, *Le Fils du
    pauvre* (Algiers, 1990), which is filled with ethnographic detail. Woven
    goods are naturally produced at home: a friend laments that his
    grandmother is too busy to make him a burnous, for buying one would
    be inconceivable.
56 G. Laoust-Chantreaux, *Kabylie côte femmes: La vie féminine à Ait
    Hichem, 1937–1939* (Paris, 1990), p. 36. On the construction of the
    Kabyle house, see M. Maunier, *La Construction collective de la
    maison en Kabylie; étude sur la coopération économique chez les
    berbères du Djurjura* (Paris, 1926), *passim*.
57 Feraoun, *Jours de Kabylie*, p. 80; translation EF. On specialized
    women's markets in Morocco, see R. Montagne, 'Coutumes et
    légendes de la côte Berbère du Maroc', *Hespéris*, 4 (1924), 8–125, esp.
    104.
58 Moroccan markets are the best studied: F. Benet, 'Explosive markets:
    the Berber highlands', in K. Polanyi, C. Arensberg and H. Pearson
    (eds), *Trade and Market in the Early Empires* (Glencoe, Ill., 1956), pp.
    188–217; M. Mikesell, 'The role of tribal markets in Morocco:
    examples from the "northern zone"', *Geographcal Review*, 48(4)
    (1958), 494–511; Hart, *The Aith Waryaghar*, pp. 69f. For the special
    case of women's markets in the Rif, see ibid., pp. 87f.
59 Mammeri, *Poèmes kabyles anciennes*, p. 85; translation EF.
60 Ibid., p. 121, translation EF.
61 E. Carette, *Exploration scientifique de l'Afrique pendant les années*

1841, 1842 (Paris, 1848), quoted in C. Lacoste-Dujardin, 'Opération "Oiseau Bleu", 1956, géostratégie et ethnopolitique', *Revue de l'Occident musulman et de la Mediterranée*, 41 (1986), 167–96, esp. 171f. For a list of craft specializations, see A. Hanoteau, and A. Letourneux, *La Kabylie et les coutumes kabyles*, 3 vols (Paris, 1857), vol. II, p. 435.

62   Aith Mansour Amrouche, Fadhma, *Histoire de ma vie* (Paris, 1946; reprinted 1990), p. 111.

63   Thus Camps remarks that it is the 'living symbol of a North African conservatism, both aesthetic and technical, which has its roots in the centuries before history began. It is thus an example of "Berber permanence"': G. Camps, *Berbères. Aux marges de l'histoire* (Toulouse, 1980), p. 213. For an exhaustive treatment of prehistoric North African ceramics, see G. Camps, *Aux origines de la Berbérie. Monuments et rites funéraires protohistoriques* (Paris, 1961). There are a number of modern works on pottery in the Maghreb, admirably synthesized recently in D. Peacock, *Pottery in the Roman World: An Ethnoarchaeological Approach* (London, 1982). See also J.-L. Combès, and A. Louis, *Les Poteries de Djerba* (Tunis, 1967); D. Gruner, *Die Berber-Keramik* (Berlin, 1973); and, for mediaeval urban production, N. Benco, *The Early Medieval Pottery Industry at al-Basra, Morocco* (BAR International 341), (Oxford, 1987).

64   Peacock, *Pottery in the Roman World, passim.*

65   See M. Devulder, 'Peintures murales et pratiques magiques dans la tribu des Ouadhias', *Revue africaine*, 95 (1951), 63–102; a good bibliography of modern studies of Berber pottery is given in Gruner, *Die Berber-Keramik.*

66   For estate production, see Peacock, *Pottery in the Roman World*; D. Peacock, F. Bejaoui and N. Ben Lazreg, 'Roman pottery production in central Tunisia', *Journal of Roman Archaeology*, 3 (1990), 59–85; on Tiddis, see J. Lassus, 'L'archéologie algérienne en 1957', *Libyca*, 6 (1958), 235–50.

67   Yacine, *L'Izli ou l'amour chanté en Kabyle*, p. 171.

68   This is probably the basis for the peaceful co-existence of large Jewish communities on Jerba and at Ghardaia – at least until the creation of Israel.

69   Bourdieu, *Outline of a Theory of Practice*, is the extreme case; in his index 'Islam' is missing, and under religion we find 'see magic'. For the Rif, see Hart *The Aith Waryaghar*, pp. 175f.

70   Goichon, *La Vie féminine*; for magic in the Rif, see Hart, *The Aith Waryaghar,* pp. 149f.

71   On the *Dii Mauri*, see M. Benabou, *La Résistance africaine à la romanisation* (Paris, 1976), pp. 309–75; E. Fentress, 'Dii Mauri and Dii Patrii', *Latomus*, 37 (1978), 2–16; G. Camps, 'Qui sont les Dii Mauri?', *Antiquités africaines*, 26 (1990), 131–53.

72   Jemma-Gouzon, *Villages de l'Aurès*, p. 162.

73   W.H.C. Frend, *The Donatist Church* (Oxford, 1952), pp. 171–84.

74 Herodotus, *History*, 4.172: 'the Nasamones swear by the men who are thought to be the most just and the best, touching their tombs. For divination they go to the tombs of their ancestors and sleep on them, after praying. They then behave according to their dreams.' On early modern practice, see S. Gsell, *Herodote* (Algiers, 1916), p. 84.

75 Jemma-Gouzon, *Villages de l'Aurès*, pp. 106f.

76 Montagne, 'Coutumes et légendes', 105. His assertion that this festival was a relic of some primitive *'nuit d'erreur'* is interesting, but not proven.

77 On Saturn, see the monumental work of Leglay, *Saturne africain*, 2 vols (Paris, 1961–6).

78 J. Amrouche, 'L'éternel Jugurtha: propositions sur le génie africain', 1946; reprinted in *Etudes méditerranéennes*, 11 (1963), translation EF.

Chapter 8   Berbers and Berberism

1 T. Yacine, *Ait Menguellet chante . . .* (Algiers), p. 13.

2 E. Gellner and C. Micaud (eds), *Arabs and Berbers: From Tribe to Nation in North Africa* (London, 1973), p. 433; M. Gast, 'La société traditionnelle des Kel Ahaggar face aux problèmes contemporains', in E. Gellner (ed.), *Islam: Société et communauté*, ser. Anthropologies du Maghreb (Paris, 1980), pp. 107–36, esp. p. 129.

3 W. Quandt, 'The Berbers in the Algerian political elite', in Gellner and Micaud (eds), *Arabs and Berbers*, p. 302.

4 F. Colonna, *Savants Paysans: Eléments d'histoire sociale sur l'Algérie rurale* (Paris, 1987), p. 205; H. Roberts, 'The unforeseen development of the Kabyle question in contemporary Algeria', *Government and Opposition*, 17 (1982), 312–25; idem, 'The economics of Berberism', *Government and Opposition*, 18 (1983), 218–35.

5 C. Lacoste-Dujardin, 'Opération "Oiseau Bleu", 1956; géostrategie et ethnopolitique', *Revue de l'Occident musulman et de la Méditeranée*, 41–2 (1986), 193.

6 Quandt, 'Berbers in the Algerian political elite', pp. 299f.

7 The following argument is based on Roberts, 'The unforeseen development' and 'The economics of Berberism'.

8 E. Burke, 'The image of the Moroccan state in French ethnological literature: a new look at the origin of Lyautey's Berber policy', in Gellner and Micaud (eds), *Arabs and Berbers*, pp. 175–99, esp. p. 190.

9 J. Waterbury, 'The coup manqué', in ibid., p. 406.

10 Said Belguidoun, personal communication; F. Colonna, 'Saints furieux et saints studieux, ou dans l'Aurès, comment la religion vient aux tribus', *Annales: économies, sociétés, civilisations* (1980), 642–63.

11 H. Ait Ahmed, 'La braise berbère', *Autrement*, no. 38 (1982), 153–8; cf. idem, *Algérie: Quelle identite?* (Paris, 1981).

12 Chaker, 'La voie étroite', p. 294; cf. idem, 'Langue et identité

berbères', *Annuaire de l'Afrique du Nord*, **23** (1984), 173–80.

13   Cf. H. Roberts, 'Towards an understanding of the Kabyle question in contemporary Algeria', *Maghreb Review*, **5** (1980), 115–24; idem, 'The unforeseen development of the Kabyle question in contemporary Algeria', *Government and Opposition*, **17** (1982), 312–34; idem, 'The economics of Berberism: the material basis of the Kabyle question in contemporary Algeria', ibid., **19** (1983), 218–35.

14   Cf. K. Sutton, A. Aghrout and S. Zaimeche, 'Political changes in Algeria: an emerging electoral geography', *Maghreb Review*, **17** (1992), 3–27.

15   Cf. Chaker, 'La voie étroite'; Lacoste, *L'Etat de Maghreb*, p. 276.

16   Cf. Lacoste, *L'Etat de Maghreb*, p. 79.

17   Ibid., pp. 95, 497–500: Ageron, *Modern Algeria*, p. 89.

18   Cf. H.T. Norris, *Saharan Myth and Saga* (Oxford, 1972), p. 33, *et passim*.

19   M. Feraoun, essays: *Jours de Kabylie* (Algiers, 1954); novels include the autobiographical *Le Fils du pauvre* (Algiers, 1950), *La Terre et le sang* (1953) and *Les Chemins qui montent* (1957). All of these have been recently reprinted by Editions Bouchène, Paris.

20   M. Mammeri, *Poèmes kabyles anciens* (Algiers, 1988); T. Yacine, *Poésie berbère et identité* (Paris, 1988); idem, *L'Izli ou l'amour chanté en Kabyle* (Paris, 1990).

21   See above, p. 223.

22   Yacine, *Ait Menguellet*.

23   S. Chaker, 'Constantes et mutations dans l'affirmation identitaire berbère', *Revue de l'Occident musulman et de la Méditerranée*, **45** (1987), 48–63.

24   *Awal Amazit*, © 1989, Tackult Software, by Arezki Nait Abdallah, University of Western Ontario.

Bibliography

Abun-Nasr, J.M. (1987), *A History of the Maghrib in the Islamic Period* (Cambridge).

Ageron, C.-R. (1960), 'La France a-t-elle eu une politique Kabyle?', *Revue Historique*, 223, 311–52.

Ageron, Ch.-R. (1972), 'La politique berbère du Protectorat marocain de 1913 à 1934', in idem, *Politiques coloniales au Maghreb* (Paris).

Ageron, Ch.-R. (1991), *Modern Algeria: A History from 1830 to the Present* (London).

Ait Ahmed, H. (1981), *Algérie. Quelle identité?* (Paris).

Ait Ahmed, H. (1982), 'La braise berbère', *Autrement*, no. 38, 153–8.

Ait Kaci, A., Bounssair, N. and Fentress, E. (1993), 'Prospections à Zana: rapport préliminaire', *Bulletin d'archéologie algérienne*, supp. 7.

Aith Mansour Amrouche, Fadhma (1946), *Histoire de ma vie* (Paris; reprinted 1990).

Akerraz, A. (1983), 'Note sur l'enceinte tardive de Volubilis', *Bulletin Archéologique de Comité des Travaux Historiques*, NS, 429–38.

Al-Azmeh, A. (1981), *Ibn Khaldūn in Modern Scholarship* (London).

Allan, J.A. (ed.) (1981), *Sahara: Ecological Change and Early Economic History* (London).

Allard-Huard, L. and Huard, P. (1986), 'La femme au Sahara avant le désert', *Etudes Scientifiques* (Cairo), 1–36.

Alport, E.A., 'The Mzab', in E. Gellner and C. Micaud (eds), *Arabs and Berbers* (New York, 1972; London, 1973), pp. 141–52; reprinted from *Man*, 84 (1954), 34–44.

Ammerman, A. and Cavalli-Sforza, L. (1979), 'The wave of advance model for the spread of agriculture in Europe', in C. Renfrew and K.L. Cooke (eds), *Transformations: Mathematical Approaches to Culture Change* (New York), pp. 175–94.

Ammerman, A. and Cavalli-Sforza, L. (1984), *The Neolithic Transition in Europe* (Princeton, N.J.).

Amrouche, J. (1946), 'L'éternel Jugurtha: propositions sur le génie africain', reprinted in *Etudes méditerranéennes*, 11 (1963).

Aron, R. et al. (1962), *Les Origines de la guerre d'Algérie* (Paris)
Année épigraphique (various issues).

Aron, A. et al. (1962), *Les Origines de la guerre d'Algérie* (Paris).

Augustin (1982), *Les Lettres de Saint Augustin découvertes par Johannes Divjak* (Paris).

Augustin (1987), *Oeuvres, 46B: lettres 1*–29**, ed. J. Divjak (Paris).

Awal: Cahiers d'études berbères (1985–).

Ayoub, A. (1984), 'The Hilali epic: material and memory', *Revue d'histoire maghrébine*, 11 (35–6), 189–217.

al-Bakri (1913), *Description de l'Afrique septentrionale*, ed. and trans. M. de Slane, 2nd edn, 2 vols (Paris; reprinted 1965).

Baldus, H.R. (1979), 'Die Münzprägung der numidischen Königreiche', in R. Horn and C. Rüger (eds), *Die Numider* (Bonn), pp. 187–208.

Banks, K. (1989), 'The appearance and spread of cattle-keeping in the Saharan North Africa', in Krzyzaniak and Kobusiewicz (eds), pp. 57–67.

Barich, B. (1987), *Archaeology and Environment in the Libyan Sahara* (Oxford; BAR no. 368).

Baker, G. (1981), 'Early agriculture and economic change in North Africa', in J.A. Allan (ed.), *Sahara: Ecological Change and Early Economic History* (London).

Barker, G. (1989), 'From classification to interpretation: Libyan prehistory, 1969–1989', *Libyan Studies*, 20, 31–43.

Barker, G. et al. (1984), 'UNESCO Libyan Valleys Survey 6: Investigations of a Romano-Libyan farm', *Libyan Studies*, 15, 1–44.

Basagana, R. and Sayad, A. (1984), *Habitat traditionnel et structures familiales en Kabylie*, Mémoire du CRAPE (Algiers), 23.

Basset, A. (1952), *The Berber Language* (London).

Bates, O. (1914), *The Eastern Libyans* (London).

Bazzana, A., Cressier, P. and Guichard, P. (1988), *Les Châteaux ruraux d'al-Andalus. Histoire et archéologie des husūn du sud-est de l'Espagne* (Madrid).

Bel, A. (1938), *La Religion musulmane en Berbérie*, vol. i (Paris).

Belkhodj, K. (1970), 'L'Afrique byzantine à la fin du VI et au début du VII siècle', *Revue de L'Occident musulman et de la Méditerranée*, 15, 55–67.

Benabou, M. (1976), *La Résistance africaine à la Romanisation* (Paris).

Benachenhou, A. (1946), 'Sîdî 'Abdallah Moul l-Gâra ou 'Abdallâh ibn Yâsîn', *Hespéris*, 33, 406–13.

Benco, N. (1987), *The Early Medieval Pottery Industry at al-Basra, Morocco* (BAR International 341) (Oxford).

Benet, F. (1956), 'Explosive markets: the Berber Highlands', in K. Polanyi, C. Arensberg and H. Pearson (eds), *Trade and Market in the Early Empires* (Glencoe, Ill.), pp. 188–217.

Bernard, A. (1921), *Enquête sur l'habitat rural des indigènes de l'Algérie* (Algiers).

Bernus, E. (1976), 'L'évolution des relations de dépendance depuis la période pré-coloniale jusqu'à nos jours chez les Iullemeden Kel Dinnik', *Revue de l'Occident musulman et de la Méditerranée*, 21, 85–99.

Bernus, S., Bonte, P., Brock, L. and Clodot C. (eds) (1986), *Le Fils et le neveu: jeux et enjeux de la parenté touarègue* (Paris).

Berque, J. (1955), *Structures Sociales du Haut Atlas* (Paris).

Berque, J. (1962), *Le Maghreb entre deux guerres* (Paris), trans. *French North Africa* (London, 1967).

Berque, J. (1978), 'Un maître de l'heure renoncé', in idem, *L'Intérieur du Maghreb* (Paris).

Berque, J. (1982), 'Une perspective nationale manquée', in Berque, *Ulémas, fondateurs, insurgés du Maghreb: XVIIᵉ siècle* (Paris).

Berthier, A. (1980) 'Un habitat punique à Constantine', *Antiquités africaines*, 16, 13–26.

Berthier, P. (1966), *Les Anciennes Sucreries de Maroc et leurs réseaux hydrauliques* (Rabat).

Bertrand, F. (1986), 'A propos du cavalier de Simitthus', *Antiquités africaines*, 22, 57–76.

Beylié, L. de (1909), *La Kalaa des Beni-Hammad* (Paris).

Bidwell, R. (1973), *Morocco under Colonial Rule* (London).

Birley, A.R. (1971), *Septimius Severus the African Emperor* (London).

Blanchard-Lemée, M. (1976), *Maisons à mosaiques du quartier central de Djemila (Cuicul)* (Etudes d'antiquités africaines) (Aix-en-Provence).

Blunt, W. (1951), *Black Sunrise* (London).

Bourdieu, P. (1977), *Outline of a Theory of Practice* (Cambridge).

Bourdieu, P. (1979), 'The Kabyle house, or the world reversed', in idem, *Algeria 1960* (Cambridge and Paris).

Bourdieu, P. (1990) *The Logic of Practice* (Paris).

Bousquet, G.H. (1974), *Les Berbères*, 2nd edn (Paris).

Bovill, E.W. (1958), *The Golden Trade of the Moors* (London).

Braudel, F. (1972), *The Mediterranean and the Mediterranean World in the Age of Philip II*, 2 vols (London).

Braund, D. (1984), *Rome and the Friendly Kings* (London).

Brett, M. (1969), 'Ifrīqiya as a market for Saharan trade from the tenth to the twelfth century AD', *Journal of African History*, 10, 347–64.

Brett, M. (1974–5), 'The Zughba at Tripoli, 429H (1037–8AD), Society for Libyan Studies [London], *Sixth Annual Report*, pp. 41–7.

Brett, M. (1975–6), 'The journey of al-Tijānī to Tripoli at the beginning of the fourteenth century AD/eighth century AH', Society for Libyan Studies [London], *Seventh Annual Report*, pp. 41–51.

Brett, M. (1978a), 'The Arab conquests and the rise of Islam in North Africa', in *The Cambridge History of Africa* (Cambridge), vol. ii, ch. 8.

Brett, M. (1978b), 'The Fatimid revolution and its aftermath in North Africa', *The Cambridge History of Africa* (Cambridge), vol. ii, ch. 10.

Brett, M. (1979a), 'Ibn Khaldūn and the Arabisation of North Africa', *Maghreb Review*, 4, 9–16.

Brett, M. (1979b), 'Jacques Berque and the history of the Maghreb', *Maghreb Review*, 4, 140–8.

Brett, M. (1980), *The Moors: Islam in the West* (London).

Brett, M. (1981), 'Arabs, Berbers and Holy Men in southern Ifrīqiya, 650–750AH/1250–1350AD', *Cahiers de Tunisie*, 29, 533–59.

Brett, M. (1982a), 'Fatimid historiography: a case study – the quarrel with the Zirids, 1048–58', in D.O. Morgan (ed.), *Medieval Historical Writing in the Christian and Islamic Worlds* (London), pp. 47–59.

Brett, M. (1982b), 'Modernisation in 19th-century North Africa', *Maghreb Review*, 7, 16–22.

Brett, M. (1983), 'Islam and trade in the *Bilād al-Sūdān*, tenth–eleventh century AD', *Journal of African History*, 24, 431–40.

Brett, M. (1984), 'Morocco and the Ottomans: the sixteenth century in North Africa', *Journal of African History*, 25, 331–41.

Brett, M. (1986), 'Continuity and change: Egypt and North Africa in the nineteenth century', *Journal of African History*, 27, 149–62.

Brett, M. (1988a), 'Islam in North Africa', in S. Sutherland et al. (eds), *The World's Religions* (London); reprinted in P. Clarke (ed.), *The World's Religions: Islam* (London, 1990).

M. Brett (1988b), 'Legislating for inequality in Algeria: the Sénatus-Consulte of 14 July 1865', *Bulletin of the School of Oriental and African Studies*, 51, 440–61.

Brett, M. (1991), 'Ibn Khaldūn and the dynastic approach to local history: the case of Biskra', *Al-Qantara*, 12, 157–80.

Brett, M. (1992), 'The Islamisation of Morocco: from the Arabs to the Almoravids', *Morocco*, 2, 57–71.

Brett, M. (1993), 'The Sons of the New Moon and the Flood of the Dam', in *Mélanges offerts à Mohamed Talbi* (Tunis), pp. 55–67.

Briggs, L.C. (1960), *Tribes of the Sahara* (Cambridge, Mass., and London).

Brogan, O. (1965), 'Henscir el-Ausaf by Tigi (Tripolitania) and some related tombs in the Tunisian Gefara', *Libya Antiqua*, 2, 47–56.

Brogan, O. and Smith, D. (1984), *Ghirza: A Libyan Settlement in the Roman Period* (Tripoli).

Broughton, T.R.S. (1929), *The Romanization of Africa Proconsularis* (London).

Brown, K.L. (1976), *People of Salé* (Manchester).

Brunschvig, R. (1940–7), *La Berbérie orientale sous les Hafsides*, 2 vols (Paris).

Brunschvig, R. (1986), 'Ibn Abdalh'akam et la conquête de l'Afrique du Nord', in idem, *Etudes sur l'Islam classique et l'Afrique du Nord* (London), vol. XI; reprinted from *AIEO* (*Annales de l'Institut des Etudes Orientales*, Algiers), 6 (1942–7), 108–55.

Buck, D., Burns, J. and Mattingly, D. (1983), 'Archaeological sites of the Bir Scedua basin: settlements and cemeteries', *Libyan Studies*, 14, 39–68.

Buecheler, F. and Riese, A. (eds) (1894), *Anthologia Latina* (Leipzig).

Bulliet, R. (1975), *The Camel and the Wheel* (Cambridge, Mass.).

Burke, E. III (1973), 'The image of the Moroccan state in French ethnological literature: a new look at the origin of Lyautey's Berber policy', in Gellner and Micaud (eds), pp. 175–99.

Burke, E. III (1976), *Prelude to Protectorate in Morocco: Precolonial Protest and Resistance, 1860–1912* (Chicago and London).

Bynon, J. (1970), 'The contribution of linguistics to history in the field of Berber studies', in D. Dalby (ed.), *Language and History in Africa* (London).

Campbell, J.K. (1964), *Honour, Family and Patronage* (Oxford).

Camps, G. (1955), 'Les Bavares', *Revue africaine*, 99, 241–88.

Camps, G. (1961a), *Aux origines de la Berbérie. Monuments et rites funéraires protohistoriques* (Paris).

Camps, G. (1961b), *Aux origines de la Berbérie. Masinissa ou les débuts de l'histoire* (Algiers).

Camps, G. (1973), 'Nouvelles observations sur l'architecture et l'âge du Medracen, mausolée royal de Numidie', *Comptes rendus de l'Académie des Inscriptions*, 470–516.

Camps G. (1974), *Les Civilisations préhistoriques de l'Afrique du Nord et du Sahara* (Paris).

Camps, G. (1980), *Berbères. Aux marges de l'histoire* (Toulouse).

Camps, G. (1982), 'Beginnings of pastoralism and cultivation in north-west Africa and the Sahara: origins of the Berbers', in *Cambridge History of Africa* (Cambridge), vol. I, pp. 548–612.

Camps, G. (1984a), '*Rex Gentium Maurorum et Romanorum*: recherches sur les royaumes de Mauretanie des VI et VII siècles', *Antiquités africaines*, 20, 183–218.

Camps, G. (1984b), 'Avertissement', *Encyclopédie Berbère*, vol. I.

Camps, G. (1984c), 'Abizar', *Encyclopédie Berbère*, vol. I.

Camps, G. (1986), 'Funerary monuments with attached chapels from the Northern Sahara', *African Archaeological Review*, 4, 151–64.

Camps, G. (1987), *Les Berbères: mémoire et identité* (Paris).

Camps, G. (1989), 'Les Chars Sahariens. Images d'une société aristocratique', *Antiquités africaines*, 25, 11–42.

Camps, G. (1990), 'Qui sont les Dii Mauri?', *Antiquités africaines*, 26, 131–53.

Camps-Fabrer, H. (1966), *Matière et art mobilier dans le préhistoire nord-africaine et saharienne* (Paris).

Camps-Fabrer, H. (1986), 'Le Sahara néolithique, centre d'art mobilier', in *Archéologie africaine et sciences de la nature* (Bordeaux).

Caputo, G. et al. (1951), 'Il Sahara Italiana: Scavi Sahariani', *Monumenti Antichi*, 41, 150–552.

Carette, E. (1848), *Exploration scientifique de l'Afrique pendant les années 1841, 1842* (Paris).

Cavalli-Sforza, L., Menozzi, P. and Piazza, A. (1994), *History and Geography of Human Genes* (Princeton, N.J.).

Chaker, S. (1977), 'Un inscription libyque du Musée des Antiquités d'Alger', *Libyca*, 25, 193–202.

Chaker, S. (1981–), 'Langue et littérature berbères. Chronique des études', *Annuaire de l'Afrique du Nord*, 20ff.

Chaker, S. (1984a), 'Langue et identité berbères', *Annuaire de l'Afrique du Nord*, 23, 173–80.

Chaker, S. (1984b), *Textes en linguistique berbère. Introduction au domaine berbère* (Paris).

Chaker, S. (1987), 'Constantes et mutations dans l'affirmation identitaire berbère', *Revue de l'Occident musulman et de la Mediterranée*, 45, 48–63.

Chaker, S. (1989), 'La voie étroite: la revendication berbère entre culture et politique', *Annuaire de l'Afrique du Nord*, 28, 281–96.

Chaker, S. (1990), 'Les bases de l'apparentement chamito-sémitique du berbère: un faisceau d'indices convergents', *Etudes et documents berbères*, 7, 28–57.

Chaker, S. (1993), 'La question berbère dans l'Algérie independante, le fracture inevitable', *Revue de l'Occident musulman et de la Méditerranée*, 65, 97–105.

Chamla, M.C. (1968), *Les Populations anciennes du Sahara et des régions limitrophes* (Paris).

Chaudhuri, K.N. (1985), *Trade and Civilisation in the Indian Ocean* (Cambridge).

Claudot-Hawad, H. (ed.) (1991), 'Touaregs, exil et résistance', *Revue du Monde musulman et de la Méditerranée*, 57.

Clayton, A. (1988), *France, Soldiers and Africa* (London).

Coarelli, F and Thébert, Y. (1988), 'Architecture funéraire et pouvoir. Réflexions sur l'hellenisme numide', *Mélanges de l'Ecole Française de Rome*, 100, 761–818.

Collins, R. (1989), *The Arab Conquest of Spain, 710–97* (Oxford).

Colonna, F. (1980), 'Saints furieux et saints studieux, ou dans l'Aures, comment la religion vient aux tribus', *Annales: économies, sociétés, civilisations*, 642–63.

Colonna, F. (1987), *Savants Paysans: eléments d'histoire sociale sur l'Algérie rurale* (Paris).

Combès, J.-L. and Louis, A. (1967), *Les Poteries de Djerba* (Tunis).

Corbier, M. (1982), 'Les familles clarissimes d'Afrique proconsulaire (Ier – IIIe siècle)', *Epigrafia e ordine senatorio* (Rome), *Tituli* V, 705–78.

Cornell, V.J. (1987), 'Understanding is the mother of ability: responsibility and action in the doctrine of Ibn Tūmart', *Studia Islamica*, 66, 71–103.

Coulson, N.J. (1964), *A History of Islamic Law* (Edinburgh).

Courtois, Ch. (1955), *Les Vandales et l'Afrique* (Paris).

Cribb, R. (1991), *Nomads in Archaeology* (Cambridge).

Cuperly, P. (1979), 'L'Ibāḍisme au XIIe siècle: la 'Aqīda de Abū Sahl Yaḥyā', *IBLA (Revue de l'Institut des Belles Lettres Arabes*, Tunis), 42(143–4), 67–89, 277–305.

Cuperly, P. (1987–8), 'La cite ibāḍite: urbanisme et vie sociale au XIᵉ siècle', *Awal: Cahiers d'études berbères*, 3, 89–114; 4, 7–14.

Daniels, C.M. (1970), *The Garamantes of Southern Libya* (Michigan).

Daniels, C.M. (1989), 'Fieldwork amongst the Garamantes', *Libyan Studies*, 20, 45–61.

Déjeux, J. (1987), *Femmes d'Algérie* (Paris).

Demougeot, E. (1960), 'Le chameau et l'Afrique du Nord romaine', *Annales: économies, sociétés, civilisations*, 15, 209–47.

Dermenghem, E. (1954), *Le Culte des saints dans l'islam maghrébin* (Paris).

Desanges, J. (1962), *Catalogue des tribus africaines de l'antiquité classique à l'ouest du Nil* (Dakar).

Desanges, J. (1978), 'L'Afrique romaine et libyco-berbère', in Cl. Nicolet, *Rome et le conquête du monde méditerranéen*, vol. 2 (Paris).

Desanges, J. (1980), 'Un *princeps gentis* à Sétif', *Bulletin du Comité des travaux historiques*, 12–14, 121–7.

Deverdun, G. (1959), *Marrakech des origines à 1912*, 2 vols (Rabat).

Devisse, J. (1988), 'Trade and trade routes in West Africa', *UNESCO General History of Africa* (Paris, London and Berkeley), vol. III, ch. 14.

Devulder, M. (1951), 'Peintures murales et pratiques magiques dans la tribu des Ouadhias', *Revue Africaine*, 95, 63–102.

Diakonoff, M. (1965), *Semito-Hamitic Languages: An Essay in Classification* (Moscow).

Diehl, C. (1896), *L'Afrique byzantine* (New York).

Di Vita, A. (1967), 'La diffusione di Cristianesimo nell'interno della Tripolitania attraverso i monumenti, e sua sopravivenza nella Tripolitania araba', *Quaderni di Archeologia della Libya*, 5, 121–42.

Dols, M. (1981), 'The general mortality of the Black Death in the Mamluk empire', in A. Udovitch (ed.), *The Islamic Middle East, 700–1900* (Princeton, N.J.), pp. 397–428.

Dufourcq, E. (1966), *L'Espagne catalane et le Maghreb aux XIIIᵉ et XIVᵉ siècles* (Paris).

Duncan-Jones, R.P. (1976), 'Some configurations of landholding in the Roman Empire', in M.I. Finley (ed.), *Studies in Roman Property* (Cambridge), 7–34.

Durliat, J. (1981), *Les Dédicaces d'ouvrage de défense dans l'Afrique byzantine* (Rome).

El Mansour, M. (1990), *Morocco in the Reign of Mawlay Sulayman* (Outwell, Wisbech).

Elmayer, A.F. (1983, 1984), 'Latino-Punic inscriptions from Roman Tripolitania', *Libyan Studies*, 14, 88–95; 15, 93–105.

Elmayer, A.F. (1985), 'The Centenaria of Roman Tripolitania', *Libyan Studies*, 16, 77–85.

Emerit, M. (1977–8), 'Hajj Ahmad Bey', in Ch.A. Julien et al. (eds), *Les Africains*, 12 vols (Paris), vol. 8, pp. 101–31.

Encyclopaedia of Islam, 1st ed (Leiden, 1913–38); 2nd edn (Leiden, 1954ff).

Encyclopédie berbére (Paris).

Ennabli, A. (1986), 'Les thermes du Thiase Marine de Sidi Ghrib', *Monuments Piot*, **68**, 1–59.

Etienne, B. (1977), 'Clientelism in Algeria', in E. Gellner and J. Waterbury (eds), *Patrons and Clients* (London), pp. 291–307.

Euzennat, M. (1974), 'Les Zegrenses', in *Mélanges d'histoire ancienne offerts à William Seston* (Paris), pp. 175–81.

Fanon, F. (1959), *L'An cinq de la révolution algérienne* (Paris); trans. as *A Dying Colonialism* (London, 1970).

Fantar, M. (1986), *Kerkouane: cité punique du Cap Bon, Tunisie* (Tunis).

Fentress, E. (1978), 'Dii Mauri and Dii Patrii', *Latomus*, **37**, 2–16.

Fentress, E. (1979), *Numidia and the Roman Army* (Oxford; BAR 53).

Fentress, E. (1987), 'The house of the Prophet: African Islamic housing', *Archeologia Medievale*, **14**, 47–68.

Fentress, E. (1990), 'The economy of an inland city: Sétif', *L'Afrique dans l'Occident Romain (Iᵉʳ siècle av. J.-C.–IVᵉ siècle ap. J.-C.)*, *Collection de d'Ecole française de Rome* (Rome), **134**, 117–28.

Fentress, E. (ed.) (1991), *Fouilles de Sétif, 1977–1984* (Algiers).

Fentress, E., Kennet, D. and Valenti, I. (1986), 'A Sicilian valley in its landscape: Contrada Mirabile, Mazara del Vallo', *Opus*, **5**, 75–96.

Feraoun, M. (1950), *Le Fils du pauvre* (Algiers; reprinted 1990).

Feraoun, M. (1954), *Jours de Kabylie* (Algiers; reprinted 1990).

Ferchiou, N. (1987), 'Le paysage funéraire pré-romain dans deux régions céréalières de Tunisie antique (Fahs-Bou Arada et Tebourba Mateur): les tombeaux monumentaux', *Antiquités africaines*, **23**, 13–70.

Ferchiou, N. (1988), 'L'habitat fortifié pre-impériale en Tunisie antique: aperçus sur le typologie des sites perchés et des sites de versant, illustrés par quelques exemples à Carthage et sa territoire dans l'antiquité', *Antiquités africaines*, **24**, 43–86.

Février, P.A. (1966), 'Inscriptions inédites relatives aux domaines de la région de Sétif', in R. Chevallier (ed.), *Mélanges Piganiol* (Paris), pp. 217–28.

Février, P.A. (1972), 'L'art funéraire et les images des chefs indigènes dans la Kabylie antique', *Actes du premier congrès d'études des cultures Méditerranéenes d'influence arabo-berbère*, Malta, pp. 152–74.

Février, P.A. (1983), 'Approches récentes de l'Afrique byzantine', *Revue de l'Occident musulman et de la Méditerranée*, **41**, 25–55.

Février, P.A. (1986), 'L'histoire auguste et le Maghreb', *Antiquités africaines*, **22**, 115–40.

Fisher, Sir G. (1957), *Barbary Legend: War, Trade and Piracy in North Africa, 1415–1830* (Oxford).

Fisher, H.J. and Conrad, D.C. (1982–3), 'The conquest that never was: Ghana and the Almoravids, 1076', *History in Africa*, **9**, 21–59; **10**, 53–78.

Fleischer, C. (1984), 'Royal authority, dynastic cyclism, and "ibn

Khaldunism" in sixteenth-century Ottoman letters', in B.B. Lawrence (ed.), *Ibn Khaldūn and Islamic Ideology* (Leiden), pp. 46–68.

Fontana, S. (in press), 'Tradizioni artigianal: e raftiguiazioni di tipi ethici nei balsamari unfigurati di produzione africana', *Quaderni dell'archeologia della Libia*, 17.

Fontana, S. (in press), 'Manufatti romani nei corredi funerarii del Fezzan: testimonianze dei commerci e della cultura dei Garamanti (I–III Seculi d.c.)', *Actes du Congrés des Sociétés Historiques et Scientifiques* (Pau, 1993), 581–4.

Forni, G. (1953), *Il Reclutamento delle legione da Augusto a Diocleziano* (Milan).

Frend, W.H.C. (1952), *The Donatist Church* (Oxford).

Frend, W.H.C. (1983), 'The end of Byzantine North Africa: some evidence of transitions', *Bulletin Archéologique du Comité des Travaux Historiques*, NS, 387–97.

Frézouls, E. (1957), 'Les *Baquates* et le province romaine de Tingitane', *BAM*, 2, 65–115.

Friedman, J. and Rowlands, M. (1979), 'Notes towards an epigenetic model of the evolution of civilisation', in J. Friedman and M. Rowlands (eds), *The Evolution of Social Systems* (London), pp. 201–76.

Galand, L. (1979), *Langue et littérature berbère (vingt-cing ans d'études)* (Paris).

Galand, L. (1989), 'Les alphabets libyques', *Antiquités africaines*, 25, 69–81.

Gast, M. (1973), 'Témoignages nouveaux sur Tine Hinane, ancêtre légendaire des Touareg Ahaggar', *Revue de l'Occident musulman et de la Méditerranée*, 13–14, 395–400.

Gast, M. (1980), 'La société traditionnelle des Kel Ahaggar face aux problèmes contemporains', in E. Gellner (ed.), *Islam: société et communauté*, ser. Anthropologies du Maghreb (Paris), pp. 107–36.

Gautier, E.-F. (1942), *Le Passé de l'Afrique du Nord: les siècles obscurs* (Paris).

Gautier, E.-F. (1952), *Le Passé de l'Afrique du Nord. Les siècles obscurs* (Paris).

Geertz, C. (1968), *Islam Observed* (Chicago and London).

Gellner, E. (1969), *Saints of the Atlas* (London).

Gellner, E. (1983), *Nations and Nationalism* (Oxford).

Gellner, E. and Micaud, C. (eds) (1972–3), *Arabs and Berbers: From Tribe to Nation in North Africa* (New York, 1972; London, 1973).

Gellner, E. and Waterbury, J. (1977), *Patrons and Clients* (London).

Giles, J.A. (trans. 1849), *Roger of Wendover's Flowers of History*, 2 vols (London).

Girard, S. (1984), 'Banasa pré-romaine: un état de la question', *Antiquités africaines*, 20, 11–94.

Gledhill, J., Bender, B. and Lanrsen, M.T. (eds) (1988), *State and Society: The Emergence and Development of Social Hierarchy and Political Centralization* (Oxford).

Goichon, A. (1931), *La Vie féminine au Mzab* (Paris).

Goitein, S.D. (1966), 'Medieval Tunisia – the hub of the Mediterranean', in idem, *Studies in Islamic History and Institutions* (Leiden; reprinted 1968), vol. XVI.

Golvin, L. (1957), *Le Maghreb centrale à l'époque des Zirides* (Paris).

Goodchild, R.G. (1976), *Libyan Studies* (London).

Gouletquer, P. and Klenmann, D. (1976), 'Structures sociales et commerce du sel', *Revue de l'Occident musulman et de la Méditerranée*, 21, 131–9.

Grandguillaume, G. (1973), 'Régime économique et structure du pouvoir: le système des foggara du Touat', *Revue de l'Occident musulman et de la Méditerranée*, 13–14, 437–56.

Grébénart, D. (1986), 'Le cuivre d'Agadez. Principaux types de fourneaux', in *Archéologie africaine et sciences de la nature* (Bordeaux), pp. 473–87.

Gruner, D. (1973), *Die Berber-Keramik* (Berlin).

Gsell, S. (1916) *Herodote* (Algiers).

Gsell, S. (1927), *Histoire ancienne de l'Afrique du Nord* (Paris).

Guernier, E. (1950), *La Berbérie, l'Islam et la France*, 2 vols (Paris).

Guichard, P. (1991), 'Pouvoirs et sociétés islamiques dans l'Espagne mediévale', *Annales, Economies, sociétés, civilisations*, 46, 1122–6.

Guiga, A. (1968), *La Geste hilalienne* (Tunis).

Guillaume, H. (1976), 'Les liens de dépendance à l'époque précoloniale chez les Touaregs de l'Imannen (Niger)', *Revue de l'Occident musulman et de la Méditerranée*, 21, 111–29.

Halm, H. (1991), *Das Reich des Mahdi* (Munich).

Hammoudi, A. (1974), 'Segmentarité, stratification sociale, pouvoir politique et sainteté', *Hespéris Tamuda*, 15, 146–80.

Hanoteau, A. and Letourneux, A. (1857), *La Kabylie et les coutumes kabyles*, 3 vols (Paris).

Harrak, F. (1989), *State and Religion in Eighteenth-century Morocco*, PhD thesis, University of London.

Harris, W.B. (1895), *Tafilet* (Edinburgh and London).

Hart, D.M. (1957), 'Notes on the Rifian community of Tangier', *Middle East Journal*, 11(2), 153–62.

Hart, D.M. (1967), 'Segmentary systems and the role of the "five fifths" in tribal Morocco', *Revue de l'Occident musulman et de la Méditerranée*, 12, 35–95.

Hart, D.M. (1973), 'The tribe in modern Morocco: two case studies', in Gellner and Micaud (eds), pp. 25–59.

Hart, D.M. (1976), *The Aith Waryaghar of the Moroccan Rif* (Tucson, Ariz.).

Hart, D.M. (1981), *Dadda 'Atta and his Forty Grandsons: The Socio-political Organisation of the Ait 'Atta of Southern Morocco* (Cambridge).

Hart, D.M. (1989), 'Rejoinder to Henry Munson, Jr, "On the Irrelevance of the Segmentary Lineage Model in the Moroccan Rif"', *American Anthropologist*, 91, 766–9.

Hawad (1991), 'Le teshumara, antidote de l'Etat', in Claudot-Hawad (ed.), *Touaregs*, pp. 123–39.

Hechd, M. (1983), 'Le chronologie relative des gravures rupestres de l'Atlas Saharien (Algérie) et le région de Djelfa', *Libyca*, 30–31, 59–142.

Henneberg, M., Kobusiewicz, M., Schild, R. and Wendorf, F. (1989), 'The early neolithic burial from the northern Fayum desert (Egypt)', in Krzyzaniak and Kobusiewicz (eds), *Environmental Change*, pp. 181–96.

Hermassi, E. (1973), *Leadership and National Development in North Africa* (Berkeley and Los Angeles, Cal.).

Hess, A.C. (1978), *The Forgotten Frontier* (Chicago and London).

Hirschberg, H.Z. (1963), 'The problem of the Judaized Berbers', *Journal of African History*, 4, 313–39.

Hirschberg, H.Z. (1981), *A History of the Jews in North Africa*, 2 vols (Leiden).

Hitchner, R.B. (1988a), 'The Kasserine Archaeological Survey, 1982–1986', *Antiquités africaines*, 24, 7–41.

Hitchner, R.B. (1988b), 'The organization of rural settlement in the Cillium–Thelepte region (Kasserine, Central Tunisia)', *L'Africa Romana*, 6, 387–402.

Hitchner, R.B. (1990), 'The Kasserine Archaeological Survey', *Antiquités africaines*, 26, 231–58.

Hopkins, J.F.P. (1958), *Medieval Muslim Government in Barbary* (London).

Horn, R. and Rüger, C. (1979), *Die Numider: Reiter und Könige nördlich der Sahara* (Bonn).

Horne, A. (1987), *A Savage War of Peace: Algeria 1954–1962*, 2nd edn (London).

Hourani, A. (1962), *Arabic Thought in the Liberal Age* (Oxford; reprinted Cambridge, 1980).

Huard, P., Leclant, J. and Allard-Huard, C. (1980), *La Culture des chasseurs du Nil et du Sahara*, Mémoires CRAPE 29 (Paris).

Hurst, H. and Roskams, S. (eds) (1984), *Excavations at Carthage: The British Mission* (Sheffield).

Ibn 'Abd al-Ḥakam (1922), *Kitāb Futūḥ Miṣr*, ed. C.C. Torrey (New Haven, Conn.).

Ibn 'Abd al-Ḥakam (1942), *Conquête de l'Afrique du Nord et de l'Espagne*, ed. and trans. A. Gateau (Algiers; 2nd rev. edn, 1948).

Ibn Ḥawqal (1938–9), *Ṣūrat al-arḍ* (Leiden); trans. J.H. Kramers and G. Wiet as *Configuration de la terre* (Paris, 1964).

Ibn 'Idhārī (1930, 1948), *Al-Bayān al-mughrib fī akhbār al-Andalus wa 'l-Maghrib*, vol. i, ed. G.S. Colin and E. Levi-Provençal (Leiden, 1948); vol. iii, ed. E. Levi-Provençal (Paris, 1930).

Ibn Khaldūn (1847), *Tārīkh al-duwal al-islamiyya bi 'l-Maghrib*, ed. M. de Slane, 2 vols (Algiers).

Ibn Khaldūn (1852ff), *Histoire des Berbères*, trans. M. de Slane, 4 vols (Paris; rev. edn, Paris, 1925ff).

Ibn Khaldūn (1867), *Kitāb al-'Ibar*, 7 vols (Būlāq); reprinted as *Ta'rīkh al-'allāma ibn Khaldūn* (Beirut, 1956ff).

Ibn Khaldūn (1958, 1967), *The Muqaddimah: An Introduction to History*, trans. F. Rosenthal, 3 vols (Princeton, N.J.; reprinted London, 1986); abridged by N. Dawood (London, 1967).

Ibn Khaldūn (1986), *Peuples et nations du monde*, selected translations by A. Cheddadi, 2 vols (Paris).

Ibn Nājī (1320H), *Ma'ālim al-īmān*, 4 vols (Tunis).

Ibn Sa'īd (1942), *El Libro de las Banderas de los Campeones*, ed. and trans. E. Garcia Gomez (Madrid).

Ibn Sallām (1986), *Kitāb ibn Sallām*, ed. W. Schwartz and Sālim ibn Ya'qūb (Wiesbaden).

Idris, H.R. (1962), *La Berbérie orientale sous les Zirides* (Paris).

al-Ifrānī (1888-9), *Nuzhat al-ḥādī*, trans. O. Houdas as *Nozhet-Elhâdî* (Paris).

Irwin, R. (1993), 'There's the rub . . . and there too: the elusive meaning of the Aladdin story', *The Times Literary Supplement*, 24 Dec. 1993, 14-15.

Irwin, R. (1994), *Companion to the Arabian Nights* (London).

Issawi, C. (1981), 'The area and population of the Arab empire', in A. Udovitch (ed.), *The Islamic Middle East, 700-1900* (Princeton, N.J.), pp. 375-96.

Jackson, J.G. (1814), *An Account of the Empire of Morocco and the Districts of Suse and Tafilelt*, 3rd edn (London; reprinted 1968).

Jacques-Meunier, Dj. (1949), 'Greniers fortifiés', *Hespéris*, 36, 7-137.

Jacques-Meunier, Dj. (1951), *Greniers-Citadelles au Maroc* (Paris).

Jacques-Meunier, Dj. (1962), *Architectures et habitats du Dadès* (Paris).

Jemma, D. (1972), 'Les artisans de l'Ahaggar', *Libyca*, 20, 269-90.

Jemma-Gouzon, D. (1989), *Villages de l'Aurès: archives de pierres* (Paris).

Jodin. A. (1977), 'Volubilis avant les Romains. Dix années de recherches dans le cité punique', *Archeoloqia*, 102, 6-19.

Julien, Ch.-A. (1951, 1952), *Histoire de l'Afrique du Nord*, 2nd edn, 2 vols (Paris).

Julien, Ch.-A. (1952), *L'Afrique du Nord en marche* (Paris; 3rd edn, 1972).

Julien, Ch.-A. (1964), *Histoire de l'Algérie contemporaine*, vol. I, *La Conquête et les débuts de la colonisation (1827-1871)* (Paris).

Julien, Ch.-A. (1970), *History of North Africa from the Arab Conquest to 1830* (London).

Julien, Ch.-A. (1978), *Le Maroc face aux impérialismes, 1415-1956* (Paris).

Kaddache, M. (1980), *Histoire du nationalisme algérienne. Question nationale et politique algérienne*, 2 vols (Algiers).

Kadra, F.K. (1983), *Les Djedars. Monuments funéraires* (Algiers).

Kedourie, E. (1980), 'The retreat from Algeria', in idem, *Islam in the Modern World* (London), pp. 213-32.

Keenan, J. (1973), 'Social change among the Tuareg of Ahaggar (Algeria)', in Gellner and Micaud (eds), *Arabs and Berbers: From Tribe to Nation in North Africa* (New York, 1972), pp. 345-60.

Keenan, J. (1976), 'Some theoretical considerations on the "Temazlayt" relationship', *Revue de l'Occident musulman et de la Méditerranée*, 21, 33–46.

Kehoe, D. (1985), *The Economics of Agriculture on Roman Imperial Estates in North Africa* (Gottingen).

Kent, S. (1990), 'Activity areas and architecture: an interdisciplinary view of the relationship between use of space and domestic built environments', in S. Kent (ed.), *Domestic Architecture and the Use of Space* (Cambridge), pp. 1–8.

King, A. (1991), 'Animal bones', in Fentress (ed.), pp. 247–67.

Kolendo, J. (1976), *Le Colonat en Afrique sous le Haut-Empire* (Paris).

Kotula, T. (1955), 'Principes gentis et principes civitatis en Afrique romaine', *Eos*, 55, 363–90.

Krzyzaniak, L. and Kobusiewicz, M. (eds) (1989), *Environmental Change and Human Culture in the Nile Basin and Northeast Africa* (Pozan).

Lacoste, C. (1962), *Bibliographie ethnographique de la Grande Kabylie* (Paris).

Lacoste, C. and Y. (eds) (1991), *L'Etat du Maghreb* (Paris).

Lacoste-Dujardin, C. (1986), 'Opération "Oiseau Bleu", 1956; géostrategie et ethnopolitique', *Revue de l'Occident musulman et de la Méditerranée*, 41–42, 167–96.

Lagardère, V. (1989), *Le Vendredi de Zallāqa: 23 octobre 1086* (Paris).

Lambton, A.K.S. (1988), 'Changing concepts of justice and injustice from the 5th/11th to the 8th/14th century in Persia', *Studia Islamica*, 68, 27–60.

Lancel, S. (1992), *Carthage* (Paris).

Laoust-Chantréaux, G. (1990), *Kabylie côte femmes: la vie féminine à Ait Hichem, 1937–1939* (Paris).

Lassus, J. (1958), 'L'archéologie algérienne en 1957', *Libyca*, 6, 235–50.

Launois, A. (1964), 'Influence des docteurs malékites sur le monnayage ziride de type sunnite et sur celui des Almoravides', *Arabica*, 11, 127–50.

Le Bohec, Y. (1989), *La Troisième Légioné Auguste* (Etudes d'antiquités africaines) (Paris).

Le Coeur, Ch. (1937), 'Les "mapalia" numides et leur survivance au Sahara', *Hesperis*, 24, 29–45.

Leglay, M. (1961–6), *Saturne africain*, 2 vols (Paris).

Leo Africanus (ed. 1981), *Description de l'Afrique* (Paris).

Lepelley, C. (1974), 'La préfecture de tribu dans l'Afrique du Bas-Empire', in *Mélanges d'histoire ancienne offerts à William Seston* (Paris), pp. 175–86

Lepelley, C. (1979), *Les Cités de l'Afrique romaine au Bas-Empire* (Paris).

Lepelley, C. (1982), 'Liberté, colonat et esclavage d'après la Lettre 24*: la juridiction épiscopale "de liberali causa"', *Les Lettres de Saint Augustin découvertes par Johannes Divjak* (Paris), pp. 331–42.

Lepelley, C. (1987), 'Spes Saeculi: le milieu social d'Augustin et ses ambitions séculières avant sa conversion', *Studia ephemeridis 'Augustinianum'*, 24, 99–117.

Le Tourneau, R. (1969), *The Almohad Movement in North Africa in the Twelfth and Thirteenth Centuries* (Princeton, N.J.).

Leveau, Ph. (1973), 'L'Aile II des Thraces, Mazices et *Praefecti Gentis*', *Antiquités africaines,* 7, 153–91.

Leveau, Ph. (1974), 'Un cantonnement de tribu au sud-est de Caesarea de Maurétanie: borne de Sidi-Bouzid', *Revue d'Études Africaines,* 76, 293–304.

Leveau, Ph. (1984), *Caesarea de Mauretanie* (Rome).

Leveau, R. (1976), *Le Fellah marocain, defenseur du trône* (Paris).

Levi, R. (1957), *The Social Structure of Islam* (Cambridge).

Levi-Provençal, E. (1944), *Histoire de l'Espagne musulmane,* vol. ɪ (Cairo).

Levi-Provençal, E. (1954), 'Un nouveau récit de la conquête de l'Afrique du Nord par les Arabes', *Arabica,* 1, 17–52.

Levi-Provençal, E. (1957), 'La fondation de Marrakech (462–1070)', in G. Marçais, *Mélanges, etc.,* vol. ɪɪ, pp. 117–20.

Levtzion, N. and Hopkins, J.F.P. (1981), *Corpus of Early Arabic Sources for West African History* (Cambridge).

Lhote, H. (1958), *A la découverte des fresques du Tassili* (Paris; reprinted 1973).

Lhote, H. (1976) 'Les gravures rupestre de l'Oued Djerat (Tassili-n-Ajjer)', *Mémoires du Centre de recherche authropologique, préhistorique et ethnographique,* 25 (Algiers).

Lhote, H. (1984), *Les Touaregs du Hoggar* (Paris).

Lombard, M. (1975), *The Golden Age of Islam* (Amsterdam, Oxford and New York).

Lopez, J. and Bazzana, A. (eds) (1990), *La Casa Hispano-Musulmana: Aportaciones de la Arqueologia* (Madrid).

Louis, A. (1973), 'Contactes entre culture "berbère" et culture arabe dans le sud tunisien', in *Actes du Premier Congrés d'Etudes des Cultures Mediterranéennes d'Influence Arabo-Berbère,* Algiers, pp. 394–405.

Louis, A. (1975), *Tunisie du Sud: ksars et villages de crêtes* (Paris).

Lourie, E. (1966), 'A society organized for war: medieval Spain', *Past and Present,* 35, 54–76.

Lubell, D. (1984), 'The Capsian palaeoeconomy in the Maghreb', in L. Krzyzaniak and M. Kobusiewicz (eds), *The Origin of and Early Development of Food-Producing Cultures in North-Eastern Africa* (Pozan), pp. 453–5.

Luni, M. (1987), 'Il santuario rupestre libyco delle immagini a Slonta (Cirenaica)', *Cirene e i Libyi* (Quaderni di Archeologia della Libia), 12, 415–18.

Maarouf, N. (1980), *Lecture de l'espace oasien* (Paris).

Mammeri, M. (1965), *L'Opium et le bâton* (Paris; reprinted 1992).

Mammeri, M. (1988), *Poèmes kabyles anciens* (Algiers). ·

Marçais, G. (1913), *Les Arabes en Berbérie du XIᵉ au XIVᵉ siècle* (Paris)

Marçais, G. (1913–38), 'Ribāṭ', in *Encyclopaedia of Islam,* 1st edn (Leiden).

Marçais, G. (1946), *La Berbérie musulmane et l'Orient au Moyen Age* (Paris).

Marçais, G. (1957), *Mélanges d'histoire et d'archéologie de l'Occident musulman*, 2 vols (Algiers).

Marçais, Ph. (1954ff), "Arabiyya', in *Encyclopaedia of Islam*, 2nd edn (Leiden).

Marçais, W. (1938, 1956), 'Comment l'Afrique du Nord a été arabisée', *AIEO* (*Annales de l'Institut des Etudes Orientales*, Algiers), **4**, 1–22; **14**, 5–17.

Mardrus, J.C. and Mathers, P. (1958), *The Book of a Thousand and One Nights*, 4 vols (London).

Marichal, R. (1979), 'Les ostraca de Bu Njem', *CR*, 436–52.

Marmier, F. and Trécolle, G. (1986), 'La céramique néolithique du type 'Hassi Mouillah', charactéristiques, diffusion, datation', *Archéologie africaine et sciences de la nature*, 235–44.

al-Marrākushi (1881), *The History of the Almohades*, ed. R. Dozy, 2nd edn (Leiden; reprinted Amsterdam, 1968).

Martin Evans, J. (1976), 'The traditional house in the oasis of Ghadames', *Libyan Studies*, **7**, 31–40.

Masqueray, E. (1886), *Formation des cités chez les populations sédentaires de l'Algérie* (Paris; reprinted Aix-en-Provence, 1983).

Massignon, L. (1913ff.), 'Ṭarīḳa', in *Encyclopaedia of Islam*, 1st edn (Leiden).

Matthews, J. (1989), *The Roman Empire of Ammianus* (London).

Mattingly, D.J. (1986a), 'New perspectives in the agricultural development of the jebel and pre-desert in Roman Tripolitania', *Revue de l'Occident musulman et de la Méditerranée*, 40–41, 46–65.

Mattingly, D. (1986b), 'Libyans and the "Limes": culture and society in Roman Tripolitania', *Antiquités africaines*, **23**, 71–94.

Maunier, M. (1926), *La Construction collective de la maison en Kabylie, étude sur la coopération économique ches les berbères du Djurjura* (Paris).

Maxwell, G. (1966), *Lords of the Atlas* (London).

McBurney, C. (1967), *The Hawa Fteah (Cyrenaica) and the Stone Age of the South East Mediterranean* (Cambridge).

McDougall, E.A. (1985), 'The view from Awdaghust, war, trade and social change in the southwestern Sahara from the eighth to the fifteenth century', *Journal of African History*, **26**, 1–31.

McIntosh, R.I. and S.K. (1981), 'The inland Niger Delta before the empire of Mali', *Journal of African History*, **22**, 1–22.

Mackeen, A.M.M. (1971), 'The early history of Sufism in the Maghrib', *Journal of the American Oriental Society*, **91**, 398–408.

Matthews, J. (1976), 'Mauretania in Ammianus and the Notitia', in R. Goodburn and P. Bartholomew (eds) *Aspects of the Notitia Dignitatum* (*BAR* Supplementary Series 15, Oxford), 157–86.

Melvinger, A. (1954ff), 'Mādjūs', in *Encyclopaedia of Islam*, 2nd edn (Leiden).

Mercer, P. (1977), 'Palace and jihād in the early 'Alawī state of Morocco', *Journal of African History*, **18**, 531–53.

Mercier, M. (1922), *La Civilization urbaine au Mzab* (Paris).

Mikesell, M. (1958), 'The role of tribal markets in Morocco: examples from the "Northern zone"', *Geographical Review*, **48** (4), 494–511.

Moderan, Y. (1989), 'Gildon, les Maures et l'Afrique', *Mélanges de l'Ecole française de Rome*, **101**, 821–72.

Moderan, Y. (1990), 'De Bellis Libycis; Berbères et Byzantins en Afrique au VIᵉ siècle', unpublished doctoral thesis, Université de Paris X.

Montagne R. (1924a), 'Une tribu berbère du sud Marocain: Massat', *Hespéris*, **4**, 357–403.

Montagne, R. (1924b), 'Coutumes et légendes de la cote berbère du Maroc', *Hespéris*, **4**, 8–135.

Montagne, R. (1930), *Les Berbères et le Makhzen au sud du Maroc* (Paris).

Montagne, R. (1951), *Révolution au Maroc* (Paris).

Montagne, R. (1973), *The Berbers: Their Social and Political Organisation* (London).

Morgan, J. (1731), *A Complete History of Algiers* (London; reprinted New York, 1970).

Morizot, P. (1989), 'Pour une nouvelle lecture de l'*elogium* de Masties', *Antiquités Africaines*, **25**, 263–84.

Mukhlis, F.A. (1964), 'Studies and comparison of the cycles of the Banū Hilāl romance', PhD thesis, University of London.

Munson, H. (1989), 'On the irrelevance of the segmentary lineage model in the Moroccan Rif', *American Anthropologist*, **91**, 386–400.

Murphy, P. (1963) 'Social distance and the veil', *American Anthropologist*, **66**, 1257–74.

Muzzolini, A. (1986), *L'Art rupestre préhistorique des Massifs Centraux Sahariens* (Oxford; BAR no. 318).

al-Nāṣirī (1954–6), *Kitāb al-istiqṣā'*, 9 vols (Casablanca).

Neumann, W. (1983), *Die Berber: Vielfalt und Einheit einer alten nordafrikanischen Kultur* (Cologne).

Nicolaisen, J. (1963), *Economy and Culture of the Pastoral Tuareg* (Copenhagen).

Norris, H.T. (1971), 'New evidence on the life of 'Abdullah b. Yāsīn and the origins of the Almoravid movement', *Journal of African History*, **12**, 255–68.

Norris, H.T. (1972), *Saharan Myth and Saga* (Oxford).

Norris, H.T. (1975), *The Tuaregs: The Islamic Legacy and its Diffusion in the Sahel* (Warminster, Wilts.).

Norris, H.T. (1977–8), 'Abdullah ibn Yāsīn et la dynamique conquérante des Almoravides', in Ch.-A. Julien et al. (eds), *Les Africains*, 12 vols (Paris), vol. XII, pp. 15–39.

Norris, H.T. (1980), *The Adventures of Antar* (Warminster, Wilts.).

Norris, H.T. (1982), *The Berbers in Arabic Literature* (London and New York).

Norris, H.T. (1986), *The Arab Conquest of the Western Sahara* (Harlow, Essex).

Norris, H.T. (1988), 'The rediscovery of the ancient sagas of the Banū Hilāl', *Bulletin of the School of Oriental and African Studies*, 51, 462–81.

O'Callaghan, J.F. (1975), *A History of Medieval Spain* (Ithaca, N.Y.).

O'Connor, D. (1982), 'Egypt, 1552–664BC', in *Cambridge History of Africa* (Cambridge), pp. 830–940.

Oliver, J. (1972), 'The text of the *Tabula Banasitana*, AD177', *American Journal of Philology*, 93, 336–40.

Oxby, C. (1986), 'Women and the allocation of herding labour in a pastoral society: Southern Kel Ferwan Twareg, Niger', in Bernus et al. (eds).

Oxford English Dictionary (1933), 1st edn (Oxford).

Pace, B., Caputo, G. and Sergi, S. (1951), 'Scavi Sahariani: Ricerche nell'Uadi el Agial e nell'Oasi di Gat della missione Pace–Sergi–Caputo', *Monumenti Antichi, Accademia Nazionale dei Lincei*, 41, 151–551.

Peacock, D. (1982), *Pottery in the Roman World: An Ethnoarchaeological Approach* (London).

Peacock, D., Bejaoui, F. and Ben Lazreg, N. (1990), 'Roman pottery production in central Tunisia', *Journal of Roman Archaeology*, 3, 59–85.

Pennell, R. (1986), *A Country with a Government and a Flag* (Outwell, Wisbech).

Peristany, J. G. (ed.) (1965), *Honour and Shame* (London).

Picard, G.-C. (1990), *La Civilization de l'Afrique romaine*, 2nd ed (Paris).

al-Qāḍī al-Nuʿmān (1975), *Iftitāḥ al-daʿwa wa ibtidāʾ al-dawla*, in F. Dachraoui (ed.), *Les Commencements du Califat fatimide au Maghreb* (Tunis).

Quandt, W. (1973), 'The Berbers in the Algerian political elite', in Gellner and Micaud (eds) *Arabs and Berbers*, pp. 285–303.

Rabinow, P. (1977), *Reflections on Fieldwork in Morocco* (Berkeley, Cal.).

Rakob, F. (1979), 'Numidische Königsarchitektur in Nordafrika', in Horn and Rüger (eds), pp. 119–71.

Randall-McIver, D. and Wilkin, A. (1901), *Libyan Notes* (London).

Rapoport, A. (1990), 'Systems of activities and systems of settings', in S. Kent (ed.), *Domestic Architecture and the Use of Space* (Cambridge), pp. 44–57.

Raven, S. (1993), *Rome in Africa* (London).

Rebuffat, R. (1975), 'Graffiti en "Libyque de Bu Njem"', *Libya Antiqua*, 11–12, 165–87.

Rebuffat, R. (1982), 'Au-delà des camps romains d'Afrique mineure, renseignement, contrôle, pénétration', *Aufstieg und Niedergang der Römische Welt*, II, *Principat*, 10 (2), 474–513.

Rebuffat, R. (1986), 'Recherches sur le bassin du Sebou', *Comptes rendues de l'Académie des Inscriptions*, 633–61.

Rebuffat, R. (1987), 'Les fermiers du désert', *L'Africa romana*, 5, 33–68.

Rebuffat, R. (1989), 'Notes sur le camp roman de Gholaia (Bu Ngem)', *Libyan Studies*, 20, 155–67.

336 *Bibliography*

Renfrew, C. (1987), *Archaeology and Language: The Puzzle of Indo-European Origins* (London).

Renfrew, C. and Cherry, J. (eds) (1986), *Peer Polity Interaction and Sociopolitical Change* (Cambridge).

Reygasse, M. (1940), 'Le monument de Tin Hinan', *Bulletin de la Société géographique et archéologique d'Oran*, 148–66.

Reynolds, J. (1977), 'The Austuriani and Tripolitania in the early fifth century', *Libyan Studies*, 8, 13.

Roberts, H. (1980), 'Towards an understanding of the Kabyle question in contemporary Algeria', *Maghreb Review*, 5, 115–24.

Roberts, H. (1982), 'The unforeseen development of the Kabyle question in contemporary Algeria', *Government and Opposition*, 17, 312–34.

Roberts, H. (1983), 'The economics of Berberism: the material basis of the Kabyle question in contemporary Algeria', *Government and Opposition*, 19, 218–35.

Rogers, P.G. (n.d. [1972]), *A History of Anglo-Moroccan Relations to 1900* (London, Foreign and Commonwealth Office).

Romanelli, P. (1959), *Storia delle province romane dell'Africa* (Rome).

Romanelli, P. (1962), 'Le iscrizione Volubilitane dei Baquati e i rapporti di Roma con le tribu indigene dell'Africa', in P. Renard (ed.), *Hommages à A. Grenier* (Paris), pp. 1347–66.

Rosen, L. (1972; 1973), 'The social and conceptual framework of Arab-Berber relations in Central Morocco', in Gellner and Micaud (eds.).

Rosen, L. (1973), 'Arab–Berber relations in Central Morocco', in Gellner and Micaud (eds), pp. 155–73.

Rosen, L. (1984), *Bargaining for Reality: The Construction of Social Relations in a Muslim Community* (Chicago).

Rostovtzeff, M. (1946), 'Numidian horsemen on Canossa vases', *American Journal of Archaeology*, 50, 265–70.

Roubet, C. (1979), *Economie pastorale préagricole en Algérie orientale. Le Néolithique de tradition capsienne* (Paris).

Rüger, C. (1979), 'Siga, die Hauptstadt des Syphax', in Horn and Rüger (eds), pp. 181–4.

Saad, E.N. (1983), *Social History of Timbuktu: The Role of Muslim Scholars and Notables, 1400–1900* (Cambridge).

Saada, L. (ed. and trans.) (1985), *La Geste hilalienne* (Paris).

Sahlins, M. (1961), 'The segmentary lineage: an organization of predatory expansion', *American Anthropologist*, 63, 322–45.

Saumagne, C. (1962), 'Les Prétextes Juridiques de la IIIᵉ Guerre Punique', *Etudes d'histoire social et politique relative à la province romaine d'Afrique de Charles Saumagne: Cahiers de Tunisie*, 10, 301–11.

Schroeter, D.J. (1988), *Merchants of Essaouira* (Cambridge).

Schwartz, J. (1984), 'The (primarily) mammalian fauna', in H. Hurst and S. Roskams (eds), *Excavations at Carthage: The British Mission* (Sheffield), vol. i.1, pp. 229–56.

Seston, W. and Euzennat, M. (1961), 'La citoyenneté romaine au temps de

Marc-Aurèle et de Commode d'après la *Tabula Banasitana'*, *Comptes rendus de l'Académie des Inscriptions*, 317–23.

Seston, W. and Euzennat, M. (1971), 'Un dossier de la chancellerie romaine: la *Tabula Banasitana'*, *Comptes rendus de l'Académie des Inscriptions*, 468–90.

Shatzmiller, M. (1983), 'La myth d'origine berbère: aspects historiographiques et sociaux', *Revue de l'Occident musulman et de la Méditerranée*, 35, 145–56.

Shaw, B.D. (1976), 'Climate, environment and history: the case of Roman North Africa', *World Archaeology*, 8, 379–403.

Shaw, B.D. (1979), 'The camel in Roman North Africa and the Sahara', *Bulletin de l'Institut français de l'Afrique noire*, 41, 663–716.

Shaw, B.D. (1982), 'Lamasba, an ancient irrigation community', *Antiquités africaines*, 18, 61–104.

Shaw, B.D. (1984), 'Water and society in the ancient Maghrib', *Antiquités africaines*, 20, 121–77.

Shaw, B.D. (1986), 'Autonomy and tribute: mountain and plain in Mauretania Tingitana', *Revue de l'Occident musulman et de la Méditerranée*, 40–41, 66–86.

Shaw, Dr T. (1738), *Travels or Observations Relating to Several Parts of Barbary and the Levant* (Oxford; 2nd rev. edn, 1756).

Sigman, M. (1977), 'The Romans and the indigenous tribes of Mauretania Tingitana', *Historia*, 26, 415–39.

Smith, A. (1989), 'The Near Eastern connection', in Krzyzaniak and Kobusiewcz (eds), *Late Prehistory of the Nile Basin and the Sahara* (Pozan), pp. 67–77.

Smith, A. (1991), 'New approaches to Saharan rock art of the "Bovidian" period', in L. Krzyzaniak and M. Kobusiewicz (eds), *Environmental Change and Human Culture in the Nile Basin and Northeast Africa* (Pozan).

Smith, P.E. (1982), 'The late palaeolithic and epi-palaeolithic of northern Africa', in *The Cambridge History of Africa* (Cambridge), vol. I, pp. 1083–1145.

Souville, G. (1986), 'Témoignages sur l'âge du bronze au Maghreb occidental', *Comptes rendus de l'Académie des Inscriptions*, 97–114.

Spencer, W. (1976), *Algiers in the Age of the Corsairs* (Norman, Okla).

Spencer, W. (1980), *Historical Dictionary of Morocco* (Metuchen, N.J., and London).

Stewart, C.C. (1973), *Islam and Social Order in Mauritania* (Oxford).

Stora, B. (1991), *Histoire de l'Algérie coloniale, 1830–1954* (Paris).

Sutton, K. Aghrout, A. and Zaimeche, S. (1992), 'Political changes in Algeria: an emerging electoral geography', *Maghreb Review*, 17, 3–27.

Sznyier, M. (1978), 'Carthage et la civilisation punique', in C. Nicolet (ed.), *Rome et le conquête du monde Méditerranéen* (Paris).

Talbi, M. (1954ff.a), 'Kāhina', in *Encyclopaedia of Islam*, 2nd edn (Leiden).

Talbi, M. (1954ff.b), 'Kusayla', in *Encyclopaedia of Islam*, 2nd edn (Leiden).

Talbi, M. (1966), *L'Emirat Aghlabide* (Paris).

Talbi, M. (1968), *Biographies Aghlabides. Extraites des Madārik du Cadi 'Iyāḍ* (Tunis).

Talbi, M. (1981), 'Law and economy in Ifrīqiya (Tunisia) in the third Islamic century', in A.L. Udovitch (ed.), *The Islamic Middle East, 700–1900* (Princeton, N.J.), pp. 209–49.

Thébert, Y. and Biget, J.-L. (1990), 'L'Afrique après la disparition de la cité classique: cohérence et ruptures dans l'histoire maghrébine', *L'Afrique dans l'Occident Romain* (Rome; *Collection de l'Ecole française de Rome*, 134), 575–602.

al-Tijānī (1958), *Riḥlat al-Tijānī* (Tunis).

Trevelyan, R. (1981), *Rome '44* (London).

Trevelyan, R. (1988), *France, Soldiers and Africa* (London).

Trimingham, J.S. (1971), *The Sufi Orders in Islam* (Oxford).

Trousset, P. (1974), *Recherches sur le limes Tripolitanus du Chott Djerid à la frontière tuniso-libyenne* (Paris).

Trousset, P. (1978), 'Les bornes du Bled Segui, nouveaux aperçus sur la centuriation romaine du Sud tunisien', *Antiquités africaines*, 12, 165–88.

Trousset, P. (1980), 'Les Milliaires de Chebika (sud tunisien)', *Antiquités africaines*, 15, 135–54.

Trousset, P. (1986), 'Les oasis présahariennes dans l'Antiquité; partage de l'eau et division du temps', *Antiquités africaines*, 22, 163–93.

al-Ṭurṭūshī (1298H), *Sirāj al-mulūk* (Cairo).

Udovitch, A.L. (ed.) (1981), *The Islamic Middle East, 700–1900: Studies in Economic and Social History* (Princeton, N.J.).

al-'Umarī, *Masālik al-abṣār*, ms. Bibliothèque nationale, Paris, no. 2327.

Valensi, L. (1977), *On the Eve of Colonialism* (New York and London).

Valensi, L. (1985), *Tunisian Peasants* (Cambridge).

Valler, M. (1990), 'Les Touaregs du Hoggar entre décolonisation et indépendance, 1954–1974', *Revue de l'Occident musulman et de la Méditerranée*, 54, 77–90.

Van Der Veen, M. (1992), 'Garamantian agriculture', *Libyan Studies*, 23, 7–40.

Vera, D. (1988), 'Terra e lavoro nell'africa Romana', *Studi Storici*, 4, 967–92.

Von Sivers, P. (1983), 'Alms and arms: the combative saintliness of the Awlad Sīdī Shaykh in the Algerian Sahara, sixteenth-nineteenth centuries', *Maghreb Review*, 8, 113–23.

Ward Gill, C. and Patterson, T. (1988), 'State formation and uneven development', in Gledhill et al. (eds), pp. 77–88.

Warmington, B. (1954), *The North African Provinces from Diocletian to the Vandal Conquest* (Cambridge).

Wasserstein, D. (1985), *The Rise and Fall of the Party-Kings* (Princeton, N.J.).

Waterbury, J. (1970), *The Commander of the Faithful* (London).

Waterbury, J. (1972), *North for the Trade: The Life and Times of a Berber Merchant* (Berkeley and Los Angeles, Cal.).

Waterbury, J. (1973), 'The Coup Manqué', in Gellner and Micaud (eds), pp. 397–423.

Wendorf, F. and Schild, R. (1980), *Prehistory of the Eastern Sahara* (New York).

Wendorf, F., Close, A. and Schild, R. (1989), 'Early domestic cattle and scientific methodology', in Krzyzaniak and Kobusiewicz (eds), pp. 61–7.

Whitcomb, T. (1975), 'New evidence on the origin of the Kunta', *Bulletin of the School of Oriental and African Studies*, 38, 103–23, 403–17.

Wright, J. (1969), *Libya* (London).

Yacine, T. (1988), *Poésie berbère et identité* (Paris).

Yacine, T. (1990a), *L'Izli ou l'amour chanté en Kabyle* (Paris).

Yacine, T. (1990b), *Ait Menguellet chante . . .* (Algiers).

Yacine, T. (1993), *Les Voleurs du feu: éléments d'une anthropologie sociale et culturelle de l'Algérie* (Paris).

al-Ya'qūbī (1892), *Kitāb al-buldān*, ed. de Goeje, *Bibliotheca geographorum arabicorum*, vol. VII (Leiden); trans. G. Wiet as *Les Pays* (Cairo, 1937).

Index

Glawa, 264, *see* el-Glaoui
GLD, 39, 72
goats, 58, 203, 215
Granada, 98, 113, 117, 156
granaries, 32, 147, 229, 246, 256, 257, 264
Greece, 33, 81, 82, 256
Gregory, exarch, 84
Grenier, Eugene, 185
Gsell, Stephane, 185
Gudāla, 101, 102
Guenziga, 200
Gulussa, 48
Gurkhas, 54
Gurzil, 66

Habsburgs, 157
Hadrian, 62, 68
Hadrumetum, 217
Hafsids, 81, 110, 113, 118, 119, 130, 139, 142, 147, 149
Ḥammadids, 95, 138
Hart, David, 8, 201, 232
Ḥarzihum, 143
Hasan ibn al-Nu 'man, 85, 96
Hasan ou Moha, 188
Hasdrubal, 26
Hassan Aga, 159, 160
Hassan II, 273
Hassani, 278
Ḥawwāra, 141
Ḥaydarān, 96, 132, 136
Hayreddin, *see* Khayr al-Dīn
heads, disembodied, 35
Hecatompylos, 32
Hellenism, 44, 45
Hellenistic
  kingdoms, 25, 27–31, 34, 35, 41
  tombs, 27, 44
Hermassi, E., 190, 193
Herodotus, 22, 76, 204, 217, 267
Hiempsal I, 42, 48
Hiempsal II, 43, 48
Hippo Regius, 32, 33
Hodna, 77, 79
Hoggar, 3, 152, 278; *see also* Ahaggar
horses, 19, 34, 58, 79, 138, 205
Hourani, Albert, 193
Ḥusaynid Beys, 161, 178, 179, 180

Ibāḍīs, 3, 89, 97, 102, 150, 151, 169,

186, 193, 254, 262–4
Iberian peninsula, 15
Ibn 'Abd al-Hakam, 85
Ibn al-'Arabī, 143
Ibn Hawqal, 102, 130
Ibn 'Idhārī, 85
Ibn Khaldūn, 4, 17, 116, 117, 124, 128, 130–5, 139–41, 148, 151, 152, 154, 156, 164, 170, 184, 185
Ibn Rushd, 110
Ibn Tūmart, 106, 108, 116, 120
Ibn Yasīn, 99
Ichoukane, 32
Idir, 280
Idrīs II, 170
Idrisids, 90, 97, 170
Iflissen, 259, 272
Ifoghas, 210
Ifrīqish, 126
Ifrīqiya, 82, 88, 89, 90, 92, 94, 95, 98, 102, 121, 122, 129, 133, 135–7, 142, 145, 146, 157, 158, 218
Ighil-Ali, 259
Igilgili, 67
Igli, 90
Ihadanaren, 208
Ihaggaren, 208
Iligh, 175
'Ilj 'Alī, 158
Imam, 101
Imazighen, 56
incubation, 267
India, 54
Indo-European, 15
ineslemen, 152, 214
Iol Caesarea, 45, 60, 77
Iran, 120, 141
Iraq, 82, 88, 139
irrigation, 56, 57, 204, 252–5
Isis, 45
islām, 83, 87, 93
Islam, 7, 81, 88, 90–4, 101, 102, 107, 109, 111, 115, 122, 124–6, 130, 136, 141, 142, 145, 146, 149, 151, 152, 158, 174, 182, 184, 193, 264, 267, 269, 274
Islamic law, 83, 101, 125, 151, 184, 226, 227
Islamization, 171, 185
Isly, 187
Ismuc, 56
Istanbul, 161, 172, 182

Printed in the United States
219780BV00005B/26/P

9 780631 207672